EXPLAINING AUSCHWITZ AND HIROSHIMA

THE NEW INTERNATIONAL HISTORY SERIES
Edited by Gordon Martel
Royal Roads Military College, British Columbia, Canada

Forthcoming titles:

WAR AND COLD WAR IN THE MIDDLE EAST
Edward Ingram

NORTH EAST ASIA: AN INTERNATIONAL HISTORY
John Stephan

RUSSIA AND THE WORLD IN THE TWENTIETH CENTURY
Teddy Uldricks

IDEOLOGY AND INTERNATIONAL RELATIONS
Alan Cassels

EXPLAINING AUSCHWITZ AND HIROSHIMA

History Writing and the Second World War
1945–1990

R.J.B. Bosworth

London and New York

First published 1993
Paperback edition first published in 1994
by Routledge
11 New Fetter Lane, London EC4P 4EE

Simultaneously published in the USA and Canada
by Routledge
29 West 35th Street, New York, NY 10001

Typeset in 10 on 12 point Times by DSC Corporation Ltd,
Falmouth, Cornwall, England

Printed in Great Britain by T. J. Press (Padstow) Ltd,
Padstow, Cornwall

British Library Cataloguing in Publication Data

A catalogue record for this book is available from the British Library.

Library of Congress Cataloging in Publication Data

Also available.

ISBN 0–415–08450–4 (hbk)
0–415–10923–X (pbk)

For Tony Cahill
Our history is together

Contents

Series editor's preface

What we now refer to as 'international' history was the primary concern of those whose work is now recognised as the first attempt by Europeans to conduct a truly 'historical' investigation of the past, and it has remained a central preoccupation of historians ever since. Herodotus, who attempted to explain the Persian Wars, approached the subject quite differently from his successor, Thucydides. Herodotus believed that the answers to the questions that arose from the confrontation between the Persians and the Greeks would be found in the differences between the two cultures; accordingly, he examined the traditions, customs and beliefs of the two civilisations. Critics have long pointed out that he was haphazard in his selection and cavalier in his use of evidence. The same has never been said of Thucydides, who, in attempting to explain the Peloponnesian Wars, went about his task more methodically, and who was meticulous in his use of evidence. Over the next two thousand years, men like Machiavelli, Ranke and Toynbee have added to the tradition, but the underlying dichotomy between the 'anthropological' and the 'archival' approach has remained. Diplomatic historians have been condemned as mere archive-grubbers; diplomatic history as consisting of what one file-clerk said to another. The 'world-historians', the synthesisers, have been attacked for creating structures and patterns that never existed, for offering explanations that can never be tested against the available evidence.

The aim of 'The New International History' is to combine the two traditions, to bring Herodotus and Thucydides together. While drawing upon the enormous wealth of archival research conducted by those historians who continue to work in the political tradition of formal relations between states, the authors in this series will also draw upon other avenues of investigation that have become increasingly fruitful since the Second World War. Ideology and culture, immigration and communications, myths and stereotypes, trade and finance, have come to be regarded by contemporary scholars as elements essential to a good understanding of international history, and yet, while these approaches are to be found in detailed monographs and scholarly journals, many of their discoveries have not been presented in a readable and accessible form to students and the public. The New International History, by providing books organised along thematic, regional or historiographical lines, hopes to repair this omission.

ix

Given the ambitions of the series, it seems most appropriate that it should begin with Richard Bosworth's examination of the 'historicising' of the Second World War, a theme that has been the subject of enduring interest to both academic and popular historians, fuelling scholastic controversies and forcing its way into the headlines and onto television. The very different ways in which various societies have attempted to understand (or chosen to ignore) their role in the war and its origins says much about the relationship between international relations and culture. Imaginative, evocative and provocative, *Explaining Auschwitz and Hiroshima* is certain to establish a place at the centre of future discussions concerning the interpretation of the Second World War.

Gordon Martel

Preface

This book has at least one claim to fame: it is more the product of 'teaching' than of 'research'. It therefore runs counter to the assumption increasingly made in my home country, Australia, that only 'researchers', elevated by grants above teaching, write books. Rather, this book's genesis was in 1978, when, with my colleague, Tony Cahill, I was given the task of developing an introductory first year course for undergraduates at the University of Sydney. What we came up with was called Late Modern European History (or LME) I.[1]

In one sense this course was highly conventional, aiming to survey European history from the French Revolution to the present. But we were also committed to introducing our students to the 'nature of history', and, to this end, our chronological 'narrative' was chopped up into fortnightly segments, each with its own historian. Either because of the compulsion of the calendar or because, as Australians, Tony and I have a terrible weakness for cricket, there were eleven such segments, and as we studied each, the major work of one historian who had written about the subject matter in question was analysed in some detail for what Arthur Marwick has called its 'witting' and 'unwitting' evidence,[2] for what it said about the past and why it said what it said. Students were thus trained to approach these secondary texts (and, indeed, everything else)[3] armed with three great questions: Who wrote the book? When exactly was it written? And why? The method was dialectical. If as much as possible could be discovered about the political, cultural and social assumptions of the authors and the works of each could be accurately set in their time and context, then much of their meaning would be revealed.

Largely because I am an Italianist, the course handbook eventually had two translated Italian epigraphs on its cover. One was a futurist playlet called *Education*:

A classroom
The Professor (Thirty years old. He is reading to his students.): Dante is a great poet. He wrote the *Divine Comedy* and . . .
(Several seconds of darkness.)
The Professor (Forty years old. He is reading with a bored voice.): Dante is a great poet. He wrote the *Divine Comedy* and . . .

xi

(Several seconds of silence.)

The Professor (Sixty years old. He is like a gramophone.): Dante is a great poet...

A Pupil (interrupting him): Why?

The Professor (surprised and embarrassed): It is printed here. Sit down and be quiet. Dante is a great poet. He wrote ...

Curtain [4]

The other was the advice of William of Baskerville, protagonist of the Italian semiologist Umberto Eco's novel, *The Name of the Rose*. William had summed up semiotics and much of the theory of post-modernism by declaring:

> Books are not made to be believed but to be subjected to inquiry. When we consider a book, we mustn't ask ourselves what it says but what it means, a precept that the commentators of the holy books had very clearly in mind.[5]

Tony and I taught LME I together in 1978, 1982–3 and 1986, and, naturally, gradually refined it. When I moved to the University of Western Australia in 1987, the course came with me and, with my new colleagues, I offered it again in 1987–8 and 1990. Tony and others have gone on teaching versions of it at the University of Sydney. Our involvement with this course and with the marvellously talented cohorts of students who have taken it, has given Tony and me more pleasure, more instruction, more enlightenment than anything else in our academic lives. We, too, have been students of LME I.

Over the years, we have discerned something else about the course which I, at least, had perceived only dimly back in 1978. LME I investigated the 'long Second World War', those processes which took humanity to 'Auschwitz' and 'Hiroshima'. But, through its critical examination of the eleven historians, it also reviewed 'the Second World War which never ended'. It studied the way in which combatant societies 'historicised', and thus explained, the terrible events of that conflict and asked why and with what effect, from time to time, and at different moments in different societies, these explanations changed. It is the analysis of that problem of change and continuity in interpretation and the role of history in post-war society which is the subject of this book.

A preface is a place to try to do the impossible – to repay intellectual debts. My first thanks must go to Tony Cahill. I think of him not only as a colleague, but also as the person who has taught me most about our wonderful discipline. He is the classic case of an academic historian who does not write a lot but who knows far more than those who do. This book, sprung from our course, is dedicated to him.

I also owe much to others who have taught LME I – Judith Keene at Sydney, Iain Brash, Rob Stuart, Judith Woodward, Jane Long at UWA. They have survived the somewhat 'totalitarian' ambitions of the course to fill every nook and cranny of their reading time and that of their students. They have been sufficiently resilient to assist me convert the course into a book. As teachers, researchers and historians, they have made university life what it ought to be, a collegial experience.

Any worthwhile historian has ambitions to write crisp, elegant and subtle prose, and not to make too many glaring errors. I can only sustain such ambitions with the help of a team of sub-editors and critics. Chief among them is Graham White, himself a superb stylist and greatly influential in the crafting of the better passages in this book. Shane White and Jonathan Steinberg took time off from their busy schedules to provide the right admixture of criticism and encouragement, especially in warning me about 'knowing too much' in the destroyed first version of the Italian chapter. Others who have read and helped with all or part of the text are Peter Monteath, David Christian, Rikki Kersten, Esta Ungar, Luisa Passerini, Mark Thornton, Harry Hinsley, Barry Laing, Ros Pesman and John Moses. Most of my colleagues in the University of Western Australia History Department have managed to survive my badgering of them for information and ideas from one or other area of their expertise, while the office staff, Dawn Barrett, Judy Bolton and Muriel Mahony, have not quailed too much whenever I have hit them with yet another set of revisions. Similarly I am grateful to the staff of the Humanities Research Centre of the Australian National University. In that flourishing and even opulent institution I spent four months, from July to October 1991, endlessly and neurotically tinkering with my text. Graeme Clarke, the director of the HRC, and Jodi Parvey and Louise Bannister among the staff seemed habituated to such outlandish behaviour from their visitors.

My other purpose in visiting the ANU was to research the final chapter on Japan, a society perilously outside my normal expertise as a Late Modern Europeanist. I am very grateful for access to the University's excellent library holdings in the Asian area and for the help which I received from scholars expert in the field. Especially, I am in debt to Gavin McCormack, the Professor of Japanese Studies at the ANU, for readily granting me access to his own files on Japanese historiographical debates, and to Sheldon Garon, a visitor from Princeton, who selflessly gave bibliographical and interpretational advice and actually seemed pleased to exchange ideas with an Italianist run wild.

Authors, especially academic ones, are playthings of the publication process. In this regard, I was flattered when Gordon Martel suggested that I contribute to the New International History series. I was relieved that he was not too taken aback when I sketched a plan of what has turned into *Explaining Auschwitz and Hiroshima*. I was sustained in the process of writing by his enthusiasm and gratified by his pleasure at the final draft. Similarly, I am in debt to Claire L'Enfant, Nick Thomas and others at Routledge for their efficiency and effectiveness in turning out a readable book.

It is the Dutch historian, Pieter Geyl, who has recorded movingly that, for him, 'history . . . became and has remained the ruling interest of my life. History such as I have always understood it: not an inventory of dead people and dead things, but a key to life. . . . Life in its fullness, life in all its shadings and aspects.'[6] I can but agree, adding only that, for me, this interest has been deepened by my marriage, for what is approaching three decades, to a fine historian, Michal Bosworth. She has read and re-read this book in manuscript form, as she has all my other publications, and it is much the better for it.

These things apart, I have not, so far, given much away to anyone seeking to ask LME I's 'who' question about the author of this book. Nor shall I, except to say that I expect its contents are coloured, to some extent, by the facts that I was born in 1943 and that I am an Australian. When Umberto Eco was asked why he had published *The Name of the Rose* as he approached fifty, he replied that, at fifty, a man should either write a novel or run off with a chorus girl. Avoiding this choice between the novel and the navel, I have opted instead for *The Grate LME I Book,* as I privately entitle it.

For it is, these days, a somewhat perplexing business being an Australian academic trained to teach and research in twentieth-century European history. Our economic weakness means that universities stagnate and there are fewer books and journals in our libraries. Members of my own generation are largely cushioned by our seniority and established contacts, but our successors will have a troublesome time merely being able to afford to work on Europe. Meanwhile official discourse in Australia flits from the menacing fatuities of 'radical nationalism' to an unlikely and somewhat pathetic attempt to persuade the powerful of Japan and South Korea that we are 'part of Asia'. In the hard decade of the 1990s, the frightening reality seems rather to be that Australia is part of nothing, no longer naturally tied to Britain, of a largely European culture but hopelessly separated from the 'real' Europe, with trade ambitions in and a still small immigration from the Asian region, in military alliance with the USA and rather rustically imitative of the Americans' non-welfarist brand of capitalism, seriously attached only to that economic wreck, New Zealand. Since white settlement,[7] Australian history has been a story of boom and bust. These are the times of bust. If, therefore, my readers find a pessimism of the intellect in these pages (though always accompanied, I trust, by an optimism of the will), the darkness owes something to my being an Australian.

But before I become even more sententious, let me return to LME I and its students. Though governments and administrators may argue that accountancy or real estate studies should be the centre of the modern university, students still flock to courses like LME I. They do so because they are attracted and intrigued, as eighteen-year-olds should be, by the epic ethical issues of the 'long Second World War', 'Auschwitz' and 'Hiroshima'. In the most recent versions of LME I, they have found the course handbook distributed to the sounds of the choral part of Beethoven's Ninth (see chapter 4 below); they have been read a long description, by the Italian journalist Curzio Malaparte, of what happened to those who could pass reading exams in the Nazi-occupied USSR (see chapter 7). Then they have heard, on a crackling tape, an extract from the *Goon Show*, a satirical and surreal British radio comedy of the 1950s. That is where this book starts, too.

Richard Bosworth

Acknowledgements

The publishers and I would like to thank the following for their permission to reproduce material which appears in the following pages (every reasonable effort has been made to trace the copyright holders; where this has not been possible we apologise to those concerned): Spike Milligan Productions Ltd, for extracts from the *Goon Show;* Maelstrom Music, for an extract from *So long Mom*, by Tom Lehrer; The Merlin Press Ltd, for an extract from 'My Study' by E.P. Thompson; EMI Music, for an extract from 'West of the Wall', words and music by Wayne Shanklin; Picador, for an extract from *Kaputt* by Curzio Malaparte; William Collins, an imprint of HarperCollins Publishers Ltd, for five lines from 'Heirs of Stalin', © Y. Yevtushenko 1966, from *Poems Chosen by the Author,* translation © R. Milner-Gulland and Peter Levi 1963.

Introduction

Bluebottle: What time is it, Eccles?

Eccles: Just a moment. I've got it written down here on a piece of paper. A nice man wrote the time down for me this morning.

Bluebottle: Oh. Then why do you carry it around with you, Eccles?

Eccles: Well. If anybody asks me the time, I can show it to them.

Bluebottle: Wait a minute, Eccles, my good man.

Eccles: What is it, fellow?

Bluebottle: It's writted on this bit of paper what it's 8 o'clock, it is writted.

Eccles: I know that my good fellow. That's right. When I asked the fellow to write it down it was 8 o'clock.

Bluebottle: Well, then, supposing when somebody asks you the time it isn't 8 o'clock.

Eccles: Oh. Then I don't show it to them.

Bluebottle: Oh. Well how do you know when it's 8 o'clock?

Eccles: I got it written down on a piece of paper.

Bluebottle: Here. I wish I could afford a piece of paper with the time written on.

Eccles: Ow!

Bluebottle: Here Eccles, let me hold that piece of paper to my ear would you?

Eccles: Yeah.

Bluebottle: Here, this piece of paper ain't going.

Eccles: What? I've been sold a forgery.

Bluebottle: No wonder it stopped at 8 o'clock!

Eccles: Oh dear!

Bluebottle: You should get one of them things my Grandad's got.

Eccles: Oh?

Bluebottle: His firm give it to him when he retired.

Eccles: Ow!

Bluebottle: It's one of them things what it is that wakes you up at 8 o'clock, boils the kettule and pours a cuppa tea.

Eccles: Oh, yeah! What's it called?

Bluebottle: My Grandma!

Eccles: Oh! Oh! Wait a minute. How does she know when it's 8 o'clock?

1

Bluebottle: She's got it written down on a piece of paper!
Greenslade: Personally, I think it's all in the mind, you know! [1]

Though at first sight an unlikely source, the *Goon Shows*, despite, or rather because of their 'goonery', their 'idiocy', their 'surreality',[2] contain important evidence for a historian of the post-1945 world. In their 'madness', the Goons reveal much about the themes of this book, that is, about the historicisation of the 'long Second World War', about 'Auschwitz' and 'Hiroshima'. (Sound of falling bomb: 'You rotten swine! You deaded me!') In the piece cited above, Eccles and Bluebottle, the (idiot) man and (snivelling) boy of the people, the *poveri cristi*, talk, except in that wretched sexist bit about grandmas, of the nature of time and the meaning of history. How do we know what the 'lessons of history' are? That is easy, for has it not all been written down on a piece of paper? But then who wrote it down? What if they happened to be forgers, those who manufacture times past? And, anyway, when did they write it down? (We all know that – at 8 o'clock. . . .) And what if it should turn out that 'it's all in the mind, you know?'

Nor do the resonances of the Goons end there. The author of the passage under discussion is Terence 'Spike' Milligan, that extraordinary 'ordinary soldier', the most authentic voice after 1945 of the Second World War as 'People's war'.[3] He had been born in 1918 to an NCO of Irish extraction serving in the British Army in India. In 1933, the father's term of service elapsed and the family returned to live on a pension of fifty shillings a week in the south-eastern suburbs of London. Life was tough, and Milligan drifted from one job to another. Like many a man ('idiot') of the 1930s, he found stimulation or entertainment not from the ideological disputes between fascism, communism and parliamentary democracy that fascinated the intellectuals of the period but rather from jazz, booze and sex. Like Eccles, he was 'merely' a 'happy-go-lucky lad'.[4]

In June 1940, Milligan was conscripted into the British Army. Henceforth he would contribute to the downfall of Adolf Hitler because those in authority said he must. Along with his mates, Milligan fought in North Africa and Italy. Despite the incompetence, self-interest and delusion of many of the officer caste, sometimes more 'naturally' his enemies than were the Germans,[5] he survived the terror and the horror of those experiences.

Indeed, by most measurements, Milligan had a 'good war'. It was the war which allowed him to meet his fellow Goons; it was the war which publicised his talents as a trumpet-player and comedian; it was the war which opened the class-bound corridors of the BBC, otherwise blocked to someone of Milligan's humble background and lack of formal training.[6] For his contribution to the King's victory, however, Milligan was to be paid not only with opportunity and eventual wealth and fame but also with unhappiness and bouts of insanity.

Milligan's war had possessed a darkness which would not fade away. In *Mussolini: His Part in My Downfall,* the fourth volume of his memoirs, Milligan recounts his 'fall'. Shell-shocked, Gunner Milligan had sought refuge in a military hospital and, by this act, he then and thereafter feared, had ratted on his mates in

2

'D-Battery'.[7] It was this war whose wages were always with him that has both inspired his creative achievements and also resulted in his occasional sojourns in a psychiatric ward. Milligan both won and lost his Second World War.

If this ambiguity may be true for an individual, so, often, is it for a society. In the following pages I shall pursue the question of the 'comfortable' or 'mad' ways in which societies which went through the Second World War have historicised and thus comprehended that experience. Historicisation is a 'process' and not a 'thing'. On occasions, the version of the past established in the historiography of a particular society, its prevailing 'myth of the war experience' (to use George Mosse's term),[8] will begin to seem inadequate. The result will usually be a bitter historiographical controversy, a 'paradigm shift', a time when '8 o'clock' no longer seems a credible answer even though it has been written down on a piece of paper. It is these shifts which, after an introduction, I shall examine in successive chapters devoted to the relevant historiographies of Britain, Germany, France, Italy, the USSR and Japan.

In each case, I shall argue that the initial traumatic effect of the war was to 'freeze time' and thus to provide a simple historical explanation about what had recently happened. Eventually, however, a thaw occurs. In Britain and West Germany in the 1960s and in France in the next decade, the dissolution of previously established interpretations seemed to enhance the significance of the conflict, and to confirm that modern politics would carry through the promises of the People's war. But, in most societies, this 'Second World War which never ended' has in turn come to its conclusion. In a process which first became apparent in Italy from the middle of the 1970s, the Second World War, in many parts of the world, has lost the overwhelming ethical force which it once possessed. By the 1990s, even in the USSR, the cultural dominance of the 'long Second World War' is over; its 'history' is 'at an end'. And the one clear political result of the conflict, the decision that Germany should not be permitted to form a nation state, has been overturned.

It was an American commentator, Francis Fukuyama, who drew the most obvious and jejune lessons from these events. In an article, published in the summer of 1989 in a journal somewhat ironically entitled the *National Interest*, Fukuyama proclaimed victory. 'The triumph of the West, of the Western *idea*, is evident . . . in the total exhaustion of viable systematic alternatives to Western liberalism.' Marxism was finished and, anyway, eccentric philosopher Alexandre Kojève had told him, 'the egalitarianism of modern America represents the essential achieve-ment of the classless society envisioned by Marx'. All in all, Fukuyama stated, 1989 amounted to 'the end of history as such; that is, the end point of mankind's ideological evolution and the universalisation of Western liberal democracy as the final form of human government.' When, a few months later, the Berlin Wall fell and Germany was re-unified, Fukuyama's prescience seemed confirmed. Maybe the longer-term future also would be as Fukuyama foresaw it. The last battle won, there would no longer be a need for self-sacrifice. 'In the post-historical period', he wrote, 'there will be neither art nor philosophy, just the perpetual caretaking of the museum of human history'. The only danger would be nostalgia for the time when 'history' did exist. 'Perhaps this very prospect of centuries of boredom at the end of history will serve to get history started once again.'[9]

It is unfortunate that the word 'history' is one of the more imprecise in the English language. It can mean both the thing studied and the process of studying it. Fukuyama's usage does not overcome this imprecision. What he appears to be celebrating is the demise not of time itself, but of the discipline of history conceived as debate. Whatever may have been true in the past, Fukuyama asserts, history, in the foreseeable future, will not be an 'argument without end' as Pieter Geyl aptly defined it soon after 1945.[10]

But, short of the commencement of the Final Conflict, Fukuyama's prophesy is certain to be mistaken. Even under the most severe tyranny, historical debate can only be pushed just beneath the surface of society, to re-emerge whenever a modicum of liberty is permitted. Humanity will always possess diverse interpretations of the past and a tolerance of that diversity is the absolute base of any democracy.

Moreover, Fukuyama has already been proven inaccurate in his forecasts. Present-day Europe is alive with rival histories, be they expressed in the Yugoslavia whose composite peoples are, in 1991, re-staging their murderously 'real' Second World wars, in the St Petersburg whose populace must hope that Tsarist history will give more comfort than have the histories of the Revolution and the Great Patriotic War or, more generally, among all those social groups which, in a world of permanent change, do not accept the immutability of the current status quo.

And yet, as has already been suggested, it will be the contention of this book that, despite the Yugoslav exception, the year 1989 did mark the 'end of the long Second World War', at least in Europe. Of course, it was not a sudden dénouement; this 'end' did not lack its own history. The processes which were then completed had moved with a different rhythm in different societies and, in some cases, had become obvious well before 1989. What Fukuyama was discerning was not an 'end of history', but rather an 'end of historiography', a moment in which historical disputation did not disappear but did shift its ground, a time when the 'long Second World War' lost its hegemony and when the ethical values of anti-Fascism, the Resistance and the People's war were finally obscured or replaced.

Fukuyama thought this a matter for rejoicing. My fear, rather, is that it is something to regret. Either point of view can be defended, but what is clear is how dominant and how durable have been the debates of the rival 'myths of the war experience'. When George Mosse coined this term in an article published in 1986, his own conclusion was that the myths of the First World War, all that was summed up in the 'camaraderie of the trenches', had been stronger and more influential than those of the Second. After 1945, Mosse claimed, there had been rather a 'failure . . . to transform the ideals of war-time camaraderie into a powerful engine of post-war politics'. Instead, 'a certain numbness, a will to forget, took the place of the Myth of the War Experience.'[11]

But, perhaps because he himself is such a child of the First World War as well as of 'Auschwitz',[12] Mosse is surely taking his brief too narrowly. This book, by contrast, will show that, for more than a generation, the politics and culture of society after society have been underpinned by interpretations of the 'long Second World War', 'Auschwitz' and 'Hiroshima'. In that sense, the Second World War, though so much the result of the First, has had the more profound and pervasive influence.

Before proceeding, I need to introduce some key terms used throughout this study. The most important are 'Auschwitz' and 'Hiroshima', the origins of which make up the 'long Second World War'.[13] This book, like so many others, is very self-consciously written after those cataclysmic events. Each term has more than one meaning. 'Auschwitz' stands for the Holocaust, for what Arno Mayer evocatively calls the 'torment of the Jews'.[14] But it also refers to a wider issue – the apparent incompatibility of 'liberty' and the 'nation state', despite the glib manner in which they were and are so frequently associated. In this instance, 'Auschwitz' signifies the frequent population transfers, the regular tyrannous attempts to homogenise the inhabitants of a state and thus force nationality to coincide with reality. It recalls all the murderous brutalities of neighbours' little wars which, particularly in Eastern Europe, were contained within what we call the Second World War. It is a reminder that in wartime Yugoslavia, for example, fascists, monarchists, liberals, communists and 'partisans', Serbs, Croats, Slovenians, Albanians, Italians and Macedonians, Muslims, Christians of one persuasion or another and Jews, killed or were killed in a complex of vicious quarrels. Finally, 'Auschwitz' implies that epic conflict defined brilliantly, again by Arno Mayer, as 'Wilson versus Lenin'.[15] The 'long Second World War' was a battleground of nationalism and communist internationalism (however swiftly abandoned in practice by the USSR, to survive, in theory, in places where 'it was all in the mind, you know').

'Hiroshima' carries almost as much cultural meaning. The military wisdom or moral virtue of President Harry S Truman's decision to bomb the Japanese cities of Hiroshima and Nagasaki can still provoke debate. But the symbol of a technological triumph, of a clean white airman releasing the device which will devastate a non-European city, remains. 'Hiroshima' forever after resonates with the power relations implicit in the term 'imperialism'. Still graver is the menace, unleashed at Hiroshima and impossible thereafter to deny, of the end of the world, the event in which 'total war' would acquire its ultimate meaning. As Spike Milligan, that 'idiot' with an 'unshakeable belief in the innate goodness of his fellow man', discerned with his usual surreal sagacity, with the Second World War over, one should 'Book now for World War III', third and last of the series.[16]

Fifty years later, that catastrophe is still not upon us. Despite the obscene size of nuclear arsenals and the fearsome proliferation of the relevant technology, the end seems not yet nigh. Rather, it may presently be suspected, historians of the post-war years will be able to conclude their accounts with much more positive words. They might even adapt a passage of Gibbon to declare that

> if a man [or woman] were called to fix the period in the history of the world, during which the condition of the human race was most happy and prosperous,

he [or she] would, without hesitation, name that which elapsed from the death of Hitler to the accession of ... [Gorbachev? Bush?].[17]

If this were to be the conclusion, its justification would be that, in 1945, the supreme moral crisis of the 'long Second World War' had been resolved, at least in the short term, in a better manner than had seemed likely. For the next two generations, having learnt the 'lessons of history', many men and women were reluctant to return either to Auschwitz or to Hiroshima. They preserved and affirmed the history and the myths of anti-Fascism, of the Resistance and the People's war, existing, writing and thinking in a more humble and re-dimensioned world. As the great Jewish psychologist and sometime inmate of Dachau, Bruno Bettelheim, conscious of having 'survived' the Holocaust, has commented:

> In World War II Auschwitz and Hiroshima showed that progress through technology has escalated man's destructive impulses into more precise and incredibly more devastating form. . .
>
> The concentration camps with their gas chambers, the first atomic bomb . . . confronted us with the stark reality of overwhelming death, not so much one's own – this each of us has to face sooner or later, and, however uneasily, most of us manage not to be overpowered by our fear of it – but the unnecessary and untimely death of millions. . . . Progress not only failed to preserve life, but it deprived millions of their lives more effectively than had been possible ever before.[18]

Bettelheim's words, none the less, are a warning that anyone who brackets Auschwitz or Hiroshima or who sets either deed in context runs the risk of being accused of seeking to relativise 'total' evil. In this book, it is certainly not my intention to derogate from the suffering of the Jews at the hands of the Nazis. Rather, I believe that this suffering can only be comprehended historically through comparison and with an admission that the 'long Second World War' had many victims.

My usage of the phrase 'the long Second World War' may also be controversial. I do not wish to join those who see the twentieth century's 'age of violence' as simply defined in a 'thirty years' war' running from 1914 to 1945. I would accept that the end of the First World War, or rather the diverse ends of the various First World Wars, did foreshadow troubles. The rivalries of 'Wilson versus Lenin' and the contradictions inherent in the formulae either of 'socialism in one country' or of liberal parliamentarism, capitalism and 'self-determination' frame all the crises of the 'long Second World War'. These rivalries and contradictions are the fundamental reasons why, by the end of 1938, no functioning parliamentary democracy existed in Europe outside Scandinavia, the Low Countries, France and Britain. Except in these societies, the 'long Second World War' commenced at that moment in which the various states required that their peoples' liberties be subordinate to their nationality. No precise definition is possible, but 1922 would be a sensible starting point for Italy, 1931 for Japan, 1933 for Germany and perhaps

1929 for the USSR. In regard to the liberal democracies, the Munich Agreement of 1938 is the turning point. It was then that Neville Chamberlain, that conscientious and liberal statesman who personified 'all that was best and most enlightened in British life',[19] flew to Germany and cheerfully betrayed Czechoslovakia, the one state east of the Rhine which still had some claims to have kept intact the Wilsonian marriage of liberalism and benign nationalism. Munich sounded the final prelude to those actual wars which would break out in Europe and the wider world between 1939 and 1941 and which are known as the Second World War.

One final matter should be noted in this introduction. I indicated above that 'history' is an ambiguous term; historiography is no different. In my surveying of debates about the meaning of the Second World War, I shall concentrate mostly on books written by professional and academic historians. From time to time, however, I shall accept that such historians do not have a monopoly on their subject and, where it is convenient, I shall turn to novelists, film-makers, and others who deal in history. Readers will have to decide whether such eclecticism is justified, just as they will have to appraise my selection of the history books which, as far as I am concerned, have commented most acutely on the meaning of the 'long Second World War'.

1

The Second World War and the historians

In the prologue to the second volume of his war memoirs, Spike Milligan juxtaposes two citations:

> Of the events of war, I have not ventured to speak from any chance information, nor according to any notion of my own. I have described nothing but what I saw myself, or learned from others of whom I made the most careful and particular enquiry.
>
> Thucydides. Peloponnesian War

> I've just jazzed mine up a little.
>
> Milligan. World War II.[1]

'*Goak*' here, the attentive reader, accustomed to A.J.P. Taylor's signal of fruitful ambiguity or aware of the post-war world's lack of faith in the certainty of knowledge,[2] should doubtless add. But it is also instructive that Milligan, voice of the 'ordinary soldier' of the Second World War, should invite this comparison of himself as historian with Thucydides and thus implicitly generalise his 'unreliable memories' about his war into a reading of all wars.

This reading from a people's historian is all the more appropriate because of the intimate relationship between war and the first origins of written history, at least in the Western tradition – though epic conflicts, battles lost and won, are also frequently near the heart of oral traditions whether Western or not. In a recent brief history of time and its constructions, G.J. Whitrow has remarked that 'historiography arose when an event occurred which in its magnitude matched the greatest events celebrated in legend', when, that is to say, the terror, the horror and the grandiosity of the present or recent past equalled that which suffused the more distant past. According to Whitrow, Thucydides, in his writing about the conflict between Athens and Sparta, became the 'Father of [Western, 'factual', 'scientific'] History', precisely because those wars, given their extent and duration and given their fraternal and fratricidal nature, irrupted into the consciousness of his Greek contemporaries, wounded and scarred them. 'History' – that is, a proper ordering of events and some attempt at their explanation – was needed because, for the years of civil war, time had seemed to stand still. This form of history was conceived as a cure for the trauma brought to Greek society by years of death and devastation. History was catharsis.

Moreover, Whitrow continues, tragedy, that classic literary vehicle of release and the channelling of ultimate emotions, was born at the same moment as history writing and this twin birth was no accident. As is the case with history, 'a short continuous crisis, the origins and consequences of which cover a long period, seems to be the double requirement of tragedy and its double relationship to time'.[3] In registering and analysing the freezing of time, both history and tragedy help to get the process of time moving again, if only by making manifest that time and society are, after all, always in movement.

Whether or not these speculations about wars of long ago are correct, there can be little doubt about the profound effect on the modern world of the Second World War. In Europe alone, 30 to 40 million died, about 50 per cent more than the total number of victims in the First World War. In Asia, where casualty figures are even more problematic, millions more perished. In Europe, about half those killed were civilians and, in Asia, this proportion was higher still. Whereas in the First War 90 per cent of deaths were military, now survival became almost as doubtful on the 'home front' as it was in battle (while Hiroshima promised that, in the Third World War, the graph of civilian casualties might soar towards 100 per cent).[4]

Where death came, so did devastation. Cities, towns and villages were flattened by bombardment from the air or the ground. At the end of the war, in Europe an estimated 16 million refugees craved hope and sanctuary. International bodies sought ineffectively to count and house them. And such agencies were then still sufficiently Eurocentric to ignore the larger number of refugees in Asia. Moreover, the war had not only devoured people's bodies, their houses, shops, factories and farms. It had also assaulted and ravished their minds in a quite unprecedented fashion. The death camps and the other macabre features of the war, notably at its epicentre in Eastern Europe, mocked belief in Progress and the Good. The American historian, Karl Schleunes, has summed up well the impact of this aspect of the Second World War:

> Violent death accompanying war in an age of industry and technology, by the 1940s, had its precedents. The institutions which most appropriately symbolise the Nazi era – Auschwitz, Dachau, Treblinka, and some fifty other concentration and extermination camps – had none.
>
> These factories of death are now permanently catalogued in the darkest annals of the human story. Their existence casts a shadow over the hopes for our own future. The realisation that some men will construct a factory in which to kill other men raises the gravest questions about man himself. We have entered an age which we cannot avoid labeling 'After Auschwitz'.[5]

Nor was 'Auschwitz' the only legacy of the war. During its course technologists had found the means and politicians the will to unleash the atom. After Hiroshima, the world had to live with the knowledge that a further conflict might liquidate civilisation itself and do so in an instant:

So long, Mom, I'm off to drop the bomb,
So don't wait up for me. . . .
Remember, mommy, I'm off to get a commie,
So send me a salami, and try to smile somehow.
I'll look for you – when the war is over,
An hour and a half from now.[6]

If any historical event deserves to be defined as traumatic, it is the Second World War. As a very recent student of the period has stated: 'no other years [in human history] have transformed so drastically the expectations of millions of men and women'.[7]

In these circumstances, it is hardly surprising that historians, those dealers in the past and in time, have laboured to explain 'Auschwitz', 'Hiroshima' and the 'long Second World War' and have built a monument of words to them. Paul Fussell, himself a historian made in the Second World War, demonstrated almost two decades ago how the First War affected the relationship between words and time. He indicated that wordsmiths of one kind or another, the artificers of 'modern memory', had given new meaning to old phrases in order to forge an armour covering over the wounds of war.[8] How much more wounding was the Second War and how much greater the need for the carapace of 'explanation'?

At first, however, the writing of a history of the war's experience, the preservation or construction of what in some circles would ironically be reduced to 'post-modern memory', occurred in an atmosphere of reverence and consensus, if, sometimes, of a rather numbed variety and in relief at having survived. Practitioners of history, in contrast with many of their fellow citizens, had often experienced quite 'good' wars. In the aftermath of the Great War, the profession had had much to explain. It had needed to hedge its commitment to 'our country right or wrong' and to justify that apparent prostitution of historical skills which had led historians to invent pasts to assist the national cause.[9] In the second conflict historians had normally occupied less exposed positions.

For some, their escape from the present had commenced in what Stuart Hughes has graphically called a sea change. As, in the 1930s, the European crisis deepened and the freedom to engage in critical history writing was curtailed, the universities of North America had offered some sanctuary.[10] The 'sea change' to this destination was inevitably incomplete, however. Whether senior or junior, the migrating scholars bore with them cultural baggage from their European past. In the New World, they would play a major role in the research and teaching of late modern European history. Every student is indebted to them for their special insights and, at the same time, is aware that they did not always shed the prejudices of their youth and origins.

It is also true that there was an intriguing tendency during the war for some refugees and many Anglo-American historians or historians-to-be to find a place in some branch of their national secret services. William McNeill, Stuart Hughes, William Langer, Carl Schorske, Max Salvadori, Felix Gilbert,[11] Hans Holborn,

10

Crane Brinton, Barrington Moore, Edward Shils, J.K. Fairbank, R.F. Byrnes, Perry Miller, Franklin Ford and David Pinkney were only a few of those employed by the OSS or other agencies of the US government.[12] In Britain, Harry Hinsley,[13] Hugh Trevor-Roper, R.W. Seton-Watson, F.W. Deakin, Basil Davidson, Arnold Toynbee and a host more worked for the overt or covert intelligence offices of the state. Perhaps this assembly of talent merely reflected history's place at the pinnacle of the humanities, and highlighted its role as the most rigorous of the generalist disciplines, with its basis in the most appropriate combination of scepticism, hard work and accuracy. But few historians showed signs of agreeing with the young Richard Cobb, later Professor of Modern History at Oxford, when he confessed his recognition of what he said, 'should be a golden rule for any historian. "Let us assume that our own country is *always* wrong".' And even Cobb, after some characteristic vicissitudes, ended up in the British Army where, as he has recalled, he was 'very lucky in all [his] postings'.[14]

In 1945, therefore, British and American historians, whose states were the least exhausted of the belligerents, were well placed to set about explaining the war, its causes, course and consequences. What did they have to say? In particular, what, following the experience of fascism, did they have to say about liberty? Could it be re-asserted after the fascist assault on the most fundamental of human values? Did freedom have a future, or a past, after 'Auschwitz'?

Paradoxically, the best way to commence answering this question is to focus not on an Anglo-American but on Pieter Geyl, a Dutchman,[15] albeit one who joined enthusiastically in English-language historiographical controversies and who was generously, perhaps over-generously, described by A.J.P. Taylor as 'one of the great historical minds of our time'.[16] It was Geyl who, in his book *Napoleon: For and Against*, published in 1949, and in his other writings, re-stated a liberal interpretation of history and of the historian's place in society. He argued the classic theses of relativism. History could 'reach no unchallengeable conclusions on so many-sided a character [as Napoleon] . . . . To expect from history those final conclusions which may perhaps be obtained in other disciplines is . . . to misunderstand its nature. . . . Truth, though for God it may be One, assumes many shapes to men.'[17] But rather than submitting cravenly in this battle of truths, historians should become activists of a sort: 'criticism . . . is the first duty of historical scholarship, criticism, again criticism, and criticism once more.'[18] Like another Coriolanus, Geyl proclaimed a stern but positive message for the post-war world. He expressed it best in a sonnet originally composed before the conflict ended.[19] For forty months he had been interned because of his 'suspect general mentality' and writing poetry had become a method of deflecting the attempts of his gaolers to dominate and destroy him. In an interview which he gave in 1961 he recalled this favourite concentration camp composition:

> The stars are fright'ning. The cold universe,
> Boundless and silent, goes revolving on,
> Worlds without end. The grace of God is gone.

11

A vast indifference, deadlier than a curse,
Chills our poor globe, which Heaven seemed to nurse
So fondly. 'Twas God's rainbow when it shone,
Until we searched. Now, as we count and con
Gusts of infinity, our hopes disperse.
Well, if it's so, then turn your eyes away
From Heav'n. Look at the earth, in its array
 Of life and beauty. – Transitory? Maybe,
But so are you. Let stark eternity
Heed its own self, and you, enjoy your day,
And when death calls, then quietly obey.[20]

But, as good students of LME I would have asked well before now, who, then, was Pieter Geyl?

In its answering, this question elicits some ambiguous evidence. Geyl had been born in Dordrecht in 1887, the son and grandson of medical doctors. He graduated from Leyden University and by 1913 was established as the London correspondent of *Nieuwe Rotterdamsche Courant*. After the First War he became Professor of Dutch Studies at London; in 1924 the title of his chair was narrowed to Dutch History and Institutions. Twelve years later he returned to the Netherlands, taking up the Professorship in Modern History at Utrecht, from which he would not retire until 1958. He made a name for himself as a historian of the Netherlands in its golden age, publishing his most famous book, *The Revolt of the Netherlands 1555–1609*, in 1932.[21]

Geyl was also a well known polemicist, challenging, for example, Henri Pirenne, the distinguished Walloon Belgian medievalist. Whereas Pirenne was inclined to see a 'natural' division between Belgium and the Netherlands, under-pinned by long-term structural factors, Geyl was not.[22] Both before and after the Second World War, Geyl was similarly critical of the French *Annales* school with its emphasis on the long term. By contrast, despite his distrust of Rankean 'scientific history',[23] he praised the very conservative German historian, Gerhard Ritter.[24]

After the war, Geyl was most scathing in his attacks on Arnold Toynbee's *Study of History*.[25] The publication of this twelve-volume work, with its theses of the rise and fall of civilisations in a rhythm of challenge and response largely controlled by creative minorities, had commenced in 1934 and continued after 1945. The twelfth and final volume would not be published until 1961. Geyl disliked Toynbee's religiosity, his pessimism and his determinism and found him guilty of selectivity and bias. Worse was Toynbee's arrogance: 'Like Faust, he tries to know more than can be known.'[26] And the wages of total knowledge ironically would be political death, passivity, fatalism, in the face of a seductive but false inevitability. Toynbee's *Study*, if believed, would end the discipline: 'The Student of History, as Toynbee calls himself, may know more of history than I shall ever do, but he is no historian. He is a prophet,' Geyl concluded dismissively.[27] In his desire to give final lessons to humankind, Toynbee was lost in the ethereal, and too near to God to understand the needs and life of ordinary men and women. History should concentrate on the real, Geyl asserted, and leave the ideal to those with time to waste.

Though Geyl wrote frequently and effectively about theory,[28] he best and most appropriately expressed his sturdy relativism and combative practicality in a piece of history writing, *Napoleon: For and Against*. It was, he acknowledged, the 'by-product of our recent experiences',[29] and, thus, his 'book of World War II'. As with the sonnet, he had begun fashioning it in his mind at Buchenwald and the other camps to which he had been transferred. Indeed, he had been interned precisely because of his contemplation of Napoleon, being arrested by the German security police (SD) after he gave a public lecture at the Rotterdam School of Economics about the Corsican conqueror. 'Occasional bursts of laughter' from the audience, Geyl has recalled, indicated that they had detected parallels being drawn with Hitler.[30]

For a liberal like Geyl, it was highly appropriate to turn back to the French Revolution[31] in order to obtain intellectual sustenance for the struggle against the Nazis and, in so doing, he reiterated his deep admiration for French 'civilization'. But, though he could not actually start writing *Napoleon: For and Against* until after his release from internment on medical grounds in February 1944, Geyl's 'resistance', his determination not to submit to fascist irrationalism, had been steeled by the discipline of history, by his conviction that history should not offer single answers, and was in its fundamental character 'an argument without end'.[32]

Napoleon: For and Against is thus a somewhat surprising book. It is certainly not a narrative of Napoleon's life, though a reader may notice that Geyl does subtly paint a compelling portrait of a cynical and self-interested dictator.[33] At its first level the book is rather a history of a history. By surveying successive interpretations of Napoleon from the 1790s to the onset of the Second World War, Geyl vividly displays history's need to talk with many voices. The past and the present are part of an unending process; one constantly reverberates with the other. Each generation or faction writes its own history with an eye on the present; but each of these presents is simultaneously a child of the past. In many instances, 'Napoleon' is more influential and powerful as a 'myth', as 'history', than the flesh and blood Emperor was when alive. While history survives, one form or other of Napoleon's spirit is with us always.

Napoleon: For and Against is a fine book which deserves to remain part of any historiographical canon. But it also contains its own ambiguities which, by the 1990s, have become more obvious than they were when it was first published. Geyl's central tenet was, as has been noted, that history is 'an argument without end'. But, in the intervening years, the argument about Napoleon has largely ended. 'Great men', especially military conquerors, have gone out of fashion. A social historian like Richard Cobb would manage to produce a study of the 'Napoleonic period' with only one slighting reference to the 'gangster dynasty'.[34] The 'myth of Napoleon' is no longer a spectre which can haunt Europe.

Geyl, then, had perceived only dimly that history can radically change course, not so much because some brilliant mind works out the final solution to a problem as because the question changes in contemporary society. His own relativism, just like his own understanding of liberty, was actually quite narrow and historically conditioned, a product of his own fleeting moment of time. For, when examined closely, it turned out that there were many, perhaps predictable, limitations in Geyl's own liberalism, numerous ironies in his deployment of history to repair the damage done by the Nazis. Historians of the last generation have by no means accepted that liberals and liberalism were uncontaminated in the great crises of the 'long Second World War'. As shall be seen in chapters 3 and 6 below, liberals did not always reject fascism out of hand in a way that a literal reading of their ideals might suggest they should have. In the 1930s, the fundamental dilemma for liberals remained what it had been for some time – the relationship between 'freedom' and the nation state. The invention and consolidation of this type of state had accompanied the rise of liberal political and cultural power. Given the evident limitations of the League of Nations and the parading of internationalism by those menacing rivals, the communists, with their commitment not so much to liberty as to equality, not so much to general freedom as to their class, liberals were often driven to conclude that they should be loyal to their nation. Sometimes they went much further than that and in so doing lost their souls since, they were forced to realise, 'self-determination' for one nation can usually only be achieved at a cost to another.[35]

And certainly Geyl's own biography splendidly illustrates this tension between liberalism and nationalism. As a youth he was drawn to socialism's promise of social justice but always preferred such 'socialism' to be of the liberal or national variety. He believed deeply in the existence of a Dutch *stam* ('stock') but failed properly to clarify what distinguished a *stam* from a race. For all his rationality and scepticism, Geyl was a decidedly romantic Dutch nationalist.[36] His commitment to his *stam* frequently underscored his arguments as a historian, for example when he rebuked the House of Orange for its elitism and cosmopolitan distancing of itself from the 'real' Dutch people. More ominously, Geyl's controversy with Pirenne could be read as providing a basis for revanchist Dutch claims on the Flemish part of Belgium. Though he detested the recklessness of those gimcrack extremists who would end up as fascists, he did act as a counsellor to and inspiration of the inter-war Flemish nationalist movement. Not for nothing did stolid bureaucrats in both The Hague and Brussels see him 'as little better than a National-Socialist'.[37] In a sense his courting of arrest during his lecture on Napoleon could be interpreted as an attempt to reject or to deny potentially unfortunate elements of his own past.

Though, by 1940, Geyl had understood something about 'Auschwitz', he never really comprehended 'Hiroshima'. Vain, with a profound sense of the respect due to him as a major scholar, Geyl was determinedly Eurocentric. Indeed, when he spoke of his reverence for French culture, what he was really applauding was 'Western civilisation', defined as all that was best and most enlightened in male and middle-class British, French, 'good German' and Dutch life. Civilisation certainly did not cross into the Soviet Union;[38] nor did it spread out into the Third World. In 1956, Geyl pronounced in favour of Anglo-French policies at Suez, thus endorsing this bathetic last fling of old-style, Western, imperialism. In 1961, he wrote off A.J.P. Taylor's *The Origins of the Second World War*, that radical exposure of liberal and conservative myths about both 'Auschwitz' and 'Hiroshima', as 'dreadful history'.[39] To his death in 1966, Geyl did not confuse liberty with egalitarian democracy. For all his proclamation of pluralism and relativism, and his passionate defence of freedom and debate, Geyl thought that strict boundaries needed to be placed on the people's victories in the aftermath of the People's war.

If, in his writings and person, Geyl only ambiguously restored a relationship between history writing and freedom, and only partially sketched the way in which liberty might be defined after Auschwitz, what happened when other historians re-addressed the question of 'fraternity' and wondered what a nation and its history meant following the catastrophic and murderous wartime attempts to make nationality coincide with reality? In particular, how did historians confront the issue of German nationality? What, in the aftermath of 1945, did they say has been Germany's place in the crisis of the 'long Second World War'?

These questions will provide much of the focus in the next three chapters of this book. But, before proceeding with these more detailed studies, it is worth reflecting on a historian whose career straddled the pre-1914, inter-war and post-1945 worlds just as his own life history had traversed Europe from Russia to Great Britain. This historian, who both lived the crisis of the 'long Second World War' and provided a crucial first analysis of its meaning, was Sir Lewis Namier.[40]

In the two or three decades before his death in August 1960, Namier was widely reputed to be the most authoritative or formidable historian in the English-speaking world. He had gained this reputation between the wars with two vast studies of the British political system during the early years of the reign of King George III (1760–1820).[41] In these works he had depicted what a follower of E.P. Thompson[42] might want to call 'a bourgeoisie present at its own making'. But what was most celebrated about Namier was the new historical method which he was deemed to have invented. He studied the functioning of power not through statesmen's great set speeches or intellectuals' ideological outpourings, but through a detailed analysis of politicians' day-to-day interests. Through such multiple biographies or 'prosopography', Namier and his acolytes, 'the Namierites' as they were called, proclaimed that they had created a genuinely 'scientific' approach to history.[43] Namier would be 'the historian's historian' and the influence of the 'Namier revolution' would affect many areas of historical investigation.[44]

But, once again, it turned out that things were not quite what they seemed. 'Who was Sir Lewis Namier?' becomes the by now inevitable first question, and immediately the plot starts to thicken. For Namier, from an earlier generation, was another of those figures who had made the 'sea change' from continental Europe to the Anglo-American world.[45]

He had been born Ludwick Bernsztajn vel Niemirowski, in June 1888, to a

Jewish family who lived in the borderlands of the Romanov and Habsburg empires. In some ways, as shall be seen below, his background was very similar to that of Isaac Deutscher, the biographer of Stalin, but whereas Deutscher's family had been self-consciously intellectual, Namier's father was an administrator for wealthy local landowners and, unusually for a Jew in that region, eventually acquired land for himself.

The young Namier was kept by his family from any contact with the local (Ruthenian) peasantry and so, in his first stirrings of identity, sought to combine Polish nationalism, non-Marxist socialism and pro-Semitism, being 'a Jew, more Polish than the Poles'.[46] When he attended Lwow University, he rapidly discovered that this credo contained an impossible mixture – as J.M. Keynes would later remark acidly, Poland's only industry was 'Jew-baiting'.[47] And certainly Namier would retain a most ambivalent attitude to Poles and to Poland.

Leaving Lwow, he moved off to the paths of exile, first to Switzerland, and then to England, where he enrolled at the London School of Economics (1907–8) and Balliol (1908–11). Though performing brilliantly at Oxford he failed to win a fellowship at All Souls. The historian, A.F. Pollard, has explained the reason: 'the best man by far in sheer intellect was a Balliol man of Polish-Jewish origin and I did my best for him, but the Warden and the majority of Fellows shied at his race, and eventually we elected the two next best.'[48]

Despite this experience of genteel English anti-Semitism,[49] Namier liked Oxford. In 1913 he became a British subject and, in an act which, for emigrants, frequently marks a ritual official sundering of ties with their own history, anglicised his name. After a brief period in the Royal Fusiliers, where his effectiveness was hampered by his extreme short-sightedness, Namier, from 1915, occupied a position in the Foreign Office, formulating expert advice on Central and Eastern Europe, during the Paris Peace Conference for example. Afterwards he liked to claim a special responsibility for dismantling the Austro-Hungarian Empire and for re-creating the Polish state. In moments of psychological doubt, he would wonder if he had thereby murdered his own (multi-national) mother. In general, however, he did not approve the terms of the Versailles settlement.

He spent some of the 1920s in the United States, punting on the stock market with fair success though he tended to spend his winnings on psychoanalysis and graphology. As his second wife, Julia, would later remark, he could believe in the diagnostic part of Freudianism but not its therapeutics.[50] In 1931 he finally obtained a proper academic position, being appointed to the chair of Modern History at the University of Manchester, a post which he did not relinquish until his retirement in 1955. Among his staff he found the young A.J.P. Taylor, who tried unsuccessfully to introduce him to nude bathing and other radical causes.[51]

Namier's great political commitment was to Zionism. In 1929 he became secretary of the London-based Zionist Jewish Agency. Typically, however, he retained major intellectual reservations. 'Though he was a Jew', Julia would state, 'he didn't basically like Jews.'[52] As the crises of the 1930s enveloped Europe, Namier, who had read *Mein Kampf*, was more and more perturbed by the Nazis and aghast at the popularity and ubiquity of appeasement. As early as April 1933, he warned that the Nazi regime really meant what it said, and, given opportunity, would eliminate its Jews.[53] Eighteen months later, he declared gloomily that capitalism was finished and that he had been left to hope that the upheaval would not be too vast so that at least 'culture' could survive.[54] He had never ceased to warn that Eastern European peasants might get out of hand and he remained a critic of the Soviet regime, which, much to his disgust, would, after 1945, sequester the Namier family estates. Trotsky, he wrote in a typical essay, was brilliant, but had engaged in self-deception when he boasted that he could communicate with the masses and control their elemental force.[55]

Namier, then, seemed to be someone whose *curriculum vitae* would make him a visceral opponent of the nation state. He certainly despised what he defined as 'linguistic nationalism' and feared the 'primeval power' which nationalist intellectuals could unleash in the masses. Unlike such Jewish Marxist historians as Eric Hobsbawm or Isaac Deutscher,[56] Namier had rejected internationalism, but he had not found satisfaction in Ruthenian or Polish or English or British or even Israeli nationality. Perhaps, as J.L. Talmon has commented, it was his 'fate to be always and everywhere an outsider'.[57]

And yet Namier had won a sort of sanctuary in Britain (especially within the culture of the great landed families of the eighteenth century about which he had written at such length and with such admiration). The British model of so-called 'territorial nationalism' did not, he opined, carry the evils present in the nationalisms of Eastern Europe. The British knew about justice and decency, particularly when their best men assembled in 'that marvellous microcosmos of English social and political life, that extraordinary club, the House of Commons. For centuries', Namier went on a little wistfully, and with a choice of metaphor replete with Freudian overtones, 'it has been the goal of English manhood.'[58]

After the Second World War began, Namier returned to London where he acted as a liaison officer between the British government and the Jewish Agency. Though frequently dismayed by what he regarded as official pusillanimity or betrayal over the Palestine question, he was eventually gratified by the decision to create the Jewish State of Israel in 1948. Characteristically he advised the Israeli leader, David Ben-Gurion, to adopt the British and reject the European way of organising parliamentary seating:

> The arrangement of benches in the House of Commons reproduces the lay-out of a playing field and fosters a team spirit. No one must intervene in a game from the flank and there is no place for a Centre party. The 'political pendulum' swings from side to side, and has only two points of arrest.[59]

Whatever else Namier might have been, he was not a liberal who, from the centre of debates, would sit so long on the fence that the iron would enter his soul.

During the war itself, the liberal British Establishment had acknowledged that Namier had 'read' Nazism better than they by giving him an important charge. In 1944 he was invited to present the Raleigh Lecture to the British Academy. The theme he chose was the history of the revolutions of 1848. He would explore the 'origins of the German problem' and thus draft the historical justification for what British policy towards a post-war Germany should be. He would lay bare the evil of German nationalism. In speaking about 1848, he would offer a commentary on German misdeeds in 1933, 1938, 1939, 1941 and 1945. In his lecture, which would be turned into a book and published in 1946 as *1848: The Revolution of the Intellectuals*,[60] he would meld the German past and the German present.

Namier had two quarries in mind. One was Germany; the second those squeamish intellectuals who, in 1919, had indulged in Wilsonian idealism and thus allowed Nazi Germany to be born. Their weakness had been a tragedy; now they would have a second opportunity to settle the German question and they must not be permitted to make it a farce. Stiffening their sinews and summoning up their blood, they must at last deal with Germany.

About a united Germany's impact on Europe, Namier held no illusions. Back in August 1942, he had already announced that 'it did not require either 1914, or 1933, or 1939 to teach me the truth about the Germans. Long before the last war I considered them a deadly menace to Europe and to civilization.'[61] In his lecture to the Academy, too, he contended that the menace had been there at the inception of the German nation state. Rather than 1848 being a 'springtime of the peoples'[62] as it had sometimes been depicted, the revolutions of that year had unveiled the fundamental contradiction between liberty and the Central and Eastern European version of nationality. In that part of the world, the nation state was 'as unsuited to living organisms as chemically pure water' and there 1848 had started 'the Great European War of every nation against its neighbours'.[63]

The epicentre of these conflicts lay in Germany. Parliamentary action or other liberal nostrums could never have united that nation: 'States are not created or destroyed, and frontiers redrawn or obliterated, by argument and majority votes; nations are freed, united, or broken by blood and iron, and not by a generous application of liberty and tomato-sauce.'[64] In their continued public idealism, Germany's liberals were the most vapid or hypocritical of the actors of 1848; besotted by nationalism, they turned German domestic 'revolution' into 'that playful cow' which would kick over the traces of Europe.[65] Nor did Germans improve their behaviour with the passage of time. As Namier pronounced brutally in another essay, Nazism was 'the correct consummation of the German era in history'.[66]

In his lecture to the Academy and in these later essays, Namier drew a picture of the 'long Second World War' with bold, clear lines. Germany, not Hitler, had caused the Second World War. Maybe Romania or Poland, given a similar population, and economic and military strength like that of Germany, would have behaved in the same manner. But it was actually Germany which had taken the world to that horror which would be understood as 'Auschwitz'. In these circumstances, the only reasonable and realistic thing to do was to divide that country and to leave it divided.

While he lived Namier continued to preach this plain lesson. For those who cared to notice, his tormented personality, so 'intellectual' and yet so dismissive of intellectuals' actions, so 'scientific' and yet so attracted by the sub-conscious, so bitterly hostile to nation states and yet so committed to Israel, so overbearing and authoritarian[67] and yet so uncertain and deferential towards those who really supped at high table, displayed the contradictions and barely suppressed violence of his own frustrated search for identity. How much worse, he seemed to imply, had been, was and would be the situation in those societies composed largely of people with similar identity crises? Peace could only be preserved, the world could only be made safe, if the Second World War had one fundamental outcome – Germany must forever after be denied self-determination. Never again could a German nation state be permitted to exist.

But Namier's work carried another implication which would soon weaken the rigidity of his argument that the enemy was the German nation and only the German nation. As has been noted, Namier was also no friend of the USSR, however much he believed that the Soviets' essence was Russian and not communist. Rather, A.J.P. Taylor has recalled, Namier 'despised Soviet Russia as the rule of the masses – the Ham, as he called them, meaning the illiterate peasants. He extended this contempt to the British and indeed the German' working class.[68] In this regard, his *1848: The Revolution of the Intellectuals* was a sort of *Anti-Communist Manifesto* in which the workers of the world congregated off stage – imponderable, malevolent, dangerous: 'The mob had come out in revolt, moved by passions and distress rather than by ideas: they had no articulate aims and no-one will ever be able to supply a rational explanation of what it was they fought for, or what made them fight.'[69] By 1948, their character had not changed. Marxists, if they pinned their hopes on such people, were deluded. 'Marx! Marx!' Namier once muttered to Sir Isaiah Berlin, 'a typical Jewish half-charlatan, who got hold of quite a good idea and then ran it to death just to spite the Gentiles.'[70]

Though he admired Stalin, accepted that collectivisation had improved the lot of the Russian peasantry,[71] and in the 1930s had advocated an Anglo-Russian alliance, Namier had already utilised the term 'totalitarian' before 1945.[72] His obsession with Germany meant that, for him, the USSR was always the lesser of two evils. But, as victory against Nazi–Fascism and Japanese militarism was rapidly followed by the onset of that prolonged international and social crisis called the Cold War, other commentators began to think that Namier's balance was wrong. The enemy lay on the (pseudo-) Left. Neither Geyl, with his concentration on liberty, nor Namier, with his iron-hard anti-German comprehension of the limitations of fraternity, had read the current relationship between past and present correctly.

The great issue of the post-war world was 'equality'; not parliamentary or intellectual freedom, not the nation, but class. Or, rather, to use less hermetic language, the real contest after 1945, and even before, was that between the 'West' and the Soviet system, which had boasted that it would unite and protect the workers of the globe and that it constituted the world historic force that would ensure the triumph of the working class in a final, stateless, and unified utopia. Marxist historians, within and without the USSR, were seen and, at least until 1956, often saw themselves as toiling in this cause. Many liberal, moderate socialist and conservative historians had different hopes and targets, and different answers, especially about the meaning of the Second World War. The real causes of that conflict were not so much the fragility of liberalism or the excesses of German nationalism, and certainly were not part of a general assault on either the USSR or the working class. Instead the war had resulted from 'totalitarianism'. Totalitarianism was evil and evil was totalitarian. The appeasement of totalitarianism in the 1930s had failed inevitably; in the 1950s it should not be attempted again. But what did 'totalitarianism' really mean and where had the term originated?[73]

The word was used first in the early days of Fascist Italy by opponents of Mussolini critical of his regime's authoritarian ambitions to intrude into civil society. By 1925, however, the *Duce* had taken over the term for his own purposes and, indeed, had made it the essence of Fascism. '*Professore*' Mussolini,[74] with his erstwhile qualifications as a primary school French teacher, was always a little uneasy in his dealings with intellectuals and fearful of their sarcasm. The idea of the '*stato totalitario*' (the totally total state)[75] gave him a useful weapon when supporters or critics suggested that his 'Fascist revolution' was a fake, lacking an appropriate ideological genealogy, cloudy in its present design. The word 'totalitarian' thus commenced its complex life as a sort of Italian advertising slogan.

It soon proved of lasting value for Fascist propagandists, however, and began to have a history developed for it. In the *Doctrine of Fascism* (1932), prepared for the celebrations of the tenth anniversary of the Fascist regime, Mussolini pronounced: 'Fascism is totalitarian, and the Fascist State – a synthesis and a unit inclusive of all values – interprets, develops, and potentiates the whole life of a people.' Though only Fascism embodied it, and the intellectuals – Charles Péguy, Georges Sorel, Hubert Lagardelle and various Italian thinkers – who sensed its coming were recent, the totalitarian Fascist state was accorded a history which went back to 1789, to the French Revolution and the Enlightenment. Its basis was 'spiritual'; it rejected 'all individualistic abstractions based on eighteenth-century materialism . . . all Jacobinistic utopias and innovations.'[76]

Many subsequent historians have doubted whether a totalitarian state was, in fact, created in Mussolini's Italy.[77] But the word has floated free from its Italian origins and they are often all but forgotten. The Nazis only rarely applied the term to themselves.[78] None the less, in the 1930s, it did start to be used for a new purpose. Especially in conservative circles, the word 'totalitarianism' began to encompass all that was abhorred in the modern world. Hitler's accession to power in 1933 and the existence of right-wing, radical, nationalist and anti-Semitic movements in every European country made it seem possible that, as Mussolini boasted, Fascism was *the* 'doctrine of the twentieth century'.

But what was Fascism?[79] This question had elicited a number of different responses. Liberals were likely to talk about a 'moral sickness', caught by Italy, Germany and other European societies in the First World War and capable of striking alike rich and poor, worker and peasant, capitalist and small shop-keeper. Predictably, Marxists thought manipulation was involved. Fascism was 'the open terrorist dictatorship of the most reactionary, most chauvinistic, most imperialist elements of finance capital.'[80] It was the state to which the bourgeoisie had recourse at a moment of desperation. If, as more perceptive Marxists admitted, Fascism possessed some sort of mass base, this base was constructed from the petty bourgeoisie, peasants or *Lumpenproletariat*, those social groups damned as 'unhistorical' by Marx and Engels in the *Communist Manifesto*.

But conservatives had a third and different answer. Perhaps their most graphic spokesman was Hermann Rauschning, a German nationalist from Danzig, who had at first flirted with the Nazis but then broken with them. Rauschning had no doubt about what Nazism was. In the words of the title of a book which he published in March 1941, it was 'the beast from the abyss', the slavering Beast of the Apocalypse. Its backers were the masses, those ordinary people who had been led into the paths of mutiny and licentiousness ever since the French Revolution. Its aim was world revolution through an orgy of war and destruction, 'the revolution of nihilism', which, paradoxically, would entail a 'vast totalitarian absolutism'.[81] For all that Hitler had gone further and faster than the Soviets in his tyranny, and had inevitably predatory designs on the USSR, his revolution and theirs were both part of the single onslaught against 'civilisation'. The criminal goal was to establish the 'Leviathan' state:

> it is the final result of man's struggle for freedom and erection of his own system, a system opposed to the divine, revealed system. It is progress in alliance with barbarism. It is the liberation that turns into total slavery. It is the earthly immortality in the form of a collective man, a mass man, a termite man.[82]

Rauschning reiterated his view that Nazi Germany was far more evil than the USSR, but the reason for this was simply that Nazism, in its practice, was still more radical than Bolshevism. Nazism, Rauschning explained, 'in its expansion of the doctrine of Socialism . . . is the legitimate and perhaps the last continuation of the process of secularization and revolutionization of the last four hundred years . . . entirely alien, . . . complete nothingness, the absolute negation of the West, of civilization.'[83]

When, a few months later, the USSR turned out to be another, and even the special victim of Nazism, these ideas fell publicly out of fashion. But they were always there to be revived should they be opportune or necessary. Their revival after 1945 is a curious tale both of the transmission of a European *Weltanschauung* to the New World and of the way in which an interpretation of the past may best fit a particular present. If once Mussolini had exploited the neologism 'totalitarian' to explain something which, he said, was already happening, so the theory of totalitarianism became powerful and pervasive (and made many an academic career) because it justified the policies of the 'West' in the Cold War.

In the 1950s three great texts were published in which the theory of totalitarianism was codified – Hannah Arendt's *The Origins of Totalitarianism*, largely written in 1949 but released in 1951; Jacob Talmon's *The Origins of Totalitarian*

Democracy (1952); and Carl Friedrich and Zbigniew Brzezinski's *Totalitarian Dictatorship and Autocracy* (1956).[84]

Each of these authors had transported overseas some sort of cultural baggage from inter-war Europe.[85] Carl Friedrich, for example, was a member of a distinguished German family; his mother was a von Bülow. Trained in the great universities of German culture, Marburg, Heidelberg, Frankfurt and Vienna, he had migrated to the United States in 1922 and from 1926 had taught at Harvard, only taking out US citizenship in 1938. Brzezinski belonged to a younger generation, having been born in Poland in 1928; his family migrated to Canada ten years later. After a brilliant career as a student at McGill, he graduated with a Harvard PhD in 1953 and took up a fellowship at the Russian Research Centre of that university.

Their text was the last of the basic studies of totalitarianism to be composed, appearing after Khrushchev's denunciation of Stalin at the Twentieth Soviet Party Congress in February 1956 and at a time when the loyalty of many Western Marxists to the USSR, its past, present and future, was waning. But it was also the simplest of the books and readily elevated to the status of a bible for Western political science, for history and other disciplines.

In their preface, Friedrich and Brzezinski acknowledged the assistance of such distinguished or soon to be distinguished authorities as Merle Fainsod, Dante Germino and Adam Ulam, as well as that of Sigmund and Franz Neumann and Hannah Arendt. They added that Carl Friedrich had already drafted a full-length analysis of the subject in the 1930s but had not published it before the outbreak of war. Now his manuscript had been re-worked on the basis of greater information, much of it garnered through seminars at the Harvard Russian Research Centre, the *Institut für Zeitgeschichte* in Munich, and a special Yale research project on 'human relations'. There had been a final re-touching of the manuscript in the light of Khrushchev's 'secret' speech, but the Russian leader had added little to what Friedrich and Brzezinski had already surmised. In any case, they predicted, the Soviet leopard, for all the talk about de-Stalinisation, had not changed its spots.[86] The authors' sales and scholarly reputations were doubtless bolstered later that year when Soviet tanks repressed the Hungarian uprising.

As was appropriate for political scientists, Friedrich and Brzezinski had a model at the base of their book. A totalitarian state, it turned out, possessed six features – a pervasive and chiliastic ideology, a mass party dominated by the charisma of one man in turn defended by a coterie of ruthless and passionate true believers, mass 'scientific' terror maximised in its effect by often being arbitrary in its direction, a near monopoly both of mass communications and any weapons in the army or elsewhere in society,[87] and a rigid state control of the economy.[88] Totalitarian states were fundamentally anti-capitalist. They also had a 'natural bent' to engage in 'world conquest'.[89] Under no circumstances should they be appeased.

In coming to these conclusions, Friedrich and Brzezinski had simplified the work of such predecessors as Hannah Arendt and Jacob Talmon. Talmon (1916–80) was of Polish birth and had migrated to Palestine, acquiring qualifications from the Hebrew University in Jerusalem, where he subsequently would teach, and at the Sorbonne and the London School of Economics. From 1944 to 1947 he worked for the Board of Deputies of British Jews, before returning to his academic post in what was about to become Israel.

A historian, if very much one of ideas, Talmon relied on his sentences rather than a model to convey his meaning. None the less, his book, too, had clear origins and clear answers. Like Friedrich, Talmon had conceptualised his work before 1939. He claimed that the ideas came to him while reading reports of the Stalinist show trials.[90] But the war had confirmed his worst fears and just as Namier, A.J.P. Taylor and others were maintaining that the roots of Nazism lay in the remote German past, so Talmon decided that totalitarianism had been born in the eighteenth century. 'From the vantage point of the mid-twentieth century', he remarked dolefully, 'the history of the last hundred and fifty years looks like a systematic preparation for the headlong collision between empirical and liberal democracy on the one hand, and totalitarian Messianic democracy on the other.' This conflict was what constituted 'the world crisis of today'.[91]

Inevitably, Talmon focused more on evil than on good, on 'totalitarian' rather than liberal democracy, as he traced totalitarianism's course from Rousseau through Saint-Just to Babeuf, the 'first communist'. Talmon's intellectual debts were largely to liberals or social democrats – Harold Laski, R.H. Tawney, E.H. Carr, Georges Lefebvre, C.E. Labrousse and Ralph Miliband among others. But his message was not so dissonant from that of Rauschning. In the Enlightenment, man had made himself 'the absolute point of reference'.[92] For this hubris, all of humanity, seduced by such versions of totalitarian democracy as Marxism,[93] would pay thereafter. Talmon spent the rest of his life studying this decline and fall; the final volume of his planned history of revolutionary iniquity would be published posthumously.

Hannah Arendt was the most individual and the most interesting of the totalitarianists. She had been born in Hanover in 1906 and graduated with a doctorate in philosophy from Heidelberg in 1929. A Zionist, she had fled Nazism, going firstly to France, and then, in 1941, to New York. Thereafter her chief ambition was to explain anti-Semitism, and, like so many post-war commentators, she sought her answers in the past. Anti-Semitism, she argued, was not new but had long been a 'subterranean stream of European history'. Its appearance was no accident: 'modern anti-semitism grew in proportion as traditional nationalism declined and reached its climax at the exact moment when the European system of nation-states and its precarious balance of power crashed.'[94]

The trouble had begun with the French Revolution. One problem was the destructive effect of equality: 'It is because equality demands that I recognise each and every individual as my equal, that the conflicts between different groups, which for reasons of their own are reluctant to grant each other this basic equality, take on such terribly cruel forms.'[95] Another negative force, she opined somewhat oddly, was 'imperialism'. Nineteenth-century man had become committed to expansion as 'a permanent and supreme aim of politics'. In these circumstances, not even the nation state could hold its own and 'the people' overwhelmed the 'individual'. The 'mob mentality' had always been naturally attracted to 'evil and crime', but the new masses, though fickle, were even more readily fanaticised. In their terrible alienation, they naturally sought (false) comfort from participation in mass movements.[96] The results were Auschwitz and the *gulag*, and there was promise of worse to come, since totalitarian regimes always aimed at conquering the globe.[97]

Arendt was more a philosopher than anything else (she had been trained by Martin Heidegger), and the intricacies of her thought were not always easily disentangled. But, for those in the 1950s investigating the crisis of the 'long Second World War', she preached a number of plain and appealing theses. Nazi Germany and the USSR were, in essence, the same. Each represented the sin, which had taken root in the political world in the eighteenth century, of a humanity believing in its own perfectability. Each battened on the masses and was sustained by them. Each must be resisted, the Soviets through present firmness, Nazi Germany through a reiterated condemnation in the historiography.

As shall be seen later in this book, many of the theses of the totalitarianists are highly dubious. But the 1950s was their decade. Indeed, with hindsight, it almost looks as though the theory of totalitarianism was deliberately tailored to fit its time. In the United States, as in other parts of the liberal capitalist world, a fear and mistrust of the USSR had a long history. Though the origins of the Cold War are still contested, most historians would acknowledge how swiftly assumptions made about the last enemy, Nazi Germany, were transferred to the next, the USSR. Indeed, in the United States, the idea of totalitarianism had become part of accepted wisdom, had achieved hegemony and become 'common sense' well before Friedrich and Brzezinski constructed their model. In 1941, the eminent commentator, William Bullitt, had defined Operation Barbarossa as a struggle between Satan and Lucifer. After 1945, the concept of 'red fascism' entered the discourse of such diverse figures as President Harry Truman, J. Edgar Hoover of the FBI and socialist Norman Thomas. Liberal Democrat presidential candidate, Adlai Stevenson, adopted the slogan 'no appeasement' for his 1952 campaign and George Meany of the American Federation of Labor defined Stalin as 'the Russian Hitler'.[98] Liberals, social democrats, conservatives – most were united in accepting both the existence of totalitarianism and the need to be eternally vigilant against its wiles.

But, ironically, the theory of totalitarianism had 'totalitarian' implications of its own. It was the right, indeed the only answer. It was also the answer for all time, or at least the foreseeable future since, while communism survived, neither the USSR nor China would change. The theory was also, at least potentially, aggressive. In the looming atmosphere of war which it justified or fostered, those who did not accept the correct answer might need to be restrained or destroyed. The idea of totalitarianism gave impulse to the nastier forms of political and cultural intolerance manifested in McCarthyism but, even where liberal values were retained, it was easy to heap scorn on critics of the totalitarianist credo because they were reading history 'incorrectly'. For much of the 1950s, the United States and other parts of the 'West', in seeking to explain the 'long Second World War', lost sight of Pieter Geyl's dictum that, in a free society, history was, or should be, an argument without end and forgot their undertakings in the People's war to defend and extend democratic pluralism.

The theory of totalitarianism, then, had alleged that fascism and communism were the opposite sides of the same coin. There was a final irony in this for, in a way, the totalitarianists were as committed to their own single answer as were their enemies, the vulgar or Stalinist Marxists, whose ideas are outlined further in chapter 7 of this book. The vulgar Marxists had gone on claiming that their present enemies, the capitalists and 'imperialists', had been the puppet-masters of Hitler and Mussolini, and were thus responsible for 'Auschwitz'. By 1949, the leading Soviet historical journal, *Voprosy Istorii*, was denouncing even the moderate *Journal of Modern History* as 'the mouthpiece of reactionary imperialistic ideas in historical literature . . . the propaganda of poisonous little ideas of bourgeois cosmopolitanism'. 'American bourgeois scholarship', it pronounced, 'having gone over to the service of American monopolistic capital, has nothing in common with scholarly research.'[99] For Stalinists, too, the villainy of the last enemy merged into that of the next.

The conservative totalitarianists especially asserted that capitalists were the particular prey of both 'Left' and 'Right' totalitarianism. Nazism and Stalinism were, in one sense, the product of each dictator's whim, but, at the same time, these vile ideologies had grown from humanity's sinful urge to be too free and its wayward desire to struggle against those elites which should always be recognised as the people's natural masters. 'Mass man' (women never entered these discussions) was the final cause of the twentieth century's 'age of violence'. Liberty might be a good thing; equality, especially social equality, was of more problematic virtue. Those people who had survived the People's war should not be too cosseted by the post-war regimes.

However, with the passage of the 1950s, these certainties began to weaken. The idea of 'totalitarianism' lost its hegemony in the 'West' at much the same time that Stalinist Marxism became subject to revision and attack. Many liberals and non-communist socialists had for a time accepted totalitarianist theory because it seemed to explain the more visible delinquencies of Stalin's regime and that of his successors. But most must have been troubled by the religious mysticism never completely absent from totalitarianist theory, however simply or 'scientifically' modelled. There were plenty of historians who wanted to go on believing in the French Revolution, the death of God and the possibility of human perfectability, and who hoped that liberty, equality and fraternity could eventually be united, even while they did not endorse all aspects of the course of Russian history since 1917. In particular, they argued, Nazi Germany could not always be paralleled with the USSR. Nazism did seem to be a movement with more middle- or lower-middle-class or peasant than working-class support. It did not look entirely like the product of 'mass man', whoever that might be. Nor did the killing in the German camps seem identical with that in the *gulag*. One regime's victims were largely defined by 'race', the other's largely by 'politics'. Nor were the methods the same. Nazi Germany killed 'scientifically', with productivity reports and time and motion studies, and using the most efficient and up-to-date technology. The Soviets murdered in a more historically recognisable fashion, by shootings and starvation, and with what sometimes looked like caprice.

In Great Britain there had always been a further problem, even for those conservatives who might elsewhere have been expected to cling loyally to the theory of totalitarianism. W.S. Churchill, conservatives said, had shown himself a truly Great Man during, before and after the war. His 'Iron Curtain' speech at Fulton, Missouri, had lifted the veil on the Soviet enemy. But Churchill was also old, ill and forgetful; by his last Prime Ministership (1951–5) in his dotage, should the truth be known. Naturally all men and women of good will now opposed the appeasement of Stalin or Khrushchev or Nasser or anyone else. But, for many Tories of the next generation, R.A. Butler or Lord Home for example, and for many in the Labour and Liberal parties as well, any historical investigation of British foreign policy carried the potential to cause the greatest embarrassment. Before the Second World War, the anti-appeasers, until at least March 1939, had been a rag-tag minority, divided among themselves, and by no means coherent or consistent in their arguments.[100] Appeasement, it was still plain, had long been popular among the British political elite and among the British people. If it were now to be discountenanced, then it must be that times had changed. That change would need historical explanation and justification.

Thus, in Britain, a corpus of scholarly work grew up around the crisis of the 'long Second World War'. In 1952, for example, Alan Bullock published his biography of Hitler, a book which later jargon would define as 'intentionalist' and which depicted the conflict as 'Hitler's war', but which also made subtle points about the *Führer* as a pragmatic, day-to-day politician.[101] Still earlier, pro-Tory historians like Keith Feiling had found reasons to defend the reputation of Neville Chamberlain.[102] Another Tory, Hugh Trevor-Roper, had edited a series of English translations of Hitler's written or verbal pronouncements, and again centred the limelight on the *Führer* and his people. 'Hitler's mind', however sinister, and however much that of a 'terrible simplifier' rather than that of a sophisticated intellectual, deserved to be understood. So, too, Trevor-Roper observed, did the backing which the *Führer* received in Germany, where he

> was able to draw around him, as willing accomplices, not only that nucleus of devoted and fanatical revolutionaries who provided him with his *élite*, but also those millions of ordinary Germans who, recognising in him the prophet and executor of their half-formulated and since disowned ambitions, followed him readily, even gladly, even to the end, in his monstrous attempt to impose upon the world a barbarous German domination.[103]

For all his own conservatism, Trevor-Roper and some who dined with him at Christ Church, were as anxious to go on fighting the last war as to gear up too quickly for what totalitarianists said would be the next.

But then came the new decade and what seemed a new atmosphere in which to pursue in a more scholarly and subtle fashion the historical explanations for 'Auschwitz' and 'Hiroshima'. The first Cold War was ending. In 1958 John XXIII, full of peasant piety and love of life, replaced the authoritarian, ascetic and 'finance capital' Pope Pius XII. In November 1960, the young, charismatic and liberal-seeming John F. Kennedy won the American presidential elections. Historiographically it was the following year which would be the most remarkable. In West Germany, Fritz Fischer published *Griff nach der Weltmacht* and launched the 'Fischer revolution'. In Israel, Adolf Eichmann was tried for genocide, and Hannah Arendt, still questing for better answers, transmitted to the *New Yorker* her moving articles on the 'banality of evil'. These served to undermine many of the more simplistic theses of totalitarianism and strongly influenced the subsequent historiography of the Holocaust. From this time, too, the term 'Holocaust' began to be used in historical analysis and thus developed a history of its own.[104] 1961 was also the year in which A.J.P. Taylor would set out his origins of the Second World War. In their different ways, Fischer, Arendt and Taylor were challenging canonic interpretations of the 'long Second World War'. Each of their works (Arendt's was not published in book form until 1963) prompted enormous controversy.

As if to mark this revival of relativism, pluralism and democratic debate, and this new enthusiasm both in culture and politics for the ideals of anti-Fascism and the People's war, 1961 also saw the publication of another key text. Its title was *What is History?*; its author E.H. Carr. This short book has not yet been bettered as an introduction to the discipline. As Carr himself would explain in an introduction to a second edition, he had written *What is History?* in a spirit of optimism and a belief in the future: 'signs had begun to accumulate that we were beginning to emerge from some of our troubles.'[105] If the hard shells of totalitarianist theory and Stalinist Marxism could be cracked, maybe there were hopeful lessons which could be learned from reviewing the meaning of 'Auschwitz' and 'Hiroshima'.

Edward Hallett Carr was a somewhat unlikely figure to initiate a great advance in history writing. He was elderly, having been born in 1892. He had spent the first half of his career working for the British Foreign Office and subsequently had been more a journalist than an academic historian. Eventually he located a haven at Balliol (1953–5) and then Trinity (1955–82) at an age when more ordinary mortals would already have retired. His enemies levelled a series of charges against him: he was a double- or triple-dyed appeaser; he had not served in the trenches during the First World War; his book *The Twenty Years' Crisis* (1939) had advocated some sort of deal with Nazism; and his mammoth history of the Russian Revolution, which he began writing after 1945 and never completed, had praised the achievements of the Soviets.[106] In a notorious obituary, Norman Stone, from 1984 Professor of History at Oxford University, concluded that, in this, as in all other matters, Carr was 'something of a coward'.

Stone was almost as scathing about *What is History?*, which he dismissed briefly as 'in places . . . [reading] like a Marxist *1066 and All That'*, and 'a version of

Fifties progressivism', successful only because 'there is a keen appetite in schools for this boring subject'. After all, the Oxford professor declared, 'it is probably as much a mistake to ask a working historian to discuss this theme as to ask a painter to give his views on aesthetics'.[107]

In his zeal as a votary of the New Right, Stone may be anxious to trivialise any who do not serve his cause. But the peremptoriness of his dismissal of *What is History?* was grotesque. For, in this short book, which began life as the G.M. Trevelyan Lectures delivered at Cambridge between January and March 1961, Carr had raised the most fundamental questions about the nature of history and about the societal role of historians. He had also signalled a new and more subtle effort to historicise the Second World War.

History, Carr declared, is 'a social process, in which the individuals are engaged as social beings'.[108] It is 'a continuous process of interaction between the historian and his [sic] facts, an unending dialogue between the present and the past.' The real purpose of history is interpretation not facts: 'To praise a historian for his accuracy is like praising an architect for using well-seasoned timber or properly mixed concrete in his building.'[109] In any case, there were, on any topic, an infinite number of facts from which the historian had to select. 'By and large', Carr stated, 'the historian will get the kind of facts he wants. History means interpretation. Indeed, if, standing Sir George Clark on his head, I were to call history "a hard core of interpretation surrounded by a pulp of disputable facts", my statement would, no doubt, be one-sided and misleading, but no more so, I venture to think, than the original dictum.'[110]

Carr's emphasis on history as debate, as process and as social criticism would be endorsed by many historians in the following decades. As the liberal, generalist historian, William McNeill, put it a generation later: 'historians by helping to define "us" and "them", play a considerable part in focussing love and hate, the two principal cements of collective behaviour known to humanity.'[111] For McNeill, the multiplicity of truth and the possibility of choice were the essence of democracy: 'historiography that aspires to get closer and closer to the documents and nothing but the documents – is merely moving closer and closer to incoherence, chaos, and meaninglessness.'[112]

Neither in the 1980s nor the 1960s did this relativism hold complete sway. Some historians still swore fealty to an authoritative and authoritarian 'historical science' which they deemed had been pioneered by the great nineteenth-century German historian, Leopold von Ranke.[113] 'Give us the historical facts', such historicists said, 'and we shall finish the job of writing our truth-filled history books.'

But especially in most recent years, the more telling attack on *What is History?* came not from this source but increasingly from the 'Left', though usage of such political nomenclature is not very helpful in this case. In some eyes, Carr's assertion of the centrality of history in human experience and understanding, and of the continuing possibility and desirability of human agency, began, in a structuralist, post-structuralist or post-modern world, to look old hat. Indeed, when the methodological and epistemological assumptions of Carr's book were set up against those of linguistic theory, literary criticism or cultural anthropology, *What is History?* seemed to the self-consciously avant-garde to be decidedly antiquated, the sort of work that might be expected from a don approaching his seventieth birthday, a last throw of English liberalism. Rather than fussing over the rival interpretations of old historical questions, the post-modern intellectual should contemplate the meaning of meaning. Maybe even that was too structured an activity since meaning was a construct, dependent in the final analysis on an artificial and capricious system of meaning. Rather than being entrapped by the falsity and narrowness of 'realism', in its very definition a contradiction in terms, or by the similarly seductive and irrelevant notion of 'politics', post-modern humanity, eschewing all systems and avoiding almost all answers, should play with the free-floating text or join Roland Barthes in contemplating the ultimate beauty and truth of a Japanese *haiku*.[114]

Some of these ideas did have a useful impact on the writing of history, notably in proffering new questions and new concepts to such new fields as feminist, oral and ethnographic history. It was important, too, to be reminded that the reader of a historical text might find there meanings and messages which the author had not necessarily 'intended' or understood (and there will be plenty of examples of such fertile 'misunderstanding' in the pages which follow). Moreover, the fierceness of the critique of everything, which was a datum of post-modernism and was sometimes even practised by its adepts, was naturally attractive to so sceptical a discipline as history. However, post-modernism turned in a more worrying direction when its practitioners slipped, as they sometimes did, into a denial of history, and when both the discipline of history and the past which it studied became no more than another pointless act in the theatre of the absurd.

In these circumstances, the historian began to wonder about the specific historical moment at which post-modernism had been engendered. The literary critic, Terry Eagleton, has advised that post-structuralism at least 'was the product of the blend of euphoria and disillusionment, liberation and dissipation, carnival and catastrophe which was 1968. Unable to break the structures of state power, post-structuralists found in [sic] possible instead to subvert the structures of language.'[115] Perhaps the 1968 'revolution of the intellectuals' was the right context into which post-modernist and post-structuralist texts should be placed. Some influence, though, should also be granted to the 'long Second World War', given the prominence of French theoreticians in this field (or of others, like Paul de Man, who seem very much to have experienced their version of 'Auschwitz').[116] The role of such thinkers might suggest the need for an exploration of how French culture (and the French intelligentsia) reconstructed itself in the era which followed the fall of France.[117]

In general, then, analysts of post-modernism might learn much from asking its theoreticians who were they? when did they write? and why? In answering those questions they might be able to comprehend why these apparent anarcho-futurists often have such a nostalgic side, frequently seem to mourn the peasant (or feudal) world we have lost and to prefer the unarticulated 'memory' of the *longue durée* to democratically contested, critical 'history'.[118] It is not my purpose to engage in a full-scale critique of post-modernism. Suffice it to say that the assumptions of this book owe more to E.H. Carr than to Jacques Derrida. In the chapters which follow I shall endeavour to make plain how societies which experienced the great moral crisis of the 'long Second World War' historicised and 'explained' that experience. My focus will generally be on individual historians. I shall assume that their texts belonged to them, just as they themselves belonged to their own societies and, often, to their own specific participation in 'Auschwitz' or 'Hiroshima'. I shall maintain that the processes of past history and of present politics are in inevitable and potentially fruitful discourse. Indeed, I shall argue that historical disputation is the final basis of a pluralist democracy.

But it is now time to return to the 1960s and to that decade's reconsideration of the meaning of the 'long Second World War'. In 1961, as the war's immediate influence flagged and the simplistic truths of the 1950s began to be discredited, as the Cold War lost its ability to freeze human minds and understanding, contemporary history thankfully returned to being an argument without end. Approached with a new commitment and a new humility, the recent past could now be scrutinised in a more illuminating and more humane manner.

2

The origins of the Third World War and the making of English social history

On 3 September 1939, two citizens of Great Britain made entries in their diaries. One was Spike Milligan, ordinary soldier-to-be. He wrote:

> HOW IT ALL STARTED.
> September 3rd, 1939. The last minutes of peace ticking away. Father and I were watching Mother digging our air-raid shelter. 'She's a great little woman,' said Father. 'And getting smaller all the time', I added. Two minutes later, a man called Chamberlain who did Prime Minister impressions spoke on the wireless; he said, 'As from eleven o'clock we are at war with Germany.' (I loved the *WE*.) 'War?' said Mother. 'It must have been something we said,' said Father. The people next door panicked, burnt their post office books and took in the washing.[1]

The other was 'Chips' Channon, socialite from the circle of the Duke of Kent and Lady Cunard, seemingly a gentleman (though actually born an American and a member of the British Establishment by marriage), MP, appeaser, and father of Paul Channon, one of Maggie Thatcher's last 'wet' Cabinet ministers:

> 10.57 a.m. The P.M. is to broadcast at 11.15 and in a few moments a state of war will be declared. The method, while to my mind precipitate and brusque, is undoubtedly popular. Everyone is smiling, the weather is glorious but I feel that our world or all that remains of it, is committing suicide, whilst Stalin laughs and the Kremlin triumphs.[2]

Two diarists; still, it seemed, 'two nations' – one fearing that 'they' had declared war expecting that 'we' would fight it; the other believing that the USSR not Nazi Germany was the real enemy. These writers provide a somewhat unfamiliar image of Britain's Second World War. The more accustomed line, reiterated in official public discourse or when the strains of *Rule Britannia* unleash patriotic emotions at a Promenade Concert, is of a Britain virtuously united against the Nazi aggressor. Donald Watt, in his recent massive account of the short-term causes of the Second World War, has refurbished this conventional account. It was 'British opinion', no longer 'divided and irresolute' as it had been at Munich, he has asserted, which decided to combat 'Hitler'.[3] This 'opinion' saw things more clearly and accurately than did members of the government. When it became necessary, Britain, all of Britain, had stood up for the right: 'In May 1945 Britain was the only power whose people could say that they had entered the war by choice, to fight for a principle, and not because their country was attacked.'[4] Britain, and Britain alone, had entered the Second World War as 'People's war', for justice and democracy abroad and at home.

It may be that Watt has a case. Few, at least, would gainsay Britain's special contribution to defeating Nazism, especially between the summers of 1940 and 1941 when, of the major Powers, Britain fought on alone. As even A.J.P. Taylor has stated, 'On the Day of Judgement men will be asked: "Where was the first defeat of Fascism?" Those who answer "The Battle of Britain" will get better marks than those who say "Moscow" or "Stalingrad" ' (though typically he added that 'those who reply "Guadalajara" [where the International Brigades briefly turned back Franco and his fascist allies] will go up to the highest place)'.[5] None the less, Watt's usage of an undefined 'national opinion' to shore up his argument obscures the many divisions of British society, both in 1939 and during the war.

These divisions can easily be located on both the military and the home front. When ordinary soldier Milligan was conscripted – there was no serious possibility that he could refuse this governmental intrusion into his life – he found an officer corps which literally spoke a different language from his own. Almost an hereditary caste, some 50 per cent of officers trained at Sandhurst were the sons of officers.[6] Milligan liked jazz; they preferred Elgar. Milligan drank beer; they drank whisky and soda. Milligan's chief sport was fumbling with his latest girlfriend in a back row at the cinema;[7] they played polo or golf and cherished those marvellous cover-drives by A.C. MacLaren and Prince Ranjitsinhji in 1902.[8] It would be the war, and only the war, which would, to some extent, democratise the British military and create a 'People's Army'. Similarly, it would be their experience of war which, at its end, would make British soldiers anxious to vote out War Hero Winston Churchill and vote in Labour's Clement Attlee.[9] That 'modest little man with a great deal to be modest about',[10] as Churchill later defined him patronisingly, promised a 'welfare state' and seemed to believe in his promise.

At home, too, it was the experience of war rather than the decision to enter it which accelerated the democratisation of Britain. The initial terror of aerial bombardment and the perceived need to evacuate children from the big cities gave the population the chance to travel, and, thus, to cross regional and class boundaries to an unprecedented degree. Angus Calder has wonderfully evoked this meeting of the two nations:

A thirteen-year-old Jewish boy, used to the friendly warmth of Stepney, was billeted in Buckinghamshire with his young sister. . . .'Rose whispered,' he writes. 'She whispered for days. Everything was so clean in the room. We were even given flannels and toothbrushes. We'd never cleaned our teeth up till then. And hot water came from the tap. And there was a lavatory upstairs. And carpets. And something called an eiderdown. And clean sheets. This was all very odd. And rather scaring.'

Nor, says Calder, was cleanliness in the bedroom automatically productive of fastidiousness elsewhere. For, he adds,

> a careful study [has] suggested that about five to ten per cent of the evacuees may have lacked proper toilet training. There was a classic case of a Glasgow mother who expostulated with her six-year-old child – in Scotland, mothers went with the school-children as well as with the infants – 'You dirty thing, messing up the lady's carpet. Go and do it in the corner.'[11]

The way in which the war blurred the previously sharp dividing lines between the military and civilians seems also to have assisted morale. The defeat in France, followed by the dramatic and popular 'rescue' from Dunkirk,[12] rallied people behind the war effort. Still more effective in constructing 'one Britain' was the blitz. German bombs did not always discriminate between the elegant dwellings of the social set and those of poor East Enders, instead engendering amid the rubble a genuine democracy, united by a hatred of the Nazi bombers, a determination to rebuild and a gladness at having lived another day.[13] Bombing seems to have had a similar effect on the German and Soviet populace,[14] as it also would have, a generation later, on the North Vietnamese.

Though productivity figures varied from week to week and factory to factory, in general British manufacture of war material rose greatly during the war. In 1939, 7,940 aircraft were produced; in 1943, 26,263; while the number of tanks and other self-propelled artillery rose from 969 to 7,476. By contrast, the output of consumer goods declined precipitously.[15] But the sacrifice involved does not seem to have generated much grumbling, let alone any widespread popular movement to extricate Britain from the war. For one thing, unemployment, such a scourge of significant parts of Britain throughout the inter-war period, was, by 1943, virtually nil.[16] For another, 'austerity' was, or seemed, designed to narrow class divisions. When a government, short of metal supplies and cloth, drew up 'utility' specifications for the manufacture of pots and kettles, set a maximum to the number of pleats in a skirt and limited female underwear to six shapes, then the effect seemed similar for the rich woman in her castle and the poor woman at her gate.[17]

But best of all was the promise of more democracy to come. If the British, as A.J.P. Taylor has alleged, remained 'a peaceful and civilized people, tolerant, patient, and generous' (and willing and happy to give up their empire),[18] and, unlike their European neighbours, not completely sundered from their national history by the war and not reduced to living in *Anno Zero*, it was at least partly because the wartime National Government recognised that sacrifices during the war must be compensated for when peace came. Planned while the conflict continued, largely legislated by the Labour Government (1945–51), and imitated by many other European and non-European societies, the Welfare State, for more than a generation, offered many ordinary people much of the time their reward for defeating fascism.[19] The Welfare State was deemed the essential product of 'the People's war that never ended'.

During the 1980s, by contrast, we have been told that the Welfare State's economic assumptions are false. Frozen in time, they hinder rather than help the development of a modern economy. That is as maybe, but already, twenty years before, the British had begun to argue about the meaning of the Second World War and about the methods and intentions with which they had entered it. In 1961, the Oxford don and media star, A.J.P. Taylor, published *The Origins of the Second World War*.[20] This book, short, pithy, craftily written – Taylor would call it, wrily, his '*goak* book'[21] – is probably the most celebrated, notorious and debated historical work of the post-war era. In it, Taylor re-viewed the British 'long Second World War', 'Auschwitz' and 'Hiroshima'. *The Origins of the Second World War,* in the short term, would encourage an unfreezing of time in British historiography and signal the commencement of the Sixties in British society. In the longer term, the resumption of debate would also permit those who disliked the People's war to re-work their version of history and, especially in the late 1980s, come up with new answers, or old answers in new words.

Though Taylor himself would claim that provocation was far from his intention,[22] controversy was not an unfamiliar intruder in the life of one who had long seen himself as the 'traitor within the gates' of the British Establishment. Alan John Percivale Taylor, born in Birkdale, Lancashire, on 25 March 1906, was the son of a prosperous Manchester cotton merchant, and came of 'radical Dissenting stock on both sides'. He would define himself as a 'hereditary dissenter' and glory in 'a collateral ancestor of [his] father's . . . killed at Peterloo'.[23] 'If there had been no troublemakers, no Dissenters', he wrote, 'we should still be living in caves.'[24] Appropriately, he was thus educated at private Quaker preparatory and secondary schools before going up to Oxford in 1924.

By then Taylor had developed a passionate love of history, 'though with no idea of what this would lead to or how to turn it to any practical use.' At Oxford, he was persuaded to work on medieval history, 'then a flourishing subject . . . . As to modern history, when we reached the Glorious Revolution, my tutor said to me: "You know the rest from your work at school, so we do not need to do any more".' The quality of the education at Oxford had not been impressive: 'I did not go to any lectures except those of Sir Charles Oman and that only because Sir Charles, being very old, was a period piece. I never saw an original document or received any guidance in historical method.'[25] Instead, 'I learnt how to choose a meal in a restaurant and that 1921 was a good year for wine . . . . I learnt how to speak with a long "a" instead of a short one, thus unintentionally losing my Lancashire accent. On a more serious level I learnt precisely nothing . . . . I increased my knowledge of history, my understanding of it not at all. I did not even learn how to write.'[26]

Partly, he admits, this failure sprang from his other great youthful enthusiasm – politics. 'Sustained by Marxist arrogance I ignored such ideas as Oxford had to offer.'[27] His parents, 'though unmistakably bourgeois in character and income', had joined the Independent Labour Party after the war and embraced 'Bolshevism'. His mother became platonically infatuated with Henry Sara, one of the founders of the British Communist Party, and Taylor accompanied them on a visit to the Soviet Union in 1925. But he was not a naturally disciplined party cadre: 'I too have tried to be a Marxist but common sense kept breaking in.'[28] He would later claim to have remained a 'lifelong Socialist', but without strong political beliefs – only 'extreme views, weakly held'.[29] At Oxford he belonged to a 'Communist' group, but drove a 'fishtailed Rover sports car – I think the only car in Oriel except for the aristocratic Cartwright's Lancia'.[30] During the General Strike of 1926, while most activist students enrolled as auxiliaries to help the police sort out the rebellious working class, Taylor drove the car on errands for the Preston strike committee. In quest of the Revolution, he had first gone to London, parking outside Communist headquarters. He 'found them bolted and barred. After much banging . . . there was a rattling of chains and an elderly Scotch Communist called Bob Steward appeared. He said, "There's no one here. I am only the caretaker. Get along hame with ye." These were the only instructions I ever received from the Communist Party of Great Britain.' However, the General Strike, Taylor maintained, 'had a deep effect on me. I developed a great admiration for the British working class and felt that I should devote my life to their service . . . . That was not all: the general strike destroyed my faith, such as it was, in the Communist party. The party that was supposed to lead the working class had played no part in the strike except to be a nuisance. What then was the use of it? The expulsion of Trotsky from the Soviet party soon afterwards completed my disillusionment.'[31]

Taylor graduated from Oxford in 1927 with first class honours in history. Under parental pressure he briefly contemplated a legal career, but quickly became bored and accepted the offer of a postgraduate research position in Vienna. There he studied under A.F. Pribram, a distinguished and patriotic Jewish-Austrian historian of European diplomacy, a really 'old-fashioned diplomatic historian'.[32] In 1930 Pribram recommended his pupil for a European History lectureship at Manchester University, where Taylor taught for the next eight years. He soon acquired Lewis Namier as his professor, though Taylor would claim characteristically that it was he who instructed Namier rather than vice versa. Taylor's Vienna research had meanwhile provided the basis of his first book, *The Italian Problem in European Diplomacy, 1847–1849* (1934).[33] His Austrian experience and the teaching of Pribram would leave him very sceptical over Italian claims to Trieste and sardonic about Italy's pretensions as 'least of the Great Powers'.[34] He moved on to study the origins of the First World War and the result in book form, *Germany's First Bid for Colonies, 1884–5* (1938) established his personal style: 'sound scholarly history and at the same time very funny, a speciality of mine.'[35] Not the sort of academic who preferred to be a recluse in the ivory tower, Taylor began reviewing for the liberal *Manchester Guardian*. Writing longer pieces on contemporary affairs as well as on historical topics, he crafted a style, as serviceable for non-academic as for scholarly readers.

Being an active member of the Labour Party, he was asked to be a candidate in the 1935 General Election but declined, preferring to retain his independence and by no means automatically adopting the party line, especially on issues of foreign affairs which interested him most:

I advocated resistance to Hitler from the moment he came to power. But I also thought that the National Government were more likely to support Hitler against Russia than to go against him and therefore I opposed rearmament until we got a change of government. In 1935 I opposed support for the League of Nations [against Mussolini's invasion of Ethiopia] by the existing government as a fraud.... With the reoccupation of the Rhineland, I decided that we must rearm even under the National Government and was convinced that if we took a firm line with Hitler there would be no war. I was one of the few people outside London who addressed meetings against appeasement at the time of Munich, and very rough they were. I have not changed the views I held then.[36]

In 1938 he returned to Oxford as Fellow and Tutor in Modern History at Magdalen College. It would remain his base until his retirement. He was never promoted to a chair, 'though there were plenty around in my time', being passed over in favour of the conservative, Hugh Trevor-Roper, in a notorious contest in 1957. 'This', he claims a little tongue-in-cheek, 'was no doubt accidental, with perhaps a tinge of disapproval for either me or recent history.'[37] He took pains not to hide his contempt for the fatuities and self-seeking of the Establishment, 'THE THING', as he loved to call it in echo of William Cobbett.[38] He would sum up his radical disdain in an article which he wrote in the year of his rejection as an Oxford professor:

Is THE THING any use? None at all except for its members. Most people lead industrious decent lives without the moral guidance of the Archbishop of Canterbury.... It would be a great improvement in every way if we got rid of THE THING. The country would be more alert, more receptive to new ideas, more capable of holding its own in the world. THE THING is on the surface a system of holding its own in the world. THE THING is on the surface a system of public morals. Underneath it is a system of public plunder. Its true purpose was revealed by a poster which the Chamberlain Government rashly displayed early in the war: *YOUR* COURAGE, *YOUR* CHEERFULNESS, *YOUR* RESOLUTION WILL BRING US VICTORY.[39]

Well before Spike Milligan wrote it down, A.J.P. Taylor also 'loved the *WE* '.

Taylor had had what a Gramscian would define as an 'organic intellectual's' Second World War. Early in the conflict, having, unlike Trevor-Roper, been rejected as a possible intelligence expert,[40] he took on adult education work among the armed forces. From 1941 he ran a radio service for the BBC in similar style – 'The World at War: Your Questions Answered'; designed to inform listeners about the world, 'it taught me radio technique'.[41] In 1940–1 he also finished another book, *The Habsburg Monarchy*. It was dedicated to Namier but, Taylor would later assert, 'though some of the views [in it] resembled those of Namier, in fact they owed little to him'. He re-wrote and expanded the book in 1947, at pains, now, to remove its residual 'liberal illusions'.[42] The war had convinced him that 'the national principle, once launched, had to work itself out to its conclusion . . . [while] mass-nationalism, where it existed, was very different from the nationalism of the intellectuals'.[43]

The most controversial of Taylor's wartime productions was, however, a survey of German history over the last two centuries. Entitled *The Course of German History*, it was, Taylor has recalled, 'my first best seller'.[44] It had been inspired by a commission from government agencies to produce a series of handbooks for army officers who were to occupy Hungary (they never got there) and Germany. When written, however, Taylor's account of the Weimar Republic's fall was rejected as 'too depressing'. But, not downcast by official disapproval, Taylor found a publisher and, indeed, expanded his original short essay into a full-length study.

The Course of German History is generally seen as a fundamentally Germanophobic and war-inspired work. Certainly some of Taylor's judgements are acerbic: 'One aim Bismarck never pursued: that of uniting all Germans in a single national state' but, even in his moderation, this Maker of Modern Germany had fundamentally destabilised Europe:

> Bismarck could not efface his own work. He had taught the Germans that conquest was the only cure for danger; and he had whipped up the dangers in order to maintain his order. In the long run, the Germans would break the bounds which he had imposed and would seek to conquer all Europe – and God too. The Bismarckian system aimed at security and peace; but it left the ruling classes of Germany no alternative – to preserve themselves they had to enter on a path of conquest which would be their ruin. Bismarck, the greatest of political Germans, was for Germany the greatest of disasters.[45]

Though, in Taylor's opinion, the German leadership did not deliberately provoke world war in the crisis of July 1914,[46] the domestic inadequacies of the German system were the major cause of the first conflict.[47] Nazism, too, was no accident. The Weimar Republic had always been an 'empty shell' and had failed completely by 1930.[48] The Nazis 'had no programme, still less a defined class interest; they stood simply for destruction and action, not contradictory but complementary. They united in their ranks the disillusioned of every class.' In England, Taylor opined in words rather alarming to an Australian reader, 'they would have been shipped off to the colonies as remittance men'.[49] Nazism meant war and 'it was naive of anyone to suppose that compromise with National Socialist Germany was ever possible on any point'. But it was 22 June 1941 not 3 September 1939 which was 'the climax, the logical conclusion, of German history, the moment at which all the forces which had contended against each other within Germany for so long, joined in a common struggle against all the world. Germany was at last united.'[50]

From a present perspective it is hard to see why this book acquired such a fearsome reputation in some circles. Taylor's fundamental argument, which he reiterated in a new preface in 1961, was that 'it was no more a mistake for the German people to end up with Hitler than it is an accident when a river flows into the sea'.[51] But this thesis of the negative *Sonderweg* ('special way') became the commonplace of German historiography during the 1960s and 1970s.[52] Similarly Taylor sketched a list of points which other historians would develop at greater length and with less panache – the authoritarianism of a Lutheran training, the alliance of 'iron and rye', the place of the military as the last redoubt of Imperial German power, the gap between theory and practice, politics and society, in Weimar. *The Course of German History* may have been depressing for those who hoped that the end of the Second World War meant an immediate return to business as usual but, for its time, it was a brilliant analysis.

The book had one other feature, little remarked on in the later commentaries but highly typical of Taylor. It had a sub-plot not so much about Germany as about the USSR; it foreshadowed an answer not only to the problem of the origins of the Second War but also to those of the Third. Throughout his book, Taylor preached against the politics which were chilling the Cold War and which would soon construct the model of totalitarianism. He tried to be even-handed about the moral worth of Anglo-French or Soviet policies in the years before 1939. 'As in 1938 the western powers had rubbed their hands at the promise of the *Drang nach Osten*, so in August 1939 the Russians folded their hands, if not rubbed them, at the *Drang nach Westen*.'[53] He reiterated how constant and terrifying had been German ambition in the east. There, he said, the Germans have appeared 'ostensibly the defenders of civilization, [but] they have defended it as barbarians, employing the technical means of civilization, but not its spirit . . . their weapons have varied, their method has always been the same – extermination. Most of the peoples of Europe', he conceded, 'have . . . been exterminators', the French, the 'English' in Ireland or on the North American plains. But, he concluded with an exaggeration not so out of place in 1945, 'no other people has pursued extermination as a permanent policy from generation to generation for a thousand years'.[54] Post-war Europe, he was advising, should not for the then foreseeable future tolerate Germany being reconstituted as a nation state and, as he would later phrase it, peace and progress would be best assisted by 'an Anglo-Soviet alliance, the most harmless and pacific of all possible combinations'.[55]

In the 1950s, Taylor's career continued in what was now its accustomed groove. He kept publishing both scholarly works and what have been estimated to be over 1,500 book reviews, many of them substantial pieces.[56] He maintained a presence in the columns of newspapers and on the radio and effortlessly adapted his lecturing style to the new medium of television. 'I was taking history to ordinary people . . . a one-man University of the air.'[57] From time to time he also resumed his political activism, campaigning against the British incursion over Suez in 1956 and denouncing that misapplication of history, that rejection of appeasement, through which the Tory Government then tried to justify its last fling at imperialism.[58] From 1958 Taylor's life was dominated for several years by his participation in the Campaign for Nuclear Disarmament – 'the best, by which I meant the worthiest, activity I ever undertook.'[59] He was a speaker at the inaugural meeting of CND in February 1958 and was swiftly co-opted onto the executive.[60] At the height of the campaign he spoke almost weekly at public meetings all over Britain, stimulated by the presence near Oxford of the major US base, Brize Norton (whence came the B47 shot down by the Russians in the July 1960 crisis). It was in the middle of this campaign – 'too busy to do much serious research . . . [but] I needed to write something'[61] – that Taylor drafted *The Origins of the Second World War*. The book was first presented in Taylor's celebrated 9 a.m. lecture series at Oxford in April–May 1960, when his voice sometimes had to combat the drone of US bombers passing low overhead. As Taylor himself has defined it, *Origins*, too, was 'a period piece'.[62]

On its publication in 1961, Taylor's book aroused enormous and sustained controversy. A number of commentators thought Taylor was absolving Adolf Hitler of responsibility for the war. A reviewer in *Time* magazine believed Taylor was attempting to do for Hitler what others had done to such 'traditional villain[s]' as 'Richard III, Metternich and Aaron Burr' (a very odd list). The writer similarly castigated Taylor for defending Neville Chamberlain and appeasement, and ended crossly: ' "A study of history is of no practical use in the present or future", Taylor, who likes to be whimsical, once said. As far as Taylor himself is concerned, his book proves his point.'[63]

Professional historians, especially the artificers or votaries of the Churchill myth, were similarly outraged. Hugh Trevor-Roper, chosen over Taylor by Harold Macmillan for the Regius chair only four years before, fired off a cannonade against the book in the July issue of *Encounter*. As far as Trevor-Roper was concerned, Taylor was trying to normalise Hitler and praise Neville Chamberlain and the appeasers. The book, Trevor-Roper concluded, was 'utterly erroneous'; in it, Taylor 'selects, suppresses, and arranges evidence on no principle other than the needs of his thesis; and that thesis, that Hitler was a traditional statesman, of limited aims, merely responding to a given situation, rests on no evidence at all, ignores essential evidence, and is . . . demonstrably false.' The only puzzle was why Taylor had done it – was Taylor insulting the ghost of 'his former master, Sir Lewis Namier, in revenge for some imagined slight'?[64] Perhaps it was a case of 'mere characteristic *gaminerie*, the love of firing squibs and laying banana-skins to disconcert the gravity and upset the balance of the orthodox'? Or did Taylor have a more sinister motive? Was he writing about the past in order to preach a lesson for the present and future? With Germany carved up, the USSR, Trevor-Roper feared, was being presented as 'the new great power' which should be allowed 'to assert its "natural weight" '. 'Mr. Khrushchev, we should recognise, has no more ambitions of world-conquest than Hitler. He is a traditional Russian statesman of limited aims, and "the moral line" consists in letting him have his way more completely than we let Hitler have his: in other words, universal disarmament.' By this argument and its other irresponsibilities, Trevor-Roper prophesied, the book 'will . . . do harm, perhaps irreparable harm, to Mr. Taylor's reputation as a serious historian'.[65]

In the September issue of *Encounter*, Taylor gave at least as good as he had got, as he picked up the detail of Trevor-Roper's attack over Hitler's role, or over appeasement, and indicated how selective and inaccurate had been his critic's reading: 'The Regius Professor's methods of quotation', Taylor concluded witheringly, 'might also do harm to his reputation as a serious historian, if he had one.'[66] Only on the comments about the USSR did Taylor stay silent.

But the conflict was not merely one between the successful and unsuccessful candidates for an Oxford chair. Alan Bullock, Harry Hinsley, Gordon Craig, and many others had their say.[67] Taylor himself wrote a fresh introduction, 'Second Thoughts', which he published in a new edition in 1963. This, in turn, prompted further comment, notably a review article in *Past and Present* by the young and independent Marxist, Tim Mason. Mason was much subtler in his analysis than Trevor-Roper had been. Taylor, he thought, had been largely successful in his narration of the short-term causes of the war and in his depiction of Anglo-French policy. His conventional methods and sources, however, made him less skilled in understanding Hitler or the foreign policy of Nazi Germany and in explaining long-term causes. 'Mr Taylor's book is not informed by any conception of the distinctive character and role of National Socialism in the history of twentieth-century Europe.' Taylor had failed to give sufficient weight to the destabilising character of the 'jungle of competing and overlapping economic organisations, interest groups and authorities, which was essential for preserving the political power of the Nazi leadership.'[68] Taylor was right to be sceptical about what would soon be labelled 'intentionalism' (the idea that everything which happened in Nazi Germany was at Hitler's behest), but he had not understood 'functionalism' (the thesis that at the core of the Nazi state lay an 'institutional darwinism', which may or may not have been 'managed' by the *Führer*).[69]

Though many of Mason's criticisms were telling, his intervention did not end the debate. Instead, it went echoing on and, in 1986, the Canadian historian, Gordon Martel, edited a new set of essays to mark the twenty-fifth anniversary of *The Origins of the Second World War*. As ever, the contributors were divided about Taylor and his book. Stephen Schuker deemed Taylor too cute by half. His 'pellucid prose and opaque meaning', his 'seamless web of aphorisms', placed him 'on both sides of almost every issue'.[70] Here was one reader who felt that the *goak* was on him and who did not like the feeling. Edward Ingram thought 'Little England patriotism' the key to Taylor's character – he was both 'a conservative posing as a radical, [and] a determinist [posing] as an idealist'.[71] Taylor's autobiography, *A Personal History* (1983), had made things worse.[72] 'Taylor', Ingram remarked tartly, 'is fond of using his own life as an exemplar of historical truth, a bad habit borrowed from him by Marxist and feminist historians in Canada, who fondly imagine that the country has reached its apotheosis in themselves.'[73]

But, as usual, Taylor did not lack defenders. Paul Kennedy argued that such later historians of appeasement as Maurice Cowling[74] had 'tended to *supplement* Taylor's version rather than replace it'.[75] Robert Young had some criticism of the detail of Taylor's treatment of France but he could not withhold praise:

It is a mark of this book's impact to be able to say that it remains central to a debate that continues to bubble away over the war's origin. Of course, scholars may persist in saying, as they have for a quarter of a century, that Taylor got it wrong, or at least much of it. They will continue to insist, as indeed they must, that his evidence is often inadequate for his case, if not overtly incompatible with it. An historical *agent provocateur*, he has invited the blows of those who find his grasp of economics rudimentary, his interest in ideology moribund, his predilection for continued aphorisms excessive. And yet he has never been chased from the field, never made to surrender. They may work around him, for a while they may even ignore him, but in the end they have to return to his field.[76]

What was it about *The Origins of the Second World War*, that '*goak* book' and 'period piece', that mere academic exercise, written by a historian who claimed 'I have no theories of history and know nothing about them',[77] which had made it the most resounding success of all historical works about 'Auschwitz', 'Hiroshima' and 'the long Second World War'?[78] The first reply to this question is stylistic. Somewhat ironically for a world enduring 'the death of the author', Taylor has confessed: 'I worried about my style as much as about my scholarship.'[79] An admirer of Gibbon,[80] Taylor is, to his own admirers, the Gibbon of the twentieth century. Like Gibbon, Taylor has frequent recourse to irony, but as a democrat who believes that 'I am no better than anyone else, and no one else is better than me',[81] his mode is the *goak* rather than the Augustan pomposity of one of Gibbon's balanced antitheses.

What, then, is the *goak*? The answer is simple; it is where Taylor, the ring-master of seven types of ambiguity, the keeper of the oxymoron, set up a debate without end within his own pages. He went closest to explaining this method in a passage at the end of an article he wrote on 'Fiction in history':

> Marx was fond of quoting Heraclitus: *panta rei*, all things move. This is the one truth we seek to recapture when we write history. We know that our version, being set into words, is itself false. We are trying to stop something that never stays still. Once written, our version too will move. It will be challenged and revised. It will take on appearances that we did not expect. We are content to repeat the words with which Geyl finished his book on Napoleon: 'History is an argument without end.'[82]

If it were not, Taylor noted in mock or *goaky* horror in his autobiography, even *The Origins of the Second World War* would become entrenched as the 'new orthodoxy'.[83] It is these *goaks*, this use of an internal dialectic, this fundamental commitment to democratic pluralism which have so frequently irritated and misled critics loyal to the Rankean view that history merely records 'what actually happened' or to the proud datum that when a historian concludes that the time was 8 o'clock, it was indeed 8 o'clock and always will remain so. It is the *goaks* which signal that, in the 1960s, Britain was abandoning the first simple interpretations of the

Second World War and was contemplating the meaning of 'Auschwitz' and 'Hiroshima' in a newly rich, nuanced, and humane manner.

In a book of this length, there is no opportunity for a detailed textual analysis of Taylor's work. One example must suffice. A sentence singled out both by the *Time* reviewer and by Trevor-Roper as particularly deplorable was that in which Taylor had typified the Munich agreement.[84] Taylor wrote that this pinnacle of appeasement was 'a triumph of all that was best and most enlightened in British life; a triumph for those who had preached equal justice between peoples; a triumph for those who had courageously denounced the harshness and short-sightedness of Versailles.'[85] Given Taylor's own unusual record in speaking out against Munich at the time, in having an 'unblemished . . . record of anti fascism',[86] it seemed an all the more contradictory a thing for him to say twenty-three years later.

But, in fact, Taylor had woven at least three meanings into his phrases. The first was that, if considered as what E.P. Thompson calls a 'thing' rather than a 'happening', if read out of time, Munich did indeed signify the victory both of British policy and of the ideals of Anglo-Saxon, 'Wilsonian', liberalism. By being accorded the Sudetenland, Germany did come closer to being a 'united nation' and to achieving 'self-determination'. If inter-war Germany – that society for which 'in international affairs there was nothing wrong with Hitler except that he was a German'[87] (*goak*) – had not been involved, a step to make nationality equate more nearly with the actual borders of the nation states of Germany and Czechoslovakia would have been highly desirable.

The second meaning was almost the exact reverse. When the contestants were Nazi Germany and the Czechoslovakia of Beneš and the Masaryks, that one half-decent regime in Southern, Central and Eastern Europe, how disgraceful was this treaty crafted by the 'best men' of Britain and France? If time were given back its movement, then Munich was a tragedy (though it and the Nazi annexation of the rump of Bohemia and Moravia in March 1939 would leave Prague largely intact after 1945, the most beautiful city of its region, to await Alexander Dubček and Vàclav Havel, those present exemplars of all that is best and most enlightened in Slovak and Czech life).[88] In occasioning the tragedy of 1938–9, the British Establishment had been as shamelessly devoted to public plunder as it usually was.

The third meaning was based on yet another reading of time. As has been noted, in the fifteen years after the Second World War, various pundits, many of them ex-appeasers, had made careers out of the slogans 'Never again', or 'No more Munichs', and had turned appeasement into a pejorative term. Their hypocrisy was one issue; their certainty that they had read the 'lessons of history' aright was the greater problem. In the post-Hiroshima world, the ability to sit down and reason together and not write off your present enemy as a madman was crucial to human survival. Personally, Taylor confessed his preference for negotiation from a position of strength, but he had become increasingly if sadly aware that England's moment of greatness was gone for ever. In any case, only some variety of appeasement and the peaceful settlement of disputes, could fend off the menace of the Third World War. So far, 'Auschwitz' was the nearest humanity had gone to the bottom-most pit of hell – 'as supreme ruler of Germany, Hitler bears the greatest responsibility for acts of immeasurable evil: for the destruction of German democracy; for the concentration camps; and, worst of all, for the extermination of peoples during the second World war', but 'his foreign policy was a different matter. He aimed to make Germany the dominant Power in Europe and maybe, more remotely, in the world. Other Powers have pursued similar aims, and still do. Other Powers treat smaller countries as their satellites. Other Powers seek to defend their vital interests by force of arms.'[89] And now in Washington, Moscow, London and Paris, political leaders had nuclear arms. In his original blundering attack on Taylor's book, Trevor-Roper had been right in at least one sense. Taylor had been writing as much about the origins of the Third as about the origins of the Second World War: 'The only great lesson of Munich, the most difficult to learn, is that there are no great lessons. Historians, useless in predicting the future, achieve something if they prevent others doing so.'[90]

The passion of the controversy over *The Origins of the Second World War* had thus been aroused for a number of reasons. Taylor's book was a 'time bomb' in the most literal of senses. It blew apart the cosy interpretations of the Second World War as Hitler's war or as the perennial product of appeased totalitarianism. It suggested that the endless reciting of the 'lessons of the 1930s' was no longer enough in a modern and still changing world. It urged that 'an historian ought to love the past, as Professor Trevor-Roper says . . . . But he ought to love the present, too, and even the future. The past is dead and there is a sterility in loving that alone.'[91] It hinted that the promises made about genuine democracy in the People's war had not always been achieved or defended, and ought to be renewed. And, most of all, in its style and with its *goaks*, it assaulted the self-image of historians as austere professionals, be-gowned professors to whom respect was automatically due. Here was an author whose sentences were frequently digested by the masses as they scanned those pages of the *Sunday Express* in which their greasy fish and chips were wrapped. And yet this same populariser had crafted more intricately meaningful sentences than had those who passed the port to each other at Christ Church high table. If Spike Milligan was the extraordinary ordinary soldier of a People's war, A.J.P. Taylor was that war's people's historian, chuffed to be recognised as such by the local dustman.[92]

And yet, Taylor, too, was, in a certain sense and over time, the victim of the 'Taylor controversy'. In his autobiography, he is almost apologetic about it: 'much to my surprise *The Origins of the Second World War* proved to be the most controversial and provocative of all my book [sic], though this had been far from my intention. I had meant to write a straightforward piece of hack diplomatic history.' A generation later, he was relieved to say, the controversy seemed over and '*The Origins* and all the unscholarly abuse it provoked are now so much water under the bridge'.[93] And, in any case, as a democrat and a historian, he had to expect his work to decay, to be overthrown, and to age in the same way that his body did. But Taylor's professional career had perhaps been altered by the debate; certainly it changed course. As has been seen, for some of his not very perceptive critics Taylor's chief drawback as a historian was that at heart he was a little Englander, 'a patriot for me'. This comment seems misapplied to a historian who had written so masterfully about German, Austro-Hungarian, Italian and other European histories. But, in the aftermath of 1961, Taylor's major books were restricted to English history. Having explained the world, he retreated, sometimes a little glumly, to that part of it which he knew and loved best. He ate his kippers for breakfast[94] and crossed his fingers lest the great men and women of the present – like those of the past 'there for the beer'[95] more than anything else – stumbled over the brink into the boiling cauldron of the Third World War. As he explained:

> In the early 1960s I was still writing under the impact of the Second World War which was the most inspiring time in our history. Now [1977] I regard the state and still more the future of my country more gloomily. Indeed I often wonder whether it is worthwhile writing history at all. The record, I think, is nearly over.[96]

In old age, he also knew that he had become something of a methodological dinosaur, writing 'narrative', 'political history': 'I kept slithering into the old fashion of writing about the "in" classes and then pulled myself up every now and then.'[97] It must be admitted, however, that these moments of arrest were generally brief. Taylor's typical sources were diplomatic documents, political papers, parliamentary speeches and the memoirs of those who ruled. His dismissal of himself as just 'an old-fashioned diplomatic historian' was thus a typical *goak*, being both true and not true at the same time. It was rather like Taylor's view of short-term and long-term causes, 'structural' determinates and 'accident' or the individual will. 'In my version of history, I am told', Taylor wrote, choosing his words with the utmost care, 'everything happens by accident.'[98] One major reason for the notoriety of *The Origins of the Second World War* was Taylor's reiterated argument in it that a week is a long time in politics, even for an ill-educated fanatic like Adolf Hitler. For Taylor, politicians' 'plans', whatever their content, always had a 'use by' stamp on them and the probable time of elapse was frequently the morrow.

But Taylor was similarly notorious in his presentation of long-standing factors. 'The first war explains the second and, in fact, caused it, in so far as one event causes another,' he declared.[99] It was Hitler's Germanness, not his personality, which was the real problem. The desire to appease lay deep in the heart of the liberal British Establishment. Taylor, in his way, is as structuralist a historian as any other.

It is doubtlessly appropriate for the Quaker-trained Taylor both to set up this dialectic between predestination and free-will and, mostly, to refuse to explore it systematically. Rather his major reference to this ultimate intellectual and ethical problem came right at the beginning of his first piece of autobiographical writing. He presented it as a wry 'story told to me by Sir Lewis Namier':

A Galician priest was explaining to a peasant what miracles were.
   'If I fell from that church tower and landed unhurt, what would you call it?'
   'An accident.'
   'And if I fell again, and was unhurt?'

'Another accident.'

'And if I did it a third time?'

'A habit.'[100]

Taylor, then, agreed with E.H. Carr: 'The fact is that all human actions are both free and determined, according to the point of view from which one considers them.'[101] Freedom and predestination, past and present, authority and democracy, the mighty and the little man or woman, were all engaged in a dialectic of endless movement and it was that movement which was both the centre of history as a discipline and, simultaneously, what it was best at explaining.

It is true that Taylor, the traitor within the gates, generally concentrated on relating the crimes and follies of the powerful. He may have loved ordinary people as he asserted, and written for them, but only rarely did he write about them. None the less, the three decades since the publication of *The Origins of the Second World War* have seen an extraordinary growth of the history of the people, of 'social history' as it came to be known. In the 1970s social history was ousting political history from many a curriculum and its more zealous proponents were declaring that it had killed off the history of kings, prime ministers and diplomats and liquidated any residual interest in merely political 'events'.[102]

By that time, in the terms of Namier's Galician peasant tale, social history had become a 'habit'. No doubt its rise to such a status had many causes. But one of prime importance was the 'long Second World War'. Indeed, it can be argued that the triumph of social history in the English-speaking world was stimulated more than anything else by the publication of one book. Entitled *The Making of the English Working Class* and published in 1963, it was written by E.P. Thompson, another for whom the Second World War had never ended.[103] Thompson's critics, hostile and favourable, have discussed many aspects of his work but they have underestimated the extent to which he was 'made' by a certainly English and perhaps romantic version of both the 'long' and the 'short' Second World War.

Edward Palmer Thompson was born in England in 1924 soon after his missionary parents returned home from India. If A.J.P. Taylor was a Lancastrian hereditary dissenter, Thompson became the Southern English equivalent. Both his parents were political as well as religious non-conformists and supported the Indian independence movement. Thompson grew up near Oxford and attended the elitist Dragon preparatory school, before going on to Kingswood, a Methodist school. Though very 'established', Thompson had not quite been trained automatically to don the purple of the Establishment.

In 1938, his much-loved and admired elder brother, Frank, entered Oxford University and, in the following year, joined the Communist Party. Though the Party denounced the war as 'imperialist', Frank volunteered for active service and fought, along with Spike Milligan, in the British 8th Army in North Africa and Sicily before being recruited by SOE, an intelligence group which liaised with European resistance movements. In 1944 Frank was parachuted into southern Yugoslavia and killed by Bulgarian fascists. To this day denied access to relevant

British archives on this event, Thompson has favoured a conspiratorial explanation in which elements of the SOE betrayed his brother as part of their attempt to prevent widespread political and social change in post-war Europe. Communist Bulgaria, by contrast, named a railway station in Frank's honour.[104]

His brother had been the dominant influence on the adolescent Edward, who also became a member of the Communist Party after entering Cambridge in 1941 and, then, as soon as he turned eighteen, joined the army. He was commissioned into the 17/21 Lancers and commanded a troop of Sherman tanks in the bitter Italian campaigns of 1943–5. This war would have a profound effect on him. He is still, as he has written, both 'haunted' by the terrible battles at Monte Cassino and inspired by his part in the liberation of Perugia. At that time, he recalls, 'there was an active democratic temper throughout Europe. There was a submission of self to a collective good . . . there was a purposive alliance of resistance to power, a "popular front" which had not yet been disfigured by bad faith. And there was also an authentic mood of internationalism which touched [both] the peasants in the Umbrian villages and the troopers in our tanks.' He and all who believed in a 'People's war' had supposed 'that the old gangs of money, privilege and militarism would go'. Later, in Thatcher's Britain, he pronounced, 'I hold the now-unfashionable view that the last war was, for the Allied armies and the Resistance, an anti-Fascist war, not only in the rhetoric but also in the intentions of the dead.'[105] For Thompson, the war, both in its 'long' and 'short' versions, was the indelible experience of his life. Though he might write about the eighteenth century, present political travail, or even science fiction,[106] that medieval history of the future, his writing was always conditioned by the values of the anti-Fascist struggle. He was another for whom the price of real democracy was eternal resistance. He would pass on an implied message to his followers that to write the people's history was meet and proper since, in the war, the people had made, as they should make, their own history.

After the war Thompson had returned to Cambridge to complete a shortened history course which gave him no research training but did introduce him to his wife, Dorothy, who would also become a distinguished historian of the English working class.[107] In 1948 he took a job as an adult education lecturer at Leeds University and, for the next seventeen years, instructed groups of working people all over Yorkshire. Here was an 'organic intellectual' working nearer to the people than did that media star, A.J.P. Taylor.

Thompson was also teaching himself how to research the nineteenth-century origins of contemporary British society and developing a serious interest in writing history. His first scholarly book was a study of the early British utopian socialist, William Morris, which he sub-titled 'romantic to revolutionary'.[108] During these years, Thompson, less sceptical and more committed or romantic than Taylor, remained a very active Communist, both locally and on a trip to the Balkans in his martyred brother's footsteps. In Tito's Yugoslavia and, more briefly, in Bulgaria, Thompson laboured with a will alongside a group of young socialist 'pioneers' on a railway project.

With the passage of the years, however, he grew impatient at the many inadequacies of the Party line. He helped found a critical Marxist journal, the *Reasoner*, and, like many another European left-wing intellectual, was expelled from the Party in 1956, after he publicly attacked the Soviet repression of the Hungarian uprising. He and fellow ex-Communists then founded the *New Reasoner* which, in 1960, changed its title to the *New Left Review*. Like Taylor, Thompson spoke up for the Campaign for Nuclear Disarmament. As shall be seen, it remains one of his obsessions, for, as he would remark, 'only historians' could 'appreciate how unlikely' was the 'making of [genuine and lasting] European peace'.[109]

In the comparative obscurity of Leeds, Thompson had planned a history of the British labour movement from the late eighteenth century to his own day, and in 1963 he published 'Chapter 1' of this project: the more than 900-page *The Making of the English Working Class*. It gave him immediate academic fame and, for the next three decades, was certainly as renowned and probably more influential than Taylor's *The Origins of the Second World War*. Thompson had discerned a new way to make the history of the English working class. He sought, as he confessed, 'to rescue the poor stockinger, the Luddite cropper, the "obsolete" hand-loom weaver, the "utopian" artisan, and even the deluded follower of Joanna Southcott, from the enormous condescension of posterity.' He would show that 'the working class made itself as much as it was made', and, thus, that it was 'present at its own making'.[110] He would display the rights of the 'free-born Englishman'.[111] And most of all, he would indicate how history, in its very essence, could not accept the freezing of time. The working class which he studied was a 'relationship' or a 'happening' and not a 'thing'.[112] In its eternal movement and eternal dissent against the comfortable corruption and injustice of the mighty, the working class eternally breathed new life into the spirit of Resistance.

Thompson was emphasising these points with a number of targets in mind. Namierite Tory historians, who had turned the history of the eighteenth century into a tale of the jobbing self-interest of relatives or clients of the Duke of Newcastle, and who had taken both the mind and the people out of history, were one group whose work was in need of revision.[113] Totalitarianists, especially those who, like J.L. Talmon, ascribed original sin to the French Revolution and Enlightenment, were also natural butts of Thompson's prose: 'so great has been the reaction in our time against Whig or Marxist interpretations of history,' he wrote firmly, 'that some scholars have propagated a ridiculous reversal of historical roles: the persecuted are seen as forerunners of oppression, and the oppressors as victims of persecution.'[114]

But Thompson's corrective ambitions did not cease there. Both in his book, and in a postscript to a revised edition which he would publish in 1968, he condemned those liberal historians who thought with Ramsay MacDonald that the story of England after the Industrial Revolution went 'on and on and on and up and up and up' and who believed that Progress was always good. He rejected the criticisms of hard-nosed economic historians like R. Currie and R.M. Hartwell who asserted that they could deploy economic statistics easily to demonstrate that the condition of the working class had improved with industrialisation. Against them, Thompson was inclined to argue that, if well-being was not quite 'all in the mind, you know', it was 'all in the relationship', all in the historical process through which free-born Englishmen and women were perpetually creating their own class and their own selves. In any case, he declared, economic statistics were always read ideologically.[115]

These debates were appropriate and useful, but also somewhat predictable. Thompson's past was as unlikely as was Thompson's present ever to accord with those of Tory or Whig historians. However, *The Making of the English Working Class* had its greatest impact neither on the Right nor on the Centre but rather within the Left. Thompson, then and thereafter, sought to revive a humanist Marxism in which, echoing those wonderful and ambiguous words at the start of the second paragraph of Marx's *Eighteenth Brumaire of Louis Bonaparte*, men and women 'make their own history'.

Thompson knew that the phrase ran on 'but not of their own free will; not under circumstances they themselves have chosen but under the given and inherited circumstances with which they are directly confronted. The tradition of the dead generations weighs like a nightmare on the minds of the living.'[116] But he chose to interpret Marx's words as an affirmation of history, especially against what, in a long polemic, he pronounced were the Stalinist or sadist rigidities of the French structuralist Marxist, Louis Althusser. In Thompson's eyes, Marxism, like the working class, was not a model, a holy writ, a 'thing', but rather a happening, a process which should be interpreted over time, a debate. 'Marx is on our side and we are not on the side of Marx.' History, he declared, knew 'no sufficient causes' but was, none the less, 'the most unitary and general of all human disciplines'. History was the subject best equipped to deal with the real world, composed of 'phenomena which are always in movement, which evince – even in a single moment – contradictory manifestations . . . . Historical knowledge is in its nature (a) provisional and incomplete (but not therefore untrue) (b) selective (but not therefore untrue) (c) limited and defined by the questions proposed to the evidence (and the concepts informing those questions) and hence only "true" within the field so defined.' 'Historical knowledge and its object' could only 'be understood as a dialogue.'[117]

Thus, although *The Making of the English Working Class* began with a (utopian?) assertion that history would eventually end, that the time of the universal proletariat would come, 'that the number of our Members be unlimited',[118] in his book Thompson sought to re-cast and re-vivify Marxism. By qualifying and, eventually, rejecting the vulgar Marxist model of an economic 'base' determining everything else (the 'super-structure'), Thompson aimed at unfreezing time for left-wing historians. No longer would they be expected merely to parrot catchcries about the inevitability of certain stages of development (including fascism and, thus, 'Auschwitz') or about the centrality of the USSR and its Great Patriotic War.[119] In taking Russia's Second World War out of time and asserting its single meaning, Stalinists were concealing and destroying the endless struggle of a 'People's war'. They must be rebutted.

In this attempt to create a 'New Left', Thompson was not alone. Commentators have noted a generation of British Marxist historians including Rodney Hilton (on the Middle Ages and the Peasants' Revolt), Christopher Hill (on the seventeenth century and the 'English Revolution') and Eric Hobsbawm (on the history of the world over the last two centuries), all of whom made major contributions to their fields, and duly inspired wide-ranging debates. All disclaimed simple-minded economic determinism.[120] In the world of political philosophy, too, the New Left was being nurtured by the writings of such humanist Marxists as George Lukács, Antonio Gramsci[121] or the 'young Marx' himself. Sloughing off Stalinism, left-wing history, inspired by such exemplars, had been turned into a process again.

The results were enormously positive. *The Making of the English Working Class* swiftly became a best-seller and had a huge impact on the 'new social history' which burst into flower in Britain, the United States and elsewhere in the 1960s and 1970s. Eugene Genovese, in *Roll, Jordan, Roll* (1974),[122] used concepts borrowed from Thompson to trigger a great leap forward in black history. Women's history, labour history, peasant history, oral history, the history of ethnic minorities, which have all become subjects in their own right since 1963, similarly almost always owe some sort of debt to *The Making of the English Working Class.*[123] E.P. Thompson, the historian who, so very self-consciously, bore proudly aloft the traditions of the people and their resistance to fascism in the 'People's war', started the movement which would give more of the people, more of a history, more of the time, than had ever been true in the past.

But, just as Taylor after his triumph in *The Origins of the Second World War* turned in on himself and found equivocal sanctuary in his Englishness, so Thompson's *curriculum vitae* has had some disappointing aspects to it since 1963. Having so superbly expressed the resistance to 'Auschwitz', Thompson, the historian, in a way fell victim to 'Hiroshima'.

Whereas Taylor had sceptically and even wearily implied that the cynicism seemingly endemic in international power-broking was an original sin which could not be lightly eliminated, Thompson demanded that it must. The 'history of power politics is nothing but the history of international crime and mass murder', he noted Karl Popper saying, but it could not remain so in the 'age of the Bomb'.[124] That age, he warned dramatically, saw the individual menaced as never before by the structures, overt and covert, conscious and unconscious, which underpinned those in power. But the 'free-born Englishman' must never lie down or be silent before this power, whether it be voiced by 'structuralist' *'lumpen-bourgeois'* intellectuals like Althusser,[125] or the hard or po-faced military technicians of 'Natopolitan culture'.[126] In the 1980s, Thompson's warnings grew more shrill. Both the USA and the USSR were 'imperialist formations', but even their rulers were tending to become puppets of a 'weapons *system*'. The world faced the imminent peril of the cataclysmic triumph of 'bureaucratic forms of exterminism':

> Undoubtedly, the MX-missile system will be the greatest single artefact of any civilization. It will be the ultimate serpentine temple of exterminism.

The rockets in their shelters, like giant menhirs pointing to the sky, will perform for the 'free West' not a military but a spiritual function. They will keep evil spirits at bay, and summon worshippers to the phallic rites of money . . . the temple will be erected to celebrate the ultimate dysfunction of humanity: self-destruct.

The people, Thompson feared, were being 'thought to death'.[127] Once they had defended their rights and liberties against the evil ideology of fascism; now they must rally anew against those who had changed their (coloured) shirts but not their spots.

As has been noted, Thompson had originally envisioned *The Making of the English Working Class* as being but 'Chapter 1' of a more lengthy study which would take the story down to this century. But the subsequent volume or volumes have never been written. In part this omission is explained by Thompson's commitment to polemical disputes with more rigid Marxists or within the University of Warwick, a very disturbed campus, at which he served as Reader in Social History until his early retirement in 1971.[128] Partly his attention had reverted to the eighteenth century, that prologue to *The Making of the English Working Class*, where he perceived the need for further campaigns against the 'mindless' 'science' of Namierism. One result was a very fine book, *Whigs and Hunters* (1975), stressing 'culture', the 'invisible rules' governing behaviour, and the special virtues of the English people whose own history had remained such a formidable vehicle of their 'free-born rights'.[129]

By the end of the 1970s, Thompson had allegedly almost finished a massive study of the mystical poet William Blake (1757–1827) as critic of his age, but this book, too, has never appeared. Instead, from 1980, Thompson became one of the founders of the European Nuclear Disarmament movement (euphoniously abbreviated as END). With his numerous appearances at rallies or in TV debates, and with his frequent books and pamphlets,[130] Thompson was soon even better known than before. In one survey, he was rated as the most familiar face in Britain after the Queen, the Queen Mum and Mrs Thatcher.[131] He was as fine a speaker as he was a writer, repeatedly exposing the selfishness, ruthlessness, and hypocrisy of those who used the 'Second Cold War' to proclaim that 'greed is good'. In the dismal decade of Thatcher (and Reagan), with the Left divided and impotent, when it was transparently plain that 'the high expectations for a deep democratisation of political and economic life which flourished on both sides of the Atlantic at the end of the Second World War were disappointed',[132] Thompson had shouldered the burden of being moral leader of the opposition in Britain. But, to historiography's loss, he had also stopped writing much history. His deepening sense that the present was too urgent a matter to be left to counsels from the past, that the 'good' Second World War was indeed over, had already been apparent in a poem which he had written back in 1973:

MY STUDY

King of my freedom here, with every prop
A poet needs – the small hours of the night,
A harvest moon above an English copse . . .

Backward unrationalised trade, its furthest yet
Technology this typewriter which goes
With flailing arms through the ripe alphabet.

Not even bread the pen is mightier than,
Each in its statutory place the giants yawn:
I blow my mind against their sails and fan

The mills that grind my own necessity.
Oh, royal me! Unpoliced imperial man
And monarch of my incapacity

To aid my helpless comrades as they fall –
Lumumba, Nagy, Allende: alphabet
Apt to our age! In answer to your call

I rush out in this rattling harvester
And thrash you into type. But what I write
Brings down no armoured bans, no Ministers

Of the Interior interrogate.
No-one bothers to break in and seize
My verses for subversion of the state:

Even the little dogmas do not bark.
I leave my desk and peer into the world.
Outside the owls are hunting. Dark

Has harvested the moon. Imperial eyes
Quarter the ground for fellow creaturehood:
Small as the hour some hunted terror cries.

I go back to my desk. If it could fight
Or dream or mate, what other creature would
Sit making marks on paper through the night?[133]

Thompson had given brilliant answers to the questions raised by the discipline
which he so adorned but, by the 1980s, his answers and those of the colleagues he
admired, especially the practitioners of social history, were either becoming
introverted, repetitive and predictable or simply seemed too arcane to carry useful
advice on how to avoid what Thompson feared was the imminent peril of the Third
World War.

A.J.P. Taylor and E.P. Thompson, in their different ways, had thus stimulated
a paradigm shift in the British understanding of the 'long Second World War'. *The*

Origins of the Second World War and *The Making of the English Working Class* were revolutionary books which, in their pages, destroyed what had seemed settled explanations either of appeasement and the structure of power in Nazi Germany or the arrival of modernity in Britain and the nature of class. Each author wrote from the Left, as critics both of present society and of the past. For all Taylor's inveterate scepticism and mistrust of mere worthiness wherever it might be found, for all Thompson's theoretical internationalism, each felt the tug of English patriotism. Their minds concentrated by their memories of a 'People's war', each both loved the people and sought to defend the individual in his or her pomp and potential majesty. At the same time, each was not disloyal to the current nation state but rather perceived a special role in the world for the English past and the English present. Each was a free-born Englishman but, having spoken his lines in the great historical debate on the meaning of the 'long Second World War', each eventually found that his message could not and should not be endlessly repeated.

Indeed, by the latter part of the 1980s, the most controversial British historians, the new and self-conscious 'radicals', were the heirs neither of Thompson's nor of Taylor's variety of leftism. They were, instead, such figures as Jonathan Clark[134] and Norman Stone who busily re-cast the past in a new conservative mould. Corelli Barnett decided that an audit of Britain's participation in the Second World War disclosed merely a story of pride and fall,[135] and Thatcherite historians were equally scathing about the causes, course and consequences of the Welfare State. In at least that part of Britain where power was held and enjoyed, where 'THE THING' was back in business, an impulse to end history had appeared well before Fukuyama heralded it. As will be found so often in the pages of this book, a film expressed the mood as well as did anything else. At the end of *The Love Child,* a 1988 production directed by Robert Smith and starring Sheila Hancock, a grimy London tenement is portrayed. It has at its base a fresco of Picasso's *Guernica* (that usual image of the 'resistance' which Taylor, for one, believed to have begun in the Spanish Civil War).[136] But in contemporary Britain, the images of *Guernica* can be seen only darkly. The fresco, doubtless painted on the best, by which I mean the worthiest, advice of some local counsellor, is now bedaubed with dirt, graffiti and excrement. 'Over and out', it seems to say from Britain's history of the 'long Second World War'.

3

Germany and the Third, Second, and First World Wars

From the very beginning it was plain to me: grown-ups will not understand you. If you cease to offer them any discernible growth, they will say you are retarded; they will drag you and their money to dozens of doctors, looking for an explanation if not a cure for your deficiency. Consequently I myself, in order to keep the consultations within tolerable limits, felt obliged to provide a plausible ground for my failure to grow, even before the doctor should offer his explanation.[1]

So Günter Grass, author in 1959 of the novel *The Tin Drum*, imagined his protagonist, Oskar Matzerath, musing. Oskar, who, aged three, had thrown himself down the family staircase, seemed to symbolise many aspects of modern Germany. Maybe he was a classic case of (self-) arrested development, this hunchback of the Notre Dame of Gdansk / Danzig, a surreal child-adult, adult-child? As once Germany's ruling elites had hoped Hitler would be their 'drummer', so Oskar could not be separated from his tin drum. Was he also then, this tinniest and most pertinacious of drummers, the master of propaganda? Certainly, with his voice that shattered glass and made every night a potential *Kristallnacht*, he could control and deploy violence. He also knew about (rye) bread (eels with sour cream and dill sauce) and circuses. And after liberation from Nazism, he could only embrace modernity from an asylum bed.

For Grass, little Oskar heralded a literary lifetime of engagement with the Nazi and German (and Kashubian, Masurian, Sorb and Polish) past of Gdansk/Danzig, epicentre of the 'outbreak of World War II' (and by the 1970s and 1980s, city of worker Solidarity). Grass would be a writer of political commitment, spokesman of the German Social Democrat Party (SPD), loyal to it, as he explained in 1989, 'because it remains mindful of history'. In that same year, he expressed his fear of a re-unified Germany, preferring a confederation or a divided 'cultural' nation to a unitary state because, he argued, only a confederation 'would include joint responsibility for German history.' Had he not, he asked, always been someone self-consciously 'writing after Auschwitz'? In 1990 he reiterated his and Germany's preoccupation: 'We cannot get around Auschwitz. And no matter how greatly we want to, we should not attempt to get around it, because Auschwitz belongs to us, is a permanent stigma of our history.' But, he concluded, it should not make present-day Germans downcast. Rather 'it has made possible this insight: Finally we know ourselves.'[2]

Now, Oskar's literary birth makes 1959 seem a year of enlightenment and opening; then, it had rather seemed to be one of renunciation and closure. In November at their party conference at Godesburg, members of the SPD finally struck the word 'socialism' from their programme and thus foreswore any lingering commitment to revolution. Historians, too, were defining themselves more narrowly. From 1959, the academics of East Germany, the GDR, no longer attended meetings of the German Historical Congress (*Verband Deutscher Historiker*).[3] They preferred their own 'national', GDR association, set up the year before. Yet, for all their efforts, outside the Warsaw Bloc only West Germany, the FRG, seemed a 'legitimate' heir of past German culture and a credible aspirant to a German future.

Two years later, this division between East and West was set in concrete in a literal sense, with the construction of the Berlin Wall. Soon, in the FRG, the USA and other parts of the liberal capitalist world, teenagers joined in singing:

> West of the Wall
> I'll wait for you
> West of the Wall
> Our dreams can all come true....
> That wall built of our sorrows
> We know must have an end
> Till then dream of tomorrow
> When we meet again...[4]

while, at the same time, readers of history were puzzling over the *goaks* in the first edition of A.J.P. Taylor's *The Origins of the Second World War*.

As has been seen in the last chapter, *The Origins*, when properly understood, represented a fundamental challenge to the ideology of the Cold War and a solemn warning lest the nations, whether over Cuba or the status of Berlin, 'slithered over the brink' into what promised to be the literally 'boiling cauldron' of the Third World War.[5]

In 1961, the philosophical, political and moral certainties of the West German historical trade were also suddenly challenged by a work which, on the surface, seemed almost the exact reverse of Taylor's '*goak* book', but which carried some remarkably similar messages. This was Fritz Fischer's *Griff nach der Weltmacht* ('grab for world power'), though its eventual English language edition would carry the less strident but more accurate title, *Germany's Aims in the First World War*.[6]

With the publication of his book, Fischer became the protagonist of what is known as 'the Fischer affair',[7] the most profound and bitter historiographical controversy, to that time, about the meaning of Germany's 'long Second World War'. In the course of that controversy Fischer would emerge as an international celebrity — Richard Evans has recalled that, in 1969, the news that Fischer was coming to give a seminar at Oxford generated intense excitement among postgraduate students.[8] He was also the object of vituperative attacks from more traditionalist West German historians. In 1964, his leading critic, Gerhard Ritter, said that, if Fischer's findings were deemed true, the 'national historical consciousness' would be 'darkened', 'even more than it was by the experiences of the Hitler period'.[9] The conservative, Christian Democrat, West German Government, so readily nervous of intellectual dissent and so armed with legislation against it, apparently even went so far as, for a time, to refuse Fischer a passport when he was invited to go on a lecture tour of the USA.[10]

What occasioned these extraordinary events and what was it about Fischer's work that aroused such heart-felt polemic? At first the reply to these questions is not obvious. Fischer himself was elderly – he had been born in March 1908 (though this made him younger than Ritter, who had seen military service on the Eastern Front in the First World War). His career seemed a model of normality. He had begun academic life in 1935. He then fought in the *Wehrmacht* during the Second World War, after which he was mistakenly detained for a time by agents of the US occupying forces who were searching for war criminals. In 1948 he became a full professor at the University of Hamburg, where he would remain until his retirement in 1973. Though he has been defined as a 'militant liberal',[11] Fischer was not a political activist and, unlike many of the historians studied in this book, seemed to have no overt ideological agenda. In his preface, he declared scrupulously that *Griff nach der Weltmacht* was 'neither an indictment nor a defence' of Imperial Germany. 'It is not for the historian to accuse or defend', he added, 'his duty is to establish facts and to marshal them in the sequence of cause and effect.'[12]

As some of his critics from the Left would eventually notice, Fischer was scarcely a methodological revolutionary.[13] In a decade of the rise and triumph of social history, he generally conformed to the traditions and principles of diplomatic history. His writing was about 'top people'; it was from 'above' not 'below'. The answers to historical problems could be found in the 'documents', that is, in the sort of papers which one top person wrote to another and which were preserved in state archives. In this world of what an Englishman would call 'chaps' (top people were by definition male), the guilty parties would reveal their guilt in the documents. Confronted by the problem of resolving the origins of the First World War, the historian's job was to be a sort of Hercule Poirot. He must assemble the *dramatis personae*, read all their papers (Fischer was an indefatigable researcher, the quintessence of what Stalin had called an 'archive rat'), and then produce with a flourish the incriminating document which would finally reveal 'the truth', that is, 'who done it'. It was certainly the case that Fischer had access to those archives which were kept at Potsdam in East Germany and that such access was banned to Ritter,[14] but Fischer, too, was still very much a traditionalist. His ambition was to be 'objective', to show 'what actually happened'. In his philosophy and practice he did not, superficially at least, seem to depart from others in the corporation or *Bund* of FRG historians.

Nor does a first reading of his book initially solve the riddle of the 'Fischer affair'. *Griff nach der Weltmacht* is lengthy; its style is sober and certainly does not aspire to the tone *allegretto molto vivace* of A.J.P. Taylor. Moreover, although it was rapidly seen as a major statement about the origins of the First World War, its actual focus is on the war years themselves. It does what its English title says it will do, that is, it sets out the changing aims of the Imperial German Government during the war.

In so doing, though it is not immediately obvious amid the plethora of 'facts', Fischer has two great emphases. One is on that sometimes forgotten First World War in which Germany was victorious, that campaign on the Eastern Front, which was temporarily resolved in the treaties of Bucharest (with Romania) and Brest-Litovsk (with the infant Soviet Union).[15] The other is on the Wilhelmine regime's economic and diplomatic policies in Central and South-Eastern Europe, its ideas about *Mitteleuropa*, and especially on its planning in this area, as evidenced most notoriously by the 'September programme' drafted in 1914 by Chancellor Theobald von Bethmann Hollweg and his adviser, the court intellectual, Kurt Riezler.[16]

What was it about these matters which struck at the heart of the established historical profession in the FRG and, indeed, at much of the political establishment? The answer is complex and, in unravelling it, a commentator must be ready, like Dr Who, to travel in time. At a superficial reading, Fischer's work focuses on 1914 to 1918 and that period may have been what Fischer thought he was writing about. But in fact the book bore messages, at once received, about 1871 to 1914, about 1919, 1933, 1938–9, 1941, 1945, 1948–9 and the 1960s.

On one level, Fischer's work sapped under the fortresses of the standard German interpretation of the beginning and end of the First World War. When he wrote about Bucharest or Brest-Litovsk, Fischer showed how draconian German policy towards the defeated states in the east had been. Russia and Romania had been forced to accept large territorial losses to Germany (or its allies) and pay punitive reparations. If the spirit of the times was considered and some comparison made, perhaps, after all, the Allies had not been as cruel to Germany at Versailles as almost all the German historical profession and most public opinion had maintained since the peace treaty had been reluctantly signed by the German delegates on 28 June 1919.

Apart from its opening chapter, *Griff nach der Weltmacht* was not directly about the origins of the war, but, in the aftermath of its publication, Fischer was drawn more and more into the controversy surrounding that issue. In 1969, he published a second detailed monograph, *Krieg der Illusionen* ('War of Illusions' as the abridged English-language version would be entitled). It concentrated on the three years before 1914 and argued, much more peremptorily (and rather less credibly), that the elites of Imperial Germany had indeed planned the outbreak of the First World War.[17] Fischer, in some ways rather like the De Felice portrayed in chapter 6 below, had been radicalised by his own controversy. By 1969 he was espousing his theses certainly in a more vehement and perhaps a cruder fashion than he had when he first sketched them in *Griff nach der Weltmacht*.[18]

Regardless of Fischer's own intent and meaning, the most public area of debate had focused on what his research contributed to the issue of Germany's responsibility for the First World War, and especially to the question of 'war guilt', as ascribed in article 231 of the Versailles Treaty. Here the special documentary key became the 'September programme' and Fischer's reading of the characters of Bethmann Hollweg and Riezler.

Though by 1961 the issue remained a matter of debate in some quarters, most non-German historians took it for granted that 'Germany' had 'caused the First World War'. Luigi Albertini, an Italian anti-Fascist, had whiled away the Mussolini years by completing a massive 2000-page, three-volume, documentary study, published in 1952–7 as *The Origins of the War of 1914*. His book seemed to give definitive proof of a German responsibility greater than that of any other power.[19] In Germany, however, such an interpretation was heretical (it was probably remembered that, in 1914–15, Albertini had been an interventionist journalist who had campaigned strongly for Italy to leave the Triple Alliance and enter the war on the Entente side).[20]

In the FRG, orthodoxy in interpreting the causation of the First War had its foremost champion in Gerhard Ritter, who had only recently organised a meeting with French historians in the spirit of the infant EEC to review the origins of the Great War as a problem on school curricula. There it was agreed that the outbreak had not been the responsibility of any individual state; in Lloyd George's phrase, the nations had slithered over the brink. Events had simply overwhelmed them.[21]

A Lutheran pastor's son, Ritter had been born in 1888. As a young scholar he earned fame defending the Prussian *kleindeutsch* tradition, his publications including studies of the army and of Luther. Under Weimar he became a leading figure in the intellectual establishment, holding a chair at the University of Freiburg from 1926. His politics were pronouncedly conservative,[22] being best reflected in his polemic against the young radical historian, Eckart Kehr. During the Nazi rise to power Kehr had written critically of such national saints as Herder, Bismarck and Tirpitz, and even dared to criticise the great nineteenth-century German historian, Leopold von Ranke, coining the term the *Primat der Innenpolitik* ('primacy of internal politics') to define the real bases of Germany's international misadventures.[23] Ritter reacted very sharply to what seemed an intrusion of Marxism and national disloyalty into German historiography. Kehr, he remarked derisively, was a 'pure-bred Bolshevik', 'this gentleman should habilitate – now, if possible – in Russia, where he naturally belongs'.[24] For Ritter, the slogan 'love it or leave it' was the beginning of historiographical wisdom.

Ritter's values were far too conservative for him to warm to every aspect of Nazism. Between 1933 and 1936 he occasionally spoke out against what he deemed Nazi departures from the ideal principles of Prussia, and in 1938 the Nazis banned him from speaking abroad.[25] None the less, his distaste for Nazi populism and for Hitler's own enormous popularity[26] did not extend to Nazi foreign policy. For Ritter, as for Meinecke and the great majority of German historians schooled in the Rankean tradition, in international relations there was nothing wrong with Hitler until it was plain that he had lost the Second World War. Ritter expressed this world view in a study of King Frederick II: 'Without violation of historical rights and without forcible conquest of power . . . there can be no great policy.' [27]

In 1944, Ritter did sympathise with the conservative, nationalist and Christian July conspirators against Hitler. On 1 November of that year, he himself was arrested by the Nazi regime and, ironically, was only saved from whatever fate the Nazis had in store for him by being liberated by the Red Army in April 1945.[28]

Back in 1940, not a good year, Ritter had stated that 'the sword is always more ready to the hand of a continental statesman, who stands in the midst of the fray of European power interests, and must always be armed to counter an attack before it is too late'. He had then gone on to agree with Mussolini that 'might is the precondition of all freedom'.[29] In the 1950s Ritter had refined these possibly embarrassing theses in his own massive study, *Staatskunst und Kriegshandwerk*.[30] In this book, Germany was still depicted as caught in a vice not of its own making. The German Army did contain in its officer corps elements who gladly accepted the prospect of war, but more doleful about that event, more 'responsible', more 'cultured', 'good Germans' in anyone's language, were liberals like Bethmann Hollweg and Riezler.

Fischer now threatened both this orthodoxy and the freshly minted Franco-German consensus on school texts.[31] The territorial aims delineated in the September memorandum and exposed by his research were so great that the annexationist Germany of 1917–18 was connected back to the Germany which had only just entered the war. Moreover, to annexation in practice in the east was added annexation in theory in both east and west. A victorious Germany, it was implied, would have behaved as ruthlessly towards liberal capitalist Britain, France or Belgium as it did towards communist Russia.

Fischer's rediscovery of the September programme contained another, still more disturbing implication (it would become much hardened in *War of Illusions*). Annexationism written down in September must have been already thought of in July. In so far as 'guilt' for the outbreak of war was concerned, Imperial Germany or its leadership had both the method and the motive. According to Fischer, Germany was not, as traditional historiography had argued, just the 'nation of the middle', granted by the caprice or malevolence of Destiny and geography too many neighbours and thus too many potential enemies. Rather it had been the Imperial German elite who so forced the pace of the Darwinian struggle between the nations before 1914 that they set all Europe awry. Worse, within that elite, Fischer now argued, it was not stern militarists who dominated civilised civilians but rather the reverse. Not to put too fine a point on it, the whole 'decision-making elite' in Imperial Germany bore full responsibility at the very least of risking continental European war (in *Krieg der Illusionen* this became more like deliberately fostering world war).

The messages in Fischer's work that were offensive to the ears of Ritter and the German historical establishment multiplied. There was that concerning the character of Kurt Riezler, for example. In the writings of Fischer and such younger supporters as Imanuel Geiss,[32] Riezler's ideas became proof of the involvement of German high culture in the origins of the First World War and thus in the whole 'German problem'. (In 1964, self-styled moderate Karl Dietrich Erdmann fuelled the fires of controversy by publishing what turned out to be a carefully expurgated version of Riezler's diaries.)[33] If Fischer and the Fischerites were correct and Ritter and Erdmann and their friends wrong, 1914 was the fault not merely of the Kaiser and his army officer corps, of Imperial diplomats, politicians and businessmen. Rather, the decision for war had been nourished by culture, by German civilisation, by the German intelligentsia, by German historiography. For all his methodological caution and moderation, Fischer, in *Griff nacht der Weltmacht,* had, among other things, initiated a full-scale debate over the validity and virtue of the Rankean tradition, over what gave German history its might and reputation both in Germany and wherever history was written.[34]

Ranke (1795–1886) had, in an extraordinarily lengthy, fertile and distinguished career, reached what has been accurately defined as 'a position of unexampled pre-eminence' as a historian.[35] Indeed, in many ways, he was the inventor of modern academic history and his authority was accepted not only within Germany but also in the wider world. The American Historical Association, for instance, was set up to translate across the Atlantic the ideas and practices of German history, though it is not always clear that the Americans got their translation right.[36] Ranke and such colleagues as the ancient historian Theodor Mommsen[37] had triumphed in the history trade as overwhelmingly as had German arms and military tactics against France in 1870–1, or as would German applied science in the chemical and electrical industries of the 'Second Industrial Revolution' before 1914. To an admiring world Ranke seemed the Bismarck of German historiography.

His successors enjoyed almost equal prestige and achievement. It was true that Heinrich von Treitschke (1834–1896), son of a Saxon general and from 1866 a fervent *kleindeutsch* nationalist, eventually seemed to his critics 'the supreme model of the historian turned [national] propagandist'.[38] For him, as Italian classicists would recall fondly in 1940, Britain was the 'new Carthage', a natural enemy of the rising power of Germany. The army was the 'very essence of the State' and 'war . . . the one remedy for an ailing nation'. Austria, Italy, France, Spain, the Vatican, women, blacks and Jews, all in one way or another met with Treitschke's disapproval. So, most of all, did democracy. 'The masses', he decreed, 'must forever remain the masses.' 'It is precisely in the differentiation of classes that the moral wealth of mankind is demonstrated.'[39]

If Treitschke sometimes went too far, his contemporaries and pupils were more cautious and acceptable. Friedrich Meinecke (1862–1954), in particular, achieved a national and international eminence which was not really shaken by his support of the Imperial German cause during the First World War.[40] It was not as though the majority of historians of Britain, France, Russia and Italy had not then also found justification for their own nation's military aims and practices. But precisely because the war had been such a 'historical event', it could thereafter, at least in the 1920s, be readily forgiven or forgotten as European historians embraced or evinced the 'Locarno spirit' and briefly preached international amity. Few were yet so bold as to argue that the world could do without German history and German historiography.

Ranke, Meinecke and the rest disagreed about many matters. Later commentators would even wonder whether Ranke was a Rankean. But the German historians did espouse a set of ideas which, it was widely believed, lay at the very base of historical methodology. History was, or should aspire to be, a 'science'. Factual error was a sin which would scar a historian's reputation for life. History must be based on documents, the real meaning of which would be elicited only by the most scrupulous reading and attention to philological nuance and detail. The periodicity of history could be scientifically determined and it was a major solecism not to assess a given society on its own terms. At the same time, however, Ranke, Treitschke, Mommsen and Meinecke, all in their different ways, distrusted the *demos*. History and life were about great ideas and Great Men. Indeed, especially for the pious Lutheran Ranke, the unfolding of German history displayed the hand of God. That unfolding occurred most notably through military conflict or diplomatic machination. Foreign policy was above party politics. For a state, the conduct of international relations represented at once its most basic and its most sublime task, the time when it was closest to God. Historians should concentrate on recounting the history of such events. In a respectful manner, they should accept the 'primacy of external politics' (*Primat der Aussenpolitik*).

Almost every item in this credo was undermined by Fischer's work, or by the debates which spread in its wake. If Riezler and the intellectual elites of Imperial Germany had risked or fomented war in 1914, maybe they had done so, at least partly, because of a German historiographical tradition which descried, in the rise of Germany to European or world power, destiny and the hand of God. Maybe these 'fathers of German history' were not pure and reproachless paladins of science and objectivity but, instead, more or less candid propagandists of German nationalism. Maybe their science and objectivity were riddled with bias, selectivity and *parti pris*. Maybe the German variety of history had 'caused the First World War'.

But even this grave charge did not end Fischer's indictment of 'German history'. Like A.J.P. Taylor's *The Origins of the Second World War*, Fischer's work was a 'time bomb' in the most literal of senses. It blew up the nation's understanding of time so carefully constructed by German historians. If the German elites and German historiography were heavily responsible for 1914, what of 1939, 1941 and 1933? What of 'Auschwitz'? Perhaps there was a continuity in German history – in old age Fischer himself became a convinced advocate of it – which ran from 1870 (or 1848) to at least 1945. Whereas, in the Imperial era, Germans had been trained to be proud of their *Sonderweg*, their special way, which was making them ever more rich, powerful and respected, now the *Sonderweg* was reversed and converted into a negative process. Maybe there was something wrong with Germany, some form of arrested development, which had prevented the Reich from following the liberal path to 'modernity' familiar in Britain or the United States. Maybe the causes of the Second World War were not so different from those of the First. Maybe, as Sir Lewis Namier had observed, Adolf Hitler was not an 'accident in the works' but the 'correct consummation'[41] of both 'German history' and German historiography.

In the aftermath of 1945, the German (both FRG and GDR) historical professions, like so many other groups studied in this book, had swiftly sought exculpation from any involvement with Nazism. The *curriculum vitae* of the history professor had not led to 'Auschwitz'. As has already been noted, Gerhard Ritter, for one, seemed to have turned thought into action through his sympathy with the July 1944 conspiracy against Hitler. Had von Stauffenberg's bomb successfully liquidated Hitler and his entourage, Ritter, it was said, would have been made Minister of Culture in a government which moderate politician Carl Goerdeler was planning.[42] This government would also presumably have cut short the Holocaust and extricated Germany from the war, at least that with the Western powers. It would have restored (conservative) German virtue.

The viciousness with which the July conspiracy was suppressed and the sadism of the punishments meted out to those conspirators who were caught made it easy to proclaim this event the supreme moment of the German Resistance, the time when good Germans said 'No' to Nazism. Especially in the writings of Hans Rothfels, a colleague of Ritter, and with a similar world view, this Resistance tradition was narrated, exalted, and attached to all that was best in the German past (or what would be good in the German future).[43] The Rankean tradition at least, it seemed, had regained its virtue.

This virtue was defended stoutly in the first major work of post-1945 German historiography. Only one year after the end of the war, Freidrich Meinecke published *Die deutsche Katastrophe*,[44] in which he promulgated all the basic theses of the conservative interpretation or myth of Germany's 'long Second World War'. *The German Catastrophe* would also tincture conservative and liberal accounts of the origins of that war in Italy,[45] in the United States, and elsewhere.

The Hitlerite regime had indeed been a catastrophe, Meinecke averred. It was a representation of all that was most sordid and evil in the human condition. Nazism was as loathsome spiritually as in every other way. However, contrary to the contemporary arguments of Edmond Vermeil, Rohan Butler or A.J.P. Taylor,[46] Nazism, according to Meinecke, had no deep roots in German history. It was, rather, a European phenomenon, brought on by the Faustian arrogance of the Enlightenment and the French Revolution, when man had the hubris to assert his own perfectability. Similarly, Nazism was an affair of the people, 'mass Machiavellism' as Meinecke defined it in a curious half-echo of those German racists who had earlier argued that the veins of the wicked Machiavelli coursed with bad Southern blood. (These same theoreticians believed Mussolini and Dante to be Aryans.)[47] Nazism was the sad culmination of the rise of '*terribles simplificateurs*', whose moment came in a Weimar in which there had been 'too little firm and continuous authority at the top of the government structure'.[48] Meinecke thus largely endorsed the thesis already put forward by Hermann Rauschning before 1945, that Nazism was 'the beast from the abyss',[49] the sort of grotesque Caliban which crawled to the surface in a society not instructed to honour God, King, social betters and history professors. Somewhat inconsistently, Meinecke also declared that the regime was indeed Hitler's. The *Führer* had been jockeyed into power by the corrupt Hindenburg entourage, by the wicked or foolish deeds of certain factions which dealt in the by-ways of politics. He had had no genuine backing, at least among the best elements of German society. In office, he simply imposed a tyranny and that was that.

Meinecke, in going back as far as the French Revolution, had been somewhat fuzzy about the history of Imperial Germany. His Germany exhibited symptoms of the coming disease from the time of Goethe onwards. However, positive elements had lingered both in the German intelligentsia and in the German body politic. These included, for example, Treitschke and Bismarck and had notably manifested themselves in the wave of national unity from July to September 1914. 'The exaltation of spirit experienced' at that time, Meinecke recalled with relish, 'is one of the most precious, unforgettable memories of the highest sort.'[50]

In the next years Meinecke's diagnosis of Nazism was duly seconded and refined by Ritter and others in the historian's *Bund*. The worst features of Nazism, Ritter explained, were imported – Social Darwinism through a figure like Houston Stuart Chamberlain from England, wayward nationalism from France, gimcrack racism from Austria.[51] In opening, in 1949, the first post-war Congress of German historians, Ritter, firm in his 'Resistance' principles, had himself warned against that selfish objectivity which confined historians to their studies and made anaemic their commitment to politics and everyday life. But in the next years he retreated from this apparent enthusiasm for democracy, just as he rigidified his periodisation of Nazi history. The Nazis were the product of a society which unnaturally sought to level people into an undifferentiated mass. Threads might connect to the French Revolution, but the unsightly knots and tears of German history had only really become manifest during and after the First World War, in Bolshevism, Versailles, the Inflation and the Depression. Nazism, it now turned out, in words which went even further than Croce's 'parenthesis' thesis on Italian Fascism, was 'a revolutionary force directed against all the central traditions of German history'[52] and, Ritter did not need to add, of German historiography.

But, in the 1960s, for those young German historians who had read *The Tin Drum* or been moved to defend Fischer, these arguments of Meinecke, Ritter and their friends smacked of special pleading. The German conservatives' version of totalitarianism (before his death in 1967 Ritter took to berating the West for not dealing with the USSR in a forcible and final manner)[53] began to seem as questionable to the new generation of German scholars as it was becoming elsewhere in liberal or left-wing circles. Nor did such questioning diminish when, in July 1962, a meeting of the Presidents of the Boards of Education of the West German *Länder* imposed the theory of totalitarianism as a truth to be taught to every school-child.[54] Reacting against such authoritarian prescription, the young historians, like so many others in the Sixties generation, took to asking that simplest of questions: 'What did you do in the Second World War, Daddy?' and the answer which the older generation gave was hedged and unsatisfactory.

Meinecke, for example, had been an 'accidentalist' (to use that splendid term drawn from Spanish history) in regard to the Weimar Republic. He had neither conspired against it, nor fought to save it.[55] Though he had disliked and mistrusted Nazism, he had not actively opposed it or fled into exile. Instead, he had devoted himself to scholastic writing, of which the central argument, at least in retrospect, seemed to remain a defence of German nationalism. Certainly he had never been actively anti-Semitic, but, even before 1933, to his own Jewish pupils he would act as the best of patrons only if they were converts to Christianity. And in *The German Catastrophe* he can still be found complaining that 'among those who drank too hastily and greedily of the cup of power which had come to them [in 1919] were many Jews'.[56]

In 1935 Meinecke had abandoned the editorship of *Historische Zeitschrift*, appalled by what he regarded as the capricious lawlessness of Nazi policies. And yet, as Georg Iggers has noted, Meinecke, very like Volpe and others in Fascist Italy,[57] sharply distinguished cruel or tawdry domestic politics from foreign affairs. In the latter sphere, it seemed, even Hitler might be touched by the hand of God. Of the *Anschluss* Meinecke wrote: 'Winning Austria has advanced all of German history with one jump and fulfilled old desires and ideals.' The demolition of Czechoslovakia and the fall of France were equally to be applauded. The invasion of the USSR was even better news, and, Meinecke opined, the world would be a happier place if Germany became the equal of the USA. Nor did he ever admit that the Anglo-American war effort was morally preferable to that of Nazi Germany, and he naturally bewailed the 'horrible expulsion' of Germans from the east in 1945 and the surrender of historic 'folk communities'.[58]

Meinecke's story, like that of Ritter, was typical of many German historians during the Nazi period. After January 1933, some 15 per cent of professors were sacked or went into exile,[59] among them Eckart Kehr who fled to the United States and died there in May. Many of those who stayed undoubtedly disapproved of much about Nazism but failed to see that they were inching their way along what Karl Schleunes has so aptly defined as 'the twisted road to Auschwitz'.[60] Many were far too scientific in their scholarship, far too Rankean in their principles and practice, to hold anything but contempt for the wilder aspects of Nazi science and Nazi culture. And yet, there was, for a long period of time, a considerable amount of fellow-travelling, just as there was by other conservative segments of the German establishment. Historians behaved as did many businessmen, army officers, judges, bureaucrats or pastors. They could see the mote in the eye of Nazism but judged it a minor irritant compared with the beam of Bolshevism (and perhaps of liberal capitalist democracy).

For some, their dealings with the regime carry an even more sinister air. Michael Burleigh has focused on the melancholy story of Germany's experts in *Osteuropaforschung*, those historians, archaeologists, linguists, geographers and other social scientists whose scholarly concentration lay to the east of the Reich, and who there helped to pave the way for the policy of *Lebensraum*.[61] Burleigh shows how natural and long-standing among these people was a visceral hatred of communism and of Russia or Poland, and an easy acceptance that, in some form or other, vast territories belonged to German culture or German administration, an alleged German past and a hypothetical German future. It was, says Burleigh, a Tübingen medievalist, Johannes Haller, who laid down the basic dictum of the *Ostforschers*: 'whoever denies the Russian threat, is himself a threat, the Russian threat in the German house.'[62]

Nor did the Nazi accession to power make a fundamental difference. Rather, the *Ostforscher* historians and pre-historians contributed to normalising the present by their nationalising of the past. 'History lent an air of apparent familiarity to chill, ahistorical, racial reality.'[63] It placed cheerful signposts on the roads to Danzig,[64] to Auschwitz and to Stalingrad. 'The experts did not challenge existing stereotypes and misconceptions; they worked within their boundaries and reified them through empirical "evidence".'[65]

There were some fanatics involved in the movement, Walter and Hans Frank or Otto Reche for example. But its more common leaders were members of the 'educated, established elite'. Typical in this regard was Albert Brackmann, co-editor with Meinecke of *Historische Zeitschrift* from 1928 to 1935. Brackmann retired after a personal dispute with Walter Frank, but he remained an important and active figure in the German intellectual and academic establishment. Earlier he had helped to bar Kehr from the archives on the specious grounds of incompetence in editing Prussian financial records. He was also a friend and patron of Gerhard Ritter and Hans Rothfels, both of whom contributed to the work of *Osteuropaforschung*. Indeed, in one collaborative production, Brackmann actually urged Rothfels to tone down the acerbity of his anti-Polish sentiments.[66]

Amid that infighting typical of the Nazi regime, Brackmann defended himself and his colleagues through his contacts with Himmler and the SS, so often one of the more 'gentlemanly' segments of the Nazi elite. In 1935 Brackmann had declared: 'We must all rationalise our academic efforts and let them be determined by one great thought: how can my work be of use to my fatherland?'[67] And this determination was not diminished by the German attack on Poland or on the Soviet Union. Indeed, Burleigh has made plain, war enhanced the level of collaboration between these scholars and the regime. Had not one young expert, Theodor Oberländer, to be a Christian Democrat Cabinet Minister in the 1950s, already stated in 1936: 'The struggle for ethnicity is nothing other than the continuation of war by other means under the cover of peace'?[68]

Nor did the catastrophe on the Eastern Front destroy the *Ostforschers*. The US Government and intelligence services were sympathetic to them, the more so because G.R. Gayre, SHAEF's (Supreme Headquarters Allied Expeditionary Force) Civil Affairs Officer for educational and religious affairs in Germany and Austria, had a pre-war background in German racial anthropology.[69] Even such zealots as Otto Reche soon regained their social position and academic prestige, Reche being accorded honorary membership of the German Anthropological Society in 1958. Whatever else the Second World War had done to Germany, there was by 1961 meagre evidence that it had 'revolutionised' or 'modernised' the German humanities and social sciences.[70] Only in the 1970s would the story of *Osteuropaforschung* become the object of critical analysis in West Germany, that is, only after the Fischer affair had been thoroughly absorbed by the German historical profession.

Fischer's book, his own later writings and the work of such historians as Hans-Ulrich Wehler[71] and what came to be known as the Bielefeld school, had firmly fixed on the continuity thesis in German history and German historiography as the basic way of understanding the 'German century' from 1848 to 1945 (or 1948–9). In the 1960s this still seemed a highly radical interpretation, with many important lessons for contemporary West German politics and society. Take the idea of the 'primacy of internal politics', for example, which Wehler (who from 1964 started re-publishing the all but forgotten work of Eckart Kehr), Imanuel Geiss (at the time a shield-bearer of Fischer),[72] Jürgen Kocka[73] and others emphasised and reiterated. The message seemed to be that the besetting sin of Imperial (and Nazi) Germany, that which pushed its leadership into the First and Second World Wars, was the failure of that leadership to accept and integrate into the German state the working class, as expressed politically in the SPD. As a result the SPD and its followers were 'encapsulated', driven in on themselves, and thus encouraged to think narrowly and in a short-term manner about their own interests, rather than being part of a German whole.

An emphasis on the primacy of domestic politics and, by implication, on the besetting self-interest of a 'ruling class', seemed almost Marxist in character. One of the half-hints, never quite brought to the surface in the 'Fischer affair', was that post-Fischer historians should not totally deride the sort of history being produced in the GDR. But, since noisy conflicts between FRG and GDR intellectuals continued unabated and the problem of the two post-war German States was not resolved, the critical historians took to arguing that their major intellectual influence was not Marx but Max Weber, first student of pressure groups and other 'structures' which lay below the surface of formal political power. Soon it turned out that other groups, the Centre Party, the *Mittelstand*, even important segments of the ruling elite, were similarly 'encapsulated'. Bismarck may have united his version of Germany but while considerable sections of the population were not politically legitimised, Germany was not yet made. It was neither a place of liberty nor of (true) nationality nor, of course, of 'modernity'.

This version of the past dove-tailed perfectly with developments in 1960s West Germany. There the great issue was whether the SPD, now that it had dropped socialism from its agenda, could, under Willy Brandt, be entrusted with government in Bonn. For hard-line conservatives it could not; they thought it symbolic that Brandt himself had been born out of wedlock, had fled after 1933, had not experienced the rigours of the 'long Second World War' within Germany (and had not been to 'Auschwitz'). A man who did not know his own father could scarcely be a bearer of German history or take up a position near to God. As Bavarian populist-conservative Franz-Josef Strauss had put it splenetically in 1961: 'We have a right to ask Herr Brandt, what did you do *for twelve years* abroad? We know ourselves what we did inside Germany during that time.'[74]

But for the majority of voters and for much of the FRG Establishment it was gradually accepted that the SPD could now become a party of the State. Indeed, during the interregnum of *Die Grosse Koalition*, 1966–9, in which Christian Democrats and SPD joined tentatively in alliance, the greater threat to West German stability seemed to come from the far Right. A neo-Nazi party, the National Democrats (NDP), founded in 1964, briefly attracted a serious level of support. Its leadership characteristically urged that 'the First World War was not Kaiser Wilhelm's war: that is known today by every historian'.[75] They also demanded action against the spread of radical ideas in universities and schools. There, nameless individuals were 'influencing the young against their own people, against their own history, and against their own fathers'. Those who were not committed to 'true history' were, party spokesmen averred, engaged in the 'glorification of treason'.[76]

However, the NDP vote soon peaked. In 1969 Brandt, with the backing of the small liberal Free Democrat Party (FDP), became Chancellor. The SPD was legitimised at last. As Brandt proclaimed, echoing the theses of the *Primat der Innenpolitik* historians, Adolf Hitler 'has finally lost the war'.[77]

Somewhat ironically, the new government's first achievement would lie in foreign affairs, in what was called Brandt's *Ostpolitik*. Among the historians it had never quite been clear whether the continuity thesis extended past 1945. At the end of the 1960s, the most obvious result of the Second World War was that the national Germany, finally united into one state in 1938, 1939 or 1941, still could not be tolerated by Europe. In a world of nations, Germany alone must remain disunited. If, as Eric Hobsbawm has put it provocatively, Adolf Hitler was 'a logical Wilsonian nationalist',[78] the package offered by Wilson at Versailles of parliamentary democracy, liberal capitalism, and national self-determination, the deal through which 'Wilson' could defeat 'Lenin',[79] could not be applied in Germany.

Many conservative Germans and successive Christian Democrat administrations, however, did not accept this omission. Cartography was one area in which Germans had retained their scientific primacy after 1945, but the maps of Eastern Europe marketed to motorists by FRG companies recorded two borders for a state like Poland – that of 1939 and that of 1945.[80] On such maps and in much political discourse, it was implied that the latter border might well turn out to be temporary. In the narrowest of legal senses, West Germany still had not agreed in 1969 that the Second World War was over.

Brandt's great achievement was to end it. Having entered office in October 1969, he moved rapidly to contact governments to the east. In August 1970 he signed a treaty with the USSR and in December with Poland, which accepted the territorial status quo and renounced force in future dealings. The *Ostforschers*, it seemed, had finally lost their brief. The SPD–FDP coalition similarly moved to abandon the rigidities of the 'Hallstein doctrine', by which conservatives had previously threatened that the FRG would break off relations with any state which recognised East Germany. By those acts 'the Federal Republic ceased to be a revisionist power in the heart of Europe'.[81] As Brandt explained after an official visit to the Auschwitz camp, his aim had been 'to accept German history in its entirety'.[82] Fischerite historiography had made plain that his actions were meet, right and to the benefit of the German people and the world.

Fischer's work had one other important influence and meaning. A break in historiographical continuity signalled change not only in the grandiose world of German external and internal politics, but also in the daily life of professors of history. As the decade of the 1960s passed, universities in the FRG, like those elsewhere, were becoming more lively and less respectful places. This process culminated in 1968, that year of the (failed) revolution of the (young) intellectuals, that moment when respect for professors went out of fashion.

As has already been hinted, the sociological base and administrative structure of West German universities in general and of the history profession in particular had been very little amended by the Nazi catastrophe. In pay and conditions, and much more importantly in social status and sense of self, German professors had remained near the summit of the social hierarchy. Whatever they said in their books or lectures, their lifestyles and pension rights, the ceremonies and titles of their universities, bespoke a world closer to Imperial Germany than to a social democracy. As A.J.P. Taylor, with his usual mordancy, had already mused about Oxford back in 1959: 'Civilization, of course, has its ups and downs, but the present talk about its decline means only that university professors used to have domestic servants and now do their own washing-up.'[83] By 1969, the assault on the Rankean tradition and its value system had German historians at least reaching for the tea-towel.

Fischer could claim some role even in effecting that particular social change. *Griff nach der Weltmacht*, it seems, was a book with many things to say. Fischer's ideas had, for example, penetrated well beyond the borders of the discipline of history. Indeed, as the years passed, the chief spokesman of the 'Fischerite revolution' and, especially, of its normalisation was not a historian but a sociologist, Ralf Dahrendorf. It was Dahrendorf who, in 1965, argued that Imperial Germany had been an 'industrial feudal' society,[84] and that this unhealthy mixture lay at the base of the 'German problem'.

Dahrendorf was a fine example of where academic life was in the decades after 1961. He had been born in Hamburg on 1 May 1929, the son of a Social Democrat Reichstag deputy who was arrested by the Nazis after January 1933. In 1944, at the age of fifteen, Dahrendorf was himself interned by the Gestapo because of anti-Nazi activities in school, and sent, briefly, to a concentration camp in which he suffered ten days' solitary confinement. In 1945 his family, which had moved to Berlin, at first welcomed Russian 'liberation', but soon they fled to the West after Dahrendorf's father refused to vote for a socialist–communist merger. Forty years later, Dahrendorf retained his animus against 'that miserable assemblage of privileged cowards which called itself the SED' and remained convinced that 'Europe ends at the Soviet border, wherever that may be'.[85] From 1947 he studied philosophy and classics at the University of Hamburg, obtaining a doctorate in

1952. Like Fischer but even more so, Dahrendorf was one of those citizens of Hamburg who remembered the traditional ties between his city and Britain, who acknowledged the fairness and decorum of British occupation policies after 1945, and who presumably forgot the British firebombing of the city in 1943. Hamburg, Dahrendorf says happily, is 'the most English city in Germany'.[86] A lifelong Anglophile, Dahrendorf studied at the London School of Economics in the 1950s and acquired there a second doctorate in 1956. He also developed contacts with the USA, the dominant centre of (non-Marxist) sociology in the 1950s. His first book, *Class and Class Conflict in Industrial Society* (1957), very much reflected those influences.[87]

But it was his next major work, *Society and Democracy in Germany*, published in German in 1965, and in English in 1966 (in Dahrendorf's own translation), which made him famous. In it Dahrendorf sought to unite history and sociology and thus to answer the question 'why Auschwitz'? or 'how was the victory of National Socialism possible in the country of Kant and Goethe'?[88] The current political analyses of the rise of the Nazis best exhibited in the work of political scientist, Karl Dietrich Bracher,[89] were, he thought, insufficient. Germany's past problems must be uncovered where they lay, deep in German society. Early in his book, he acknowledged his admiration for Fischer. The 'bitterness and intensity' [of the Fischer controversy], he wrote, 'are understandable only if we remember that Fischer has pulled the centrepiece out of the whole, useful conception of history the profession has built up'.[90] His own ambition, he might have added, through his new and probing investigation of the relationship of politics and society from 1870 to 1945 and beyond, was to replace that lost centre with his own ideas and even with his own person and thus to preside over a Thermidor in German academic life.

In *Society and Democracy* Dahrendorf argued that Germany was 'the faulted nation', the place of 'authoritarianism without authority'. The real problem with Weimar, he wrote characteristically, was its 'contradiction . . . between a political system that permitted, and a social system that forbade democracy'.[91] The trouble had been neither the Weimar constitution, nor the policies and fortunes of this or that political party, nor the propaganda skills of the NSDAP, but the retention of traditional hierarchical values in the army, bureaucracy, judiciary, the academic world, the family, the trade unions, and even in a nominally mass and democratic party like the SPD.[92] Germany before 1933 was a place resistant both to 'liberty' and to 'modernity'.

Thus, it was only the Nazis who finally unleashed the 'German revolution': 'Whatever their ideology, they were compelled to revolutionize society in order to stay in power.'[93] The much trumpeted Resistance, notably that of 1944, was, by contrast, largely a result of tradition, illiberalism and authoritarianism.[94] 'Islands of tradition' remained in both post-war Germanies, and especially in the West, but there was no doubt that a great deal had been achieved and would go on being achieved so long as the banner of liberty was held high. 'The German Question is . . . not a political question put to others, but a social question put to ourselves.'[95]

Dahrendorf's emphasis on the social humus which nurtured politics perfectly caught the intellectual spirit of his times and gave him public as well as academic fame. In turn, he developed political ambitions, in 1967 joining the Free Democrats, a party which sought to represent the liberal history of 'good Germans' and which would hold the balance of power should the Grand Coalition break down. In 1969 the FDP, despite doing relatively poorly (5.8 per cent) in the polls, duly gave Willy Brandt the backing which he needed to become SPD Chancellor. Dahrendorf, from his position as parliamentary secretary of state in the Foreign Ministry, now became a crucial agent of *Ostpolitik*.

He had already acquired the nickname *politische Senkrechtstarter*, the 'politically vertical take-off' professor,[96] when, in 1970, Brandt nominated him to be the German representative on the Commission of the European Community in Brussels. But in the next two decades it has become less clear what should follow this scintillating beginning. Dahrendorf has written frequently and passionately, and has become a 'guru' summoned, for example by the Italian radical weekly, *L'Espresso*,[97] to make weighty comments on a wide range of matters. In 1990 it was even rumoured that the Italian Communist Party, desperate to demonstrate that it was in charge of its own history and that this history had nothing to do with the USSR and Eastern Europe, had suggested to Dahrendorf that he stand as a PCI deputy to the Europarliament.

But Dahrendorf's greater success has been in the Anglo-Saxon world where, after 1974, he became an effective director of the London School of Economics, presiding over that body's return to normality following the excitment of 1968. In 1987 he was appointed Warden of St Antony's College, Oxford,[98] a post earlier held by the distinguished British historian and retired intelligence agent, F.W. Deakin.[99] Dahrendorf had been made an honorary KBE by the Thatcher Government for his services to British public life, and in the 1990s he is often called 'Sir Ralf'. He was also a close friend of the Liberal leader, Sir David Steel, and advised him on party policy and the formation of the 'Alliance' with the 'Owenites' and the 'Social Democrats', which, in some eyes, promised to open a 'third way' in British politics and, in others, divided the Left thus ensuring the domination of Thatcherism throughout the 1980s. Dahrendorf also has many ties with the USA, where he has worked for the liberal capitalist Russell Sage Foundation in New York. He has even visited far-off Australia in order freely to disburse advice on issues ranging from the meaning of liberty to whether Australia should mine and sell uranium.[100]

In 1984 he did return for a while to Germany, taking up a chair in Social Science at Konstanz and declaring that he would help to re-structure the Free Democrats. In his absence, they had withdrawn from coalition with the SPD and gone back to the CDU, thus permitting Kohl to be the 1980s German equivalent of Thatcher and Reagan. But the re-structuring did not proceed apace, and Kohl remained in power as further momentous events began to unfold.

The 'European Revolution' of 1989 duly seemed to confirm many of Dahrendorf's ideas about the 'new liberty' and particularly his view that modern society was less interested in (costly) social welfare than it was in (presumably cheap) 'cultural freedom'. 'Closed worlds' must everywhere be rejected and replaced by 'open societies'. But, at the same time, Dahrendorf was not a full-blooded advocate of German re-unification and admitted that a resuscitated fascism, perhaps of an up-dated variety, had now become the greatest peril in the East.[101] Meanwhile, despite his fame, his political career had languished and England had become his real refuge. Back in 1987, he himself had taken to saying wrily: 'Now I'm an intellectual who is "out", far from political power. In my life I've always commuted between being "in" and being "out".'[102]

Dahrendorf's, then, is a most curious and suggestive *curriculum vitae*. He is the German liberal, the heir of those Germans who, in 1848 or 1870, facing the dilemma of the relationship between freedom and the nation state, between liberalism and nationalism, were, in the famous words of Lewis Namier, 'bitten by the Pan German dog [and] caught rabies'.[103] But he, the good, if frustrated, European, the almost Englishman, cannot be thus accused. What he could more credibly be charged with, though he himself would deny it, is 'objectively' being the sort of liberal whose ideas and actions, after the first legitimation of Brandt in 1969–71, helped to weaken and divert social democracy and eventually to install its enemies in power. It is almost as though, on closer study, Dahrendorfian liberalism, which, as it rose on its vertical take-off once seemed a shiny means to transport humanity to God, or at least to freedom and equality, does not really exist.

For some time now, Dahrendorf, the Bielefeld school and even Fischer himself have become the object of serious attack. In critical eyes, the 'Fischer revolution' has turned out to be another *rivoluzione mancata*. English social historian, Richard Evans, for example, has emphasised just how traditional was Fischer's own methodology and just how limited would be the interest of the Bielefeld school in 'genuine social history', in *Alltagsgeschichte,* the study of 'daily life'. Much German historiography was still narrowly bound by 'politics' and by the 'event' and thus had not been enriched by the study of 'structures' and the '*longue durée*' especially associated with the *Annales* school in France. Evans was equally troubled by the Fischerites' dogmatic dismissal of the claims of Imperial Germany to belong to a distinct and self-contained era of history, their reiteration of the continuity thesis. Such an insistence, he has written, overlooks auspicious aspects of Wilhelmine society, and ignores those positive continuities which were thwarted or not yet obvious, the processes which were advancing the cause of women, for example.[104]

But the most effective assault from the Left on what by the 1970s was already being labelled the new conformism in West German historiography came rather from two other Englishmen, Geoffrey Eley and David Blackbourn (though Eley would flee the effects of the Thatcher counter-revolution and in the 1980s take a position in the United States). This background, it might be noted in passing, is a token of how internationalised 'German' history had by then become and how open West German historians were to this internationalisation of their discipline (in striking contrast to many historians in France, Italy and, in its different way, Britain).

In two essays which would eventually be brought together and published in

English as *The Peculiarities of German History* (1984), Blackbourn and Eley looked afresh at the whole problem of the negative *Sonderweg*.[105] In so doing they challenged the conclusions about social imperialism associated with H.-U. Wehler and Jürgen Kocka and denied that Imperial Germany was merely a place in which the elites successfully diverted the masses from domestic revolution and socialism by the deployment of foreign adventures, nationalism and war. But their special target was Dahrendorf.

There are, Blackbourn, Eley and Dahrendorf's other critics assert, three great problems with his theses in *Society and Democracy in Germany*. The first is the argument that Germany did not have a 'bourgeois revolution' until after 1933, that those who manipulated the Nazis into power, who thought Hitler was no more than a drummer for hire, represented the feudal side of the industrial-feudal equation, that what was wrong with Germany in 1933 was that German politics and society were insufficiently 'modern'. On the contrary, Blackbourn, Eley and their academic allies argue that Germany did have a bourgeois revolution in the nineteenth century, though its political or economic expression was different from those in Britain and France. Moreover, they say, allegedly feudal sections of German society such as the Army Officer Corps were decidedly 'modern', for example in their attitude to and knowledge of military technology, or in their sponsoring of mass pressure groups. Equally unsatisfactory may be the claim that 'feudal' behaviour patterns were ubiquitous in German society; according to Dahrendorf, working-class fathers or SPD politicians with lingering 'feudal' attitudes were as blameworthy for Nazism as were von Papen or von Hindenburg. For his critics, Dahrendorf's arguments have the ring of falsehood about them. Worse, they are, beneath the surface, highly self-interested. What Dahrendorf, the Bielefeld school, and the heirs of Fischer are engaged in is an act of disculpation, of answering the question 'why Auschwitz?' with the classic and even crude response 'it wasn't me, sir' or my ideology.

In the accounts of political scientists like Bracher, or indeed in the very early work of S.M. Lipset,[106] one of the great issues of the Weimar Republic was 'the case of the disappearing liberals'. Why, as the Nazis rose to power, did not the electoral fortunes of the Catholic Centre Party, the combined Left (SPD and KPD) and even the hard-core conservatives of the DNVP, radically decline when those of the DDP, DVP and the assortment of small bourgeois parties did? A first psephological reading makes it look as though there is evidence for Nazism being a 'fascism of the centre', a political movement whose firmest electoral base was among ex-liberals and among the other ex-bourgeois parties. Similarly, more nuanced historical and sociological analyses have often shown that Nazism, for all its ambitions to be an inter-class movement, had its strongest support from bourgeois and lower-middle-class sections of society[107] or from businessmen, engineers, lawyers and other professionals, teachers and university students, in other words from segments of society which, in more ordinary times, might be expected to form the ideological redoubts of liberalism. In blaming feudal ideas of hierarchy and tradition for paving the way to Nazism, Dahrendorf and his associates have sought to restore the virtue of German liberty and German modernity, of German liberals and the German bourgeoisie.

The claim that Nazism, after 1933 and despite the wishes of its leaders, became the 'German revolution' has a similarly useful corollary. It refurbishes the idea that Nazism was a parenthesis in German history. Maybe it was the Terror and the Horror which Germany had to have but, once endured, it was over. In a sense those Junkers hanging from piano wire after their failed coup in 1944 signalled, in however macabre a fashion, the 'end of German history'. Though islands of tradition doubtless lingered on in the German Republics, they could, in those regimes, be contained and more gently and more gradually removed. The past may have been grievous, but the future would be happy (though Dahrendorf himself has frequently viewed the present with pessimistic eyes).

The other problem with the social-imperial, industrial-feudal argument is that constant comparative implication which is so hard to keep out of any discussion of Nazism. Germany followed a wicked *Sonderweg* to catastrophe; others did not. If only Germany had accepted the British, French or US models of development, the path to 'Auschwitz' would have been barred. The Anglo-American model, it seems, is the best one, proferring truth and justice in its own 'special way'. As Dahrendorf was still remarking wistfully in 1990, building a proper civil society was a difficult task; current East European intellectuals did not have the good fortune of Edmund Burke whose England had won its Magna Carta 500 years before.[108] Dahrendorf's disculpation thus extended beyond the German variety of liberalism. A real commitment to liberalism, he repeatedly and urgently proclaimed, still offers humanity and the world the greatest happiness of the greatest number.

For a radical Marxist like Geoff Eley, living in the Britain of Heath, Callaghan and Thatcher, and then in the United States of Reagan and Bush, this severing of all other than German history from the problem of fascism was unacceptable. It implied that there was no longer a need to be vigilant against tyranny and authoritarianism and that 'modernity' would be a sort of nirvana in which true 'liberty' was effortlessly achieved. It promised that the construction of an open society was an easy matter whether in good times or bad. All that was necessary was to shrug off the past. Dahrendorf seemed to be stating that, for the United States, history had ended in 1776, for France in 1789, for Britain in 1688. To those more aware of social conflict, deprivation and repression and more convinced that history is a relationship and not a thing, it was not a convincing proposition.

Nor were Blackbourn and Eley alone in challenging the hegemony of the social imperial school of historians, political scientists and sociologists in (West) Germany. In the second half of the 1980s, a new controversy, at least as bitter in its polemics as the Fischer affair, shook German academe. It was denominated the *Historikerstreit* ('The Historians' Quarrel'). Among its keener participants were those who attacked established interpretations not from the Left but rather from the Right. Fischer had not, therefore, won a total victory and Oskar's expectation that Germany would be able fully to explain itself and find a plausible and agreed version of its national history remained unfulfilled.

4

The *Historikerstreit* and the relativisation of Auschwitz

From 25 August to 1 September 1985, over 2,000 delegates gathered at Stuttgart in West Germany for the Sixteenth International Congress of Historical Sciences. That quinquennial ceremony which has claims to be the Olympic Games of World History was now being held in Germany for the first time since the war.[1] Prominent among the organisers and speakers were what looked like a present coalition of moderate FRG historians – Erdmann, Wehler, Kocka and Broszat. Of the seers of the past, Max Weber was invoked most frequently and only Eric Hobsbawm made a curmudgeonly and serious attempt to suggest that Marx was still alive; the Soviet delegates, by contrast, reflecting what would soon be called 'the years of Brezhnevite stagnation', were elderly or wordless or both.[2]

With appropriate courtesy, official Stuttgart mobilised itself to hail the assembled historians. At a civic reception, those present could listen to a welcoming speech by the Lord Mayor of Stuttgart, a Mr Manfred Rommel. On the Wednesday night the Stuttgart Philharmonic Orchestra performed a finely crafted programme, beginning with Charles Ives, moving on to Dmitri Shostakovich, before climaxing in Beethoven's Fifth. Attentive listeners may therefore have discerned that North Americans had a high culture too; that there were some good Russians the quality of whose high culture was not in doubt; but that, as likely as not, they would encounter a German at the summit of all cultural endeavour. Who better than Beethoven, welcomer of the French Revolution, brave critic of Napoleon when he turned Destroyer of that Revolution, and composer of the Ninth choral symphony, most grandiose evocation of Liberty and now accepted as the Hymn of the new Europe?

In 1985 it was not only the hills of Stuttgart which were alive with the sounds of history. That year was, after all, the fortieth anniversary of the end of the Second World War in Europe. On 30 April 1945, Adolf Hitler had committed suicide in his bunker in Berlin and a week later Nazism, too, was dead. Four decades later, Germany and the world were still grappling with this past that would not pass away.[3]

Though many politicians and some historians now sought to make mellifluous the echoes of that sad time, a new discord would soon overwhelm their best efforts. By 1986, the *'Historikerstreit'*, the 'quarrel among historians', had begun.

From 1983 the FRG had, in the Christian Democrat Helmut Kohl, a Chancellor who had himself once been a history student[4] and who, in Michael Stürmer, possessed a professional historian as a key adviser.[5] Kohl had shown at least as much interest as Willy Brandt in locating a usable past for his brand of German politics. Born in 1930, too late, as he would somewhat insouciantly remark during an official visit to Israel,[6] to be a direct participant in Nazi atrocities, Kohl had welcomed the anniversary of the fall of Nazism as an opportunity publicly to 'normalise' German history.

As a preliminary, he had, in September 1984, met President François Mitterrand at Verdun. Their handshake had refreshed Franco-German friendship,[7] implicitly refurbishing the pre-Fischer interpretation of the origins of the First World War as a regrettable accident occasioned by human error and a presumably malevolent God, and quietly hinting that neither First nor Second War should continue either to jar Europe or to dog Germany's reputation.

Kohl had also actively favoured the opening of two grand new museums of German history, the House of History (*Haus der Geschichte*) in Bonn and the German Historical Museum (*Deutsches Historisches Museum*) in West Berlin.[8] This latter, planned to be positioned on an especially sacred site next to the Reichstag, whose burning had given the Nazis their justification for the Enabling Act and for the imposition of untrammelled tyranny, aroused great controversy. Public disputation was not allayed by Kohl's utilisation of Stürmer and other conservative historians as experts on an advisory committee (though they were joined by Jürgen Kocka among others).[9] Critics declared that the variety of social and *longue durée* history to be favoured in the museum's exhibitions downplayed Nazism, and that this obfuscation was evident even in the museum's positioning.[10] Inevitably the new edifice would draw attention away from the Reichstag, as symbol of German liberal democracy and of the anti-parliamentary crimes of the Nazis (and from that Russian soldier photographed planting the Red Flag of victory and revolution on the ruins of Berlin in 1945). It certainly did seem to be true that the *Deutsches Historisches Museum* was meant to out-match East Germany's own Museum for German History[11] and to defeat the GDR's increasingly desperate efforts to obtain legitimacy through history. (In 1983 a major exhibition in East Berlin had sought to connect the communist system with Luther, born 500 years before. As its economy and society withered away, the East German regime became ever more cynical in setting aside the Marxist canon in order frenetically to claim that history was on its side.)[12] Would not Stürmer, in 1986, explain his purpose with almost embarrassing frankness: 'in a land without history, whoever supplies memory, shapes concepts, and interprets the past will win the future'?[13]

At that time, few had any sense that the dissolution of the GDR and of its vulgar Marxist variety of official history would come so swiftly. There is little evidence that Kohl, Stürmer or others in the FRG leadership anticipated the 'European revolution' of 1989. Then, suddenly, the great contest was over and what so long had seemed a near-run thing, for the foreseeable future turned into a rout. Whatever the tensions and difficulties of their history, Germans more readily embraced a liberal capitalist present than the empty façade of communism typified by such tired (and venal) old men as Erich Honecker. By the early 1990s, Kohl's original proclamation that the *Deutsches Historisches Museum* would make the young comprehend 'whence we come, who we are as Germans, where we stand, and where we are going'[14] had a newly triumphant ring to it, though not everyone was yet sure of re-united Germany's actual destination.

This dispute over 'public history' and over what 'usable past' a museum should purvey acted as a backdrop to the *Historikerstreit*. So did other political and cultural events. For, after he returned from Verdun, Kohl planned further occasions to make manifest his Germany's reconciliation with the past. Most redolent was to be a state visit from the titular head of the Free World, US President, Ronald Reagan. He and Kohl would shake hands at Bitburg, a military cemetery near Hanover, in which both German and American soldiers were buried.[15]

This second handshake proved more tricky to stage-manage than the first. It was true that, from a conservative German perspective, Ronald Reagan held unexceptional views. He deemed Nazism the fault of one man, Hitler, who had imposed vicious 'totalitarian' rule over Germany. Reagan was thus an out-and-out 'intentionalist', to borrow the jargon of one of the current historiographical debates about Nazism. He could remark cosily that both Jews and German soldiers were Hitler's victims.[16] In honouring the fallen of the *Wehrmacht* he was certainly not intending to traduce those sacrificed in the Holocaust (or alienate his Jewish vote). From a purist perspective, it was perhaps a shame that his knowledge of history was shaky – in the mode of celluloid 'hero' 'Ronald Reagan the movie',[17] he seemed at least once to forget that he himself had been alive between 1939 and 1945. And, on a number of occasions, he suggested that the enemy in that war had not been Germany but the 'evil empire' of totalitarianism.[18] But the sneers of censorious and 'confrontationist' intellectuals at such a homely proneness to error and confusion, then or later, could not dent Reagan's image and popularity. For Kohl, who liked to portray himself as the spiritual 'grandson' of Konrad Adenauer,[19] to be clasped in friendship by so charming an old buffer as the US President could only be for the good. In Kohl's scenario, Reagan was cast for the part of benign foreign uncle who would gallantly and urbanely forgive a small and only half-remembered childhood sin.

But Kohl had miscalculated. Among the German dead were not only soldiers of the *Wehrmacht* but also members of the *Waffen SS*. Scholarship might point out that the SS attracted a considerable number of intellectually talented and socially respectable young Germans and other Europeans to its ranks; it might also allege that the difference between the *Wehrmacht* and the SS in the 'barbarisation of warfare' to the east was not so great.[20] But such fine distinctions were irrelevant in an event like Bitburg. Reagan, it seemed in some circles, had been asked to salute totalitarian murderers.

A public outcry began. Liberal Jews like Raul Hilberg[21] and Saul Friedländer[22] argued that the *Wehrmacht* and the SS could not easily be separated, and reminded their readers of the tensions perennially underlying Germany's relationship with its past. In France, there was suggestion that among the SS dead might have been some who had participated in the massacre at Oradour (see p. 100).[23] From so prominent a Jew as Elie Wiesel came firm advice that the visit should be cancelled.[24]

In the event it was not, although Reagan grudgingly agreed also to attend a ceremony at the nearby Bergen-Belsen concentration camp (however appalling a place, not a site in which mass gassings had been perpetrated). Through all the debate and controversy Reagan kept smiling, even when his enemies said that he condoned murder while he smiled. 'You know, I don't think we ought to focus on the past', the President explained disarmingly. 'I want to focus on the future, I want to put that history behind us.'[25] If history could not be comfortable, maybe that old anti-Semite Henry Ford was right. It was bunk.

Kohl, who had first planned the event and who knew more about history than did Reagan, had greater difficulty brazening it out. His own speech at Bergen-Belsen reflected his embarrassment. As Charles Maier has indicated, Kohl offered some apologies:

> Germany under the National Socialist regime filled the world with fear and horror. That era of slaughter, indeed of genocide, is the darkest, most painful chapter in German history. One of our country's paramount tasks is to inform people of those occurrences and keep alive an awareness of the full extent of this historical burden.[26]

It is also clear that what Maier has construed as Kohl's sensitivity had its limits. The West German Government had not forgotten that its slogan for the ceremonies had been 'Freedom or Totalitarianism'.[27] Kohl's own speech had included words which Gerhard Ritter might have written: Nazism, he stated, was caused by the 'accelerating disintegration of values and morals. In the final analysis, the totalitarian State was the product of the re-negation of God.'[28]

Kohl's equivocations and the bad odour left by them seem to have prompted the popular and liberal FRG President, Richard von Weizsäcker (himself the son of a leading official in the German Foreign Ministry under Nazism),[29] to try to clear the air in a speech to the Bundestag of 8 May. What Weizsäcker said was well received and has remained an object of praise in the later historiography, though a critical reading might suggest that Weizsäcker cleaved to only one version of German history while reiterating the antithesis of freedom and totalitarianism.

Certainly he was at pains not to deny responsibility. The Holocaust was indeed 'unparalleled in history' and Germans, however great their subjection to Nazi evil, had participated in it: 'At the root of the tyranny was Hitler's immeasurable hatred against our Jewish compatriots. Hitler had never concealed this hatred from the public, but made the entire nation a tool of it.' An intentionalist Weizsäcker remained, but a rather more sophisticated and humble one than was Ronald Reagan.

In relation to certain other areas of historiographical debate, Weizsäcker was a less mutedly conservative spokesman. The massacre of the Jews was to be deplored but that of Russian soldiers and POWs was a more complex matter. Stalin, observed Weizsäcker in sibylline manner, had accepted the Ribbentrop–Molotov Pact knowing that it would incite Hitler to act against Poland, though, he added hastily, the Soviet dictator's Machiavellian lucubrations did not mean that the USSR was responsible for the Second World War. Rather it was 'Hitler's war', and had many, too many victims, but 'at the end of it only one nation remained to be tormented, enslaved and defiled: the German nation'. This torment, slavery and defilement had had a catharsis, however. Nazism was over. 'There is every reason for us to perceive 8 May 1945 as the end of an aberration in German history.' At the same time, Weizsäcker stated in words which would resonate during the *Historikerstreit,* Hitler's death marked the finish of the 'European civil war'. With Nazism duly defeated and confined to the past, Germany was liberated. Still today, Weizsäcker concluded, 'we Germans are one people and one nation'.[30]

In 1985, while politicians fumbled over the moral to the story, historians of Nazism seemed most readily divided into the sober-sounding categories of 'intentionalists' and 'functionalists'. In that year Ian Kershaw, the careful and moderate English historian of modern Germany, published a survey of the historiography emphasising this division. Before long, he had to up-date his survey to take account of the *Historikerstreit*, though he would continue to argue that the quarrel engendered more heat than light.[31] Indeed, he declared disapprovingly and with more than a hint of residual Rankeanism,

> the *Historikerstreit* . . . has been in essence a political discourse . . . about the way the society of the highly developed, prosperous, and stable Federal Republic can cope with living with its Nazi past. This is an unending debate in which the expertise of historians offers no great advantage or special privilege.[32]

But, as Kershaw had himself implied, a political agenda also played some part in the disputes between intentionalists and functionalists. Intentionalists, heirs to those first analysts of Nazi Germany described earlier in this book, maintain that the Third Reich was in essence governed by the 'intention' of Adolf Hitler. It represented a 'triumph of the will'. There may have been fragmentation in the power structure of Nazi Germany and some contradiction in day-to-day policy, but these apparent conflicts were as likely as not fostered by the *Führer* himself and served his own interests, those of *divide et impera*. What characterised Nazism was its relentless determination to do certain things – to murder the Jews, to go to war for *Lebensraum*, to wipe out all forms and expressions of opposition and resistance, and to achieve a totalitarian society.

Intentionalist historians, subscribers to these theses and their corollaries, are often politically conservative. Hitler, the 'master of the Third Reich', is usually depicted as the agent of discontinuity, the malign 'accident in the works'. The years from 1933 to 1945 are self-contained and do not necessarily connect with the rest of German history. The more natural link is with other fascist regimes, or, if they are deemed too few and equivocal, with Stalinism, that evil system which is 'a sickness of the modern world', through the model of totalitarianism. Moreover, since Nazism stands for pervasive tyranny, it is by definition an inter-class movement and regime. Trying to tease out which social, regional or gender group did best in the Nazi years is pointless, a futile attempt to make sense of happenstance, or what is worse, a bid to attach Nazi guilt to the guiltless. To echo Weizsäcker or Reagan, for the intentionalists all Germans, more than any other people except perhaps the Jews, were the real victims of Nazism.

Functionalists (or structuralists as they are sometimes rather confusingly denominated) possess a much more articulated reading of Nazi Germany. Any study of Hitler, they allege, must admit how bohemian was the *Führer's* lifestyle, how impossible it was to corral him into the familiar patterns of executive activity. Rather, the real story of Nazism was, as an American historian put it back in 1969, one of the 'limits of Hitler's power',[33] or at least of the unpredictability and caprice with which that power was exercised. Hitler, in the challenging words of West German historian Martin Broszat, was a 'weak dictator'.[34] His world view was banal; his 'policy' often a triumph of the whim. Anti-Semitism, *Lebensraum*, anti-communism, war, the people's community and domestic order, all were ideas fully or partly shared by other Germans, many in highly influential positions either in the Nazi Party or in the German state. Indeed, except for the totally unacceptable – Jews,[35] homosexuals, gypsies, the intellectually handicapped, and openly political critics – the Nazi regime resembled in its own distorted manner a free society, if freedom is taken to mean the opportunity for the ruthless and greedy to maximise their own power and ambition. This Germany was the place of 'institutional Darwinism'; its road to Auschwitz was as twisted as its proferring of 'social opportunity'. David Schoenbaum had summed it up in 1966 at the conclusion of his *Hitler's Social Revolution*:

> Like a super Elks Club, the Third Reich pampered the familiar human weakness for distinction on a scale probably without precedent. As early as 1935, the party listed over 200,000 'representatives of authority' (*Hoheitsträger*). Functionaries of various satellites like the corporatist groups, professional and welfare organisations, totalled nearly 1½ million, not including the representatives of still embryonic institutions like the Hitler Youth or the SS. This, in the form of jobs, medals, uniforms . . . was status distribution in the grand manner . . . . The Third Reich proved that a house divided against itself *can* stand, provided, at least, that the occupants have no alternative place to go and that the landlord pays attention to the wallpaper, if not to the walls.[36]

In so far as the *Führer* was concerned, for some functionalists it was almost as though he 'didn't really exist'. As has already been noted this, in a sense, had been one of A.J.P. Taylor's fundamental messages in *The Origins of the Second World War* and, in 1977, he repeated his views in a mordant review of far right-wing English historian David Irving's *Hitler's War*. Justly excoriating Irving for his ponderous prose, extreme literalness in reading documents and general lack of intellectual subtlety, Taylor none the less acknowledged that he had received one insight from the book, 'though not what Irving had intended':

> Historians have often discussed the background of Hitler's so-called ideas. They have pointed to geopoliticians and racialist writers. [But] I see now the true source of Hitler's inspiration. It was Karl May, a German who wrote thrillers about Red Indians. Hitler always saw himself in the dramatic role of a Red Indian brave. Why, for instance, did he set up his headquarters in the barren wastes of East Prussia when he could have directed the war far more effectively from Berlin? Simply because it was more romantic and dramatic. Dozens of huts had to be built; security forces had to be drafted in; telephone lines had to be laid. And with it all Hitler was cut off from the centres of information and command.
>
> What was the work which kept him up all through the night? As all his records have been destroyed, we shall never know for certain. But it seems likely that he was labouring on futile trivialities, loyal to his Red Indian vision. His real interventions in the war and in politics came by fits and starts with no method behind them. He had great successes but he was essentially a nullity, an empty man and the least interesting of all dictators the world has known.
>
> His end was characteristic. He announced that he would remain in Berlin and die fighting at the head of his troops. He did no fighting. He led no troops. He directed imaginary armies and, in a last gesture of irresponsibility, committed suicide. Throughout the war he had seen himself as the Last of the Mohicans. When reality caught up with his imagination he simply vanished as though he had never been. So far as he existed at all he was a bad man with no redeeming features. I hope we shall have no more books about him.[37]

Though readers of recent biographies of Hitler will find it hard not to burst into spontaneous applause at this point, they might also have to admit that Taylor has here engaged in an exercise in nose-thumbing at historiographical cliché extreme even by his standards. In any case, Taylor was not the sort of historian to be naturally shackled by such ponderous terms as functionalist, structuralist or intentionalist. And yet if the *goaks* were decoded and the statement translated out of Taylorese, the lessons about past and present were very much those of the functionalists. Nazi Germany was not a simple place to reckon with; it certainly could not adequately be defined by the words, 'Adolf Hitler' or 'totalitarianism'.

By the mid-1980s a whole host of historians, utilising their real research to catch up with Taylor's imagination, had continued to nudge scholarship towards a more nuanced reading of Nazism. In English there were the subtle and independent Marxist, Tim Mason, and Ian Kershaw himself. Kershaw, by then, was working closely with Martin Broszat who, in the previous decade, had launched the 'Bavaria Project', under the auspices of the Munich Institute of Contemporary History, applying the techniques of *Alltagsgeschichte* mentioned in the previous chapter to the history of Nazism. It was time, Kershaw and Broszat said, to write about the Third Reich 'from below', to study what 'everyday life' had meant in Hitler's Germany.[38]

The classic general study of this genre was Detlev Peukert's *Volksgenossen und Geneinschaftsfremde – Anpassung, Ausmerze Aufbegehren unter dem Na-tional-sozialismus* (1982) which appeared in English translation as *Inside Nazi Germany: Conformity, Opposition and Racism in Everyday Life* in 1987. The book's aim, Peukert declared appropriately, was 'to understand more precisely how "Auschwitz" . . . was possible, why it was tolerated and, indeed, in part endorsed.'[39] Peukert drew a picture of Nazi Germany of which few functionalists would disapprove. 'Nazi labour policy', he explained in words recalling the previous findings of Tim Mason (though Peukert firmly dismissed the research of what he termed 'vulgar Marxists'), 'was if anything an anxious attempt to diminish the risks of political disaffection among the workers by making social and welfare concessions'. Despite the harangues about a people's community by Hitler and Nazi leaders, Germans after 1933 became significantly more consumerist. Even 'Coca Cola consumption rose . . . in the thirties.'[40] Resistance was less the work of the July conspirators than a sort of passive refusal to give consent (rather like that Luisa Passerini was discovering in Turin under Fascism).[41] Peukert documented 'numerous expressions of dissatisfaction and instances of non-conformist behaviour, ranging from the deliberate refusal to cook an officially prescribed Sunday stew . . . to the giving of shelter and support to victims of persecution.' If anything, war increased non-conformist behaviour and a number of young Germans turned into 'teenage rebels', sceptical of Nazi moralising, 'apolitical', 'bored' and rebellious in dress, songs and lifestyle. (In the novel *The Tin Drum* little Oskar meets up with some, and becomes their leader as the Red Army approaches Danzig.) Peukert cites one adolescent from further to the west advising his mate: 'Be a proper spokesman for Kiel, won't you? i.e. make sure you're really casual, singing or whistling English hits all the time, absolutely smashed and always surrounded by really amazing women.'[42]

This wonderful and graphic detail, so 'day-to-day', so 'real', so much 'from below', a reader gradually discovers, also carries messages which connect to other debates about Nazism and about German history as a whole. Nazism in its ideology, Peukert argues, had a short-term clarity and an abiding ambiguity (a mixture ideal for propaganda). Therefore, in many long-term matters the Third Reich displayed 'no divergence, either positive or negative, from the earlier course of development of industrial class society'. For all the rhetoric of sacrifice, heroism and war, the 'polycratic' nature of Nazi rule, its very inconsistencies and contradictions, and its tyranny, encouraged private values to prevail over social ones. 'The "nationalisation" of society by Nazism was followed by the "privatisation" of the state.' Thus, Peukert avers, Nazism meant 'the dawning of the new achievement-orientated consumer society, based on the nuclear family, upward mobility, mass media, leisure and an interventionist welfare state (though much of this still lay in the realms of propaganda and had not yet come into being.)' Of course there were always 'the encroaching shadows cast by a project of social order based on racialist doctrines and terror', but, according to Peukert, Nazi Germany was a place of many continuities from the pasts of the Second Reich and Weimar to the presents of the FRG and the GDR. As he had explained at the beginning of his book, *Alltagsgeschichte* would tend to blur the great interpretations and the easy moralisings. When studied from below, he wrote, 'the stereotypes of the utterly evil fascist and the wholly good anti-fascist dissolve'.[43]

In early 1985, just before Reagan and Kohl met at Bitburg, Martin Broszat, the doyen of the new social historians, underlined these points and their meaning in a challenging short paper. In it he urged the need for a '*Historisierung*' or 'historicisation' of the Nazi period. 'The moral impact of the Nazi past', he feared, 'has progressively exhausted itself.' It had 'lost much of its singularity in light of new catastrophes and atrocities, and we are left with a set of convictions, as safe as they are vague, that no longer carry any moral force.' Only a 'more nuanced historical analysis' could 'make them morally useful again'. This new approach would be best if it were some sort of combination of functionalism and *Alltagsgeschichte*, since 'the vague populist attractiveness of National Socialism carried more weight than [its] . . . ideological indoctrination'.[44]

But Broszat had other more general and more provocative things to say. The current historiography, he noted, was 'still dominated by the overwhelming impact of the catastrophic end and final condition of the regime'.[45] The Nazism of war and defeat, the Nazism of the practice of genocide, the Nazism of Auschwitz, eclipsed all other possible Nazisms. In addition, Germany itself remained incomplete while its past was enshrouded in total obloquy. 'West Germany is a provisional entity that resulted from a break with national history.' For some, that provisionality was to be deplored as it hindered the natural marriage of history and nationalism. But Broszat was troubled rather by what he saw as the reverse effect: 'precisely because the FRG is integrated into Western political culture and can only become an object of national identification to a limited extent, the memory of the last days of a united Germany has remained alive at a deeper level of the collective consciousness.'[46] Ironically this fundamental inadequacy was shared with many citizens in the GDR. There were ghosts which still needed to be exorcised, and which could only be removed through a new history, better attuned to ordinary people's consciousness and to the 'structures' of the '*longue durée*'.

Broszat's views duly provoked controversy, notably in a series of public letters exchanged with the liberal Jewish-American historian, Saul Friedländer. For the latter, the problem with the somewhat cloudy concept of *Historisierung* was that it could easily slip into a sort of neo-Rankean absence of judgement. The 'abnormal and criminal' would merge into the 'normal and every-day'. Auschwitz and the Holocaust would lose their uniqueness. Since 'the history of Nazism belongs to everybody', he urged, it should never be 'normalised'.[47]

While this debate was proceeding in a reasonably courteous and measured fashion, it was overtaken by another which would be much more widespread and vitriolic. The *Historikerstreit* had begun.

The opening shots were fired by the independent left-wing philosopher, Jürgen Habermas, in an article which he wrote for the liberal weekly, *Die Zeit*, on 11 July 1986. An unholy alliance, he claimed, had been reached between three leading conservative historians, Michael Stürmer, Andreas Hillgruber and Ernst Nolte. The purpose of their pact was exhibited both in the new museums of Bonn and West Berlin and in a number of recent books and articles. What was planned was a re-minted German nationalism, which would explain Nazism away and re-connect present-day Germany with a glorious past. As part of that process, both Nazism and the Holocaust were to be relativised.[48]

The immediate stimulus for Habermas had been another newspaper article. On 6 June 1986, Ernst Nolte had written it under the title 'The past that will not pass away' in the conservative *Frankfurter Allgemeine Zeitung*. This paper was edited by Joachim Fest, a biographer of Hitler,[49] who would soon publicly align himself in the debate on Nolte's side.

The key to Nolte's argument lay in what he alleged to be the inevitable comparison between Nazism and Russian communism: 'The following question', he wrote,

> must be deemed admissible, indeed necessary: Did the National Socialists carry out, did Hitler perhaps carry out an 'Asiatic' deed only because they regarded themselves and their kind as the potential or real victims of an 'Asiatic' deed? Wasn't the 'Gulag Archipelago' more original than Auschwitz? Wasn't class murder on the part of the Bolsheviks logically and actually prior to race murder on the part of the Nazis?[50]

If the comparison were allowed, Nazi Germany did not represent absolute evil, and the Holocaust was not unique. Hitler's anti-communism, Nolte would get around to saying, was 'understandable and, up to a certain point, indeed, justified'.[51]

Nolte is a rather idiosyncratic member of the *Bund* of West German historians. Born in 1923, he was trained as a philosopher by that ambiguous figure, Martin Heidegger,[52] before taking up the study of history. He became and has remained a historian of ideas and has always rejected any Marxist contention that ideas in essence spring from their social humus. Nolte made his name with the publication in 1963 of *Der Faschismus in seiner Epoche: Die Action française, der italienische Faschismus, der Nationalsozialismus*, which appeared in English (1965) as *Three Faces of Fascism*.

These publication dates coincided with the revival of fascism studies and with the new scholarly imprint given to them by the work of Hans Rogger, Eugen Weber, Renzo De Felice, and especially by contributors to the *Journal of Contemporary History* which commenced publication under the editorship of George Mosse and Walter Laqueur in 1966.[53]

Nolte's book made a number of contributions to the lively debate then occurring about fascism. Though fascist movements were confined by 'the unyielding framework of national self-assertion and autonomy', he explained, there was something generic called fascism which could be studied across national borders (and national histories). Rather than re-hashing what then seemed the exhausted model of totalitarianism and endlessly contrasting Nazism and Stalinism, more promising insights could be gained from a systematic comparison of Nazi Germany with Mussolini's Italy and with other fascist movements, even if, like *Action Française* in France, they did not actually achieve power. Nolte had not entirely abandoned the alleged parallel with communism however, since his 'first-level' definition still identified fascism as ' "anti-Marxism" seeking to destroy the enemy by the development of a radically opposed yet related ideology and the application of nearly identical, although typically transformed methods'. But for the moment, commentators marked the fact that Nolte was taking fascist ideas seriously. Moreover, with his third-level explanation that fascism was 'resistance to transcendance'[54] – something rather like what psychologist Erich Fromm[55] had defined as the 'fear of freedom' – Nolte implied, though he did not openly state, that ideas were rooted in certain specific societies. The brilliant work of George Mosse[56] and his students in investigating who crafted these ideas and in whose interest the crafting was done did not seem antithetical to a Noltean mould.

Nolte had one other important case to make and that was, as his German-language title implied, that fascism had belonged to a special 'epoch'. One corollary of this, picked up for example by Renzo De Felice, the great Italian biographer of Mussolini,[57] was that fascism was over; 1945 marked the end of the 'fascist era'. The genesis of fascism was, however, more fluid. Neither 1933, nor 1919, nor 1917, nor even 1914 represented its beginning. As Nolte put it in a style awkward in German and worse in English translation:

> The history of the Action Française forms a symptomatic component of the history of a country which from 1789 to 1919 was always politically a few steps ahead of the rest of Europe. . . . The practice of the Action Française anticipates, in the clear simplicity of the rudimentary, the characteristic traits of the infinitely cruder and more wholesale methods used in Italy and Germany. Seen by itself, the Action Française is not an epochal phenomenon. Yet it is, as it were, the missing link demonstrating fascism as a stage in an overall and much older struggle.[58]

What Nolte was saying seemed unexceptional at the time. It could be and was used either by conservatives certain that the 'origins of totalitarian democracy' were located in 1789 or by Marxists and neo-Marxists anxious to argue that fascism was the system to which a bourgeoisie in crisis would more or less inevitably have recourse. But hindsight suggests that Nolte was also already groping for a past that might pass away, for a 'guilt' which Germany could share with others (and who better than France?).

Whatever the case, Nolte never regained the academic pinnacle he had reached with *Three Faces of Fascism*. He had a rough time in 1968 and has remained a bitter critic of student politicians and their academic fellow-travellers.[59] His own prose style meanwhile had grown ever more tortuous and few seemed to notice when he argued in *Germany and the Cold War* (1974) that US actions in Vietnam were essentially crueller than the Nazis' at Auschwitz,[60] in *Marxism, Fascism and Cold War* (1982) that 'the central *idea* of Marxism is the idea of annihilation',[61] or in *Marxism and the Industrial Revolution* (1983) that communism had provided fascism with its fundamental motive.[62] He had also mused that 'the German radical students are the children of contemporary history research' and, given his views on the students, he was not being flattering about contemporary history. That subject, he had remarked, was particularly difficult: 'it is never research *alone*, but is always at the same time interpretation, indeed a struggle for self-understanding, for liberation'. The FRG, he explained further, was itself 'a state of contemporary history, emerging out of catastrophe and erected for the overcoming of the catastrophe'.[63]

What Nolte wrote in 1986 was thus scarcely new and surprising. Nor was it, given Nolte's idiosyncracies, particularly important. Its significance lay rather in the linkage made by Habermas to the sort of new nationalist public history advocated by Michael Stürmer, and to the work of mainstream conservative historian, Andreas Hillgruber.[64] In adding Hillgruber to his target, Habermas identified taxing conundrums both about the moral critique of Nazism most applicable in the 1980s, and about that whole tradition of the German historical profession, which had already produced such heated exchanges during the Fischer affair. To this already explosive mixture was added the greatest questions of all in the historiography of the 'long Second World War': did the Jews, the Germans or the Russians suffer the most in that tormented time and who had been responsible for the suffering?

Andreas Hillgruber was an elderly and distinguished professor at the University of Cologne. Born in 1925, he had grown up in the 'lost' province of East Prussia and fought briefly on the Eastern Front before becoming an able, if traditional, military and diplomatic historian. He had regularly campaigned against Fischer, and against the ideas of Dahrendorf and others about the sins of the Second Reich. The re-publication of the works of Eckart Kehr, he opined, was a matter to be regretted, an example of the foolishness of trendy *Marxisants* and Wehler, the worst of such people, had 'quasi-totalitarian' ambitions. He and his friends were 'cultural revolutionaries' who needed to be resisted and defeated.[65]

Such comments could perhaps be disregarded as no more than the sort of thunderous rhetoric common in German scholarly wrangles, but, in early 1986, Hillgruber went one step further. He published a short volume under the title *Zweierlei Untergang. Die Zerschlagung das deutschen Reiches und das Ende des europäischen Judentums* ('Two sorts of Demise. The shattering of the German Reich and the end of European Jewry').[66]

The central focus of this book was on the terrible months in 1944–5 when soldiers of the Red Army were advancing over German territory towards Berlin, while the *Wehrmacht,* reduced to an increasingly rag-tag condition, sought to resist them. It was a bloody conflict and Hillgruber emphasised the extent of rape and pillage, killing and deportation inflicted on the German populace. This part of the book is essentially an elegy for a lost ruling class (that Prussian aristocracy which, according to Hillgruber, had regained its honour in the July 1944 conspiracy), and for the 'lost territories'. The 'centuries-old area of German settlement, . . . the home of millions of Germans who lived in a core land of the German Empire – namely, in eastern Prussia, in the provinces of East Prussia, West Prussia, Silesia, East Brandenburg, and Pomerania', lands 'lost forever for Germany and for its German inhabitants'.[67] Hillgruber, now in full nostalgic flow, had harsh words for Roosevelt and Churchill, and for Allied plans to punish all Germany for the Second World War. But always he returned to his suffering co-expellees and to the limitless barbarism of the Red Army, Stalin and the USSR.

All of this has been accepted by many commentators with a shrug, as the sort of obsessive epitaph for a social and political system which might be expected from someone of Hillgruber's background. Plainly, the Red Army neither conquered nor ruled with kid gloves though, given the nature of the Nazi and *Wehrmacht* invasion, and the brutality of Germany's administration of its temporary conquests in the USSR, Soviet vindictiveness towards defeated Germans was scarcely surprising. Hillgruber's historical arguments were made more alarming because Kohl's own commitment to the achievements of *Ostpolitik* had sometimes wavered – in 1985 the Chancellor had endorsed German claims to its borders of 1937 and failed to leave a meeting at which expellees unfurled banners reading 'Silesia stays German'.[68] At the very least Hillgruber's words were a reminder that the possibility of an eventual revision of the post-Second World War settlement had not been abandoned by some Germans of his generation and politics.

But a menace to the settlement in the east was not the factor which most kindled the fire of this controversy. Though Hillgruber had never in any sense condoned Nazi anti-Semitism, now, like Nolte, he was thinking comparatively. Probably, again, his real target was the Russians (and their East German satellite) – one of his themes was that a more rapid surrender by the Germans in, say, 1944, which would obviously have curtailed genocide, would actually have caused more German suffering. Germans fought on against so implacable an enemy as the Red Army because of necessity. As a consequence, millions more Jews died and, though he did not say so openly, Hillgruber implied that much of the responsibility for those deaths lay with the USSR (and perhaps with their allies). But, again, it was his second theme which seemed more outrageous. 'Auschwitz' was 'one sort of demise'; the loss of the eastern mark , or border territories, of Germany was another. Europe in the twentieth century had endured an extended civil war – 'all Europe was the loser in the catastrophe of 1914' (which certainly had not been caused by Imperial Germany alone); its result was a destruction of the European Centre (for which both the non-European Powers, the USA and the USSR, were to blame).[69] In that catastrophe, the Jews were not the only casualties.

The controversy now began in earnest. Kocka, Hans and Wolfgang Mommsen, H.A. Winkler and Eberhard Jäckel joined Habermas in repelling what was seen as a 'conservative offensive'.[70] Fest, Klaus Hildebrand, Hagen Schulze[71] and, somewhat surprisingly, Imanuel Geiss, were among those who defended Stürmer, Nolte and Hillgruber. Ian Kershaw has tallied 'hundreds' of articles which appeared on the matter in the German press.[72] Already in October 1986, the right-wing Hans Martin Schleyer Foundation, named after a victim of leftist terrorists in the 1970s and committed to 'restoring German values', held a conference on the theme 'to whom does German history belong?' Hillgruber used the occasion to warn afresh against what he regarded as the current GDR leadership's attempt to capture 'German history' for its own dastardly regime.[73]

Meanwhile, as usual, German history turned out not to belong to Germans alone. Jewish historians were naturally alert; four major English-language books on the current state of West German historiography rapidly appeared;[74] and even Italian diplomatic historians, who had done their best to ignore the Fischer affair and its ramifications, now turned their attention to German debates.[75] Perhaps the best symbol of the impact of the *Historikerstreit* (and of the continuing unlimited interest in the history of Nazism outside Germany) was Ian Kershaw, an English historian, being employed to summarise it in the Italian periodical, *Passato e Presente*, and being able to express his ideas on the 'Hitler myth' in the *Annales*, that French periodical which is 'the most famous history journal in the world'.[76]

In his own book on the historiography of the Nazi dictatorship, Kershaw has remarked that the *Historikerstreit* was, in the end, a sort of fake, which 'resulted in no new and lasting insights into a deeper understanding of the Third Reich'.[77] He has also concluded that Habermas was being unfair; actually the views of Stürmer, Nolte and Hillgruber were 'three quite heterogeneous contributions'[78] and these historians had not formed a conservative triple alliance designed to turn back the tide of German historiography. If the bombast and special pleading were stripped away, he declared, and explosive terms like 'relativising Auschwitz' defused, the views of a leftist like Broszat and a rightist like Hillgruber were capable of being joined in historiographical compromise. What Kershaw and others[79] have implied, somewhat wistfully, is that it is a pity that the history of Nazism cannot settle into the magisterial Braudellian calmness of the *longue durée*.

But undoubtedly the most sensitive and wide-ranging account of the *Historikerstreit* was written by Charles S. Maier, Professor at Harvard University, and himself emotionally involved in the history of Nazism. He explained his dilemma in his preface: 'the historians' dispute has recalled questions I first confronted when, in the summer of 1955, as a sixteen-year-old exchange student of German-Jewish ancestry, I went to the Federal Republic of Germany and had to reconcile my own awareness of Nazi crimes with the decency, warmth and affection of my host family'.[80]

Equally, it was not as though US historians had been imperturbable in their debates about Nazism. Indeed, news of Bitburg and the *Historikerstreit* reached the USA at the very moment at which the 'Abraham affair' was ending. David Abraham was a young scholar, who, in 1981, had published with Princeton University Press an account of the rise of the Nazis entitled *The Collapse of the Weimar Republic*. Abraham was a neo-Marxist, who was intending to analyse the nature of hegemony in German society and wanted to re-focus attention on the role of at least some sections of German business in Hitler's accession to power. Though his work was praised by such serious and discerning critics as Geoff Eley, Richard Evans, Arno Mayer and Ian Kershaw, it was devastatingly attacked by the conservative American historians, Henry Turner and Gerald Feldman.[81] They concentrated their fire on what they deemed an unacceptable level of factual error in Abraham's work (he had, indeed, been rather careless.) And, although a revised and corrected edition of *The Collapse of the Weimar Republic* appeared in 1986, the force of these criticisms destroyed Abraham's career and converted him into a mature-age student of law.

In 1985, Henry Turner, the most unyielding of Abraham's opponents, published his own *German Big Business and the Rise of Hitler*. It is a fine book and much better written than Abraham's but it, too, carries a hint of a political agenda. The real problem of Weimar in 1930, Turner states, was one that would grow more familiar after 1945 (for example in the USA of the 1980s): 'whether, in a time of economic contraction, social programs should be maintained, regardless of the cost, in order to help those most affected by the hard times, or whether these programs should be curtailed in order to permit the private capital accumulation needed to spur investment and renewed growth.'[82] Business worries, then, deserved sympathy, all the more because historians, unfortunately, 'generally have little or no personal contact with the world of business. Like so many intellectuals, they tend to view big business with a combination of condescension and mistrust'[83] (as had Eckart Kehr, another historian of whom Turner disapproved,[84] in the 1930s). In any case, Turner concludes, the Nazis rose because of 'the primacy of politics', not that of economics. All, he says, must accept 'responsibility for the Third Reich is not a valid cudgel with which to belabor [the existing capitalist] economic system'.[85]

Although the Abraham–Turner debate sounded very like some of the discussions occurring in West Germany, Maier, except for passing advertence, made no attempt to draw parallels with the US controversy.[86] Instead, his major references, apart from those to Germany, were to the USSR and to Israel. The two key questions, he said, were 'what are the stakes of the uniqueness [of Auschwitz and Nazism] for Germans? And from the other side . . . what are the stakes for Jews and other victims'?[87] For, he added, 'if the Final Solution remains non-comparable . . . the past may never be "worked through", the future never normalized, and German nationhood may remain forever tainted, like some well forever poisoned.'[88] And, if this situation were maintained, historians would feel the burden first and foremost since, he argued firmly, they 'must believe in national communities persisting through time'.[89] The malleability of time in turn deepened the problem. Since 'all participants have recognised that there can be no discussion of a national community without a confrontation of the darkest aspects of the national past, the controversy is also about the German future. It resonates'.[90]

Maier went on to describe and analyse the *Historikerstreit* and its background at Bitburg and in the controversy about museums. 'Western societies have been living through an era of self-archaeologisation,' he stated wittily, and then identified more than 500 museums opened in the FRG during the 1960s and 1970s.[91] Nor had satiety been reached. 'The hunger for memory', he explained, 'has been a remarkable cultural feature of the last decade.'[92] In his recounting, Maier had many wise things to say but he concluded by urging that historians not become immodest. 'No one can master the past; one can only interrogate it.'[93] Despite his own earlier views on the historian's commitment to the nation, he was anxious to point out that 'national identity' is never the single and necessary result of the past, not least because, to adapt E.P. Thompson's famous phrase, such identity is a 'happening and not a thing'. 'We need to know history, therefore, to understand identity; but history will not suffice. If it did, countries would move in worn grooves, and trajectories of development would be predictable. German history, above all, teaches that national behaviour has scope for unexpected veerings and craziness, atrocious (and corrective) possibilities beyond what historical knowledge can prepare us for.'[94] In any society with pretensions to democracy, the debate, it seems, will have to continue (though that debate might be more palatable and productive without the fury and the insults of the *Historikerstreit*).

But what of Maier's own explicit or implicit comparisons? As has been mentioned, one was with the USSR. Though Maier did ponder the extent to which the quarrel was stimulated and exacerbated by a fear in the FRG of the early promise of the Gorbachev reforms, the USSR did badly in his analysis. His table of victims of the 'long Second World War' largely excluded the more than 20 million Soviet war dead. He had no time for Western liberal attempts to distinguish 'Stalinist excesses [allegedly] committed in the name of historical progress, and Nazi crimes'. This, he said, was a sort of earlier attempt to relativise the Gulag by harping on Auschwitz.[95] And he accepted the continuing validity of the term 'totalitarian'. Maier, it is plain, was not a partisan of Soviet historiography's ambitions to assign to their 'Great Patriotic War' the real 'uniqueness', to have themselves recognised as the special victims of Nazism.

On the other hand, Maier was troubled by too easy a matching of the death tolls of 'Hitler' and 'Stalin'. Like most historians, he re-asserted the view that there was something appallingly and numbingly special about Auschwitz. It alone was intended to be a genocide in the complete meaning of that term; it alone was 'scientific' (conversion to a particular brand of politics could not bring salvation), 'industrial' and 'bureaucratic'. It alone had the single design: death.

These conclusions eventually led Maier to another comparison. For whom, he asked, with a word choice which exhibited the continuing visceral tensions of the matter, is the Holocaust an 'asset'? His first answer was Israel: Zionism, and Jews whether Zionist or not, and whether they lived in Israel or not. 'Postwar Jewish identity', he pronounced bluntly, 'depends upon the Holocaust.' Then came a liberal qualification: in Israel, the Holocaust 'helps legitimate the state, even if it cannot legitimate any particular frontiers or policies'; and good advice about enlightened and humble ambiguity:

The obligations of memory thus remain asymmetrical. For Jews: to remember that although they seek legitimation of a public sorrow, their suffering was not exclusive. For Germans: to specify that the Holocaust was the Final Solution of the Jewish problem as its architects understood it. The appropriateness of each proposition depends upon who utters it.[96]

Maier's phrases were a reminder, if such was necessary, that the people whose identity is enmeshed more than any other in the myths and history of the 'long Second World War' are the Jews. No historian of Late Modern Europe can ignore the enormous contribution made to the subject by Jewish historians, or overlook the fact that those historians come in almost infinite variety and can scarcely be usefully categorised by being called Jews. No serious student of modern politics would wish to deny that the Holocaust gives the present State of Israel a special legitimacy, though of course it has many other valid claims to existence.[97] At the same time it has to be admitted that Zionism was another of the nationalisms invented in the declining Habsburg Empire, comparable in many ways with those nationalisms which so tortured Central and Eastern Europe before 1945, and that Israel is another of the products of the 'long Second World War'.[98]

Similarly, it must be recognised that the Mandate of Palestine after the First World War and the new Israel after the Second were assigned their borders through the methods and assumptions of imperialism. While Israelis can be saddened and encouraged by 'Auschwitz', nationalist Palestinians can seek their justification in 'Hiroshima'. Thus history makes still more profound the terrifying, tragic and unsolved enigma of the contemporary Middle East. There, most of all, the 'long Second World War' drags on forever. There, most of all, historians should be aware that, though national communities may indeed exist over time, they can also be imagined and invented by the cynical and self-interested, and especially by what Eric Hobsbawm has memorably denominated the 'lesser examination-passing classes'.[99]

This question or contradiction of 'Auschwitz versus Hiroshima' is naturally present in the historiography of Nazism. Among Zionist historians of the last generation, the most compelling has been Lucy Dawidowicz (1915–90). In her memoirs she has briefly described her background. Before the First World War her family had fled to New York from Russian Poland, such a rich seed-bed of future histories of the 'long Second World War'. Though not particularly religious, they had, Dawidowicz says, a clear view of their own distinctiveness:

Our sense of being Jews and therefore being different from non-Jews was nurtured in me and my sister from infancy. We were raised to know that the world was divided into two irreconcilable groups: We and They. *They* were the non-Jews, who hated us and wished to destroy us. But *We* would prevail, largely because of our moral virtues and mental endowments. We took pride in being Jewish despite – or perhaps because of – the tragic circumstances of our history.[100]

After a brief period as a Communist, which ended when it dawned on her that Communists lie for tactical purposes, she began to devote herself to Jewish studies. In 1938 she left the USA for Vilna, then a centre of Jewish learning in Poland. It was, she has remarked drily, 'not an auspicious year to travel to Eastern Europe for business or pleasure'.[101] She stayed there for a year, aghast at the anti-Semitism endemic in Polish society and especially in Polish education, and stunned by the news from across the German border. In late August 1939 she escaped on almost the last train through Germany to find temporary sanctuary in Copenhagen. She had thus listened to the devilish overture of the Holocaust, but avoided the main performance. She was also there for the coda, returning to Europe in 1946 with the daunting task of interviewing and helping refugee Jews. These appalling experiences confirmed her adamantine character. During the war, she wrote that, 'in my daytime fantasies I imagine that I, too, in Europe searching for my friends, hoping they had survived, would kill a German or two. I never quite pictured how I'd do it, but the fantasy comforted me in my frustration, in my hopelessness.' Back in Germany after the war, she confessed: 'Hatred for the Germans, continued to consume me . . . though my rage was somewhat appeased by the knowledge that Germany was a defeated nation, its cities in ruins, its land divided into four zones and occupied by the victorious Allies.'[102]

Eventually, Dawidowicz became an academic and journalist in Israel and the United States, writing regularly for *Commentary* and acting as a spokesperson for conservative and patriotic Jewish-American and Israeli causes. She also wrote on the history of Nazism, and did so as a staunch intentionalist, fearing that the real purpose of functionalism was a relativisation of Nazi evil. For her, the meaning of the Second World War was simple, and Hitler's purpose single. As the title of her most famous book announced, Nazism had been no more and no less than 'the War against the Jews 1933–45'.[103]

Though she praised George Mosse, 'the preeminent explicator and demythologiser of the ideas that shaped German nationalism', her roll of historian-villains was a long one. A.J.P. Taylor (because of his alleged contempt for ideas), David Irving, Meinecke, Ritter, all Soviet historiography, all Polish historiography (which was still worse), even Hannah Arendt (for claiming in *Eichmann in Jerusalem* that some Jews collaborated) – none of these met her standards. Her favourite was K.D. Bracher, 'the first German historian, indeed the first non-Jewish historian anywhere, who has recognised that from the start the Nazis assigned primacy of place, in doctrine and in action, to make hatred of the Jews . . . a cardinal feature of . . . policy.'[104] But, in the end, her own claim to uniqueness for her side is total. The Holocaust is unique; the Nazis, the practitioners of Auschwitz, are unique; Hitler himself is unique; while the Jews are 'the quintessential people of history . . . [they] originated the idea of the God of history and they produced a written record of the past at least four centuries before Herodotus'.[105] In the face of Israel's history, all other nations are mere pretenders.

Before her death Dawidowicz was outraged[106] by a publication written by an American Jew, whose background and politics were very different from her own.

Arno J. Mayer's *Why did the Heavens not Darken? The 'Final Solution' in History* directly attacked Dawidowicz's interpretation of the meaning of Nazism and was, in its own argument, far more radically revisionist than were the works of any of the competing historians in the *Historikerstreit*.[107] In a curious attempt to import *glasnost* and *perestroika* into the Western historiography of the 'long Second World War', Mayer argued that the real quarry of Nazism, the first of their chosen victims, was not so much the Jews as communism and the Russian state and peoples.

As he explained in his preface, Mayer had been born in Luxembourg in 1926 into a middle-class family of 'fully emancipated and largely acculturated' Jews. The family's wealth, distinction and political acuity enabled most of its members to escape the Holocaust, but one grandfather died in a concentration camp and his wife survived to relate the harrowing tale to her grandson.

The Mayers fled across France, pursued, so it seemed, by German bombers and the German Army, and, after access to Franco's Spain was pitilessly blocked, they managed to reach French North Africa and eventually the United States. Transit visas had been illegally obtained 'in the manner portrayed in the film *Casablanca*'. From his American sanctuary, Mayer watched the terrible events of the Second World War unfold in Europe. In 1944 he was inducted into the US Army where his experiences 'finally helped me appreciate the link my father had made between left-wing antifascism and secular Zionism. During basic training in armored warfare in Fort Knox, Kentucky, I encountered fierce expressions of anti-black racism and anti-communism, and was personally exposed to anti-Jewish outbursts'.

Mayer's political beliefs hardened when he was transferred to an Intelligence unit. Apart from interviewing captured *Wehrmacht* and *Waffen SS* officers, he was assigned the special job of keeping up the morale of Nazi scientists moving over to the West:

> I was officially initiated into the ironies of the Cold War when I was given strict orders not to dispute any of their justifications for having served Hitler, including their favourite self-interested claim that except for persecuting the Jews, the Nazis had served their country and Europe well by saving Germany from the deadly scourge of communism and by fighting to keep bolshevism out of the European heartland.[108]

After a period in the army, Mayer enrolled at the City University of New York, where he completed a BA in 1949. His MA was gained from Yale in 1950 and his PhD from the same institution in 1953. He rejected the prevailing conservative, McCarthyite ideology of the Cold War and, on visits in 1950 and 1954, also distanced himself from what he saw happening in Israel, where Israeli nationalism was triumphing over what he regarded as the more proper commitment to democracy and socialism. He was particularly troubled by the developing division between Jews and Palestinian Arabs.

As has already been noted, Mayer, in succeeding decades, became an important historian of Late Modern Europe, based, after 1961, at Princeton (or 'Frenchville' as it was coming to be known), where he remained a firm proponent of *histoire*

91

évènementielle and spurned the attractions of post-structuralism and the *longue durée.*[109] He had made his name with a lengthy, two-volume, account of the post-First World War peacemaking, which was controversial in its location of a 'first cold war' of capitalist nationalism against communism in 1918–19 ('Wilson versus Lenin'). In other books he further explored the counter-revolutionary side of the European crisis in the twentieth century.[110] But it was *Why did the Heavens not Darken?* which brought all his work together and gave it a new and radical clarity.

He, too, was interested, he explained, in finding a responsible way to 'historicise' 'Auschwitz' (or the 'Judeocide' as he called it).[111] Like Nolte and Hillgruber, Broszat and Maier, he pondered the question of which comparison would best enable a comprehension of its horrors, for, as his first sentence would proclaim, 'the mass slaughter of the Jews of continental Europe during the first half of the twentieth century was an integral part of an enormous historical convulsion in which Jews were the foremost but by no means the only victims'.[112]

Mayer then proceeded to separate the long-term and the short-term causes of the Holocaust. One comparison was temporal: during the Thirty Years' War or in the Middle Ages, Jews had similarly been hunted down and murdered. The other was geographical and political: in what Mayer also defines as a 'European Civil War' from 1914 or 1917 to 1945, the Germans were not the only ones to kill Jews – most of the peoples of Central and Eastern Europe and especially their old elites either sympathised with the Final Solution or participated in it. Nor were the Jews the only enemy. 'If Hitler's world view had an epicenter, it was his deep-seated animosity toward contemporary civilization, and not his hatred of Jews, which was grafted on to it.'[113] 'Ultimately, Nazi Germany's dual resolve to acquire living space in the east and liquidate the Soviet regime provided the essential geopolitical, military, and ideological preconditions for the Judeocide.'[114] The Holocaust did not commence in 1933, but in 1939 or, more properly, in 1941–2 after Operation Barbarossa and the Wannsee Conference. Without the attack on the USSR there would and could have been no Jewish catastrophe, no 'Final Solution'.[115] The Nazis, with their allies' help, killed the Jews because the German armies had failed to over-run and defeat the USSR, because their forces were in retreat, and because, in an almost accidental way, they had the whole world of Jewry in their hands. They murdered in a politics of cultural and social despair. As Mayer would write in the afterword to the paperback edition of his book: 'It soon struck me as impossible . . . to grasp and characterize the singularity of the suffering of the Jews without comparing it to the enormous suffering during World War II of Russians and Poles in particular, but of other peoples as well.'[116]

And who was responsible for this torment? Again Mayer had an answer unpleasing to Dawidowicz and, indeed, to all conservative historians. Nazism was evil, that was understood, but it had come to power at the behest of and been condoned thereafter by 'industrial-feudal Europe', though Mayer agreed with Dahrendorf that it was the feudal part which was the more guilty. The European Civil War had seen 'the elites and institutions of Europe's embattled old regime. . . locked in a death struggle with those of a defiant new order.'[117] Just as Marxism was collapsing in Eastern Europe and Fukuyama was proclaiming the 'end of history', Mayer was re-stating (with a Dahrendorfian liberal admixture) a version of the first Marxist interpretation of fascism.

The *Historikerstreit* itself was finally quietened by the momentous events of 1989, though it is hard to believe that the re-unification of Germany will still the controversy about the meaning of German history and the role of that nation's past in its future. Similarly, it is likely that Germany's history will continue to be appraised by non-Germans; it will continue to 'belong' to them, too. In the endless debates about the meaning of the 'long Second World War', Germany is destined to remain the land of the historiographical 'middle'.

The middle it may be, but, contrary to much legend, unique it is not. The desire of historians to compare will survive and will further nourish historiography. Comparison will be made with the USSR (the model of totalitarianism) and Israel, with Britain and the United States (the model of the *Sonderweg*), with Italy and Eastern Europe (the model of fascism). This last model may remain the most apposite one because, presently, the successor states of the Soviet and Russian empires seem more likely to retrace the sad inter-war story of exacerbated nationalisms than do the new generation of Germans who, in the main, are so 'European' and 'democratic' and so hostile to nationalist excess.

Comparison will be made because that is the way history operates as a discipline. As Nolte put it, in regard to Nazism and Stalinism: 'two phenomena can appear to be both unlike and alike under different perspectives is, after all, nothing else but obvious'.[118] Comparison will be made for another reason. Not all of Arno Mayer's theses have to be accepted in order to recognise that the conflict of 1939–45 was a People's war, and that the crisis which led up to it was perhaps a world and certainly a European phenomenon. Germany's historiography may have been 'the historiography of the middle', but other historiographies, other societies, have also had to comprehend, to seek to master, or at the least to interrogate their own experience of the 'long Second World War'.

This analysis of the *Historikerstreit* has had a curious, even perplexing, sub-theme. West German historians of the Left and the Right, Ian Kershaw, Charles Maier in his epilogue – all these have yearned for sanctuary in the timeless (or almost timeless) world of the *longue durée*. Even Arno Mayer, who was so determined to study the 'event' of the Judeocide, claimed in the end to have written in the memory and spirit of Marc Bloch, patron and saint of the *Annales*.[119] Although the Kaiser may be written off as a man of straw, or Hitler defined as a weak dictator, the Emperor Fernand Braudel, it seems, rules OK in the historiography of the new Europe as it confronts the problem of German re-unification and, in the East, the end of what had so long seemed 'the Second World War which never ended'.

5

The sorrow and the pity of the fall of France and the rise of French historiography

At the very end of the epilogue to *The Unmasterable Past,* Charles Maier wondered whether the *Historikerstreit* represented the final arrival of 'post-modern historiography' in (West) Germany. Basically he thought it did. Nolte and his colleagues, he said, had launched 'a sharp attack on history as a would-be social science and a critique of any implicit theory of progress or redemption'. 'Post-modern historiography', he added, following Habermas:

> is attempting to fill a void left by the erosion of the earlier social-democratic premises of post-1960 [post-Fischer] history and politics. Fill it with history as ritual, discourse, or carnival. Sometimes the purpose has been to explore the hitherto neglected ways by which actors without formal power could nonetheless contest the hierarchies that regulated their everyday lives. In such a case the new history still presupposes a world of real power and struggle. But in some historical and anthropological reconstructions, politics loses any instrumental rationality. It no longer embodies socially purposive aspirations, whether for emancipation or for domination, and appears only as ritual or theater, the state as cinema. Whatever the new and allusive subject, the major thrust of post-modern historiography is the unmooring of politics from any unambiguous correspondence with social structure.[1]

Speak of ritual, discourse and carnival and you think of Roland Barthes, Claude Lévi-Strauss, Michel Foucault, Jacques Derrida; you think of France. Restrict yourself to historians and you turn to Marc Bloch, Lucien Febvre, Fernand Braudel, Emmanuel Le Roy Ladurie and Marc Ferro; you read *The Royal Touch: Sacred Monarchy and Scrofula in England and France,*[2] *The Mediterranean and the Mediterranean World in the Age of Philip II,*[3] *Montaillou* or *Carnival in Romans,*[4] you contemplate the *Annales, mentalités,* the *longue durée, histoire totale*; you invoke *The Identity of France.*[5]

Here, then, is a paradox. In the disciplines of linguistics, anthropology, criminology, sociology and history, the world since the end of the Second World War has seen the rise of a French Empire and has applauded victory after victory won by 'post-modernist' French intellectuals. In 1945 these triumphs would have been hard to foresee. Then France lay in overwhelming and humiliating defeat, in military, political, social and psychological ruin. Truly post-modernism is a phoenix arisen from the ashes of France's utterly calamitous, short Second World War.

Yet, for all the impact of the war on intellectual life, there is a strange void in French historiography. French historians, indeed French intellectuals, it seems, will not greatly assist anyone trying to explain 'Auschwitz' and 'Hiroshima' or investigating why such explanations tend to be contested. Anyone who studies France's historicising of the 'long Second World War' confronts the dilemma posed to Sherlock Holmes by the dog which did not bark in the night. It is not the history of that war which instructs, but the absence of a history.

For, neither France's 'long' Second World War nor its 'short' one have occupied a major place in French academic discourse since 1945. Typical evidence of this omission came in 1989, Bicentenary of the French Revolution and a time of many celebrations. Then an English language version of *Unanswered Questions: Nazi Germany and the Genocide of the Jews* appeared. It was edited by François Furet, presently the most famous historian of the Revolution. However, on this occasion Furet had studied not 1789 and all that, but, as the title indicates, vexed issues relating to a much more recent conflict. The book had originated in a seminar organised in 1982 and, in his introduction, Furet confessed that there was something a little disappointing about it. The experts who had been drawn to Paris to discuss the matter had come from all over the world. They were not French.[6] Even the paper which most directly touched on France's experience from 1940 to 1944 was written by two Americans, Michael Marrus and Robert Paxton.[7] The only contribution from a Frenchman was that by Pierre Vidal-Naquet who, in the last chapter, exposed the absurdities of those so-called 'revisionists' (including the Frenchman Robert Faurisson) who argue that the Holocaust never happened.[8]

But Maier's somewhat convoluted phrases hint at a further irony in post-war France's historicisation of its recent past. 'Post-modernists', Maier noticed, were inclined to treat the state as cinema; yet, in France, it was through cinema, and specifically through the documentary film, *Le Chagrin et la pitié* (1971), that cosy myths about the Second War began to unravel.[9] Here was a film director doing what French historians had not done, treating the state and society both metaphorically and directly. Only with the documentary's screening was it at last possible to have some sense of the sorrow and the pity of the French experience in defeat, under occupation and after liberation.

Of all the Great and pseudo-great Powers involved in the Second World War, France fared worst. In any objective sense the French Republic and the French people proved themselves inadequate before what Arthur Marwick has aptly called the 'test of war'.[10] The French state performed more feebly even than the Italian, which, then and thereafter, was so frequently made the butt of derisory comments about its unpreparedness and unsuitability for military combat.[11] The extent of France's humiliation and calamity can be paralleled only with that of Poland, epicentre of the Holocaust. But Poland's national mythology made it almost predictable that yet again it was the suffering 'Christ among nations', to be transported to 'Golgotha'.[12] Moreover, Poland's war was a recognisable one of death and destruction, of Warsaw levelled to the ground, of villages left in smoking ruins, of the end of any pretence of civilisation. Though such contrast may be invidious, France, except for a few weeks in 1940, and during the months before and after the Allied invasion in June 1944, had a relatively soft war. It was a softness which, for a country of France's traditions and history, made defeat all the harder to bear (although it may have also rendered it all the easier, after the event, to forget or to obscure).

The fall of France can be seen in a number of ways. Most obvious was the military loss. After months of 'Phoney War', in which French propaganda continued to define the Maginot Line as impregnable, the Nazis, on 10 May 1940, attacked in the west, using the obvious stratagem of sweeping through the Ardennes, Luxembourg and Belgium. By 20 May, their forces had reached the sea. On 9 June, an attempt by the French armies to stand on the line of the rivers Somme and Aisne collapsed and, a few days later, German troops reached the Loire, well to the south of Paris. Before the end of May, the French Government had fled, first to Tours and then to Bordeaux, and there on 16 June the Prime Minister, Paul Reynaud, resigned. His replacement, Philippe Pétain, the aged hero of the defence of Verdun in 1916 and until recently Ambassador to Franco's Spain, announced the next day that he was seeking an armistice. The Third Republic had withered away before the might of Nazism.

This debacle could not be explained simply in military terms. The Germans did have a punishing supremacy in the air, but on the ground they won not so much because of a superiority in numbers or equipment, but rather because their generals had the better tactics and their soldiers the greater will. Put simply, the German system had functioned more efficiently than had the French. As a recent student of the campaign has concluded:

> In war between comparable forces victory goes to the side which suffers fewer delays and confusions and in which the chain of command is more lucid and effective. The best French troops and their equipment and morale were fully equal to those of the best German troops. They were defeated because too often they were not in the right place at the right time.[13]

While the armies disintegrated, so too, for a brief period, did *la régle du jeu*, the rules of the game of everyday life. Especially in Paris, that city of light which had always regarded itself as the inspiration of France and the world, the bonds of society crumbled into nothingness. Hundreds of thousands of the citizens of Paris fled,[14] out on to the roads of France to join perhaps 5 million others forming a clogged caravanserai of automobiles and hand-carts, a motley throng clutching its most cherished or useful possessions. Some, strafed by passing German *Stukas*, were killed. But most photographs of the time show a bedraggled and bewildered populace crammed to one edge of a road while German motorised divisions, superb in their technology and confidence, roar past, contemptuous of the people they had conquered and, in their opinion, now reduced to homeless gypsies.

Other accounts tell a tale which prompts anger as much as sorrow at the pity of it all. Of the 40,000 civilians who died in this retreat some were victims of the Germans and others simply perished in the confusion. Others still died in more deliberate acts. There were stories of hospital staff, ordered to evacuate their buildings, killing their patients before they left rather than attempting the burdensome or distasteful task of carrying them with them; of local inhabitants who rounded on and shot officers brave or foolhardy enough to attempt one last resistance. Even the ultimate basis of family life did not always survive: 'For weeks afterwards newspapers carried advertisements for babies who had been lost, or found without means of identification.'[15] At this moment, it was as though France, its institutions, its people, and their history, did not exist. The French state and the French nation, it seemed, had fallen into the abyss of *anno zero*.

But this time of disintegration was short. Well before 24 October, when Pétain and Adolf Hitler exchanged greetings in front of the photographers at Montoire, law and order and a state system had been restored. There were some complications, it is true, in this temporary peace settlement. Germany had re-annexed Alsace and Lorraine, and the areas around Lille and the Pas-de-Calais were placed under the German military administration based in Brussels. The Nazis' Italian allies had their own zone in the far south-east. The rest of *la belle France* was also split. German troops occupied the north, but a large section of the south was left unoccupied until November 1942. It was there, briefly at Clermont-Ferrand[16] and later at the nearby spa of Vichy, that the new French Government under Pétain assembled. It would be officially denominated *L'État français* but soon would be familiarly called the Vichy regime.

Historians have continued to debate whether or not this regime was fascist. In France, the most common view among historians,[17] as expressed, for example, by the very conservative René Rémond,[18] has been that fascism 'came from the left'. Fascism, he and others claim, is a term which should be restricted to such Paris-based rabble-rousers as Marcel Déat and Jacques Doriot. Vichy, by contrast, was merely 'reactionary' or 'counter-revolutionary'; its famous catchcry '*travail, famille, patrie*' (work, family, fatherland) deliberately phrased to shout down '*liberté, egalité, fraternité*', the slogan which, since 1789, had allowed the Great Revolution to go on reverberating. Other historians, notably Anglo-Saxon ones,[19] have been less sure, and many have argued that, at the very least, Vichy afforded a classic example of 'fellow-travelling' by conservatives. For such analysts, the French wartime regime demonstrated that fascism originated more on the right than on the left.

This argument about a right-wing genesis of fascism can be located in France, too, but perhaps discussion of it has been feebler there because, in French circles, the more resonant and contested word has been 'collaboration'. The great questions have been to what extent did the Vichy regime, or the French populace, actively or passively collaborate in the Nazi New Order? Did the French gladly, or because there was no help for it, do Hitler's work for him?

On the surface, there is much evidence that, after the panic was over, life became sweet in wartime France, at least in comparison with elsewhere in Europe or Asia. In 1941–2, French industry expanded in the service of the German war machine.[20] As Gerhard Hirschfeld has recently put it: 'no other occupied country during the Second World War . . . contributed more to the initial efficiency of Nazi rule in Europe than France.'[21] Some far-seeing businessmen were troubled by the consequent subservience to German big business, but most French men and women seem happily to have accepted their improved profits or their regular wages. Only in 1943–4, as the Nazis sought enhanced profits from the French part of their empire, did times start to become more arduous. In particular, German demands that French labour 'volunteer' for transfer to the Reich caused special resentment of a kind that working for Nazi paymasters in France never had.[22]

In 1941–2, Paris, too, had turned its lights back on and become the cushiest posting for a soldier of the *Wehrmacht* or SS looking for some R and R after service on the Eastern Front. The theatres boomed,[23] as did the brothels. Paris intellectuals in the cafés, or in their small magazines, resumed their subtle debates. Pierre Renouvin, the great and conservative French diplomatic historian, would even say that, though he had lived in Paris throughout the war, he had never seen a German soldier. He had gone each day from his flat to the archives and back again without let or hindrance.[24]

The film industry also flourished, assisted by elements in Vichy patriotically anxious that it not be submerged by its German rival. The preferred cinematic mode was light comedy or historical romance. Only the very occasional feature film was overtly propagandist, though the shorter documentaries more frequently displayed a political intent.[25] Mostly it was *outré* figures who hitched their wagons to the Nazi star – like the bitterly anti-Semitic and misanthropic novelist, Louis-Ferdinand Céline, who would claim characteristically that 'all of France has committed treason except me', and that 'an immense hatred keeps me alive. I would live for a thousand years if I were certain of seeing the whole world croak';[26] or his ostentatiously rash colleague, Robert Brasillach, a youth determined not to survive his youth.[27] Many Parisians, many French intellectuals, and many of the French people, by contrast, treated the war and their own lives in it as a curious sort of holiday as long as they could. It was not a time to be too serious and, if a carping or puritanical critic perceived some corruption or prostitution, well, such was the way of the world. If deprivation, hunger and death might be just around the corner, now was not the time to repine such a fate.

In relation to one matter, however, it is hard to smile at such cynicism, more troubling to accept such passivity. When it came to the Jews of France, the Nazis meant business, genocidal business. Here, then, is another sense in which, between 1940 and 1944, the identity of France was assaulted. For the Vichy regime was a participant, in many ways an active and a willing participant, in the murder of the Jews.

On 3 October 1940, the Vichy administration enacted its own *Statut des juifs*,[28] and in March 1941 it appointed Xavier Vallat, a one-eyed Catholic war hero, as Commissioner for Jewish Affairs. Though personally maintaining an old soldier's mistrust of the enemy from the last war, Vallat actively promoted anti-Jewish legislation, before being replaced in May 1942 by the frenetically anti-Semitic Louis Darquier de Pellepoix.[29] Historians have commented that, in compiling lists of Jews and in imposing restrictions on them, the French often behaved with more celerity and more conviction in their own zone than did the occupying Germans. 'There were', Marrus and Paxton have pointed out, 'important links between the Nazis' "final solution" and the . . . work of French governments – policies usually supported by French public opinion.'[30] Certainly, French anti-Semitism was far sharper and more pervasive than was Italian. At least from November 1942 to September 1943, the Italian zone offered the best sanctuary for the Jews of France if only, as Jonathan Steinberg has so acutely argued, because the Italians, with a mixture of corruption, outraged national pride, sly Germanophobia and Catholic mercy, were able still to express 'the banality of good'.[31]

Most ethically detestable were the French authorities' disgraceful attempts, from the very beginning, to distinguish foreign Jews from 'their own', and their nightmarish efforts to harden this distinction through legislation. In the inter-war period, France, for both political and economic reasons, had been a major venue for immigration, and in 1939 some 50 per cent of an estimated total of 350,000 Jews resident in France were not French by birth.[32] As early as 22 July 1940, with the armistice yet to take full effect, the Vichy Government had established a commission to review, with obvious and baleful intent, those naturalisations which had occurred since 1927.[33]

In the end some 70,000 French Jews were transferred to the east, there to be liquidated.[34] In an interview screened in *The Sorrow and the Pity*, Comte René de Chambrun, the son-in-law of executed Vichy Prime Minister Pierre Laval, pursued a common Vichyite line by arguing that, after all, only some 5 per cent of 'French' Jews had died. As his interviewer at once reminded him, he had thus omitted the tens of thousands of Jews, resident in France at the start of the war, who subsequently perished.[35] Others who sought to justify themselves or the regime state that, after all, 'only' 20 per cent died, and this figure was lower than that of the Netherlands (some 85 per cent killed), or of Quisling's Norway (50 per cent). Such playing with numbers is macabre and distasteful and does not alter the point that French anti-Semitism, far more than Dutch or Norwegian, was engendered within France and to a considerable degree was self-sustaining. As Marrus and Paxton have rather mildly stated:

> in its widely acclaimed Révolution Nationale, capitalizing on a popular disposition to seek scapegoats for a humiliating defeat, Vichy France energetically issued a series of new laws which defined Jews, excluded them from the army and the civil service, interned many of them, and set the stage for their elimination from economic life.[36]

It also set the stage for their liquidation. There can be little doubt that Vichy France helped to map out its own path to Auschwitz.

What then of the Resistance, of those French men and women who sometimes quite self-consciously before 'liberation' sought to restore France's honour by combatting the German victors and who, after the defeat of Nazism, were paraded as proof that the 'real France' had never submitted? As shall be seen, a historiographical debate about the character of this body continues but almost all would now agree that they were a variegated group of men and women.[37] There were the 'Free French' in London, with a doubtful claim, by no means accepted by the Allies, to be a government-in-exile. Their enigmatic leader, Charles De Gaulle, was a man who, to adapt a famous saying of Napoleon III, was half-legitimist, half-nationalist, half-militarist, half-socialist and half-mad. There were the Communists, until 1941 somewhat sullen believers in the Ribbentrop–Molotov Pact, thereafter likely to top the Resistance's body count, but never in the service only of France or its people. There were the other resisters – socialists, Christian Democrats, monarchists, republicans – a varied crew, few in number at least at first, motivated frequently by honesty, decency and love, and sometimes by chance, opportunity and hatred. They were killed and they killed, and in so doing they and the French people were exposed to the viciousness of German reprisals, most notoriously the sacking of Oradour-sur-Glane. There, on 10 June 1944, the Germans meted out what they defined as condign punishment (even if they mistook the place they really wanted), and 642 out of a village population of 652 died, the women and children being incinerated in the local church.[38] Thereafter this atrocity gained even further force because some of the 'Germans' involved were actually Alsatians who, after 1945, had again become 'French'.

For many, however, then and later, the agony of this sort of war paled into insignificance compared with one final disaster – the purge instituted after liberation. The Allies had invaded France on 'D-Day' (6 June 1944) without having decided with any finality which political force or forces in liberated France they intended to back.[39] Roosevelt did not even seem to have made up his mind whether the new France should be a Republic or not.[40] But he, like De Gaulle and other politicians, had to reckon with what happened in France itself, especially when rapid German retreat temporarily produced a political and power vacuum. Some recent historians of these events have concluded that 'there was not one Liberation of France, but several'. High politics, intellectual and ideological disputation, international diplomacy, all often 'lagged well behind the decisions made "on the ground", on the roads and villages of France', whether by the populace, by a local Resistance group or by individual military commanders who happened to take charge of a particular place at a particular time.[41]

During this confusion and after it, there was violence. Gradually the occupation had become less benign and, in the last months before D-Day, had been decidedly unpleasant. Some people were reduced to near starvation[42] while, faced with both active and passive resistance (for example, to the labour round-ups), German rule increased in brutality. Almost inevitably the violence did not end with the arrival of Allied troops. As Herbert Lottman has put it, 'the liberation of France also liberated anger'.[43] Spontaneous acts of revenge against collaborators caused some 10,000 deaths in the first weeks after the expulsion of the Nazis. The Resistance had already killed some 2,500 before 6 June.[44] Its leadership, whether within France or arriving with De Gaulle from exile, agreed that there should be a purge, an *épuration*, to wipe out the blot of Vichy and of collaboration. Beginning in 1943, internment lists had been drawn up, and more than 125,000 persons were actually seized (though 36,000 of these were soon released). Before the trials were ended in 1951, 110,000, including such cultural notables as Céline, Roger Peyrefitte, Maurice Chevalier and Edith Piaf, went before the courts. Almost half were sentenced to the humiliation of *indignité nationale,* while 767 were executed.[45] Those 767 included novelist Brasillach and politician Pierre Laval whose trial was hardly a model of judicial impartiality and whose execution was a grim farce – he had taken cyanide but his stomach was pumped for long enough for him to be dragged out and shot.[46] Pétain, amid controversy, was also sentenced to death, but De Gaulle commuted his sentence, and the erstwhile hero of Verdun died in prison, aged ninety-five, on 23 July 1951.[47] His demise symbolically ended what conservatives were already calling 'the Franco-French civil war'.[48]

Such conservatives had endeavoured to give Pétain a Christ-like apotheosis or, at least, following his death to propagate the view that he and Vichy represented the counter-revolutionary reading of French history. While his body lay in its mortuary chapel, four girls garbed in the costume of the Vendée, famous centre of resistance to the Revolution, stood beneath the windows and a Vendean peasant solemnly chanted: 'Saints et saintes de France, priez pour notre vieux chef.' An Honour Committee for Pétain, formed three years before and headed by the historian, Louis Madelin, once a zealous advocate of French friendship with Fascist Italy, had been dissolved. Shortly after the death of 'Le Maréchal', however, French officialdom did concede the right to found an *Association pour défendre la mémoire du maréchal Pétain.*[49] Active among those wanting to honour Pétain was Jacques Le Roy Ladurie, peasantist Minister of Agriculture under Vichy but eventually also a member of the Resistance, and the father of the *Annales* historian.[50] If Pétain was dead, the battle to historicise France's Second World War had scarcely begun.

The complex of events between 1939 and 1945 seemed destined to have a major impact on French historiography. In some eyes, after all, historiographical division then lay at the very root of France's crisis, while in others, a historiographical conjuring trick would soon permit France to regain its 'identity', and to deny or to forget that the mere 'events' of the Second World War had ever happened. If words and their echoes had troubled France before 1940, they could act as a soothing balm after 1945.

Ever since 1789, France had been the country of the historical caesura. The Revolution had broken French history into two and more than a century later, in 1914, France was still a European oddity – along with tiny San Marino and idiosyncratic Switzerland, the only republic in a world dominated by the persistence of what were, at least constitutionally, *anciens régimes*. By most standards France was then Europe's most democratic or meritocratic society (though French women would not get the vote until 1945 and freedom had not been rashly conceded to the subject peoples of the French Empire). The touchstone of this democracy for metropolitan men, was, or was believed to be, the Revolution. The republican education system, so powerful a machine for 'making Frenchmen',[51] purveyed a certain myth of the Revolution – liberty, opportunity for equality, nationalism; these were what composed, or were meant to compose, republican *virtu*.

As already noted in the first chapter of this book, Pieter Geyl, himself an old-style republican and admirer of (his myth of) the French Revolution and French culture, used the occasion of his Second World War to recount the French Revolution-as-history. In *Napoleon: For and Against*, he told of a modern French history profession led from the Sorbonne by such republican worthies as Alphonse Aulard, Charles Seignobos and Georges Lefebvre.[52] Predictably enough, Geyl applauded the socialist Lefebvre's austerely scientific[53] commitment to relating what actually happened (though equally predictably he was on the look-out for any 'determinism'). And in general, Geyl explained in 1949, 'the argument [about the Revolution] is going merrily on';[54] the *universitaires'* characterisation of Napoleon or Robespierre was being and had been contested by another group of historians. They were the *académiciens* and included such scholars as Madelin and Jacques Bainville. Members of the French Academy, they worked outside the professionalised academic system. They wrote a sort of popular history, were more cavalier with facts and were more given to rhetorical flourishes than was, say, Lefebvre.[55] Generally, they objected to the Revolution. Jacques Bainville (who died in 1936),[56] and his acolyte, Pierre Gaxotte, were writers active in the cause of the proto-fascist *Action Française*. During the Stavisky riots and the rightist *journées* of February 1934, the Popular Front of 1936–8, and over the years 1939–40, French historians, just like French society, polarised readily enough into those essentially in favour of the Revolution and those against it, into 'revolutionaries' and 'counter-revolutionaries'.

With Vichy would come the opportunity for counter-revolution, the chance to 'turn the clock back' (though the regime also possessed a sort of 'apolitical', 'technocratic' promise of 'modernity'). Charles Maurras, for two generations the intellectual leader of *Action Française*,[57] who later would be sentenced to life imprisonment, tried to develop a new history of France, the *uchronie* as he called it. It condemned or simply omitted anything which could be construed a result of the Revolution.[58] A less strident but perhaps more characteristic figure under Vichy was Jérôme Carcopino, appointed Minister of National Education in 1941. A distinguished classical historian and Italophile, or, more precisely, a Romanophile (he had become head of the French School in Mussolini's Rome in 1937),[59] Carcopino regarded the teaching profession as the backbone of the regime. He warned darkly how febrile a place a class-room could be. Teachers' words, he said, could 'arouse in your students profound reverberations . . . the slightest doubt may trouble them'. Thus obedient pupils should be told to salute the triumphs and rest under the wings of Marshal Pétain 'who, alone among so many, from 1914 to 1918, had acquired enough glory to win the admiration of the victors, to stop the invasion of 1940 and whose presence at the head of the government symbolises and guarantees the unity of France and its empire'.[60] In 1944, Carcopino was duly arrested as a collaborator and was badly beaten up before being dumped among the internees in the camp at Drancy near Paris.[61] His trial followed but, like so many others, by the 1950s he was back at his desk and had resumed his scholarly career.

Other historians, by contrast, joined the Resistance at one time or another. The most celebrated cultural figure among its fallen was Marc Bloch. Indeed, after 1945, Bloch became the quintessential martyr of the war. He was one intellectual absolutely guiltless of the '*trahison des clercs*'.

Bloch had been born in Lyons in July 1886, to a family of Alsatian Jewish extraction. His father eventually rose to lecture in classical Roman history at the Sorbonne. Bloch himself attended the *École Normale Supérieure* from 1904 and, after research in Germany, commenced a doctoral thesis on medieval history. He had disliked what he had seen across the Rhine and particularly rejected what he perceived as an excessive commitment by German historians to the positive role of the state. In his *Weltanschauung,* by contrast, liberty and the nation intermingled and this unity had a genuine popular base; for Bloch, republican *virtu* sprang, in the final analysis, from the people.[62]

In the light of this world view, it is not surprising that, in 1914, Bloch went gladly to war, serving on the Western Front and in Algeria. By September 1917 he had been promoted to intelligence officer for his regiment. None the less, he had retained a historian's scepticism and was openly critical of a national education system (and the history it taught) which had produced what he deemed the deficient army leadership of 1914. He had also discerned that, in his words, 'great crises move slowly',[63] that France's and Europe's predicaments were occasioned by what would later be called structural problems.

After the end of the war, the three-times decorated Bloch returned to an academic career and in 1920 his thesis was passed by its examiners. During the next few years, he worked in the provinces, notably at Strasbourg where, in 1929 with Lucien Febvre, he set up a new journal called *Annales.*[64] In 1936 he was elevated to the Sorbonne.[64]

Bloch returned to a Paris scoured by deepening political turmoil and by rising anti-Semitism. In 1938, he was advised by Febvre to withdraw his candidature for the directorship of the *École Normale Supérieure* lest it allow Gaxotte or other right-wing commentators to talk about Jewish conspiracies. With the outbreak of war, although now in his fifties, he volunteered for military service, and would write a moving account, *Strange Defeat,* of the military and psychological reasons for the fall of France.[65] On that defeat, he joined the Resistance, while also for a time teaching on the staff of the University of Strasbourg-in-exile based at Clermont-Ferrand.[66] In 1944 he was captured by the Nazis, tortured and killed, a death which, like those of the villagers of Oradour, was all the more poignant because it occurred after liberation had begun. Bloch's last words, it is said, as he went before the firing squad, were 'Vive la France!'[67] These words and his deeds have made him a natural saint for the anti-Vichy cause in France's 'civil war of the mind'.[68]

That a national France could not only survive but flourish after 1945, that it could bind up the wounds of defeat, humiliation and civil war, owes much to Charles De Gaulle[69] and to his manipulation of his own myth as the Saviour of France, the heroic and virile foil to that sad and doddering collaborationist, Pétain. Yet, in relation to the more long-standing history of the 'civil war of the mind', it was difficult to identify De Gaulle with either the 'Revolution' or the 'Counter-Revolution'. At first it seemed clear that he, the first organiser and inspiration of the 'Free French', must embody the Resistance, though by the 1950s and 1960s the Gaullists' ranks included many who had passively sat out the Vichy period. It also seemed that this greatest of patriots incarnated the nation, but some nationalists wondered about that, too, when in 1962 De Gaulle accepted Algerian independence and energetically repressed those who opposed it.[70] Instead, the key to De Gaulle's success, the reason why he was able to create a moderate conservative consensus was to be found further back in the French past. In his person and ideas he blurred the old divide between those who were for and those who were against the Revolution. No one could be sure where De Gaulle would have stood had a time-machine transported him to 1789. And in this ambiguity about more distant history he helped to paper over the recent crisis of the Second World War.

Though the comparison is risky and is certainly not exact, the historiographical equivalent of De Gaulle, the force best designed to moderate French cultural conflict and to mute the more menacing echoes of national history, is that which had grown up around the journal founded by Bloch and Febvre in 1929. Indeed, the *Annales*, or rather those *Annalistes* of the 'second generation' who flourished after 1945, more successfully restored or constructed a French cultural empire than De Gaulle or his successors managed in the political field. The *Annalistes*, and their post-modernist colleagues in anthropology, linguistic theory and philosophy, again turned Paris into the city of light and gave France a cultural imperium unknown since the Enlightenment. The seeds of this victory became obvious only in the aftermath of defeat and war. As the Belgian historian Jan Dhont has recalled, with the conflict over, he suddenly found his fellow students 'imbued with the spirit of the *Annales*. I never discovered how that came about. It certainly had nothing to do with the professors. It must have just been something in the air.'[71]

The *Annales* has attracted so many superb historians and inspired so many commentaries on their work that it is hardly possible in a book such as this to review the resultant scholarship in any detail. But what of Dhont's conundrum? What was it about the spirit of the times, the *mentalité*[72] of the post-war period which assisted the rise of the *Annales* to world power? What special variety of history would make the *Annales* at that particular moment 'the most famous history journal in the world'?

It is now two decades since Jack Hexter, in his article 'Fernand Braudel and the Monde Braudellien . . .', wittily parodied the style of the *Annalistes* and at the same time analysed the *Annales* triumph using an imperial metaphor. For Hexter, Febvre was 'a bit like Machiavelli's image of Romulus, powerful, domineering, fierce, pugnacious, a warrior, almost a brawler at heart . . . a man of ecumenical intellect but not of irenic spirit.'[73] His successor, Fernand Braudel (1902–85) who, born in a village in German-occupied Lorraine, had joined the *Annales* team in 1937 and who, on Febvre's death in 1956, succeeded him as editor of the journal, was, instead, 'an academic statesman of more judicious temper'.[74] Perhaps Hexter should have moved his image a little forward in time. If Bloch (before and after deification) and Febvre had won their gallic and other wars, Braudel was the Augustus who solidified the empire, codified its systems and philosophy, and promised to make it endure.

The *Annales* was a product of the periphery. It was founded in Strasbourg, a city unable to compete with Paris, but one which did have a resonance of its own. Capital of regained (and then to be lost again and re-regained) Alsace, in the post-1945 period it was fated to become, perhaps appropriately, one of the capitals of 'Europe'. The enemies of the *Annales*, naturally enough, resided in Paris. They were the *universitaires*, especially the more methodologically conservative professors such as Seignobos or Pierre Renouvin; French Rankeans, who thought that their studies of Great Men, Diplomacy and Political History were relating all that actually mattered.

But the *Annales* historians had another target, rather less remarked on because it was composed of amateurs beneath the contempt of any *Annales équipe*. These readily vanquished playthings of the *Annales* were the *académiciens*. The typical field of their defeat was the Middle Ages. They had made that era a time of romance, of heroic kings and virtuous princesses, of Catholic piety, of envied *Gemeinschaft*, of a properly functioning corporatist order which a monarchist or conservative fascist regime might hope to emulate. The *académiciens* could not, however, footnote it, graph it, or put it in a table. That the *académiciens*' version of the Middle Ages was wrong and silly was not difficult to prove. The cardinal feature of the *Annales* became not so much their rewriting of medieval history as their offer to French historiography (and France) of a 'third way' between the *universitaires* and *académiciens*, between radicals and conservatives, while all the time being more 'scientific' than either. By implication and at first quite unconsciously, they promised to end the cultural war between those for and those against the French Revolution. And, indeed, after three generations of *Annales* hegemony, as shall be seen below, there was precious little left of the French Revolution to celebrate in 1989.

But still the issues of why the *Annales* flourished so mightily after 1945, and what instruction their scholarship offered to those afflicted by the fall of France have not been resolved. To answer such questions, it is necessary to examine Braudel's exposition of *Annales* methodology in more detail. For Braudel, time, like Gaul or the Almighty, could be divided into three parts – the short term, the middling-term and the *longue durée*. The short term produced the 'event', the middling the 'conjuncture', and from the long duration came the 'structure'. This movement from the fleeting to the long term was also a movement of understanding. The event was (to adapt the title of a contemporary French satirical novel) little more than 'froth on the day dream'.[75] The conjuncture or the structure were what were significant; ironically they were where the action really was. The diverse currents of history, too, could be separated. The event was political; the structure social and economic, or even geographical, geological and climatic. Thus typical *Annales* articles would be entitled 'the history of rain and fine weather', 'amenorrhoea in time of famine (seventeenth to twentieth century)';[76] thus, Braudel, in his most grandiose book, seeking to write the history of everything from the fifteenth to the eighteenth centuries, would engage in 'a weighing up of the world'.[77]

But what has all this to do with the Second World War? Perhaps the first answer to this question is found in another of Braudel's books, his two-volume study of the identity of France. Composed in his old age and meant to be a sort of will and testament, this book is full of a profound national piety. His reverence for France perhaps even exceeds Ranke's for Prussia, and certainly shows that the Braudellian *Annales*, though it may have many new short-term characteristics, also fits rather older structures of a national intelligentsia.

> Let me start by saying once and for all that I love France with the same demanding and complicated passion as did Jules Michelet . . . . The historian can really be on equal footing only with the history of his own country; he understands almost instinctively its twists and turns, its complexities, its originalities and its weaknesses.[78]

De Tocqueville and Taine had been incorrect to start French history in 1789; Zeldin wrong to look to 1848 – so much for revolutionary caesuras. Rather, France began in pre-Roman Gaul with patterns of village construction or the appearance of blood groups (not for nothing would Astérix, heroic comic-strip Gaul, from that little Breton (!) village, never occupied, without a single collaborator . . . be launched in 1959).[79] For, Braudel argues, 'it should be understood that for no nation does the obligatory and increasingly burdensome dialogue with the outside world mean an expropriation or obliteration of its own history. There may be some intermingling but there is no fusion.'[80]

Later in his book, Braudel, as is appropriate for the greatest historian of his generation, shies away from the nastier implications of these comments.[81] He admits that 'France is not one society . . . but many societies.' But, time and again, he none the less subscribes to highly conservative causes. The borders of France, he claims, were plain by the twelfth or thirteenth centuries: 'the old frontiers stood the test: they would endure.' Hierarchy is the natural state of humanity, 'for no society is built on equality: the only way any of them can be presented schematically is as a pyramid.' 'Immigration without tears' in contemporary France, as at any other time, is possible only through a policy of assimilation. Recent events sometimes matter (the dates he chooses are the resonant list of 1815, 1871, 1914 and 1940 – not 1789, 1830, 1848 and 1968 . . .) but, in the final analysis, 'the crucial events occurred in fact millennia ago'.[82]

There is one modern event which prompts him to a special lyricism. It is, of course, the fall of France in 1940, that moment of 'the indescribable disorder of defeat' when 'we the defeated, trudged the unjust road towards a suddenly-imposed captivity, [then we] represented the lost France, dust blown by the wind from a heap of sand'. Naturally, such a 'rent in the canvas' could eventually be repaired: 'in time even these monstrous wounds heal, fade [and] are forgotten'. But, even as the Vichy regime was being installed, Braudel had found a comforter.

> The real France, the France held in reserve, la France profonde, remained
> behind us. It would survive, it did survive .... Ever since those days, already
> so long ago, I have never ceased to think of a France buried deep inside itself,
> within its own heart, a France flowing along the contours of its own age –
> long history, destined to continue, come what may.[83]

And, it was as a POW at Lübeck that he conceived his great work on the Mediterranean which he would publish in 1949. Listening in his mind to the rhythms of that sea and of the people who lived on its littoral was the best way, in 'gloomy captivity', to escape the 'chronicle' of the 'difficult years' from 1940 to 1945. In a Nazi prison near the grey and sombre Baltic he would understand that the long view was 'wise man's time'.[84] Braudel may have been the great historian of this long view, the liberal humanist open to all the sciences of the human mind, the pluralist aspiring to a total history of the world, but his reflections and writings seem inspired more than anything else by his personal experience of an event, his participation in the sorrow and the pity of the fall of France, and his desire to gloss over its full horror.

Though Braudel is the most formidable of the *Annales* school, the Great Man of the structuralist historians, his *curriculum vitae* is by no means unique. Recently Pierre Nora has launched what he calls '*ego-histoire*', 'an attempt to set up a sort of laboratory in which historians try to make historians of themselves . . . a new genre for a new age of historical consciousness'.[85] Though the real novelty of this 'new science' may be doubted – Nora could have read in E.H. Carr the dictum: 'study the historian before you begin to study the facts'[86] – the popular psychoanalytic trappings of the statements from historians which Nora has published do indeed provide fresh insights into French historiography.

Not all Nora's subjects are *Annalistes* (he includes René Rémond, for example, and the extreme nationalist diplomatic historian René Girardet).[87] But those, like Braudel, who may be regarded as belonging to the *Annales* school, do seem to have been prompted in their choice of discipline and topic either by the years between 1940 and 1944, or by the events of what might be deemed France's 'long Second World War' (it is still probably too short a period to be properly defined as a 'conjuncture'). And, somewhere in the story, as likely as not, Braudel himself will also appear in the role of friend, patron, monarch or divine afflatus both of the new history and its adepts.

Take Pierre Chaunu, for example. This brilliant author of a twelve-volume study of the 'Atlantic world' and student of the history of death[88] explains: 'I am a historian because I am the child of death and because the mystery of time has haunted me since infancy.' Chaunu, it turns out, was born, in 1923, in the Côtes de Meuse near the front of the Great War. His childhood, he says, was peopled by the immense dead trees between Metz and Verdun. In this wasteland he constructed his 'historical space. In that space, as in my memory, there would [always] be the war. Everything, whether at Metz or Verdun, every activity which enclosed me was for the war.'[89]

Thereafter his story was more humdrum. He had a soft Second World War; after denying, in 1942, his initial attraction to medicine, that brittle refuge against death, he enrolled as a history student at the normally functioning Sorbonne. He was already developing an interest in social and economic history, and, when the war was over, he met Braudel. . . .[90]

The younger Maurice Agulhon had a not dissimilar tale to tell. His radical republican school-teacher parents made him conscious of his own isolation and membership of an elite, even as they preached about the viciousness of history – 'the *Patrie*, violence and war, detestable things'. This abhorrent past, he now explains virtuously, was that of *histoire événementielle*. Agulhon himself, however, would escape such unfortunate matters for, at a Lyons *lycée*, which he attended from 1943 to 1946 before transferring to the *École Normale Supérieure*, he heard of the ideas of Bloch and the *Annales* through a school-teacher who was also in the Resistance.[91]

Like many of his contemporaries, Agulhon joined the French Communist Party (PCF) after the war, impelled by his family tradition of disciplined leftism and by the inspiration which he had gained from the social ferment of the Resistance. As a young history student he was anxious to study a twentieth-century issue: 'we wished to serve our cause, through a militant science.'[92] At the Sorbonne, he found the conservative Renouvin was the established expert in the contemporary field; most other professional historians derided attempts to understand recent times.[93] It was Ernest Labrousse, a socialist and socio-economic historian and an out-rider of the *Annales,* who managed to persuade Agulhon to commence research on 'the origins of the Republican tradition' in his own region of the Midi. These 'origins' were deemed to have occurred in the previous century and, in pursuit of them, Agulhon, in the French manner, threw himself into years of archival labour. In 1969 he completed his 1,500-page thesis which, by then, had been narrowed down to an exhaustive account of a single department.[94] He had left the PCF in 1960, and had kept in contact with the *Annales*, but remained somewhat anomalous because of his conviction that the nineteenth century was 'the birth of modernity', and because he always retained a political commitment, though it was now toned down to a kind of reformist socialism.

But certainly the most revealing of self-analyses in Nora's book is that by Jacques Le Goff (born 1924). His background was full of contradictions. A pious Catholic mother gave him a firm sense of ethics and of the need for political belief, but as a youth he was more radical than his patriotic parents, supporting the Popular Front, hating Munich, opposing Vichy, and taking to the *maquis* in autumn 1943.

His anger against the collaborationists still smoulders. School-children, he asserts, should be taught that 'Pétain is the greatest blot on the history of France. I learned through him, as did many Frenchmen, how to be bruised in my national being.'[95] After the war, he says, it would have been natural for him, like Agulhon, to have joined the PCF. But, in 1948, he happened to be in Prague studying and returned 'vaccinated'. In any case, he had always had a nagging mistrust of the French Revolution. His schoolboy's sense of precision, order and continuity had, he recalls, been offended by the revolutionaries' tinkering with the calendar.[96] In his eyes, there was no romance in calling months Brumaire or Thermidor but only petty change for change's sake.

Shortly after coming back to Paris, he met Braudel. His recollection of that event is extraordinarily effusive: 'I thus had the joy of entering the promised land and the further joy of discovering that it was an even happier place than I had imagined.' In 1969, Braudel 'gave' him 'one more fabulous gift'. Along with Ferro and Le Roy Ladurie, he was made an editor of *Annales*.[97] By then, through his experience as a historian, he had regained the France which he must have feared had been lost in 1940:

I am more and more persuaded not only that the French possess a privileged, all but neurotic, relationship with their past, but also that the historic spirit has been the principal artisan of the French state and the French nation. France, more than other states and nations, is based on a historical consciousness.[98]

By 1971, Le Goff had become prominent outside France, among those peoples who, he was presumably learning, had a historical consciousness inferior to his own. In the wide-ranging journal *Daedalus*, he published a trenchant exposition of the *Annales* philosophy and method. 'The *Annales* school', he explained, 'loathed the trio formed by political history, narrative history and chronicle or episodic (événementielle) history. All this, for them, was mere pseudohistory, history on the cheap, a superficial affair which preferred the shadow to the substance. . . . Once the backbone of history, political history had sunk to being no more than an atrophied appendix: the parson's nose of history.' Under the magisterial leadership of Braudel, the *Annales* would remain vigilant against the 'old political history' which, with amended metaphor, Le Goff now defined as 'a corpse that has to be made to lie down'.[99]

In retrospect, the year 1971 was an odd and even unfortunate one in which to make these drastic statements. For while the *Annales* had been spreading the gospel of the structure and refreshing the allure of the Middle Ages, the history of the fall of France was still largely ignored. Henry Rousso, the historian of the 'Vichy Syndrome' as he calls it, has provided a very *Annales*-looking graph (Figure 5.1) to plot the historicisation of France's Second World War (though a statistician might be troubled by its scientific base). It shows that, at least after the trial in 1954 of those responsible for the massacre at Oradour, the 'fever' of memory diminished in the French body politic. Its temperature would only rise again to a dangerous

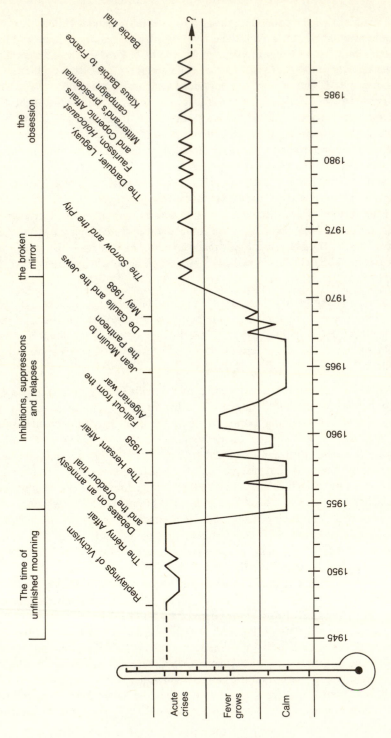

Figure 5.1 The temperature chart of the Vichy Syndrome

Source: after H. Rousso, *Le Syndrome de Vichy (1944–198. . .)*, p. 234.

level in 1971, with the screening in a small Latin-quarter 'art' cinema of a lengthy documentary film. It was entitled *Le Chagrin et la pitié* and was the work of André Harris, Alain de Sédouy and Marcel Ophuls,[100] who in 1967–8 designed it for French TV. But the Gaullist bosses of ORTF refused to take up their first option on the film until 1981 (when François Mitterrand was installed as socialist President of France).[101] With the television outlet blocked, the movie version, ten years earlier, had none the less run for eighty-seven weeks to an audience of 600,000 even though it was denounced, by an ex-member of the Resistance now a Senator of the Republic, as 'destroying myths of which the French still have need'.[102] In the absence of French historians, Marcel Ophuls and his colleagues had done what Pieter Geyl had specified as the first job of the critical historian; they had demolished 'myth in spite of those who did not like it'.[103]

Predictably, Ophuls had had his own reckoning with the Second World War. His father, Max, had been a distinguished film director. Of Jewish extraction, he had left Germany after 1933, and worked both in France and in Fascist Italy. In 1941 he had fled to the USA, taking his young son with him. Under Weimar, in the 1930s, at Hollywood, and back in France in the 1950s, Max Ophüls made a series of romantic comedies and melodramas. Typical among them was *La Ronde* (1950), adapted from a play written by Arthur Schnitzler in pre-1914 'gay Vienna'. As Roy Armes, the historian of the French cinema, has put it: 'for [Max] Ophüls the essence of the cinema lay in the play of light, the juggling with surfaces. . . . The themes of the transitoriness of pleasure and the precariousness of happiness recur again and again, their reappearance emphasised by the continual recourse to dream-world turn-of-the-century settings.'[104] Max Ophüls was one Jew who preferred to situate himself back in a (fake) Vienna and dance to a light Oskar Straus waltz rather than openly confront that path to Auschwitz which other Jews had been forced to take. In making *The Sorrow and the Pity*, Marcel Ophuls was, like many another young European in 1968, asking 'What did you do in the war, Daddy?' and not receiving a very satisfactory reply.

With a fine sense of place, the makers of *Le Chagrin et la pitié* concentrated on the occupation of and the collaboration in Clermont-Ferrand. That central-southern heavy industrial town was the nearest city to Vichy and had a large Michelin plant on its outskirts; Clermont-Ferrand was where Bloch taught at the University of Strasbourg-in-exile (and, for those who like to decode *Astérix* comics, its main square was dominated by a statue of Vercingetorix, while the Plateau de Gergovie, where the Gauls fought their celebrated battle in 52 BC in the high-point of their 'resistance' to the Romans, was nearby and there this first 'French national triumph' was regularly commemorated).[105]

The treatment of collaboration and resistance in the movie has had its critics,[106] most notably the American historian, John Sweets, who, in his own book on 'choices in Vichy France' (which also focuses on Clermont-Ferrand) has remarked that 'although it was a huge success in France and other countries, the film is highly unsatisfactory from a historical perspective. The examples chosen by Ophuls for dramatic or entertainment value often abuse the historical reality beyond recognition.'[107]

Sweets himself seems sometimes to have a rather literal understanding of how to 'read' a movie (or other forms of 'historical evidence'). But the real point about *Le Chagrin et la pitié*, which Sweets fails to underline, is that it must be placed in the context of its making, that is, in the years from 1967 to 1971, and be set among previous French reflections on Vichy and the fall of France.

It is here that Henry Rousso's book is especially useful. Rousso notes how, from the very beginning, the victorious Gaullists were anxious to deny any legitimacy to Vichy and to assert total backing from the French people (and from French history). De Gaulle's speech on 25 August 1944 to liberated Paris, for example, proclaimed that the city had been 'freed by itself, freed by its own people with the support of the armies of France, with the cooperation and support of the whole of France, of the France which fights, of the only France, of the true France, of the eternal France'.[108] To Georges Bidault, then De Gaulle's ally and later his bitter enemy, he put it more succinctly: 'Vichy was always and has remained null and void; it did not happen.'[109]

Without such blank spots, it was soon evident, it would be difficult 'to construct a united national memory' of the Second World War.[110] In striking contrast to the Great War, the cities and villages of France did not ostentatiously commemorate the second conflict,[111] and De Gaulle himself, presaging Nolte or Arno Mayer, slipped easily into talking about the 'thirty years' war'.[112] He could thus embody the *union sacrée* of 1914 and the stoic victories of the Western Front and turn attention away from the disgrace, dishonour and division of the period from 1940 to 1944.

As has already been noted, De Gaulle's ambitions to re-unify and re-nationalise France and to control and harness its history did not satisfy all tastes. Indeed, for more than a decade, the main historical account of France's Second World War was a bland but pro-Vichyite narration published in 1954 by Robert Aron, a moderate conservative Jew.[113] His chief competition as historian of the war, apart from some paleo-Marxists loyal to the PCF, who, predictably, tried to claim the Resistance as their own, was De Gaulle himself in his multi-volume memoirs.[114] But, in 1968, the great man's myth of himself would be challenged and almost overturned in the second European 'revolution of the intellectuals'. It was the spirit of 1968 which was the real genesis of *Le Chagrin et la pitié*. The documentary was certainly pro-Resistance – its least sullied heroes were the appropriately named Grave brothers, socialists, peasants, men of the people, red-blooded fighters, drinkers of red wine, real, serious, visceral resisters. But those interviewed in the film also gave a much more nuanced image of France under occupation than was then accepted by the Gaullist regime. The German *Wehrmacht* captain, Helmut Tausend (who incarnated the Fischerite continuity of German history) recalled that life as an occupier of Clermont-Ferrand, especially when contrasted with that on the Eastern Front, was pleasant. You could get a glass of wine or beer, and the women were not distant, especially at night.[115] Similarly, not all resisters were galahads, *sans peur et sans reproche*. Emmanuel d'Astier de la Vigerie said somewhat tongue-in-cheek: 'I think you could only have joined the Resistance if you were maladjusted.' As he recalled nostalgically, 'it is the only period in my life when I lived in a truly classless society.'[116] Even the volunteer for the French *Waffen SS*, Christian de la Mazière, was not depicted as a simple thug, but as reflecting a genuine and long-standing current of French history.

The real counterpoints to the Grave brothers were two other characters. On the one hand, there was the heavily brilliantined Maurice Chevalier singing his vapidly happy little songs for whoever would pay; on the other, the Clermont-Ferrand pharmacist, Marcel Verdier, a real republican and no friend of the Germans, anxious to stay out of the limelight and keep his and his family's stomachs full and noses clean, an unheroic, sensible and democratic *attentiste*.

In retrospect, it is hard to see why *Le Chagrin et la pitié* caused quite such a fuss. In the main, its theses seem reasonable and right and not presented with the same deliberate provocation with which, a decade before, A.J.P Taylor had assaulted conservative myths about Britain's Second World War. (Anthony Eden is another of the characters of *Le Chagrin et la pitié* and is adroitly permitted to express in his own words, sometimes in French, sometimes in English, the virtues and limitations of being the embodiment of liberal British fair-play.)[117] But, despite Ophuls's apparent preference for letting all sides speak, at least partly, for themselves, censorship, condemnation,[118] and controversy were aroused by his film.

And the controversy continued, although, in 1973, a history book and not a film rekindled passion and debate. Ironically, the book was written by an American, Robert Paxton, a professor at Columbia University. With scrupulous scholarship and lots of footnotes, Paxton argued a case much like that of *Le Chagrin et la pitié* and condemned both the Gaullist line of the naturally united French, apart from a few criminals, resisting to a man and a woman, and Aron's interpretation of Pétain's double-play, which had Vichyites cunningly supping with the Germans while aiming eventually to do them a bad turn.[119] In the face of Paxton's evidence, logic and good sense, one outraged patriot even wondered, in a newspaper review of his book, how such a person could hold down a chair, and huffed and puffed about the temerity of foreigners who interfered in what was the business of the French and the French alone.[120]

But, once begun, the debate was impossible to suppress. By the decade's end, a reform in archive law had given access to some of the documents previously kept hidden. There was a burst of thesis-writing, notably at the *Institut d'histoire du temps présent* where Rousso had a post. After Mitterrand's election, to which the new openness about the past contributed, the Vichy period could for the first time be seriously discussed in French high schools. In 1987 Ophuls screened his documentary of the trial of Klaus Barbie, the SS 'Butcher of Lyons', who had been captured and returned to French justice in 1983. It was a sort of *Sorrow and the Pity 2*[121] and, in 1989, that bicentennial year, rather than provoking alarums and excitation, it won an Oscar as best documentary. Half a century after, France had, in most senses, settled its account with 1940.

Yet there is still something rather unsatisfactory about the current state of French historiography. At the very moment that the history of Vichy has, in some senses, come into its own, French historians, especially those of or near the *Annales,* have been busily deconstructing or destroying the French Revolution. Read François Furet, Mona Ozouf and the rest, consult the new dictionary of the Revolution and you learn that, if it was not the sinister birthtime of 'totalitarian democracy', the French Revolution was little more than an 'event', one of those despised and trumpery moments of 'mere politics'.[122] Its politicians lied and pirouetted in the macabre revolutionary dance but they seldom mattered. A structurated French Revolution will, it seems, no longer exist, and its history will no longer divide the French.

As so often, this newly established historical orthodoxy was expressed most crudely in a film, *Chouans!* made by Philippe de Broca in 1988 as a sort of curtain-raiser for the great and expensive cultural celebrations of the Bicentennial. The movie's topic, the conflict between revolution and counter-revolution in Brittany (and the Vendée) in 1793 and after, seemed full of possibilities. There was a distinguished cast of actors, including Philippe Noiret as the wise old Count de Kerfadec. The story-line sounded epic. The count's legitimate son, Aurèle (a philosopher king in the making?), off in America in 1789 but later returning to fight alongside the peasant *Chouans* for God, King and Country; an adopted son, Tarquin, a child of the people, educated by the benevolence of the count (but perhaps destined to be tyrant, rapist and worse), becomes, after 1789, a revolutionary chief. To this tale of family division was added a love interest – Aurèle and Tarquin were competing for the hand of Céline (also graciously educated by the count). Played by Sophie Marceau, Céline was portrayed as a sort of reconstituted, pouting Brigitte Bardot 2. She must have represented the heavenly body of France!

After much derring-do, the film reaches its dénouement. Philippe Noiret, who, very wise old aristocrat that he is, has invented the airplane a century or so before the Wright Brothers or Blériot, rescues his real son and Céline, pent up in a coastal fortress by the wicked revolutionaries. Knowing that he will be killed, the count sacrifices his own life to cram Aurèle and the girl into the airplane. It takes off and heads out over the sea, to the West, to America (capitalism and free market economics). Awaiting the revenge of the revolutionaries, Philippe Noiret wraps himself in a handily available tricolor, takes as his winding sheet the symbol of French nationality and French history, and . . . *fin.*[123]

Fin, indeed. This cinematic French Revolution has reached a level of confusion and contradiction which it would be hard to exceed. But French historiography in the 1980s and 1990s is similarly characterised by a new complexity and a new uncertainty. Among the *Annales*, most commentators would agree, the third generation has failed to retain the unity and discipline imposed by Braudel.[124] Some critics admit that it may no longer be clear just what composes the '*Annales* method'.[125]

Most interesting in this regard is Marc Ferro, a historian of the Russian Revolution who will be discussed further in chapter 7 and who regards himself as something of an outsider in the *Annales* leadership.[126] Under Ferro's influence, the *Annales* has regularly published articles on 1917 and on Stalinism, on what looks like 'political history', 'events' and the twentieth century. Apart from his work on Russia, Ferro has written about film and war.[127] Where Braudel had asked 'is not the secret aim and underlying motive of history to seek to explain the present?'[128] Ferro was troubled lest history do no more than 'control the past . . . master the present . . . legitimise dominion and . . . justify legal claims'.[129] Generally Ferro softened the totalising ambitions of the *Annales* in order to preach plurality.[130] Recalling his own youthful experience as a teacher in Oran, he has urged a new respect for the history of the Third World. Similarly, for Ferro, life in Algeria built up questions in his mind which he would later seek to answer as a historian of the USSR even though he has also said 'my personal life is never mixed up with [my writing of] history'.[131]

Perhaps under Ferro's influence, these days an issue of *Annales* is likely to carry articles about any part of the globe in any period of time. That eclecticism underlines the triumph of the school's methodological empire but it also reflects its new weakness. Like the Roman Empire of the third century it now has too many borders. The *Annales* retains its prestige as 'the greatest historical journal in the world' but, in the long term and considered structurally, the *Annales* 'French historical revolution', as it has been called, may turn out to be a phantasm. After all, the one article on Vichy published in the journal between 1985 and 1990 began by asking whether it was possible to write the history of a time which was still so fraught with contestation. It ended by asserting 'Vichy est . . . surtout, le fruit de la défaite, le fruit de l' événement, de l'irréductible événement' ('Vichy is . . . above all the fruit of defeat, the fruit of the event, of the inescapable event').[132]

By the time that article was published, Ferro himself had done what once would have been unthinkable; in 1987 he produced a biography of Pétain, enlarging on his view that 'Vichy existed before 1940 just as Nazism did under Weimar', and, indeed, that it represented a species of fascism.[133] (Four years earlier, Ferro had also written a case study of Suez and 'the birth of a third world'.)[134] Now, in the introduction to *Pétain*, Ferro gave a fascinating account of what brought him to that most dangerous topic.

He dedicated the biography to Braudel. Though such a dedication may have seemed anomalous, Ferro explained that it was not. Rather the ex-POW, Braudel, who had never ceased wondering about the origins of the 'strange defeat', had, just before his death, suggested the idea to Ferro saying 'it is necessary at the end to understand everything'. Braudel had also asked, shrewdly, whether his friend and student had found any new documentation. . . .[135]

But Ferro was troubled about venturing into a field where, it seemed, you had to be 'for' or 'against'. A historian, he averred, scientifically situated above the ruck, 'must preserve, make plain, analyse, diagnose. He must never judge.'[136] And yet Ferro himself had once been a fighter in the FFI (the non-communist Resistance). Then, he recalled, he and his fellows hated Laval but they tried not to talk about Pétain. That would have been divisive. Forty years later, as he began his work on Pétain, however, Ferro promised ambitiously, 'I shall hide nothing about him.'[137]

In a sense, Ferro is as good as his word. Largely ignoring the Pétain of the Great War and Third Republic, he narrates the years from 1940 to 1944 in some 600 pages, and then spends another hundred on the story of Pétain's *épuration*. He prefers, in this as in his other books, not to follow the accustomed rules of historical narrative (his practices in that regard may be a legacy of his *Annales* training). The book is crafted as a succession of short, cinematic-like scenes, sometimes including flashbacks, perhaps reflecting Ferro's own interest in film[138] – he himself says he wrote the biography in order to content his publishers when what he really wanted to do was to study the relationship of film and history. Ferro also reviews critically the post-1945 attempts to read a simple moral lesson into Pétain's life. Neither those 'for' nor those 'against' are right. But, hostile as he is to demonisation, Ferro still leans to the 'against' side, accepting what he defines as the 'révolution paxtonienne',[139] and admitting the technocratic, 'modernising' character of Vichy. He argues, further, that Pétain's regime had another characteristic and one with a high cost. In his dealings with the Nazis, Pétain, for all his hope to do otherwise, found 'the price was often the honour of the nation'.[140] Ferro may be right but this is not an especially new, profound, nor subtle conclusion for a representative of the third generation of the *Annales* to draw about those events which had given so much impetus to its cultural empire.

It may be that in concentrating on Ferro, this account of the *Annales* is misleading. Many other leading historians of that school have gone on renewing the history of pre-modern times and fostering 'a return to the Middle Ages'. The best known work in this regard is Emmanuel Le Roy Ladurie's *Montaillou*, first published in 1975 and a best-seller all over the world. It is easy to tell that it is written by one of the editors of the *Annales*, given its awareness of anthropology, geography and the other social sciences. Although it is a case study of a small French village in the Pyrenees for only a thirty-year period (1294–1324), it uncovers such grandiose matters as the *mentalité* of the local peasantry, their body language and sexuality, their concepts of love and death, of time and space, of the divine and the human. It is a beautiful book, though its sales must also have been helped by its implicit nostalgia for the peasant 'world we have lost' and the splendid, if sexist, character of one of the book's protagonists, the priest, Pierre Clergue, who emerges from the Inquisitional records as possessed of an 'irrepressible libido'. Le Roy Ladurie tells of Pierre's 'dozen authenticated mistresses' (including his own sister-in-law) in a 'list [which] is certainly incomplete'.[141]

But *Montaillou* should also be contrasted with another, and, on the surface, a very similar and equally delightful book, *The Cheese and the Worms: The Cosmos of a Sixteenth-Century Miller*. Its author is the Italian historian, Carlo Ginzburg, himself an insightful critic of the *Annales* and the son of a Jewish intellectual martyred in the Italian Resistance. Like *Montaillou*, *The Cheese and the Worms* is based on the archives of the Inquisition. Like Le Roy Ladurie, Ginzburg eschews the traditional historian's narrative style and is aware of the fraternal social sciences. But Ginzburg's book has one plain hero, Menocchio the miller.[142]

However, Menocchio is a very different historical personage from Pierre Clergue. The miller is a natural resister; he does not believe what he is told; he struggles to express his own humanity, to look for a time of liberty, equality and fraternity, which will foreshadow living in a 'truly classless society' or in love and charity with his neighbours. He is an activist. The priest, by contrast, for all his charm and slyness, is more passive. He wants the authorities to stay out of his life but his real preference is to eat, drink and be merry. Like Maurice Chevalier, he thanks heaven for little girls. He is a natural *attentiste* but he will collaborate if he must and while he can.

This is a notable distinction. For all the *Annales'* manifold achievement, by the 1970s what Fukuyama would later call the 'end of history' (i.e. 'depoliticisation', the 'end of ideologies', the victory of one and only one, capitalist-democratic understanding of the past) was widespread in a post-modernist France which remained so anxious to forget the terrible events of 1940 to 1944. In the 1980s, this hoped-for oblivion was further reinforced under the presidency of François Mitterrand, that socialist *sans doctrine*[143] or second 'sphinx without a riddle' to attain an eminent position in national political history. In 1981, Mitterrand, POW, escapee and resister,[144] seemed to the more joyous of his supporters to embody 'the spirit of the Resistance' and to promise a restoration of meaning to liberty, equality and fraternity. A decade later it is hard to be so sanguine. A France, without a Revolution contested by a Counter-Revolution, without a Resistance struggling against a Collaboration, and with those endless historical debates finally quietened, might promise to become a less and not a more democratic place. It might feebly accept Braudel's final summary of the future: 'France will, alas, have to undergo its destiny rather than choosing it, I fear.'[145]

That recipe for a pessimism of the will was, in Braudel's opinion, simply justified. As he put it in the last words of his last book: 'men do not make history, rather it is history above all that makes men and thereby absolves them of blame.'[146] In the *longue durée,* even 'Auschwitz' and 'Hiroshima' do not require judgement and *attentisme* is the best policy. But for those who wish to avert a collapse into a time of consensus, a time of indifference, and who believe that liberty and equality are best defended and extended by an eternal vigilance, an eternal and self-critical optimism of the will, and by an eternal re-assertion that men and women indeed make their own history and are responsible for it, a saying of Marc Ferro might inspire greater comfort: 'It is the heart of liberty [equality and real fraternity] to allow several historical traditions to co-exist and even to fight it out.'[147]

6

The eclipse of anti-Fascism in Italy

In 1976, Carlo Ginzburg or Menocchio might still invoke the spirit of the Resistance. At that time, Italian culture and Italian historiography seemed, at first glance, as anomalous as did Italian politics. This last was characterised by an idiosyncratic multi-party system in which one short-lived government swiftly succeeded another, though their personnel usually remained the same and the central party, the Christian Democrats (DC), had held office uninterruptedly since the war.[1] Italy was also *sui generis* in possessing the West's largest Communist Party, the PCI. In the national elections of June 1976, more than one in three Italians voted for this party which boasted proudly of its incorruptibility, efficiency, moderation, independence and good sense. With its vote at a record high, the PCI already controlled large parts of Italian local and regional administration and had made the elegant and prosperous city of Bologna, site of one of the oldest universities in the world, its special show-case.[2] To the dismay of the US Government[3] and other anti-communist forces outside Italy, the PCI appeared destined soon to join a coalition government in Rome. To prophets both optimistic and pessimistic, the PCI seemed to have entered a process of legitimation like that through which, in the late 1960s, the SPD had obtained respectability and office in West Germany. Certainly Aldo Moro, renowned as the most canny of DC tacticians, and a politician who, a decade and a half previously, had stage-managed the legitimising of the Italian Socialist Party (PSI) in the so-called 'Opening to the Left', had accepted the inevitable. The second half of the 1970s, he assumed, was time for the PCI.[4]

Fifteen years later, these prophesies seem misguided and these assumptions false. The time when it was the time of the PCI can now only dimly be remembered. Moro, cold-bloodedly slain by Red Brigade terrorists in May 1978 after two months of cruel and humiliating imprisonment, is dead.[5] So, too, is the PCI at least in the sense that, in early 1991, it sloughed off its name and metamorphosised into the nebulous 'Party of the Democratic Left'. It had already lost a third of those voters which it had attracted in 1976 and the pundits of today foresee its further decay and possible demise. Though, in many ways, Italian politics remain distinctive, the organisation which gave Italy its most obvious claim to uniqueness and made Italy most like a 'border state', a not totally reliable or necessarily permanent member of 'the West', has been destroyed. As this process took effect, the PCI surrendered its future and its past (and Carlo Ginzburg, for one, distanced himself from too overt a political commitment).[6] By 1990, even Menocchio might have had to agree with Fukuyama that, in Italy, history was at an end.

A decade and a half earlier, the PCI seemed to have many things going for it. In Antonio Gramsci, it possessed a modern patron saint, a lay Saint Francis of Assisi (or 'the Marxist you can take home to mother', as an American commentator unkindly dubbed him).[7] Ever since the Second World War, Gramsci's allegedly humanist Marxism had been extraordinarily useful to the Communists (and the release onto the cultural market of his wide-ranging *Prison Notebooks* had been carefully stage-managed by them).[8] Gramsci, the martyr to Fascism – his judges had been told to stop his mind working for twenty years – had been cleansed of any potential Stalinist corruption by being penned in a Fascist gaol for the decade before his death in 1937. In that calvary, he became the progenitor of the Resistance, the philosopher of revolution by consent, the historian who indicated the special path which could lead the Italian people from the ambiguity of the incomplete revolution of the Risorgimento (the '*rivoluzione mancata*') through the valley of tears of Fascism to the upland of the present republic and its potentially luminous future. Gramsci, or those disciples who took charge of his writings after his death, had charted the *via italiana al socialismo* (the Italian way to socialism).[9]

Although Gramsci was the PCI's figurehead in the 1970s, the party asserted that its title to a future was posited on a more general claim to the past. The PCI had roots; the PCI had a history – before its formal beginning in schism with the Socialists in 1921, before 1917 and the Russian Revolution, before the foundation of the Italian Socialist movement. The PCI was a part, a natural part, even the best part of a timeless history of the Italian people and the Italian nation.

Thus, the PCI's 1976 election slogan became 'venuto da lontano' (come from afar). In fact this phrase had been cribbed from a speech by Palmiro Togliatti, Gramsci's machiavellian successor as PCI leader (1927–64).[10] In that original speech, Togliatti had said aloud what the PCI now mentioned in less stentorian tones, perhaps because, though they wanted political legitimation in a coalition with the DC, it was becoming less plain what they would actually do in office. But, for Togliatti, in the simpler days of the recent defeat of Fascism, it was precisely because the PCI had come from afar that it had far to go and could aspire to a destination certainly of power and perhaps of revolution. So long as the PCI possessed a past, he had pronounced, it would have a future.

For the enemies of the PCI, this proclamation of a usable past bespoke manipulation on a grand scale. The enveloping menace of communism and Italy's other woes they ascribed to what they called 'the official culture of anti-Fascism'. For the Communists and their dupes, they said, it was convenient to label their opponents and critics 'Fascists'.[11] Italy's present, they argued, was jarred by a misconstruction of Italy's past and, especially, by a misrepresentation of the Fascist era and of Italy's 'long Second World War'. Such anti-anti-Fascists quailed when a historian like Leo Valiani, a Socialist rather than a Communist, a Jew who had indeed resisted Fascism, now a Senator and a man of respect, declared that Fascism was identical with Nazism and that the Fascist peril persisted. He had been glad, Valiani went on, that the spirit of anti-Fascism had, in 1960, been mobilised to defeat the Tambroni Government,[12] a DC attempt to avert the Opening to the Left through alliance with the neo-Fascist MSI (the Italian Social Movement). Such mobilisation, he warned, might again be necessary to deflect the abidingly malevolent fascist purpose and he rejoiced that, in Italy, the spirit of the Resistance still wandered where it wist.[13] Valiani and many another self-consciously anti-Fascist historian remained determined and even ostentatious partisans of a Second World War which had never ended. The 'generation of the Resistance', they maintained, bore a historic consciousness essential for all subsequent Italian endeavours.[14]

If Valiani or the PCI were to be believed, Italy had historicised its 'long Second World War' in a unique fashion. In Britain, Germany and France, the first interpretations of the tumultuous recent past had been conservative in character and had only slowly been countered by the revisionism of such left-wing critics as A.J.P. Taylor, Fritz Fischer and Marcel Ophuls. In Italy, by contrast, it seemed that it was the Left which, in the post-war years, had crafted the most pervasive 'myth of the war experience'. It was the Left's comprehension of the Italian 'Auschwitz' which held historiographical and political sway. But was Italian historiography really as unusual as it seemed? And if it was, how was that version of the past which seemed established in 1976 so utterly overthrown by the 1990s?

Italy had, of course, endured a very lengthy inter-war crisis. In Italy, liberty had had to bow the knee to nationality and to tyranny as early as October 1922, when Benito Mussolini, the Fascist *Duce*, obtained power through a characteristic mixture of political jockeying and the threat of armed might. Mussolini, the first Fascist and the only one to hold office for a generation, would go on ruling Italy until he was captured and killed by Communist members of the Resistance in April 1945.

Despite this evident durability and apparent achievement, the *Duce*, as far as many foreign commentators have been concerned, could be dismissed as 'Dictator Minor'. His regime, they said, had a somewhat farcical air, its pretensions to totalitarianism were false, its body count could not begin to match those of Hitler or Stalin. Though doubtless a Fascist, Mussolini was no more than a 'sawdust Caesar'.[15] As A.J.P. Taylor, who seems never to have forgotten why, in 1945, he argued that Trieste should be assigned to what he believed were the real partisans of Yugoslavia, put it caustically in *The Origins of the Second World War*:

> Fascism never possessed the ruthless drive, let alone the material strength, of National Socialism. Morally it was just as corrupting – or perhaps more so from its very dishonesty. Everything about Fascism was a fraud. The social peril from which it saved Italy was a fraud; the revolution by which it seized power was a fraud; the ability and policy of Mussolini were fraudulent. Fascist rule was corrupt, incompetent, empty; Mussolini himself a vain, blundering boaster without either ideas or aims.[16]

In the 1970s this interpretation was repeated and refurbished by Denis Mack Smith, the great English radical historian of the Risorgimento, who had directed his pen less persuasively onto the Fascist era.[17]

Italians, perhaps rightly, feared that this Anglo-Saxon derision for Mussolini carried vestiges of those nineteenth-century racial theoretics which had assigned Italians, or, at least, the 'Mediterranean race', such a lowly place in the world. Italians were inclined to talk with more gravity and circumspection about the Fascist repression of political parties, socialist and Catholic trade unions, the press, liberal values and much else. They recalled the Fascist beatings, gaolings, or outright murder of such critics as the socialists Giacomo Matteotti and Carlo and Nello Rosselli, the liberals Giovanni Amendola and Piero Gobetti, the Catholic Don Giovanni Minzoni, the Communist Gramsci and numerous members of his party's rank and file. They regretted Fascist violence and Fascist war.

On this final topic, anti-Fascist Italian and foreign interpretations of Mussolini could generally re-unite. Italy, though still the least of the Great Powers, had played a highly significant role in the approach of the Second World War. Fascist Italy had set an already anxious world awry with its cruel invasion of Ethiopia in 1935–6, with its pitiless use of poison gas, and with the callous boasting by members of Mussolini's family and entourage about the beauty of watching, from the safety of the air, bombs tear apart Ethiopian villages and Ethiopian lives. Thereafter, Mussolini's Italy continued to disturb the good order of Europe. Fascist Italian 'volunteers' had gone to help Franco in Spain, though the volunteering was usually compulsory and the Spanish neither liked nor admired their Italian aides.[18] On Good Friday 1939, Italy had invaded Albania, adding that unstable Balkan kingdom to the Fascist Empire either out of jealousy at Hitler's triumphs or because Mussolini's son-in-law, Foreign Minister Galeazzo Ciano, hoped to make a financial killing. By that time, too, Fascist Italy had introduced anti-Semitic legislation and it was gradually extended by a *Duce* who had once mocked racism as a barbarous German disease. Most Italians disliked this legislation and did their best to avoid its provisions but, at least in 1943–5 during the so-called 'Salò Republic', many Fascists did Hitler's work for him in assembling and transporting to the death camps both Italian Jews and those of their co-religionists who had taken refuge in Fascist Italy.[19]

In most of the historiography, it was the war, then, which especially damned Fascism and its fellow-travellers. In Greece, in Ethiopia, in North Africa, on the peninsula itself, in every factory and piazza, defeat had followed defeat, both for Fascism and for the Italian nation state. As with Caporetto in the First World War, the loss was not merely military but social. Which country's economy was unprepared for war and which alone did not grow under war's demands? Which populace regarded bombing as a reason for surrender rather than for stiffening morale and fighting on? Which country's soldiers were the most ruthlessly exploited and derided by its major ally? Which rulers botched an attempt to change sides, leaving the King, Prime Minister and military chief to flee the capital city without telling the citizens or even the Ministry of Foreign Affairs that they were going? Which relatively weak country challenged the might of a United States that, for two generations, had been the dearly sought venue of emigrants pursuing their 'foreign policy of the poor', and thus required that Fascist soldiers war against 'paradise'?[20] The answer is always Italy.

The only major European state whose vanquishing is comparable with Italy is France and, as has already been noted, the French Republic had the great advantage, at least for after-the-event explanations, of losing militarily in a single campaign. If ever a country had reached '*Anno Zero*' in 1945, it was Italy.[21] At that time of defeat and degradation, the Italian nation state seemed to lack a past, a present and a future.

But what part had history played in driving Italy to such a predicament? And did the war, Fascism and the Resistance really mark a historiographical caesura after which the Republic, voted into existence in 1946, would be constructed on a radically novel reading of its past, one which would be crafted by Italian anti-Fascists?

The history of Italian history before 1945 has some parallels with that of Germany. Each nation state was, after all, an essentially new creation. Neither a German nor an Italian domain with the borders in existence after 1870 had ever existed before. But this novelty, this revolutionary break in European state systems, was cloaked by an appeal to the past, by the forging of a lineage which began in the mists of time, and by that recourse to public history which Eric Hobsbawm has so well denominated the 'invention of tradition'.[22] In this imagining of an Italian community, intellectuals assumed a special role, if only in the hope that the liberal state would give recognition to their talents and opportunity for their political and economic advantage.

Romantic poet, Ugo Foscolo, had bequeathed a slogan to his nation: 'Italians, look to your histories.'[23] Prophet of the nation, Giuseppe Mazzini, had proclaimed that the Risorgimento or rising again of Italy was underpinned both by geographical determinism – God had made it the best defined country in Europe – and by historical inevitability. Italians, he averred, cleaved together through their belief in a common origin and a common end. Past created present and future; history was indissolubly linked to contemporary behaviour as the new man, the new national man, the new Italian man, combined thought and action. 'In Rome', Mazzini wrote portentously in 1871, 'great memories have ever been the germs of new life.' Now that Rome had been 'restored' as Italy's capital, Roman Italians should preach the 'gospel of civilization' for a 'third time' and shortly set out to 're-conquer' the Trentino, Istria and Nice.[24] In more humdrum hands Mazzini's preachings turned into what has been defined as the '*rivoluzione nazionale*' (national revolution) interpretation of the Risorgimento.[25] Italy had been created because of its populace. The Italian masses had won liberty and nationality; equality could not be far behind.

In the next generation, Italian historians continued to pile up evidence for this version of the events of national unification. However they could not emulate the fame accorded to contemporary poets and philosophers[26] and they had no Rankes or Treitschkes in their midst. To the regret of some conservative post-Fascist commentators, the liberal era signally failed to mark out a *Sonderweg* which might lead the 'Third Italy' from past to future. So clear-sighted a figure as Giustino Fortunato, a liberal southern landowner and intellectual, always half-fearful that his illiterate peasants would burst into his study, murder him and burn his books, was left to advise a friend ironically: 'Let's bless unification . . . and forget the past.'[27]

In the new century, this apparent lack of a national mission, this uneasy sense that liberal Italy had shallow historical roots, increasingly obsessed Italian intellectuals. For many, the best solution to this deficiency was to ignore what they deemed the sullen, divided and imponderable peasantry of the 'Italies' and argue instead that, in Italy and the world, in past and present, only men of ideas mattered. There may not have been an 'Italian people' before 1860, but there had been Italian intellectuals. The sociologists and political scientists, Vilfredo Pareto and Gaetano Mosca, and the historian–philosopher, Benedetto Croce, pronounced that both future and past belonged to such active minorities. Any who surveyed the Italian past, Croce advised, 'must not give primacy to the negative element, to the inert and reluctant mass (which exists in every people, and in southern Italy was perhaps still more inert and heavy and reluctant than elsewhere), but to the active element, to that intellectual class which represented the developing nation and which alone was truly the nation.' The highest creations of this active element were ideas. And, he went on, among these ideas, the most pressing requirement was history: 'Neither individuals nor peoples can live without a myth of their past, present, and future potentialities.'[28] But, where could a 'real' history be found? That, for Croce and others, was the rub.

Responding to the question of how to locate a usable past and then how to deploy it in order fully to nationalise the Italian masses was so difficult that some new-generation intellectuals tried to reject history altogether. For them, Italy's special claim to fame would lie in deriding the past and in focusing only on the future. The fragile and highly self-conscious cleverness of the Futurists instructed them to abandon the Sisyphean task of building bridges from past to future. Unlike their *fin de siècle* colleagues in Germany, they would not practise the politics of cultural despair or be tempted by reactionary modernism. Their modernity, at least rhetorically, would be honest enough to eschew all those fake historical references:

> Italy has been too long the great second-hand market. We want to get rid of the innumerable museums which cover it with innumerable cemeteries. Museums, cemeteries! Truly identical in their sinister juxtaposition of bodies that do not know each other. . . . Indeed, daily visits to museums, libraries and academies (those cemeteries of wasted effort, calvaries of crucified dreams, registers of false starts!) is for artists what prolonged supervision by the parents is for intelligent young men, drunk with their own talent and ambition. . . . Let the good incendiaries with charred fingers come! Here they are! Heap up the fire to the shelves of the libraries! Divert the canals to flood the cellars of the museums![29]

123

But sundering a nation from its history was not as easy as the Futurists assumed. Preparing to enter and then participating in a world war were rather more serious activities than penning wicked or delicious lines, and cried out for historical justification, especially if, as philosopher Giovanni Gentile (later a Fascist) proclaimed, intervention in the war meant 'Italy's entry into the great history of the world'.[30] Service in the alpine trenches of Monte Grappa or on the barren plateau of the Carso gave Italians a First World War as terrible as that of Flanders or of Eastern Europe (though the unreality of Italy's pretensions to have entered the historiography of the world is evidenced by the cavalier manner in which commentators on the war still avoid reference to its Southern Front).[31] The defeat at Caporetto made the war even worse, not so much because of its military[32] as for its social causes and consequences. When, in 1917–18, a considerable section of Friuli and the Veneto fell into Austrian hands, the civil authorities, the representatives of Italian state and Italian history, fled. Nor, though the fact has been long hidden, did the local populace, the *paesani* (villagers) of the Italies, mind much. Priests emerged as the natural leaders of their communities; peasants went about their business, especially happy if the landowners had disappeared along with the *sindaco* (mayor) and *carabinieri* (police).[33] In this as in other instances, the *contadini* were still connected with a past, but it was their own, not that of the Italian nation state.

Nevertheless, as far as Italian culture is concerned, what is most interesting about Italy's First World War is its unchanged reputation as a 'good war'. As Martin Clark has noted, a whole generation, Fascist and anti-Fascist alike, drew their patriotic credentials from it.[34] They did so through their special version of history, because the war for *sacro egoismo* was more grandiosely represented as the 'Fourth War of the Risorgimento'. It was another, greater, *rivoluzione nazionale*. And this interpretation would prove extraordinarily durable. With the exception of the belated and idiosyncratic *Brigata di Sassari* of Emilio Lussu, there was no inter-war Italian equivalent of the great anti-war literature of Hašek or Remarque, Barbusse or Sassoon.[35] Similarly, after 1945, no Italian historian followed Fritz Fischer's example in probing the possible continuity between Liberal and Fascist foreign policy, even though there can be no doubt that Liberal politicians deliberately chose to take Italy into the war in May 1915.[36] And Rosario Romeo, the most technically able of Italy's non-Marxist historians of the post Second World War period, hailed the First War as 'the greatest triumph in our history'.[37] It is hard to imagine a serious historian from any other of the participants in the First World War coming then to so cheerful or so brazen a conclusion.

Italy's First World War was, of course, rapidly followed by a return to international reality and humiliation at Versailles, by class conflict and political turmoil, and by Fascism. How did the Italian historical profession react to Fascist dictatorship? The answer to the question is contested. For Renzo De Felice and the anti-Marxist faction of current Italian historiography, Fascism attempted to control culture, but Italy's historians and other intellectuals were too resilient and subtle for this supervision ever to be complete. The special symbol of Fascist interference was Cesare De Vecchi di Val Cismon, the ex-Quadrumvir and war hero, who, through Mussolini's personal fiat, policed the Italian history profession in the 1930s.[38] In 1933 De Vecchi became president of the *Società nazionale per la storia del Risorgimento* and thus took editorial charge over one of Italy's leading academic journals, the *Rassegna storica del Risorgimento* which, through the infusion of Fascist finance, was given a major uplift.[39] De Vecchi, who had always remained a monarchist, had been promoted to Minister of National Education and in that capacity instituted separate chairs in the history of the Risorgimento at several Italian universities.[40] The new professors, he hoped, would re-assert the natural relationship between the Savoy dynasty and Fascism, past and present.

There were some ambiguities here, but, for the De Feliceans, the real point is that De Vecchi lacked the concentration and intellectual skill to hone historiography into a sleek Fascist weapon. Indeed his reliance on such eminent historians as Gioacchino Volpe, who all admit had become a 'great manager of the culture of the regime',[41] meant that, apart from occasional verbal sallies and the sacking of some Jews after the introduction of the 1938 racial legislation, the Fascists were harnessed by the experts rather than vice versa.[42] According to De Felice, Volpe, as *padrone* of the Fascist historical profession, presided over a cultural 'free zone'.[43] And even De Vecchi could on occasion express views apparently at odds with a totalitarian state, as for example in November 1934, when he launched the *Giunta centrale degli studi storici* by stating his preference for 'an absolutely scientific profundity in investigation and analysis, a detailed and wide-ranging study of the archives, publication of such research with the same meticulous care for any historical period, including the most recent, [and] a serene and fearless critique.' Such an approach was possible, he said, because 'Italy does not have and never has had need of history written "by decree".'[44]

Most commentators would interpret these words as pious platitudes which did not reflect De Vecchi's genuinely Fascist intentions. But who were his opponents? Who were Italy's anti-Fascist historians? For some, the antithesis of De Vecchi's crudity and corruption was the liberal Croce. He was the most praiseworthy representative of anti-Fascism and personal voice of Italy's liberal humanist traditions. He kept the light of liberty burning by his insistence on avoiding the nationalist contamination.[45] Far more than the blood-stained partisans of 1943–5, or the quarrelling *fuorusciti* (exiled intellectuals and politicians), he was the real Resister.[46]

A more critical assessment of Croce is certainly possible and has been enunciated most succinctly by Mack Smith. For him, Croce's life in his elegant and comfortable palace in Naples is a symbol of his elevation above the ruck perhaps of Italian politics and certainly of Italian life and makes him the bearer of less ideal traditions than is often assumed.[47] Croce's pessimism – war, he opined, is inevitable from time to time[48]; 'the party which governs us or misgoverns us always turns out to be the same party'[49] – and his aristocratic disdain – Fascism, he would say after its fall, was a 'parenthesis' in Italian history, it was not worthy of study, it pained him (gave him '*fastidio*') – made him more an a-Fascist than someone who actively contributed to the downfall of the regime.[50]

If Croce's role in Fascist Italy can be questioned, there is much more reason to be doubtful of the *curriculum vitae* of such a mainstream inter-war historian as Gioacchino Volpe. It is typical of the new conservatism of recent, 'lay', Italian historiography, that Volpe has been experiencing a major revival. His books have been republished by a family publishing house. He has been widely praised as the greatest historian of his generation, an Italian Meinecke or Marc Bloch, who was alert to the '*Annales* revolution', and knew, well before Fritz Fischer or Eckart Kehr, all about the 'primacy of internal politics' and had even prefigured George Mosse's ideas about the 'nationalisation of the masses'.[51] But these claims are exaggerated and underplay the extent to which Volpe was committed to Fascism and was indeed an exemplar of the strengths and weaknesses of that regime. Separating Fascists and a-Fascist nationalists in Mussolini's Italy is as taxing a task as judging whether Croce's intellectual resistance was the equal of those who took up armed struggle against Fascism.

Mario Isnenghi, a contemporary historian, has noted that, for many intellectuals, the best meeting place amid the diverse currents of Fascism lay in 'patriotism', even though that patriotism was now 'more resentful and verbose than in the past'.[52] Isnenghi's language is indirect. But what he hints at was true. Italian intellectuals in general and the historical profession in particular saw little wrong with many aspects of Fascism and especially with its foreign policy. In 1935–6 they were sure enough that the Ethiopian adventure was 'Mussolini's masterpiece', to use De Felice's controversial definition. Even Croce donated his Senator's gold medal to assist the national and imperial cause. Younger figures like Federico Chabod readily allowed themselves to be swept away by patriotic fervour as Fascist troops stormed into Addis Ababa. The anti-Semitic legislation of 1938–9 was more questionable – it was so blatantly tyrannous, capricious, unscientific and uncouth. Worse, it could readily seem a humiliating mimicking of Nazi Germany, evidence of national weakness. But perhaps it could be explained away as meant only for domestic consumption, as meaningless as those Fascist party games of the later 1930s when balding and paunchy hierarchs leaped over bayonets or through fiery hoops for the benefit of the masses or the camera, seeking thus to inspire the Fascist 'new man'.

But the acid test certainly of the Italian and Fascist state and perhaps of the Italian historical profession came, in June 1940, with entry into the Second World War. Was this intervention a matter only of a dictator's murderous obsession or caprice? Did the decision and the responsibility lie, as Churchill, the first 'intentionalist', maintained (for highly politic reasons), with 'one man alone'?[53] Or was the Second World War, as some propagandists with historical training claimed, the 'Fifth War for the Risorgimento', and a destined part of a necessary historical process? Was it the culmination of Italian history and Italian historiography? Was there a special Italian version of the Second World War?

If Nazi Germany was, to many a member of the Italian Establishment and to Mussolini himself, a somewhat disagreeable friend, the liberal democracies of Britain and France were by no means unpleasing enemies. Italy's historians can be

126

read as preparing for a war against them in a way that is partially comparable with the *Ostforscher* 'planning' of Germany's drive to the East. Take Volpe, for example, firm in his chair at Rome University and in his leading role in the Fascist Academy.[54] Volpe had become the most senior Italian figure in the institutionalisa- tion of history which occurred between the wars. In that capacity he had no time for League of Nations-style liberal internationalism and pacifism, his Fascist eyes seeing the world with a greater clarity and realism. Italy should play its due part in international historical conferences and he himself should remain a worthy member of international historical associations, but Italian history, he reiterated, must stay in Italian hands.

But Volpe's actions and ideas also had more direct implications for foreign policy. From 1925, he fostered the *Archivo storico di Corsica* and in January 1939 he chose to publish his *Storia della Corsica italiana* which, though moderate in tone, hailed Corsica as Italy's 'lost child' at precisely the moment that Fascist agitators were demanding that Tunis, Nice, Savoy, Djibouti and Corsica be brought home to the Italian *Reich*.[55] In 1935 Volpe blessed the precursors of Empire[56] and in June 1939 praised the creation of the *Centro di studi per l'Albania*.[57] His speeches frequently applauded the greatness of the *Duce* and enthused over every Italian nationalist achievement or prospect, urging, for example, that emigrants be saved from assimilation into their countries of adoption and instead be re-unified in their *italianità* by such bodies as the *Fasci all'estero*.[58] From time to time, he argued that Malta, Nice, Dalmatia, Tunis, Alexandria and the rest of Egypt were Italian lands. Without a sense of history, he said, a statesman was a nullity.[59] Though certainly not a practising anti-Semite, Volpe can also be found admitting that he preferred to avoid Jewish colleagues.[60] His apologists have stated that, by 1939, Volpe tended to ignore what he regarded as the sillier intrusions by the Fascist Party into his life and to downplay the party's historic specificity.[61] That he could be so independent is not a sign of his a-Fascism however, but rather that he was powerful enough to defend his own version of Fascism.

For what is most important about Volpe, and about the great academic institu- tions of Fascist Italy to which he was patron and adviser – the *Enciclopedia italiana,* the *Istituto per gli studi di politica internazionale* (financed from 1934 by Pirelli in Milan) or the *Dizionario di politica,* was not his or their ideological position on this, that, or the other Fascist policy or ambition. Rather it is the vaguer and more general influence they exerted. Volpe, in ironical agreement with his enemy Croce, preached that all history was contemporary history, while emphasising that the true purpose of the subject was to justify the present national cause.[62] Furthermore, Volpe asserted, and Walter Maturi, Augusto Torre, Federico Chabod, A.M. Ghisalberti[63] and others of his students seem to have believed him, that this is a wicked world. To survive an iron realism was needed, a realism which, if circum- stances demanded, might mean alliance in war with Nazi Germany. And, by cheerfully or fatalistically embracing this sort of cynicism or practicality, the Italian historical profession had become actors in a sub-plot of those tragedies which set the calendar of the Italian nation state at *anno zero* in 1945.

The disasters of the war, and the violent conflict on the Italian peninsula itself between Anglo-American forces and the Germans and, especially, between one (puppet) Italian regime and another after September 1943, cried out for historical explanation. Perhaps they did so all the more insistently because, as Isnenghi has argued provocatively, there had been a shared vocabulary in the war of words, because the ideals proclaimed by Salò *repubblichino* Nazi-fascist and communist, liberal, socialist or catholic partisan, were so similar. Each side killed or died for *Patria, Italia, Nazione, Popolo, Risorgimento,* Garibaldi and Mazzini. 'Neither during the war of independence nor at the moment of intervention in 1915, nor in any other phase of its post-unification national life', Isnenghi concludes, 'had the word *Italy* ever mobilised so much civic passion and active participation.' Italian history might have arrived at *Anno Zero* but, whether knowing it or not, the participants in this 'Italian civil war' did have a mutual past.[64]

Isnenghi's use of the term 'civil war' now bespeaks a conservative revisionism in which violent and murderous Fascists are scarcely distinguished from violent and murderous resisters. But, in the immediate aftermath of the conflict, Volpe, whose current devotees like to claim was the only intellectual purged because of his Fascism, had already endeavoured to write off the Resistance as 'a bloody story of civil war'.[65] By contrast Pietro Silva, an a-Fascist who had made a successful career in the inter-war period but had remained a conservative monarchist sufficiently uncontaminated to have his classically 'realist' textbooks still used in Italian schools in the 1960s, revived an older refrain. *Professore* Mussolini, Silva said, for all the pomposity of his title, was not a real intellectual. As a leader his lack of 'cultivation' had unleashed the 'crudity' of the people, who, ultimately, were the ones to blame.[66]

Few went as far as this in exculpation. Rather, especially in the last stages of the war, many historians and other intellectuals participated in one part or other of the Resistance, sometimes no doubt out of self-interest but also with a genuine sense of the need for expiation either of the misdeeds of the Fascist era or of the humiliating character of Italy's military defeat. At the same time they often retained a firm sense of their own importance. Because they were men of ideas, they remained the best and the brightest of Italian society. As Giaimè Pintor, himself a martyr in the Resistance, would express it in his posthumously published diary: 'Italy is born [again] through the thought of a few intellectuals.'[67]

A typical exemplar of this perceived need to merge thought and action in the way that Mazzini had once advised was the young historian, Enrico Serra. His social and cultural background was orthodox; as an aspirant expert in international affairs, he had sought to work closely with Chabod and ISPI, but had also served his nation in war, being wounded in a tank while fighting for Fascism in North Africa. After September 1943, he discerned the genocidal character of the SS and joined the Resistance, associating with Valiani and Ferruccio Parri, leader of the highly intellectual *Partito d'Azione* (Action Party) and destined to be Prime Minister for a few short months in 1945. In his memoirs, Serra recounts his admiration for Parri and his gratitude that this politician ensured the rapid re-establishment of a post-Fascist ISPI, which, Serra averred, would thereafter act as necessary counter-weight to Italians' natural parochialism.[68]

If many intellectuals sought to re-state liberal values of some kind, others including Delio Cantimori, De Felice's teacher and not uncritical first patron, became Communists. In the 1930s Cantimori had written for Fascism but he had disliked the German alliance and rejected anti-Semitism. By the end of the war, he had switched his allegiance to the PCI and would duly support it in the post-war years. He was, however, dismayed by the naked display of Soviet imperialism in Hungary and, as a result, along with a number of Italian intellectuals (and the young De Felice) left the PCI before his death in 1966.[69] Cantimori's discipline had given him more consistent comfort than had his political commitments. History, he had advised in a characteristic phrase, was like parsley: 'It should be taken with everything.'[70] Its essential scepticism gave piquancy to what might otherwise be the incoherence of real life.

Perhaps it was the complex nature of his own *curriculum vitae* which made Cantimori relish this recipe. But, any individuals apart, because the Resistance contained so many diverse currents the meaning of its history was always destined to be contested. The PCI, whose cadres had undoubtedly been the most numerous, best organised and toughest of the fighting partisans, though sometimes with mixed motives, was particularly anxious to assert its seniority and superiority in opposing Mussolini,[71] and to proclaim that the soul of the Resistance must go marching on. Veterans of the *Partito d'Azione*, by contrast, blamed Communist cynicism for the failure of Parri's Government and declared that it was they who best expressed the spiritual values of anti-Fascism. Catholic and socialist commentators, too, sought to demonstrate that their movements had donated blood and ideas to the cause and that they constituted anti-Fascism's best elements.

In these circumstances, despite the size and significance of the Italian Resistance and its frequent recalling in post-war political and cultural discourse, it is not astonishing to find that the history of Italian history after 1945 was less anomalous than is sometimes alleged. Indeed, the first reaction to the immediate past had often been that numbness and silence which has already been described in other combatant societies. One example of this desire to deny or ignore Mussolini was Croce's statement that Fascism had been no more than a 'parenthesis' and did not belong to Italy's 'real history'. But a more typical way of transmuting or fudging the history of Fascism was given representation in Roberto Rossellini's film, *Roma, città aperta* (*Rome, Open City*) which was first screened in 1945.

Rossellini, who had once been a Fascist young man-about-town, now deployed the techniques of what would be called 'neo-realism' to craft a moving and memorable film which, rare for its genre, was also a commercial success. Its grainy images of Rome under German occupation had a verisimilitude which has seldom been equalled. Less remarked by commentators is the 'national populism', far more extreme and manipulative than any of Gramsci's, which the film expresses. In its plot, men and women (and small boys) of the people, local Fascist policemen, Communists, priests, even *Wehrmacht* officers, are, in essence, good. Evil is confined to the sanguinary sado-masochists of the SS. In *Rome, Open City*, Rossellini thus was offering a reading of contemporary history that was almost the exact reverse of that of Pietro Silva. Nazi–Fascism was evil but its real practitioners were few. The people, the real people, poor and rich, powerless and even powerful, had avoided its corruption and had not practised its violence.[72]

Its depiction of the humanity of the Italian people made *Rome, Open City* seem very different from the blatantly self-interested efforts of Croce or Silva, Meinecke or Ritter, and other conservative commentators to detach their own class or caste from any responsibility for Fascism. And yet Rossellini, and his many imitators, both among historians and speechifiers in the years after 1945, were also offering an easy way out. In Italy, as compared with Germany or France, the 'people' might be more regularly invoked in books or at ceremonials, but 'the lessons of history' were not so different south of the Alps. Fascists were violent, wicked men. They had possessed no real or natural following. They would be easy enough to detect in the unlikely event of their seeking to return. Of course, Fascism should be condemned but it had not really mattered in the *longue durée* of Italian history. Thus, despite the publicity given in Italy to certain Marxist intellectuals, the 1950s readily became a decade of restoration historiographically. Whatever had happened to historians' ideas during the collapse of Fascism, the personnel of the Italian historical profession exhibited almost complete continuity. Now began the age of those young men who had been the pupils and clients of Volpe in the 1930s.

Most praised, and most deserving of praise, was Federico Chabod. He had spoken up for Liberty and for Europe (and, perhaps more equivocally, for the Mazzinian Risorgimento) against Nazi racism, and eventually had joined the partisans, using the appropriate fighting name of 'Lazzaro' (Lazarus).[73] In 1945 he had almost single-handedly saved his home region, the Val d'Aosta, from the unreconstructed territorial ambitions of Charles De Gaulle. In the post-war period, he worked zealously to rebuild the international structures of the historical profession, being rewarded with honours and the chance, as early as 1955, to hold the Tenth International Congress of Historical Sciences in Rome. Subsequently, he became president of that body's central committee.[74] Chabod was generous to the defeated Germans, repeatedly emphasising his own debt to Meinecke, but somewhat critical of Antonio Gramsci whom he thought over-rated.[75] Especially in the United States, Chabod was hailed as the head of the Italian historical profession.

Chabod's greatest triumph as a historian was his *Storia della politica estera italiana dal 1870 al 1896*, which he had commenced in the 1930s but did not publish until 1951.[76] Though not always a marvel of organisation or clarity, it is indeed a very fine book. Its insistence that foreign policy springs from 'the whole life of a nation' and that geopolitical determinism is never a proper explanation of action since a diplomatist always faces at least two alternatives, illuminated the way for the more subtle, 'structuralist', analyses of international relations of the post-Fischer, post-*Origins of the Second World War* generation.

Yet there are a number of odd features about Chabod's *Storia della politica estera*. The most obvious is the extent to which it is so applauded by conservative, lay, Italian historiography[77] and yet so ignored in the actual writing of diplomatic history. Another is the long gestation period of the book which, in its combination of realism and patriotism, can be seen to retain the imprint of its Fascist or Volpean birth. There are other, more general points of interest. Chabod was one of those intellectuals who had no time for what he wrote off as the 'passions of the mob'.[78] It was also a little odd that his reputation should have been largely constructed on his history of foreign policy, given that, as the years passed and the victories of social history accumulated, that topic would no longer seem crucial.

But Chabod's success had a further reason behind it. Admiring Chabod's structuralist book about the foreign policy of Liberal Italy served a double purpose. It took minds back to a period when pursuing an expansionist foreign policy was a worthy or predestined activity. And if structuralism illuminated the diplomacy of Liberal Italy, paradoxically it became easier to go on insisting that 'intentionalism' was the appropriate way in which to comprehend Fascism. The value of Chabod's *Storia della politica estera italiana* was thus best expressed in a curiously contradictory syllogism. Since Chabod was reputed not to be and never to have been a Fascist, and the Italy whose history he recounted was not Fascist, then the methods which he used in that recounting should not be applied to Fascism. That regime must continue to be defined as 'Mussolini's Italy'.

In the 1960s, however, the re-composition of Italy's liberal humanist inheritance exemplified by Chabod, the re-marriage in historiography of liberalism and nationalism, began to look shaky. Historiographically, the year 1961 brought crisis not so much over a book about the meaning of the 'long Second World War' as in Britain and West Germany, as over certain carping criticisms of the centenary celebrations of the Risorgimento. The PCI, with its increasingly insistent proclamation of Gramsci's *rivoluzione mancata* thesis, was one annoyance. The greater irritant was a book written by a foreigner, Englishman Denis Mack Smith's *Storia d'Italia*. Its scintillating prose successfully penetrating the popular market was to be deplored or envied. Its chief theses – that there was indeed a continuity from the Risorgimento through Liberalism to Fascism, that Mussolini was the 'revelation' *(rivelazone)* of Italian history – were still worse.[79] Volpe might accuse Mack Smith of 'socialist propaganda' in his reduction of the heroics of the Risorgimento to 'squalor'.[80] Romeo might end years of vituperative attack by writing off Mack Smith as a historian in whose works the relationship between words and 'historical reality' was 'merely coincidental'.[81] But the status quo could not stand. Mack Smith's book had similar implications and a similar effect to that of *Griff nach der Weltmacht* in Germany. Romeo's pious hope that (his version of) the history of the Risorgimento would bind Italians together[82] was evidently false. Worse still, by 1968 history students were no longer always deferential towards their professors.[83] For two decades Italian historiography would go into crisis. Its crisis would be a curious backdrop to the general crisis of the Italian Republic.

Then, as has been noted, a superficial reading of Italian culture once again made it seem that victory had gone to the Marxists. Though historians seldom had the starring role assumed by sociologists, film-makers, novelists and even semioticians,[84] many members of the Italian intelligentsia and, indeed, of the political class took to reiterating their ethical origins in the Resistance and their detestation of Fascism. Roberto Battaglia, a communist author of the standard history of the Resistance, explained carefully in his memoirs how, in 1943, he had transmuted from a respectable art student into a partisan who had given 'pain' (*fastidio*) to more than one German.[85] In this process, Battaglia said in words echoing the messages which Rossellini had purveyed twenty years before in *Rome, Open City*, he had merely imitated thousands of Italian folk of the most humble and varied backgrounds who were determined to save Italy and to restore human values to an entire globe emerging from 'Nazi–Fascist oppression'. If the Risorgimento had been the achievement of an intellectual elite, the Resistance had been the time in which the whole Italian people spontaneously displayed their fundamental goodness and humanity.[86] Then intellectuals did not lead, they were merely, as Gramsci had foreshadowed that they should be, part of an organic process.

Fascism, Battaglia and other communist commentators[87] sometimes admitted, had not assaulted intellectuals directly, and had not expelled or imprisoned them as Nazism had done. But Mussolini had also hated and feared the freedom which was a natural part of true culture.[88] Only after Fascism's demise could 'culture' again be properly expressed. As independent socialist philosopher, Norberto Bobbio, put it emphatically: 'where there was culture, there was not Fascism. Where there was Fascism, there was not culture; there was never such a thing as Fascist culture.'[89]

However, when studied more closely, this apparent unanimity about the ideals transmitted by anti-Fascism to the present tended to dissolve. There were problems on the Left. The disrespectful students of the generation of 1968, called '*cinesi*' (Chinese) by their enemies and often admirers of Chairman Mao's 'cultural revolution', had little time for the discipline of history. Physics, chemistry, mathematics and philosophy, they agreed, were 'indirectly ideological' subjects. But history they, like their Soviet predecessor of the 1920s, condemned as a purely ideological business.[90] Its only purpose was propagandist; historians were the natural hirelings of some hegemonic group. More sinister were the left-wing terrorists, and especially the Red Brigades (BR). They were as terrifyingly literal in their reading of phrases like 'revolution now' as they were in their belief in the supposed continuity between Fascist past and Christian Democrat–capitalist– historic compromise present. Their timeless world, with its rejection of historical specificity, meant that they could readily see themselves as Maoists, Tupamaros, Cuban revolutionaries, Vietnamese soldiers and Second World War partisans, and, at the same time, as unmaskers of the hydra-headed beast of Nazi–Fascism and its latest manifestation, the 'Imperialist State of the Multinationals'. When a respectable left-wing historian like Guido Quazza said that 1968 had marked a radical turning point both in the nature of Italy and in its historiography, and declared both that the Fascist peril remained and that current historiographical disputes between Left and Right over Fascism and anti-Fascism were a 'paradigm of national life', they took him at his word.[91] As Renzo Del Carria, the historian most sympathetic to the extreme Left, opined, the Resistance could only find its meaning as an 'interrupted revolution'.[92] Now was the moment to resume its partisanship. Now was the time for action. A 'folksong of the 1970s' expressed this 'applied (vulgar) Marxism' simply and with considerable menace:

THE FINE BIG FAMILY

There's a lovely big family
which really loves me
but if I should stop and not work
they would not know what to do.

At the head is the padrone
who gives me a job
and for that reason I love him
and have only to collaborate.

The padrone's son
is called 'salary'
he's very small
who knows if he'll grow.

The padrone's other son
is called 'profit'
he was born starved
and now all by himself eats everything.

The padrone's grandfather
is called 'fascism'
he's deaf and can't reason
but he can still talk.

The padrone's daughter
is called 'police'
she's interested in her safety
and not in mine.

Oh what a lovely big family
at the head is the padrone
my padrone's son
the other son of my padrone
the grandfather of my padrone
and the daughter of my padrone.
They should all be killed.[93]

But, in the long term, by far the greater threat to an 'anti-Fascist culture', by far the more serious undermining of the idea that the real history of the new Italy began in the Resistance, came not so much from the extreme Left as from the moderate Right. Its most public leader was Renzo De Felice, a historian engaged in writing an exhaustive and exhausting biography of Mussolini. [94] In 1975–6 this historian was the protagonist of the 'De Felice affair', the Italian controversy which, at first sight, parallels those Fischer and A.J.P. Taylor debates which have been narrated above.

As a historian, De Felice seems almost the quintessence of normality and professionalism. He was born on 8 April 1929 at Rieti, a provincial town to the east of Rome on the opposite slopes of the Apennines to Volpe's much loved birthplace, Paganica.[95] Like Volpe, and such leaders of conservative Italian historiography as Rosario Romeo[96] and Emilio Gentile,[97] De Felice seems reasonably defined in Gramscian terms as a 'Southern intellectual'. Proud of his training by both Chabod and Cantimori, De Felice began his career as a student of Italian Jacobinism, though it is not clear whether he had assumed from J.L. Talmon that the 'origins of totalitarian democracy' lay in the years before 1789. In his first research what De Felice was best at was locating and processing documents.[98]

In 1961 he commenced his study of Fascism by publishing with Einaudi a lengthy and detailed history of the experience of the Jews under the regime.[99] That in turn led him to a biography of Mussolini. At first he had some competitors, notably Roberto Vivarelli,[100] a radical heir of the anti-Fascist Gaetano Salvemini, but De Felice's efforts were greater and his publications more swift. In 1965 his first volume, *Mussolini il rivoluzionario*, appeared; in 1966 the first part of the next volume, *Mussolini il Fascista: la conquista del potere 1921–1925*; in 1968 the second part, *Mussolini il Fascista: l'organizzazione dello stato fascista 1925–1929*.

His devotion to archival research was and is extraordinary, making him in that regard the Italian equivalent of Fritz Fischer. Actually his labours in the archives have outdone even those of Fischer, and can have had, over the last generation, few equivalents anywhere in the world. If ever a historian has known the 'facts', it is De Felice. Similarly, he has busily, and usually scrupulously,[101] collected and published diaries and other texts from the Fascist period, and since 1970 he has edited the very professional *Storia contemporanea* which promulgates the findings of his school. From 1971 he received international recognition by promotion to the editorial board of the *Journal of Contemporary History*.

But it was the early volumes of the biography which had made De Felice's name. He was everywhere recognised as the major historian of Italian Fascism. Nor had his books produced much controversy. There were some left-wing doubters about the theme of his first volume. Orthodox Marxism decreed that Mussolini must always have been a wicked Fascist in the making, and certainly could not accept that the *Duce* was still a 'revolutionary' as late as 1920.[102] Had Mussolini not left the Socialist Party for French or Italian capitalist money in 1914 and founded the 'reactionary' Fascist movement in 1919? None the less, De Felice had also properly acknowledged his debt to Gramsci,[103] and it was hard to argue with the immensity of his documentation and his mastery of the 'facts'. Perhaps some readers were stunned by the length of De Felice's sentences, which were inclined to twist and turn from one qualification to another, or by his fondness for what in Anglo-Saxon historiography is condemned as 'scissors and paste history', the massive citation of documents linked only by shortish explanatory passages. In these first two volumes of the biography, however, the documents did seem 'to speak for themselves' and to say little more than that Mussolini was a bad man with many backers in high places, and that his 'Fascist state' was tyrannous. It was as if all the finer points could be left to scholastic debate within the ivory tower.

Then in 1974, De Felice published the next volume; subtitled 'the Years of Consensus', it covered the period 1929 to 1936, from the Lateran Pacts to the triumph in Ethiopia. So great was the controversy it provoked that Laterza arranged an interview with De Felice in which he defended his work.[104] His interviewer was Michael Ledeen, a young American post-doctoral student visiting the University of Rome after working with George Mosse at Wisconsin. De Felice explained that he had talked with Ledeen because only such an outsider would be uncontaminated by the personal and ideological disputes of Italian academic life,[105] and, at the time, he could hardly have known what an intriguing career Ledeen would afterwards pursue.[106] As if to confirm De Felice's commitment to history-as-science and to objectivity, Laterza delayed publication of the interview until after the fiercely contested regional elections of June 1975 (in which the PCI made vast gains) allegedly for fear that this historiographical debate might interfere with the political process. The following year the book became a run-away best-seller and, in the national elections of June 1976, the 'affare De Felice' informed many of the vivacious ideological discussions of that political apogee of the 'crisis of the Italian crisis'.

This travail of the Italian Republic had begun in 1974. Then the ruling Christian Democrats, or a faction of them led by Amintore Fanfani, had campaigned against divorce in a referendum. It was unwise to attempt to undo so necessary a reform; it was silly for a party which had been in power since 1946 to use the slogan: 'Vote for the Family, the one institution in Italy that really works';[107] it was dangerous for the MSI to be made the DC's only ally.

The referendum resulted in a 59:41 victory for the combined forces of communist, socialist and 'lay' Italy. In its aftermath, the DC began a long period of debate about internal 'renewal' and whether or not it had been 'worn out' by all those years of power. (Master tactician Giulio Andreotti would eventually make the cynical comment that only the absence of power is tiring.) Commentators began to wonder if the DC's central role in Italian politics was finished. But what would replace it? The answer to this question nobody knew and, as the economy staggered under the effect of the oil crisis and right- and left-wing terrorism increased, menacing historical parallels began to be adduced. Perhaps the Christian Democrats were a regime and not a party; perhaps the First Republic would be followed by a Second; perhaps Italy was Weimar? Or was it instead like Russia in 1917? Was DC leader Aldo Moro perhaps a Kerensky?

If, at that time, conservative Italy was confused about its past and its future, the Left seemed united and emboldened by its commitment to anti-Fascism and to 'the myth of the Resistance'. Then the PCI had been in alliance with socialists, liberals and catholics sprung from 'a genuinely popular base'. Then all good men and women and true had come to the aid of the party. So they should now lest the Fascist beast, once the 'revelation' of the negative course of Italian history, again devour the Italian body politic. In 1975–6, it seemed, history was working for the legitimation of the PCI. History was the main propellant of what PCI leader, Enrico Berlinguer, with unconscious irony, called the '*compromesso storico*' (the historic compromise).

But De Felice's research, as expressed in *Gli anni di consenso* and the *Intervista*, was undermining this particular reading of history and exposing the frailty and self-interest of this 'myth of the Resistance'. Who had the Fascists been? Marxists had argued that they were threatened landowners, decaying artisans, criminal and sexually perverse *déracinés*, *petit bourgeois* fearful of proletarianisation. No, said De Felice, the Fascists' main base was the 'emerging middle classes', those who had boarded the locomotive of history during the time of economic growth occasioned by the First World War. Marxists deemed Fascism reactionary in its final purpose. No, said De Felice, the presence of these emerging middle classes guaranteed that Fascism always possessed a genuinely revolutionary side. It was true that Mussolini had truck with King and Pope, army and big business, in what De Felice defined as 'Fascism regime'. But at the same time there was a positive, optimistic, spontaneous and genuinely popular side to the period. De Felice called it 'Fascism movement'. And, he added, Fascism, despite considerable bureaucratisation and a consequent hardening of administrative arteries in the 1930s, retained an *élan vital*. Mussolini himself, buoyed by his high reputation abroad,[108] had pushed for a 'cultural revolution' through which would be constructed the 'new Fascist man' (and woman). He was near to success after the triumph in Ethiopia, a conflict which, De Felice averred, deserved to be called 'Mussolini's masterpiece' and gave Fascism a greater 'consensus' than that achieved by any predecessor (or perhaps successor).

Moreover, Fascism had its own specificity which was hidden by unnecessary emphasis on continuity or Fascism *rivelazione*. 'The Fascist era' in Italy was over and could not be revived. 'It is a closed chapter, and because of this', said De Felice in pious echo of Ranke, 'it is possible to study it historically, with a historical method and a historical mentality.'[109] Italian Fascism was also unique. Attempts to build a model of 'European fascism' were doomed; movements like the Legion of the Archangel Michael in Romania or the Arrow Cross in Hungary were no more than 'false fascisms'.[110] And De Felice had a final argument, one crucial to so many debates about the meaning of the 'long Second World War'. The 'myth of the Resistance' had conflated Italian Fascism and German Nazism and so harnessed the guilt of 'Auschwitz' in the anti-Fascist cause. But, De Felice proclaimed determinedly, Fascism was radically different from Nazism. The Italian ideology was positive and forward-looking, the German negative and retrospective. Even Italian anti-Semitism, however deplorable, was internally generated and should not be confused with German. Fascism, De Felice would get around to saying, carried not a shred of real guilt for the Holocaust.[111]

In 1975–6, the first enunciation of these theses created an enormous controversy which may well in turn have hardened De Felice's allegiance to them. Outraged critics accused De Felice of being a 'documentary fetishist' (which perhaps he is) or a philo-Fascist (which he plainly is not) and made desperate attempts to argue that Fascism was at least as wicked as Nazism. The Right, within Italy and outside, claimed De Felice as their own. Journalist Indro Montanelli, always on the lookout for a useful cause, bemoaned the 'attempted lynching' of De Felice by 'left-wing culture', and, in the atmosphere of terrorism then prevailing, it must indeed have been frightening for De Felice to receive death threats.[112] George Urban of Radio Free Europe lured the still residually cautious De Felice to draw appropriately totalitarianist parallels between the PNF and the PCI:

> Clearly, the political and intellectual history of Fascism and Communism are very different, and the regimes they have generated, or might generate in Italy, have been, and would be, different from one another when seen through the intellectually fastidious microscope of historical analysis. But for the man whose preoccupation in life is to stay alive, give himself and his family two hot meals a day, a roof above their heads and enough freedom to breathe like human beings and refuse to have their backs broken by tyranny, there is precious little to choose between the two. The difference between being thrown into the sea and being thrown into a lake is rather academic if you don't know how to swim.[113]

Only Nicola Tranfaglia on the Left made sensible points about De Felice's prolixity, and the complexity and even contradictoriness of much of his actual historical writing, while noting suspiciously that the *Confederazione generale dell'industria*, Italy's big business league, had favoured the distribution of the *Intervista* among its clients and members. To Tranfaglia's disgust, the past according to De Felice, they had stated, was the only legitimate, 'non-political' one;[114] it was the one they liked best.

Of course, in many ways, De Felice, in his revisionism, was pushing through an open door. Virtually no Italian critics remarked on De Felice's curiously old-fashioned methodological assumptions about 'objectivity' and the 'science' of the historical study of 'past' eras, or about his reiterated idea that the Fascist period was still so close that the first necessity was to compose its history and that only then could it be interpreted. Neither De Felice nor his critics had much sense of E.H. Carr's relativist view that historians always write themselves into their own histories. Rather, De Felice was using the same simple historicist methodology to demolish the 'myth of the Resistance' which its supporters had used to construct it.[115] In these circumstances, his victory was hard to deny because he had done the work in the archives and they had not.

In terms of a philosophy of history, then, what De Felice was offering Italy was neo-Rankeanism. In the 1980s this offer was accepted in many circles with such alacrity that it was almost as though no other way of writing history could be imagined. 'Scientific history', often accompanied by a political conservatism and a nationalism which Ranke himself might have recognised, became all the rage. So, too, did De Felicean interpretations of Italian Fascism. In TV programmes, popular biographies and museum displays, as well as in academic history, the Fascist period was granted a dignity of its own and the previous ethical rejection of Fascism downplayed. The 'Great Economic History Show' staged in the Colosseum during the autumn of 1984 provides a typical example. At least according to Tim Mason, the Marxist English historian then living in Rome, this exhibition managed to illustrate the 'ordinary lives' of inter-war Italians, in an atmosphere of a-Fascism and by ignoring the poverty and oppression then experienced by the poor, women and southerners. Instead, all was a cheerful and patriotic spectacle of the spread of modernity, cars, mod-cons, and new and rather dashing fashion. De Felice himself acted as 'general historical consultant' to the display, the immediate organisation of which was in the hands of the New Rightist, ex-Fascist, Giano Accame. The Socialist Prime Minister, Bettino Craxi, was an enthusiastic supporter, but so were some Communists. The exhibition said what it should have to all those who sought in the 1980s to build a stronger republican state and forget the turmoil of the 1970s, when they had been reduced to believing 'Italians exist [only] because they exist in history'. Now history served a clearer if humbler purpose. As Mason put it sadly, the 'apoliticisation of the historical consciousness' proceeded apace. 'In order to de-politicise the present it is essential to de-politicise the past.'[116]

Becoming more set in his views over time, De Felice continued to push this new conservatism. His own public interventions, though rarer, for example, than those of his irascible friend Rosario Romeo,[117] became more open and less ambiguous. Authoritarian regimes, he said, were no longer possible in non-communist Europe; the MSI was not a serious threat and was on a path to extinction; the 'historic compromise', if ever revived, would be the *coup de grâce* for Italian democracy; the unionisation of professors would be a sad day for academic freedom; the Resistance was really only a myth – echoing those words once used by Volpe, De Felice now agreed the 1943–5 period was better defined as 'civil war'.[118]

But it was in the Christmas–New Year of 1987–8 that De Felice made his strongest statements so far. Craxi had had a meeting with Gianfranco Fini, a new generation yuppy who had succeeded ex-*repubblichino*, ex-Salò Republic Fascist, Giorgio Almirante, as leader of the MSI. As a result, De Felice was contacted by a journalist from *Corriere della sera* to give his opinion of this incongruous spectacle of Socialist and neo-Fascist leader supping together. Once again, De Felice said that there was no reason to worry about the MSI. He then went on to a series of more drastic statements. Fascism was not responsible for 'Auschwitz'; the Fascist ruling class was illiberal, but was it so much worse than that of the republic? The formal ban on the open re-constitution of a Fascist party was 'grotesque' and 'ridiculous'. Craxi was to be praised for detaching himself from past prejudices. All in all, one matter was plain: 'It is logical that the great alternative of Fascism and anti-Fascism now falls. It does not make sense any more either in public consciousness or in the reality of the daily political struggle.'[119]

De Felice's words brought an immediate response. Valiani, Paolo Spriano, Mack Smith, Tranfaglia, Alberto Asor Rosa and even Andreotti spoke out against this final abandonment of the history or the myth of the Resistance. Montanelli, Luigi Settembrini and a number of Craxian Socialists sprang to De Felice's defence. But he could manage quite well on his own. On 7 January, he replied to his critics. The 'official culture' of anti-Fascism must go. 'Anti-Fascism, acting as an ideology of State, historically, politically and culturally, is not a useful discriminator to establish what a genuine democracy is.' In March, De Felice expanded his reference outside Italy. 'The Soviet Union did not have a positive role in the struggle against Nazi–Fascism'; rather, 'Nazi Germany and the Soviet Union were made from the same pasta.' 'To the Soviet Union we owe nothing. Our liberty', he concluded in words which may have made Denis Mack Smith sit up in bed, 'if we owe it to anybody, we owe to the English.'[120] There seemed scarcely a need any more for those awaited two or three thousand pages which would conclude the biography of Mussolini.

In 1990, De Felice provided 1,576 of them as he traversed the period from 1940 to 1943 in what he admitted was the most difficult to write of the volumes of his book. The trouble, De Felice opined, had lain with the existing historiography which was a sort of 'historical journalism'. It was much to blame for 'the mediocrity of Italian culture today' as it successfully converted Mussolini and Fascism into 'the only scapegoats of the defeat'. De Felice, by contrast, averred that he would hide nothing from his intrepid or perservering readers 'but, on the contrary, give them the elements to form *their own* [sic] opinion, *their own* judgement'. De Felice did not let modesty overwhelm him, however. The overall '*taglio*' (interpretation) which he gave to events was, he explained in his introduction, 'the only possible and correct one both scientifically and in view of the readership'.[121]

The story which De Felice thereafter narrated was indeed one lacking in overt political passion or morality. Mussolini was as accurate as any of his contemporaries in his diagnosis of the war's issues. But, unluckily, he could not persuade his German ally that in the Mediterranean sector lay the epicentre of the Second World War (here De Felice differed from Andreas Hillgruber whose work he otherwise applauded). The great conflict, it seemed, had been 'objectivised'; nobody much died in it or at least did not die in an exceptional manner. The most regrettable thing about the war was 'the ethical–political weakness' it revealed in all Italians. In a better world, De Felice ran on, Italians would not have displayed their 'lack of moral preparation to confront the test of war at least with a faith in their own capacity; as a community, [their failure] to have as dignified a part as did other national communities.'[122]

In this, as in other writings, De Felice had relegated the Italian version of the 'long Second World War' as People's war to the attic of historiography. The future might be uncertain but the 'second *dopoguerra*', the era since 1945, was over and its historiographical base destroyed.

Under De Felice's aegis, thus, Italy had experienced a paradigm shift about the meaning of the 'long Second World War' which was almost the exact reverse of that experienced in Britain and West Germany in the 1960s, and France in the 1970s. In Italy the conservative empire struck back and effortlessly had accepted the sort of historical interpretations which had got Hillgruber or Stürmer into so much trouble in the FRG. In Italy, it seemed, the Right had won the historians' quarrel. Italy's 'long Second World War' had now been historicised in a way which best fitted both the 'second Cold War' and those Western victories in it which, Fukuyama proclaimed, had meant the 'end of history'.

Of course, this conclusion is exaggerated. In the 1990s Italy is no more the place of one and only one interpretation of the present and the past than it was in the 1970s. Persuasive De Felice's version of Mussolini may be; unchallenged it is not. A settled definition of the 'emerging middle classes' is not made. The antithesis of 'Fascism movement' and 'Fascism regime' is a useful concept but individuals seem to have been perfectly able to be 'fascist' and conservative at the same time. Mussolini's reputation outside Italy is scarcely what the De Feliceans claim; typically their reading of the 'documents' is literal, their methodology primitive, and they neither comprehend unspoken assumptions nor utilise the many new approaches to 'reading' the past. Is Fascist Italy really guiltless of Auschwitz? That it should be allied with Nazi Germany for cynical or Machiavellian reasons rather than credulous, ideological ones does not seem a full excuse. And was the regime really no more than cynical in 1938, 1940, 1941 or 1943–5? What, too, of Fascism's violent policies in its empire? De Felice regards them as positive or at least in need of 'objectification', but other conclusions are possible. Did Fascism really have a 'consensus' or was its 'popular base' more complicated, as Luisa Passerini's brilliant oral history has indicated at least for the working men and women of Turin?[123] To what extent had Fascism really nationalised its masses? The military effort in the Second World War, the behaviour of Italian soldiers and POWs, suggest doubts there too.

Nor has neo-Rankean 'objectivity' triumphed on every front. Paola Di Cori, a leading Italian feminist historian, in urging an emergence from 'the anti-ideological bath of the last decade' and the avoidance of 'an excessively accelerated depoliticisation', with its destruction of 'any form of collective identity or commitment in the public arena', has suggested that the most powerful agents of present research in Italy are women's history and oral history. These fields, she says, previously marginalised by the methodological and professional conservatism of both Left and Right, are revealing fresh concepts and fresh techniques which, deployed in a professional manner and with a new humility about the historian's social role, may construct new and fruitful versions of 'individual and collective historic memory'.[124]

Similarly, invocations of anti-Fascist ethics have not entirely been eliminated from Italian political discourse. Indeed, the greatest advances of neo-conservatism in Italian politics and culture ironically occurred during the Presidency of Sandro Pertini. This 'grandfather of all Italians' never ceased to endorse the myths of the Resistance. His autobiography with its title *Six Times found Guilty, Two Prison Escapes* mocked those who preach civil passivity on all occasions.[125] And, after his departure from office in 1985, he and his world have not entirely been forgotten.

They can, however, no longer be taken as read. Francesco Cossiga, Pertini's successor as President, approached contemporary history in a very different manner. For him, the 'myth of the Resistance', the repeated summoning of the anti-Fascists to go on fighting the good fight, caused the terrorism of the 1970s. Then a generation was led astray by 'false teachers' (*cattivi maestri*). Such teachers, manipulated by communism and its false appeal, had, through their insistence on the virtue and permanence of the Resistance, sponsored violence. It is a pity, he has added, that, while many terrorists have been convicted and gaoled, those who twisted the past to fit their version of the present have not. And, he concluded with some menace, unrepentent they still hold down their jobs in Italian universitites.[126]

This hint of a purge is probably no more than that. Cossiga, as his presidential term drew to a close, was an unpopular and embattled figure. In the 1990s it is not illiberalism which threatens the practitioners of Italian history but rather irrelevance. In the 1970s, when the rival currents of the People's war still so publicly ebbed and flowed through Italian politics and culture, history seemed to matter. Students then read and re-read Gramsci's wonderful letter from his deathbed to his son:

Dearest Delio,

I feel rather tired and can't write you a long letter. Go on writing to me about everything that interests you in school. I think you like history, as I liked it at your age, because it concerns living men; and everything that concerns them – as many men as possible, all the men in the world, insofar as they unite in society and work and strive to improve themselves – must necessarily interest you more than anything else. But is this the case for you? A hug.

Antonio.[127]

In the 1990s, by contrast, the age of accountants, economists and infotainment is '*anche in Italia*' (also in Italy) as the advertising hoardings somewhat self-consciously put it. It is time to re-read some words from Croce, that 'lay Pope' whom Gramsci had so envied and admired:

During periods in which reforms and upheavals are being prepared, attention is paid to the past, to that from which a break is to be made and to that with which a link is to be forged. During uneventful, slow and heavy periods, fables and romances are preferred to histories or history is reduced to a fable or romance.[128]

De Felice and his associates, through their re-reading of Fascism and anti-Fascism, are glad to have participated in the destruction of the PCI's past. What is of most concern now is that they have also eclipsed the ethically desirable features of the Italian version of a People's war. Without that past, Italy's present and future may be the poorer.

7

Glasnost Reaches Soviet historiography

When Ronald Reagan went to Bitburg, *Izvestia* was not amused. It objected to his failure to recall Soviet sacrifice in the Second World War and thought that he had got his history wrong: 'The head of the American administration . . . intolerably distorted historical truth in Bergen-Belsen, where he confined the crimes of the Nazi regime solely to the extermination of the Jewish population.'[1] What *Izvestia* would have preferred was reference to the some 20 million Soviet citizens who were direct casualties of the German invasion. It might also have expected acknowledgement of the other terrible statistics of Operation Barbarossa and its aftermath, some reflection on the tally of POWs who died in captivity in the Second World War – 4 per cent of Anglo-Americans in German hands, 27 per cent of Anglo-Americans captured by the Japanese, up to 37.4 per cent of Germans held by the Soviets and 57.8 per cent of Soviets taken by Nazi Germany.[2] In his recent general history of the conflict, Alastair Parker has remarked that the Second World War was really two wars, a European one and an Asian–Pacific one.[3] Soviet readers, armed with the memories of German invasion, would disagree. They would point to at least three Second World Wars – the conflict with Japan, the rather gentlemanly sideshows of Western and Southern Europe, and, most importantly, the mortal combat in Eastern Europe, the 'real Second World War', the 'Great Patriotic War' as their textbooks call it, their war, their history. This war, which they had suffered, endured and won, they were loath to share with anyone, not even the Jewish victims of the Holocaust.

There have been many complex attempts to explain the survival of a kind of Stalinism in the USSR for a generation after the death of the dictator. But there is one obvious reason for the social conservatism of the 1960s and 1970s USSR, its leaderships' lack of political or economic imagination, and refusal to utilise modern expertise or to accept that sociological change which has made the Soviet peoples urban and educated rather than peasant and unskilled.[4] In the post-war period and even after Stalin's death, the *mentalité* of the Soviet ruling class was 'frozen in time'. Though the course of history continued, the political bosses viewed the world through the prism of their wartime experience (and through their knowledge of the 1930s and of the Revolution after 1917, through Russia's 'long Second World War'). In the early 1980s, the elderly Brezhnev or, even better, Konstantin

Chernenko who, staring down at the great patriotic parades on Red Square, always looked as though he had been rouged, wheeled from the mortuary and propped up to do his bit, splendidly represented the fact that the Soviet Union before Gorbachev was still governed by these 'old fighters' from the war, by men whose world view was governed by their past, and by a simple reading of their own history. In a sense, they did not and could not exist without it.

' "The state is like a jug", runs a Russian proverb,' which Marc Ferro has recalled, ' "when it cracks, water flows". After February 1917', he has gone on to argue with some exaggeration, 'society itself began to move. . . . The February Revolution had been the greatest in all history. In the space of a few weeks, Russia got rid of all her former leaders – the Tsar and his law-makers, the police, the priests, the landowners, the civil servants, the officers and the employers. Not one citizen could fail to feel quite free – free to determine at any time what he would do, in the present or the future. Within a short time, virtually everyone had his own notion of what should be done to achieve national regeneration. It was, as the poets of the Revolution wrote, a new era in the history of Man.'[5] Russia had become 'a sheet of sand'[6] and in its friability what the revolutionary leadership and many of the masses hoped they could bury was history, Russia's history of Tsars and priests, of the knout and the whip, of poverty and backwardness.

Lenin himself, the 'Great Headmaster' as Edmund Wilson so brilliantly defined him,[7] was a highly intellectual person. US journalist John Reed, author of the first and for a decade the most authoritative contemporary narration of the Bolshevik Revolution, called Lenin 'a strange popular leader – a leader purely by virtue of intellect'.[8] A member of the intelligentsia Lenin may have been, and, indeed, in his time a fine historian, but, once in power, the past did not preoccupy him. Rather, with his eyes set on the present and the future, he aimed at revolution and then 'Soviet power plus electrification of the whole country'. His Marxist determinism notwithstanding, still he would force the pace of time and of history.

Nevertheless a party leader could not altogether eliminate historical reference. Trotsky, that other even more intellectual revolutionary, looked to the great revolutions of the past, especially the French, to provide guidance if only about mistakes a present-day revolutionary should avoid. In 1903–4, for example, he had quarrelled with Lenin and his Bolsheviks, comparing them with Robespierre and the Committee of Public Safety. Jacobin utopianism was to be eschewed: 'They cut off heads; we enlighten them with class consciousness.' After 1917 the main 'lesson of history' for Trotsky became Thermidor. How could the revolutionaries avoid repeating such a calamitous result in this, the final revolution? Ironically, party members who disliked Trotsky's intellectuality, arrogance and Jewish roots were soon suggesting that the triumphant Commissar of the Red Army was the looming Napoleon. In eventual exile, Trotsky would gain some intellectual revenge by defining Stalin's regime as Bonapartist.[9]

Such historiographical disputes weighed little in the momentous years after 1917. When the Soviet system began to establish itself and impose an educational programme to foster the 'sovietisation of the masses', history was not high on the list of useful and appropriate subjects for the new Russia. Indeed, M.N. Pokrovsky, a leading Marxist scholar who had graduated with a degree in Russian history in 1891 and who now with A.V. Lunacharsky and Krupskaya, Lenin's wife, was a member of the triumvirate which administered education through *Narkompros*, 'the Commissariat of Enlightenment', discounted history and traditional historians. The subject, he wrote, was hopelessly scarred by bias. It was the 'most political of all sciences'. Or rather, it was not a science at all but only the expression of ideology. 'History *tout court*', he told Krupskaya severely, 'does not exist! It is always the history of something.' 'All ideology', he added, 'is a distorting mirror which gives a quite unfaithful representation of real life.'

Thus school curricula in the 1920s avoided history. As a historian of Soviet education has put it:

Pokrovsky believed that all the historical knowledge necessary to the Soviet schoolchild was a handful of sociological generalizations which were of relevance to his understanding of the vital contemporary issues presented in the school programme of *obshchestvovedenie* (social studies). In fact, during the 1920s history was not taught as a separate subject in secondary school; and a move to have it reinstated . . . was defeated.[10]

But this proclaimed 'end of history' was not final. Indeed, the more firmly it was denied the more obstinately it kept slipping back into public discourse. For one thing there was the story of the Revolution where history and ideology mixed. Equally the enormous extent of the crisis of state and society between 1917 and 1921, and their only partial reconnection thereafter, made it all the more urgent for the Bolshevik rulers to portray themselves as servants of a Great Tradition, even if, at first, it was Marxian and not Russian.

Yet Russian traditions were hard to ignore. In a recent book, Nina Tumarkin has traced the growth of the 'Lenin cult' in the post-revolutionary period. Though the first revolutionaries piously proclaimed 'we Bolsheviks are not inclined to push individuals into the foreground',[11] Lenin's blessing was impossible to foreswear. While he was injured or sick, and especially when he was dead, ambitious politicians almost inevitably sought to exploit his myth and charisma to their own benefit. Their devotion to his history was fostered by the fact that, after the assassination attempt in 1918, during Lenin's long final illness, or at his funeral ceremonies, popular enthusiasm for the Great Man, the new Tsar, the *vozhd'*, spontaneously manifested itself. As yet illiterate peasants took Lenin into their folk-tales and, perhaps with some nudging from the authorities, converted him with predictable metaphor into a lay Christ: 'I have heard that Lenin is a good person. Handsome. Diligent. Wise. Affectionate. He defended the oppressed and the poor. He loved children very much. He knew lots of things. . . . Little Lenin had pretty curls and forehead.'[12] Party and people agreed that he must have a special tomb; his body, like that of Tutankhamen,[13] must be embalmed. It should not moulder in a grave while his soul (or interpreters of it) went marching on into the revolutionary future.

Indeed, in the Great Patriotic War, it would be lovingly deployed as the most potent relic to stiffen the sinews of the Red Armies; as the Germans threatened Moscow, Lenin was moved from his tomb in Red Square to Kuibysev for the eventual rallying and the final victory.[14] This Lenin now incarnated the history of the Revolution in the most literal sense and, somewhere between life and death, acted as great and god-like ancestor for the new *vozhd'*, Joseph Stalin. After all, Stalin liked history to have a practical and useful side. 'Study history,' he would tell his daughter, 'then you can do what you want.'[15]

This limitless cynicism about the lessons of the past eventually may have characterised both the dictator and his regime but, in the 1930s, the chief preoccupation of Soviet educationalists and politicians rather had been anxiously to train technocrats and administrators to combine 'electrification and Soviet power' in what, after Nazism's accession to power in 1933, seemed an ever more menacing world. Engineers and accountants were a first priority, especially if they were children of the working class or peasants; their training should be swift and practical and not dally too much with humanist values or Marxist theoretics.[16] History, too, needed as a discipline to be simplified and regularised, to be converted into something rather like engineering and accountancy. The last thing the 1930s USSR required was an argument without end.

And arguments, personal, ideological and professional, there had been. Some 20 per cent of pre-revolutionary historians had perished in the Revolution and Civil War.[17] During the 1920s, however, many 'bourgeois experts' survived in this as in other fields even though Pokrovsky, as head of the Historical Section of the Institute of Red Professors, tried to educate his own Bolshevik personnel, including such figures as S.M. Dubrovsky and I.I. Mints. From 1928, the reverberations of the Shakhty affair and the subsequent trial of foreign bourgeois 'wreckers' and their assistants were also felt in the history trade.

Though disputation could lead to sacking or worse (in 1930–1 some 130 historians were arrested),[18] history still did not come up with a single answer. Instead it was apparent that Pokrovsky's reading of the past was contested even within the Party. The more tough-minded of the leadership were now growing tired of these conflicts, particularly because history was the sort of subject which regularly threatened to spill over into politics and administration. In 1931, Lazar Kaganovich, before the revolution a poor and ill-educated Jewish bootmaker but now become a myrmidon of Stalin in the Politbureau,[19] warned Pokrovsky menacingly:

In the field of history, the activities of the Communist Academy have still not been subjected to an extensive and merciless self-criticism; this, however, is not evidence of the absence of mistakes, but only of the fact that these mistakes until now have not been revealed.[20]

Pokrovsky, though ill, stubbornly defended his clients and his version of history. But by October 1931, he had a still more dangerous critic – Joseph Stalin. The Party Secretary intervened to denounce an article by the historian, A.G. Slutsky, which he deemed 'Trotskyite' and 'disloyal to Lenin'. But he also now remarked regretfully on Pokrovsky's fondness for determinism and his 'cosmopolitan' background. History or sociology, what did it matter? But one or the other should have a simple message: 'Who, save hopeless bureaucrats, can rely on written documents alone? Who, besides archive rats, does not understand that a party and its leaders must be tested primarily by their deeds, and not by their declarations?'[21] History, it seemed, must put its house in order. In 1931 the Central Committee resolved that history should return to the curriculum as a basic subject 'requiring systematic teaching'. In 1932 it complained that the new programmes had not yet been written, but demanded 'a more historical approach to the teaching of literature, geography and social studies'; in 1933 it was resolved that a general textbook be prepared; in 1935 that teaching emphasise 'chronological historical sequence in the setting out of historical events, firmly fixing in the minds of the pupils important historical events, historical personages and dates.' These should be preferred to the 'abstract sociological schemes' or the 'abstract definition of socio-economic formations.'[22] In 1937, the Historical Section of the Institute of Red Professssors was suppressed. Pokrovsky, who perhaps fortunately for him had died in 1932, had had his radical ideas relegated to the trash-can of . . . sociology. Instead education was policed by S.M. Budenny, a fiercely-mustachioed former Tsarist cavalry sergeant now a notoriously drunken general who, in 1935, toured the USSR to supervise the re-imposition of rote learning and class-room discipline. The time when Krupskaya could talk mistily of life as the best textbook was over,[23] though the 'formational approach', which elsewhere would be called sociology, soon crept back in practice to become the conceptual base of all Soviet history until the 1980s.

The culmination of this return to the past would occur in 1938 when Stalin supervised the completion by a collective of party historians of the *Short Course,* the *History of the Communist Party of the Soviet Union (Bolsheviks).* To the regime it represented the revised standard version of the historical truth, and it was spread through the Soviet Union and, in innumerable translations, the wider world.[24] Contemporary rumour said that Stalin had not only encouraged its production, but had actually written it himself.[25] Whatever the case, history in the Soviet Union had been absorbed into the Stalinist system.

It is possible to see this absorption merely as a triumph of the dictator's whim. But in recent times the new social historians of Stalinism have been making another stimulating and credible suggestion. Ferro has remarked with typical *Annales* insight that there were, in 1917, many time zones in Russia; history had not run with the same rhythm throughout that vast and complex country and among its varied peoples.[26] Though the calendars may have indeed said '1917' in Petrograd or Moscow, in provincial towns the 'real time' was some decades earlier and in much of the countryside centuries before. Driven by these diverse currents of time, there were, averred Ferro, many potential or actual social revolutions in 1917 apart from the political one commandeered by the Bolsheviks as they stormed the Winter Palace.

146

What Ferro was also implying was that Russia remained a place of many histories or potential histories. Different nationalities, different classes, different age groups, all might want to read the past differently. Certainly the *muzhiki*, the vast peasantry which still made up 70 per cent of the population, would.

The early Bolsheviks were well aware that their version of history did not match that of the peasantry. For Lenin and many others it was precisely 'peasant backwardness', their clinging to the past and retention of their own history, which was the greatest obstacle for the Soviet regime as it turned its eyes to the future. For some sensitive members of the Bolshevik elite, then and later, this real or potential divorce from the people could stimulate guilt:

Oh, your hands – they're so lovely! [the egg girl in a Tartar village in 1934] said. . . . She had been struck with genuine admiration for my delicate, white, manicured fingers. They showed up to advantage against her large, work-coarsened, brick-red hands with their swollen veins, chapped fingers, and broken nails. She had not meant to hurt me, but I found myself bursting into tears with these two hands – hers and mine – in close-up before me, as if in the cinema. I felt a burning sense of shame. With these delicate hands of mine, I had come to teach her how to construct Communism.[27]

These ideals and emotions in turn prompted the Soviet regime to seek ways of nurturing its own experts and expertise. 'The working class must create its own productive-technical intelligentsia capable of standing up for its own interests in production,' Stalin had declared in 1931.[28] But there a first problem was that the working class, or rather the peasantry – since even with industrialisation and urbanisation in the 1930s many 'workers' had only recently abandoned village life – possessed, as they had already shown during the emergence of the Lenin cult, their own sense of history. Now they demanded that the regime's teaching bear some resemblance to that history.[29] Thus the initial pressure for curriculum change in the schools seems to have come at least as much from below as from above. History, the people believed, should tell a simple moral tale. There should be strong individual figures, an emphasis on the *vozhd'* whom Russia needed from time to time. His strength and power would be in part magical.[30] Great deeds were always in a sense 'superhuman'. The past should be plumbed for tales like those presently associated with the regime's policy of *stakhanovism*[31] or, indeed, with Stalin's own 'personality cult' (which had so overwhelmed that of Lenin).

The new social historians, then, began saying that there were Stalinists who endorsed the world view of the dictator, himself the son of a peasant turned drunken cobbler. And those Stalinists, who were rising in the hierarchy of power in the 1930s, were often the *praktiki*, practical men like Kaganovitch or Budenny with virtually no academic training, or the *vydvizhentsy*, 'the accelerated ones', those who had done specially abbreviated courses in humdrum subjects like management or mechanics. They were the 'new men' of the Soviet Union whose *mentalité* old members of the intelligentsia, whether Bolshevik or not, began to find unfamiliar. As one liberal, Nadezhda Mandelstam, recalled, her family had 'belonged to the intelligentsia by birth and had grown up in an atmosphere of our own intimate small talk, bound together by common interests. Suddenly, without any transition we found ourselves in a new world, among utterly strange people who did not talk our language. I had the odd sensation of looking around and feeling I no longer knew anybody – the words, ideas, concepts, and emotions were quite different'. So, of course, was the history. That subject, Mandelstam concluded bleakly, was most to blame; it should be cursed since it 'never serves as a warning to posterity, as a deterrent, but only puts a "modern" gloss on the mistakes and crimes of previous generations, decking them out in glittering new rationalizations.'[32]

The *Short Course* had, indeed, a short way with the nuances and ambiguities of more subtle histories. Its moral lines were strong, as, for example, when it got around to explaining the purges:

> These Whiteguard pigmies, whose strength was no more than that of a gnat, apparently flattered themselves that they were the masters of the country, and imagined that it was really in their power to sell or give away the Ukraine, Byelorussia and the Maritime Region. These Whiteguard insects forgot that the real masters of the Soviet country were the Soviet people, and that the rykovs, bukharins, zinovievs and kamenevs [sic] were only temporary employees of the state, which could at any moment sweep them from its offices as so much useless rubbish. These contemptible lackeys of the fascists forgot that the Soviet people had only to move a finger, and not a trace of them would be left. The Soviet court sentenced the Bukharin-Trotsky fiends to be shot.[33]

It was a variety of history not only well suited to tyranny but also acceptable to a 'new class' with things on its mind other than humanist pluralism.

This alliance of Stalin and the Stalinists was duly cemented by the Second World War, or the 'Great Patriotic War' as it was rapidly denominated. Once, the Civil War had created a unity of peasant and Bolshevik fused by service in the Red Army and a cleaving to the Army's systems, myths and versions of history. Now the Second World War repeated the process in a much more profound manner. For it was indeed Russia's war in a way not always accepted in the West. Certainly the peoples of Russia, along with the Jews and some other East European minority groups, were the special victims of the conflict. The horrendous death rate of Soviet POWs who fell into German hands has already been noted. Furthermore, the majority of the 20 million or more Soviet dead were civilians. As Israeli historian Omer Bartov, in his honest acknowledgement of the 'barbarisation of war' on the Eastern Front, has commented, much sympathy is extended to the French for enduring the punitive SS 'action' against the village of Oradour but can that really be compared with the 1,710 towns aznd 70,000 villages, at least according to Soviet figures, devastated by the *Wehrmacht*?[34]

The disastrous unpreparedness of the Stalin regime for the German onslaught in June 1941 produced those other extraordinary statistics – by winter the USSR had surrendered areas which produced 63 per cent of its coal, 68 per cent of its pig iron, 58 per cent of its steel, 60 per cent of its aluminium, 38 per cent of its grain and 85 per cent of its sugar; 98,000 out of an estimated total of 200,000 collective farms fell to the Germans in the first year of the war (and were eventually destroyed). In 1941, by contrast, the Nazi regime had not yet imposed 'total war' on its population and was famously producing quantities of cuckoo clocks and hair oil. In the USSR the people had to support a 'total' war from the start; indeed that adjective seems inadequate to define the contribution levied from the Soviet people by the war. In some regions, the *kolkhozy* or collective farms, deprived both of male labour and their livestock, took to harnessing eight or ten women to the plough in order to get their precarious sowing done.[35]

The USSR would eventually benefit greatly from US and British supplies. But in that stubborn resistance which would lead to the turning point at Stalingrad in January 1943, in the mammoth siege of Leningrad, which lasted from August 1941 to January 1944 and in which perhaps a million starved to death, and in every area which German armies penetrated, the war was truly fought on the heads and over the bodies of the Russian people. Defeat, they had every reason to believe, would mean the loss of their material possessions, their culture, their history and their lives. That highly untrustworthy Italian war correspondent, Curzio Malaparte, for once tells it like it was in what is surely the most moving of all descriptions of the Great Patriotic War: one day he watched as the Germans assembled some prisoners of war. They

> were lined up in the yard of the *kolkhoz*. Along the walls of the yard and under the large sheds were piled, haphazardly, hundreds of agricultural machines – reapers, cultivators, mechanical ploughs, threshing machines. It rained and the prisoners were soaked to their skins. They had been standing there, in silence, leaning against each other; they were big, fair boys with close-cropped heads and light eyes in their broad faces. Their hands were flat and thick with squat, arched, calloused thumbs. Almost all were peasants. The workmen, mostly engineers and mechanics from the *kolkhoz*, could be distinguished among them by their height and their hands; they were taller, leaner and lighter skinned; their hands were bony, with long fingers, and smooth finger-tips glazed from gripping hammers, planes, wrenches, screwdrivers and controls. They could be distinguished by their stern faces and glazed eyes.

A German sergeant-major or *Feldwebel* informed them that they were to have a reading test.

> Those who passed the examination well would be drafted as clerks into the offices of the prisoners' camps; the others, those who failed, would be sent to work on the land or be employed as labourers and dockworkers.

Some officers joined the throng and were watching a little glumly as the examination began.

Five prisoners took a step forward. Each of them stretched out a hand, took a paper that the officer held out to him – they were old issues of *Izvestia* and *Pravda* found in the office of the *kolkhoz* – and began reading aloud. The colonel raised his left arm to look at his wristwatch. He kept his arm breast-high and his eyes fixed on the watch. It was raining and the newspapers were soaked; they drooped in the hands of the five prisoners whose faces were either red or extremely pale and sweating as they stumbled over the words, halted, stammered, blundered the accents and skipped lines. They could all read with difficulty, except one very young man who read with assurance, from time to time raising his eyes from the paper. The Sonderführer [a civilian technician assisting the Germans] listened to the reading with an ironical smile in which I seemed to sense a vengefulness – as interpreter, he was the sole judge. He stared at the readers, shifting his eyes from one to the other with a deliberate and nasty slowness. 'Stop!' said the colonel.

The five prisoners raised their eyes from the papers and waited. At a nod from the judge, the Feldwebel shouted, 'Those who have failed will go and stand on the left; those who have been promoted, over there, to the right.' The first four failures at a sign from the judge went dejectedly to cluster on the left, and a youthful ripple of laughter ran along the ranks of the prisoners, a gay, mischievous, peasant laughter. The Sonderführer also laughed. *'Oh, bednii* – Oh poor fellows!' the prisoners called to those who had failed. 'You will be sent to work on the roads, *Oh, bednii*, you'll carry stones on your backs,' and they laughed. The one who had passed, all alone on the other side, laughed more than the others, chaffing his unlucky comrades. They all laughed except the prisoners who looked like workmen; they stared at the colonel's face and were silent. . . .

Again, one of the five prisoners in the third batch read excellently, fluently, pronouncing each syllable, and from time to time he raised his eyes to look at the colonel. The newspaper he was reading was an old issue of *Pravda*, dated June 24, 1941, and the page read: 'The Germans have invaded Russia! Comrade soldiers, the Soviet people will win the war and will crush the invaders!' The words rang out under the rain, and the colonel laughed, the Sonderführer, the Feldwebel, the officers laughed, everybody laughed, and the prisoners also laughed, looking with envy and admiration at their companion who could read like a schoolmaster. 'Well done!' said the Sonderführer and his face shone. He seemed proud of the prisoner who could read so well: he was happy and proud as if the prisoner had been his pupil. 'You, to the right, over there,' said the Feldwebel in a good-natured voice giving him a kindly push with his hand. The colonel glanced at the Feldwebel, started to say something, but checked himself, and I noticed that he was blushing. . . .

The examination lasted for about an hour. When the last batch of three prisoners completed the two minutes of reading, the colonel turned to the

Feldwebel and said, 'Count them!' The Feldwebel began counting from a distance, pointing at each man with his finger, '*Ein, zwei, drei. . . .*' On the left were eighty-seven, on the right were thirty-one who had passed successfully. Then, at the colonel's bidding, the Sonderführer began to speak. He seemed like a schoolmaster dissatisfied with his pupils. He said that he was disappointed, that he was sorry to have failed so many, that he would have preferred to pass them all. At any rate, he added, those who had not succeeded in getting through the examination would have no reason to complain, provided they worked and displayed a greater skill than they had displayed at school. While he spoke, the group of the successful prisoners gazed at their less fortunate comrades with a compassionate air, and the younger ones dug their elbows into each other's ribs and giggled. When the Sonderführer had finished speaking, the colonel turned to the Feldwebel and said: '*Alles in Ordnung. Weg!*' and he walked off toward his headquarters followed by the other officers who looked back occasionally and exchanged whispers.

'You'll stay here until tomorrow, and tomorrow you will start for the labour camp,' said the Feldwebel to the group on the left. Then he turned toward the group on the right who had passed and harshly ordered them to fall in line. As soon as the prisoners formed a close line touching one another's elbows – they looked pleased, and laughed, glancing at their companions as if making fun of them – he counted them again quickly, said, 'Thirty-one,' and made a sign with his hand to a squad of SS men waiting at the end of the courtyard. He ordered, 'Right about, turn!' The prisoners turned right about, marched forward stamping their feet hard in the mud and, when they came face to face with the wall surrounding the yard, the Feldwebel commanded 'Halt!' Then turning to the SS men who had lined up behind the prisoners and had already raised their tommy guns, he cleared his throat, spat on the ground and shouted, 'Fire!'

When he heard the rattle of the guns, the colonel, who was within a few steps of the office, stopped, turned abruptly; the other officers stopped and also turned. The colonel passed his hand over his face as if wiping away sweat and, followed by his officers, entered the building.

'*Ach, so,*' said the Melitopol Sonderführer walking past me. 'Russia must be cleared of all this learned rabble. The peasants and workers who can read and write too well are dangerous. They are all communists.'[36]

In the face of such barbarous invaders, the regime exploited any weapon which might turn them back. The past, the history of the Russian people, seemed the best-equipped of remaining armouries. Atheism, zealously preached since the 1920s, was now renounced and religious services resumed. The Orthodox Church was, after all, the Russian Orthodox Church and thus a reliquary of cherished national traditions. The armed services remembered Tsarist victories, unfurled regimental banners, restored pre-revolutionary practices; they, too, bore national glory from past to present. Providing the usable facts about these pasts were, as likely or not, 'bourgeois historians', non-Bolshevik left-overs from Tsarist days whose careers had flourished with the blighting of Pokrovsky's reputation.[37] And there was a return to history in a more precise sense. In a speech on 7 November 1941, the 24th anniversary of the Revolution and what many suspected might be the last to be celebrated, Stalin called on heroes of battles past to assist him: the shades of Alexander Nevsky, Dimitri Donskoi, Alexander Suvorov and Michael Kutuzov must steel the Russian armies and embolden the Russian people. The invasions of Teutonic Knights, Poles, Lithuanians, Swedes, and the French had been endured; now the Germans, in their turn, would be expelled from the Russian homeland. And Stalin, Marshal Stalin, that crude, suspicious, banal and violent man, would be refulgent with the glory of Peter the Great and Ivan the Terrible.[38] Whatever doubts there may still have been at the end of the 1930s, war had confirmed that Stalin was indeed the *vozhd'*, the instrument of history.

Perhaps the most accessible exemplification of this historiographical process lies not in the turgid and unreadable pages of the *Short Course* but in the films of the greatest of revolutionary directors, Sergei Eisenstein. This brilliant offspring of the unhappy marriage of a Jewish engineer father and a Russian mother was born in 1898 and brought up by a Russian peasant nurse who later became his house-keeper, the only person who 'could accept him'.[39] With this background, it was as though Soviet power plus electrification plus the *muzhik mentalité* were joined in Eisenstein's *persona*.

He was, indeed, an intellectual child of the Revolution. His father opted for the Whites but, as a biographer has put it, Sergei, being 'part of the intelligentsia, wished to be one of the new men worthy to build the rich and free world lying beyond the anguish of civil war'.[40] Following employment decorating troop trains and in revolutionary 'Proletkult' theatre, Eisenstein produced, in 1925, *Battleship Potemkin* and then, in 1927–8, *October*. The first movie was an enormous success at home and abroad, prompting Eisenstein, with due revolutionary probity, to proclaim: 'The only thing I need is contact with the people.'[41] If *Potemkin* portrayed the 1905 Revolution, *October* aimed to re-stage the 'ten days that shook the world', to be history on film. As a historian Eisenstein was well aware that he had a part to play. He took pleasure in rediscovering Nicholas II's chamber pot and was photographed lolling on the imperial throne. He hired a cast of thousands. At his request, the *Aurora* was brought out of mothballs, sailed up the Neva and ordered to shell the Winter Palace. At least according to some sources, far more damage was done to the Palace during the filming than had actually occurred in 1917, a curious case of reality imitating art or of historiography doing those things which it said history had done.[42]

But the film was also 'difficult', avant-garde in its cinematographic techniques, self-consciously revolutionary and intellectual. Despite, in 1927–8, Eisenstein's rapid cutting of the Trotsky scenes, it was condemned as being too arty and symbolic.[43] The people, it seemed, did not necessarily need contact with Eisenstein and his career languished. He spent time abroad, travelling to the United States where the American Right hailed him as 'Hollywood's Messenger from Hell'. Returning to the USSR in 1932 he was shocked by what he found. 'Everything is so ugly. The new architecture we are building is cheap and bad. If only they would think a little.'[44]

In 1935–7 he began making *Bezhin Meadow*, a film about collectivisation, which involved a wicked *kulak* father killing a good, pro-collectivist, Bolshevik son. But this theme of family murder was unacceptable. *Pravda* condemned the film's 'harmful formalistic exercises' and it was suppressed.[45]

If Eisenstein was again to portray the past, he would need to keep an eye on the present. In 1938–9, with a co-director as watchdog, he produced *Alexander Nevsky*. 'My subject is patriotism,' he declared defensively, and the film duly glorified the medieval expulsion of those 'proto-Nazis', the Teutonic Knights.[46] Stalin, in what must have been a somewhat chilling conversation, remarked after viewing the movie: 'Sergei Mikhailovitch, you are a good Bolshevik after all!'[47] A good Stalinist was certainly adaptable. In the aftermath of the Ribbentrop–Molotov Pact Eisenstein forgot about Teutonic Knights for a while, *Nevsky* was withdrawn from circulation, and he used his talents to design the set and costumes for the 1940 Bolshoi production of Wagner's *Valkyrie*.[48]

The German invasion necessitated more changes. The Russian film industry was transported east, along with the rest, and found temporary quarters at Alma Ata, near the Mongolian–Chinese border. There, in 1942–3, in extraordinarily difficult technical circumstances (even film was often lacking), Eisenstein shot the first part of what was planned as a trilogy on the sixteenth-century Tsar, Ivan IV *Groznyi*, Ivan the Terrible. In the middle of the Great Patriotic War, Ivan's image was to stand for Russian history just as, in a medieval battle, the icons of Saints Cyril and Serge had once symbolised Russian state and society.

The story of Ivan's reputation is a fascinating one. Though, in the revolutionary 1920s, the Pokrovsky school had no time for Tsars or other such detritus of the past, in the next decade Ivan's reputation improved. By the Second World War a number of celebratory histories about him had appeared, those by such older-generation survivors as R.Y. Wipper and S.V. Bakhrushin, for example. Like so many others, these historians had commenced their careers under Nicholas II and then gone into eclipse before reviving in the 1930s. Their new theme was that Ivan was a Maker of Modern Russia, a proto-Stalin. His reliance on the *oprichnina* gentry to curb the feudal boyars seemed to have parallels with Stalin's dependence on the 'people', or at least on the *praktiki* and *vydvizhentsy,* and with his purging of those potential modern boyars, the Old Bolsheviks and intelligentsia. Like Stalin, Ivan had confronted enemies to the East and West, but he had fought them in battle and trumped their knavish tricks, gaining strategic and economic advantage by opening contact to England through the Arctic Sea. As long as the historical record was not studied closely, it seemed Ivan, too, had won his patriotic wars.

In scholarly circles, however, this Ivan revival did not last. As early as May 1956, Dubrovsky, the sometime pupil of Pokrovsky and expert on Stolypin who had suffered imprisonment under Stalin, delivered a paper to the Moscow Institute of History on 'the cult of personality in certain works on historical issues (on the evaluation of Ivan IV and others)'. Thereafter Ivan was to be buried, at least in academic circles, rather more swiftly than Stalin.[49]

But there is another side to the Ivan story which has been marvellously evoked by Maureen Perrie. Ivan 'lived' not only in the pages of history books but also in folklore. In popular tales and songs, it was frequently recalled that the *narod* had summoned Ivan's help against the prepotence of the boyars. Ivan's murder of his eldest son was criticised but his notorious cruelty was otherwise approved or accepted as what could be expected from a magical figure. His exemplary sentences – nailing the hat of a foreign ambassador or a Jew to his head, executing corrupt officials in public by slicing bits off them, the death of a thousand cuts – were remembered as half-humorous punishments made to fit the crime. Few even held it against Tsar Ivan that, when he introduced the liquor shop to Russia, he at first only permitted the *oprichniki* to have access to it. As Perrie concludes: 'the paradox remains, that [Ivan's] image in folklore is much more favourable than his historical reputation would seem to warrant.'[50]

In making his film about Ivan the Terrible Eisenstein was approaching a historical subject whose story could appeal to Stalin, the peasantry and the 'new class' alike. In *Ivan Part I,* finally screened as the war ended, Eisenstein got his history and his characterisation 'right'. Ivan both heroically overcame Kazan (the Mongols were portrayed as strikingly 'Asiatic' or Japanese), and checked the threat from the West. Domestically, he confronted a sea of troubles stirred up by the plotting boyars, but he thwarted their wicked designs especially by using the *oprichniki* and his 'all-seeing eye' Malyuta, 'a man of the people', who was pictured as a proto-Beria (and whose characterisation Stalin himself admired).[51] The film moved in stately fashion from one set scene to the next; for a partially literate audience, the baddies were easy to pick.[52] Leader of the boyars was Ivan's aunt, Euphrosinia, who magnificently evoked folkloric images of the wicked fairy or step-mother; potential replacement for Ivan was Euphrosinia's son Vladimir, a slobbering idiot, 'the boyar's tsar'.

The film's reception was triumphant. Eisenstein was awarded the 1946 Stalin Prize and rumour had it that when he completed *Ivan*, he would make the historical parallels crystal clear by filming the life of the dictator himself. Meanwhile Stalin engaged Eisenstein in a wonderfully resonant conversation:

Stalin: 'Did you study history?'
Eisenstein: 'More or less'.
Stalin: 'More or less? I also have a little knowledge of history . . . . Czar Ivan was a great and wise ruler. If one compares him with Louis XI . . . then Ivan the Terrible was in a much higher class. Ivan the Terrible's wisdom was that he championed the national point of view. He did not let foreigners in – he safeguarded the country against penetration by foreign influences . . . . Peter I was also a great sovereign, but he was too liberal in relation to foreigners . . . . Ivan the Terrible was very ruthless. One can show that he was ruthless. But you must show why *it was necessary to be ruthless*.'[53]

There was the rub. As the battles of the Great Patriotic War ceased, the battle for history resumed. In *Ivan Part II* Eisenstein would get his history 'wrong'. There was a scene in which Malyuta exhibited slain boyars and Ivan murmured 'too few'. There was another in which Ivan had 'drunk much but [was] absolutely sober'. There were more executions which Ivan justified:

> Not in anger, not in malice. Not in Fierceness. But for treason. For the betrayal of the whole people's cause. . . . Not for myself, not for ambition's sake. But for the Motherland. Not out of savagery. But for reasons of state.

The *opritchniki* were not all incorruptible; they engaged in a (colour) orgy scene.[54]

Stalin was displeased. The Central Committee complained that Ivan had been portrayed as 'weak and indecisive, somewhat like Hamlet'. *Ivan Part II* was suppressed until 1958 and Eisenstein forced to make a public recantation. What he should have exhibited on the screen, he now said, was 'Ivan the builder, Ivan the creator of a new, powerful, united Russian power', and he apologised for characterising the 'progressive *opritchniks* . . . as a gang of degenerates something like the Ku Klux Klan'.[55] Perhaps he had thus again become a good Bolshevik after all, but there would be no *Ivan Part III*, no *Life of Stalin*. On 9 February 1948, Eisenstein died. While Stalin lived and even after he was no more, on both screen and page there would be within the borders of the Soviet Empire one simple version of history.

War was followed by prolonged international tension and, as has already been noted in chapter 1, this Cold War rapidly engendered its own historiography. Outside the USSR, the builders of the model of totalitarianism happily argued that Russian communism and German Nazism were opposite sides of the same coin, even while totalitarianist history was itself something like the opposite of that static version of history which had created the *Short Course*. As Sheila Fitzpatrick ('Ms Sheila Fitzpatrick' to her right-wing critics)[56] would recall:

> Not even rhetorical peace and friendship existed between Western and Soviet historians during the mid-60s. In Soviet eyes, Western scholars who wrote about the post-1917 period were virtually all Cold Warriors and 'bourgeois falsifiers'. Western historians were scarcely more flattering about their Soviet counterparts ('party hacks') and viewed even the factual content of their publications with suspicion.[57]

The great exception to this manichean division was Isaac Deutscher. His career deserves a moment's reflection because of the enormous popular success of his biographies of Stalin and Trotsky[58] and because his own life story is such a splendid example of the way past and present mingle in the history of the history of the 'long Second World War'. Deutscher was born in 1907 into a Jewish family in Cracow, then part of the Habsburg Empire. He was a precocious child in a learned household and by the age of sixteen was reading his poems in public and had had a book of them published. Resisting family pressure to become a rabbi, he turned into what he would later define as a 'non-Jewish Jew'.[59] Though he was attracted to Polish politics and to socialism, he was warned by his father against surrendering to provincialism: 'German is the world language. Why should you bury all your talent in a provincial language? You have only to go beyond Auschwitz'[60] (then an insignificant town in the hinterland of Cracow).

In 1927, a year after Polish parliamentarism was overthrown by Marshal Pilsudski's nationalist-militarist coup in the commencement of Poland's 'long Second World War', Deutscher joined the Polish Communist Party. But, he retained his independence and a visit to the USSR in 1931 confirmed his fears about developments there. Returning home, he formed an anti-Stalin, pro-Trotsky faction in the PCP but in 1932 was expelled for 'spreading panic about Nazism' – he had rejected the Comintern's 'catastrophist', 'the worse the better' and 'social fascist' lines. As the biographer of Stalin would later explain, he thus belonged to those whom Stalin had cruelly defeated. And, in September 1936, he was one of the first Marxists publicly to denounce the show trials.[61]

In April 1939 he fled to England, but his parents and other members of his family were caught by the Nazis and died at Auschwitz some time after 1942. By then, Deutscher, who had taught himself English with extraordinary rapidity, had become a journalist, writing for *The Economist* and *Observer*. But he abandoned his commitment neither to Marxism nor 'revolution' and, indeed, in the 1960s became one of the intellectual parents of the Anglo-American New Left.

Shortly after the Second World War, Oxford University Press commissioned from Deutscher a biography of Stalin, which he wrote in 1947–8 and had published in 1949. It was an odd task in many ways – biography was not the most obvious activity for a genuine Marxist and moreover as Deutscher put it: 'I had never been a devotee of the Stalin cult and the cold war was not my war.'[62] His Stalin would be neither that of the *Short Course* nor of the totalitarianists.

Deutscher had one other characteristic which made him an unusual historian of the 'long Second World War'. His sense of himself as being a non-Jewish Jew was that he belonged to a borderland people and that he need not opt exclusively for one nationality or another:

> As Jews [he and his ancestors] . . . dwelt on the borderlines of various civilizations, religions and national cultures. They were born and brought up on the borderlines of various epochs. . . . Their minds lived on the margins or in the nooks and crannies of their respective nations.[63]

Their most significant figures – Marx, Trotsky and Rosa Luxemburg, Freud too – were superficially 'rootless', but 'had the deepest roots in intellectual tradition and in the noblest aspirations of their times. . . . Their manner of thinking is dialectical, because, living on the borderlines of nations and religions, they see society in a state of flux.'[64] The Zionists were wrong. Israel was an 'act of Jewish despair'. In their internationalism, the Jewish pioneers of socialism and Deutscher himself had best resolved the problem of nationality which so signposted the twisted road to Auschwitz, and which so underpinned the crisis of the 'long Second World War'.

Deutcher's identity was co-terminous with his Marxism: 'I have never hesitated in my Marxist *Weltanschauung*,' he would write shortly before his death, 'I just cannot think otherwise than in Marxist terms. Kill me, I cannot do it. I may try; I just cannot. Marxism has become part of my existence.'[65]

Deutscher's biography of Stalin was beautifully written (some of his more small-minded critics would say that was what was most deplorable and dangerous about it)[66] and contained brilliant psychological insights: 'There was no sense of guilt, not a trace of it, in his socialism. . . . In Djugashvili [Stalin, the apprentice Bolshevik] class hatred was not his second nature – it was his first.'[67] None the less, for all his proclaimed origin in the ambiguities of border peoples, Deutscher was confident in his conclusions. Khrushchev's revelations about the cult of personality, which the historian Pospelov had helped to draft, did not make Deutscher want to alter a line of his own book.[68] Nor did he wish to moralise too much: 'The truly astonishing aspect of the purges . . . is how little they changed the surface of Soviet Russia.'[69] In personal terms, Stalin was cruel, ignorant and banal; yet he presided over Herculean tasks – industrialisation, literacy, the victory against Nazism. In this regard, Deutscher wrote, 'the greatest reformers in Russian history, Ivan the Terrible and Peter the Great, and the great reformers of other nations too, seem to be dwarfed by the giant form of the General Secretary. . . . The ideas of the second revolution were not his. He neither foresaw it nor prepared for it. Yet he, and in a sense he alone, accomplished it', the terrible task of driving 'barbarism out of Russia by barbarous means'.[70]

Deutscher's Stalin, then, lived in a wicked world; as the *vozhd'* himself expressed it in 1931: 'We are fifty or a hundred years behind the advanced countries. We must make good this lag in ten years. Either we do or they crush us.'[71] Certainly Nazism and perhaps international capitalism threatened from outside, but within the Soviet Empire there was the heavy problem of 'backwardness', the *muzhiks*, their traditions and *mentalité*, the sad legacy of Russian history. The new intelligentsia, Deutscher noted in words prefiguring the ideas of 1980s social historians, were educated above all to be practical. Their 'chief interest was in machines and technical discoveries, in bold projects for the development of backward provinces, in administrative jobs, and in the arts of business management' but not in humanist ethics.[72]

Deutscher's Stalin had been responsible for much evil, but still the achievement and hope of the tragic, self-contradictory but creative revolution soared above individual folly or crime. The war had been won; the idea of eventual equality was compelling. A determination to educate the people was praiseworthy and, whatever its faults, Soviet society was greatly to be preferred to the USA where 'the vulgarity of the. . . press, radio, film, and book-selling trade is really overwhelming'.[73] And, Deutscher was predicting in the 1960s, by the end of the century the standard of living in the USSR would probably equal that of the USA and would certainly surpass that of Western Europe. The working hours of ordinary Russians, he surmised, would decline to two or three per day, and the people, not stunted by the capitalist mass media, would use their leisure creatively and well.[74]

Not surprisingly these opinions made Deutscher a target of the Right. In the 1970s Leopold Labedz was still complaining crossly in *Survey* that the commercial success of Deutscher's book was sad testament to the gullibility of the times.[75] But by then new currents were beginning to eddy through the historiography of Russia's 'long Second World War'.

One rather idiosyncratic 'new historian' of the USSR was Marc Ferro, the 'third generation' editor of *Annales* mentioned at the start of this chapter. He had sought to take *Annales* history from France to the world and from the Middle Ages to contemporary fields and in the early 1960s, as a young Research Fellow, had won some privileged access to Soviet archives, a by-product of the then close relations between the USSR and Gaullist France. As a result, in 1967 he published a first volume on the revolutions of 1917 which would be translated into English as *The Russian Revolution of February 1917* in 1972. A second volume, on the October Revolution, appeared in 1976 in French (and in 1980 in English).[76]

What is most interesting about these two books, neither of which completely represents a luminous application of the '*Annales* method', is their reception in the USSR. The first, with its argument that the February Revolution was a fact before it happened, was received warmly, especially considering it was the work of a 'Western' scholar; the second was studiously ignored. What had gone wrong with Ferro's attempt to bring 'the people' back into accounts of the Revolution, to show that 'compared to the social upheavals, the political stage with its gestures and speech-making, seems in retrospect a kind of shadow-play where the same actors trotted yet again through their roles, before an audience less and less attentive, and increasingly occupied elsewhere'?[77]

The answer is simple enough. Ferro concluded that not only had the Revolution (or Revolutions) come 'from below', but so had their violence. 'The terror' of 1918, he wrote, 'was clearly no deviation [nor was it] solely the doing of the Bolshevik leaders'; rather 'it came up from the depths.'[78] Stalinism also, it seemed, was a fact before it happened. Moreover, he implied, if a regime used barbarous means to drive out barbarism that regime stayed barbarous, at least while the generation which implemented the barbarity survived.

Brezhnev's Russia could not tolerate such brutal honesty, but even as it stagnated and its old men determinedly forgot, new opinions about history were expressed within the USSR itself. After 1956, the Khrushchev 'thaw' had to some extent extended to historiography. A new edition of the official history was prepared and took care to credit the 'victories' of the Five Year Plans or the Great Patriotic War not to Stalin, but to 'the Party'.[79] Some useful research was done, notably by V.P. Danilov and others on Stalin's 'errors' in the pursuit of collectivisation, but the (partial) revision of contemporary history at this time owed more to such novels as *Doctor Zhivago*[80] and *One Day in the Life of Ivan Denisovich*,[81] or to a memoir like *Into the Whirlwind*,[82] than it did to historiography.

A new freeze was not long in coming. When in 1965, S.P. Trapeznikov, a loyal assistant of Brezhnev, was appointed head of the Central Committee's Department of Science and Education Establishments, the old order returned. Danilov's latest work on the agony of the 1930s peasantry was suppressed and he himself was downgraded academically. As if to illustrate that there was again a single truth on this and other matters, S.P. Trapeznikov published a 'definitive', traditionalist account of collectivisation. And Soviet school-children went on chanting: 'By defeating Hitler's Germany, the Soviet Nation saved mankind from annihilation or enslavement by German Fascism, and preserved world civilization. This great exploit of Soviet citizens will never fade from the memory of a grateful mankind.'[83]

Though many must have carried doubts in their hearts, those who did not toe the party line on this and other matters found their careers blighted and retreated into silence, conformism or arcane scholarship. (It was sometimes possible to think radical thoughts on the 'Third World' and the 'Asiatic mode of production' while Eurocommunism for a time in the 1970s encouraged some mention of Gramsci.)[84] One who did not thus divert his interests, who suffered but did not stay silent, was Roy Medvedev. Over the next two decades, he would become the most famous 'liberal', 'dissenting' historian working in the USSR.

Medvedev was born in 1925 into a distinguished Soviet intellectual family,[85] having neither the pessimistic polish of a Mandelstam nor the rough and ready narrowness of the *vydvizhentsy*. His father was a commissar in the Red Army and an instructor in philosophy at the Military Academy, who would die a victim of Stalinism on the Kolyma. 'This was the tragedy', Medvedev has recently commented, 'which changed the course of my life and my ideas about society.'[86] His twin brother, Zhores, was a prominent biochemist who led the final denunciation of T.D. Lysenko and other creatures of Stalin in the scientific field, and who, after a scandalous period of psychological confinement, left the USSR in 1973.[87] Roy Medvedev was an educationalist but, after 1956, he became fascinated with the history of Stalinism.

In 1961 he began a large-scale work on a history of the dictatorship which he completed in 1968. By then he was in bad odour with the regime which, perhaps egged on by emigré rightists (*Posev,* a journal in West Germany, published a critical letter written by Medvedev but apparently sent to them by the KGB), expelled him from the party.[88] His book was first published in North America, in 1971, under the title *Let History Judge*. It would not be officially released until the Gorbachev era and Medvedev could not join in public debate in the USSR until 1988. Meanwhile, he kept writing[89] and built up many contacts with the West, especially through such bodies as the Bertrand Russell Peace Foundation, or through individuals such as Isaac Deutscher's widow, Tamara.

Let History Judge, none the less, was Medvedev's most important statement. Its basic thesis was simple, and, for a 'liberal Marxist' at the time, predictable – 'Stalin created Stalinism'. The Stalin period was vile, cruel and murderous, and all that its most bitter critics, Robert Conquest and the other totalitarianists in the West, said about it was true. But their attempts to explain Stalinism by linking it to other aspects of Russian history were wrong. Stalin was not Lenin's fault, or that of the Revolution and the Party. Nor was Stalinism the fault of the people, 'for it was the masses, aroused by the socialist revolution, who managed to check and later to overcome many of the harmful consequences of the cult of Stalin's personality'. The present lesson of history, Medvedev preached, was that

> the Soviet Union passed through a serious disease and lost many of its finest sons. When the cult of Stalin's personality was exposed a great step was made to recovery. But not everything connected with Stalinism is behind us, by no means everything. The process of purifying the Communist movement, of washing out all the layers of Stalinist filth, is not yet finished. It must be carried through to the end.[90]

This heartening rhetoric might have sounded encouraging to the Bertrand Russell Peace Foundation, but others in the West thought of themselves as both intellectually and politically tougher and more rigorous. For them, Medvedev had only glimpsed the beginning of wisdom. Though the model of 'totalitarianism' had been attacked and damaged in the 1960s, its paladins had never surrendered their theory or their control over many of the fortresses of academe. Rather, from the firmest of bases in the United States and, for example, West German academic establishments,[91] the totalitarianists came again. In the 1980s of Reagan, Thatcher and Kohl, the idea of an 'evil Empire' at least as evil as Nazism became a staple of conservative political discourse and gained renewed strength in intellectual circles. The pile of academic works preaching its cause mounted impressively.

Robert Conquest had not let up in his denunciation of the purges[92] and his followers used more and more sophisticated statistical techniques to 'prove' that tens of millions had fallen victim to Stalinism.[93] Critics complained that the techniques were fine but the original 'facts' were less so – as one radical historian put it 'because there are no convincing statistics, all calculations are quite subjective and appear to reflect the point of view of the person making the calculation.'[94] But such criticism was scorned and its author berated. Richard Pipes at Harvard University wrote what might be called a 'Course of Russian History' which, although it lacked the stylistic brio of A.J.P. Taylor's war-inspired *Course of German History*, intended to show 'why in Russia – unlike the rest of Europe to which Russia belongs by virtue of her location, race and religion – society has proven unable to impose on political authority any kind of effective restraints.'[95] Rather than Stalin being wholly to blame, it turned out that the seeds of Soviet totalitarianism lay in the tradition of 'patrimonial government' in Russia, or even in its frozen soil; Russian productivity was always too low to allow the sort of surplus in grain production on which liberty was ultimately dependent. When he was not exploring past history, Pipes was interested in present politics. From the pages of *Commentary*, he exhorted the Reagan regime to be firm in its international dealings and not to resile from a belief in war as the only solution to the Russian problem since, Pipes had decided, change from within was inconceivable for such a state.[96]

The chief advocates of totalitarianism remained the political scientists, whose discipline had crafted the models of the 1950s. Zbigniew Brzezinski had transferred from academe to high politics to become Jimmy Carter's National Security Adviser. That job turned out not to be an easy one. Despite the best efforts of Brzezinski, who would later bewail his President's (or his other advisers') reluctance to stage a coup in time in Teheran,[97] Carter was portrayed by conservative America as a wimp, soft on the Russians and soft on the Ayatollah. When Carter fell, Brzezinski fell with him. But other political scientists kept up the totalitarianist barrage and dealt peremptorily with mutiny in their own ranks, as Jerry Hough, for example, would discover.[98]

Puissant the totalitarianists certainly were, and their arguments were convincing to many, but for all their power and certainty, they never obtained hegemony in the West. In the 1980s, indeed, a challenge to them grew from the new generation of social historians, belonging to what might be termed the 'functionalist' school of the history of Stalinism. One of its leaders was Sheila Fitzpatrick, an Australian who migrated to the United States from Oxford, and who, for a time, was the wife of Jerry Hough.

For an outsider, it is hard not to be pleased by this tardy entry of social history into Russian studies. Ritual denunciations of Stalin or Lenin or the Bolsheviks or the Russians pall after a while. Moreover, though the theory of totalitarianism may have its uses, there remains little reason to regard Nazism and Stalinism as especially comparable regimes, and the static nature of the political science model is almost by definition offensive to historians, whose very discipline concentrates on the demonstration and explanation of change. Most of the new social historians are also committed to archival research in a way that has scarcely been true of older-generation experts on the USSR (hindered as they were by being banned from the archives in a country whose terrible history had hardly made it a paradise for archivists or encouraged the careful conservation of documents).[99] Indeed, Fitzpatrick has sounded very moderate in explaining her personal methodology. Too much theory, she fears, gets in the way of the facts: 'I am still a positivist at heart,' she has declared wrily, 'I value the illusion of objectivity.'[100]

Of course the new cohort of social historians provides no final solution to the problem of Russian history (plainly no such thing exists or ought to exist). The recent Fitzpatrick-inspired debates in the pages of *Russian Review* and *Slavic Review* show the width of the spectrum of opinion on Stalin and the USSR's 'long Second World War'.[101] Despite fulminations from the Right (as Peter Kenez put it: 'consciously or unconsciously [the new historians] de-demonise Stalin and his Politbureau, so much so that Stalinism disappears as a phenomenon'),[102] a single school with a single answer has thankfully not appeared. Rather too much of the conflict is linked as ever to wars of power and promotion in the US history profession and in US society. As Gabor Rittersporn has noted, 'to a large extent this debate is not about Soviet history, but about Western *mentalités*.'[103]

There is one other factor which deserves underlining. Many of the new social historians would doubtless say that they love and respect the Russian people and sympathise with their suffering both in the Great Patriotic War and under Stalinism. Many also have some sort of allegiance to leftist ideals. And yet their work tends to have a decidedly pessimistic conclusion, at least about revolutions, and is almost the exact opposite of Medvedev's stubborn cheerfulness. For the new social historians, it seems, the tyranny and error, the extreme social and cultural conservatism of Stalinism before and after 1953, occurred because the 'people', or at least that part of them chosen, at random, through events in the Civil War, access to party membership, the famous accelerated courses of the late 1920s and early 1930s, or the opportunity for social mobility available to peasant veterans of the Great Patriotic War, took control of the Revolution. Those with chapped hands ousted (and often killed) those with white hands; they administered an empire and won a war, and then stagnated like so many returned soldiers, recalling a time of troubles and their triumph over it as the happiest days of their lives. Endless tales of how the T34 vanquished the Nazis at Kursk assisted neither the growth of that pluralist democracy nor the development of that post-computer technology which an effective modern economy requires.

Eventually, the old men of the Great Patriotic War, the patriarchs of the Five Year Plans, collectivisation and the purges, died. In March 1985, there was a symbolic changing of the guard among those occupying the summit of Soviet power. The new General Secretary was M.S. Gorbachev, who had been trained in the 1950s in law and agricultural economics, and who had not been an old fighter in the Second World War. It is true that in his first speeches he continued to emphasise his generation's commitment to that supreme test, that glorious triumph: 'Our victory has not receded into the past. It is a living victory crucial to the present and the future.'[104] But he also wanted new efficiency, greater purpose, higher productivity. Progress in such matters could only occur, it soon became apparent, if there were cultural and historiographical changes. Stalin would not be buried until the Stalinist version of the past was successfully interred.

Gorbachev and his supporters did not move to this task eagerly or early. Indeed, in April 1986 the General Secretary was still warning: 'If we began studying the past, we would use up all our energies and set the people at loggerheads.'[105] In his heart he may well have agreed with Academician Mints, who back in the 1930s had managed to distance himself from the fall of Pokrovsky and who now in his nineties accepted *perestroika*,[106] but only because it might make Soviet historians more effective in debates with their Western counterparts. But what the senior politicans or gerontocratic academics wanted no longer mattered; again Russian society had moved and in its moving had sought consolation, advice and armour from different readings of history. These readings would appear first not from the historians but from poets, film-makers, novelists, dramatists – and, it seems, the 'people', or at least from that educated youth who had had to sit through boring and irrelevant compulsory lessons on Stalinist Marxist dialectics, but who also had been influenced or inspired by the humanities. Out of the new generation was growing a new intelligentsia with all the true and false ideals, ambitions, self-delusion and sensitivity that that term entails. As one self-consciously dissident intellectual would proclaim arrogantly, 'the future of culture is the future of the country'.[107]

There was one obvious metaphor with which to begin. For some time now, the problem had not been how to praise Stalin but how to bury him. On the frontispiece of her beautiful memoir about the purges, Evgenia Ginzburg had quoted from Yevtushenko's *The Heirs of Stalin*:

> So I ask our government
> To double
> To treble
> The guard
> Over his tomb.

These hopes of the 1960s had scarcely been realised, but in the second half of the 1980s they were expressed anew. The best early symbol of them was a film, *Repentance (Pokayanie),* made by Tengiz Abuladze and screened in January 1987. Perhaps appropriately for his task, Abuladze was a Georgian though, something of a latter-day radical, he had been born in 1924. With wit and skill, his film told of a town's attempt to bury a corrupt and cruel town boss, 'Varlam Aravidze', symbol both of Stalin and of the past. But whenever individuals tried to get rid of the body, up mysteriously it popped again. While there was silence about Varlam's crimes by those who had participated in and turned a blind eye to them, there could be no genuine repentance.[108]

Novels (notably Alexander Bek's *New Appointment* [1987] and Andrei Rybakov's *Children of the Arbat* [1987]), similarly engendered critical debate. By 1987, the *Literaturnaya Gazeta* had a circulation of 3.1 million and, as R.W. Davies has remarked, 'people stood in queues from six in the morning for these publications and then passed them from hand to hand'.[109] Gorbachev himself began to amend his rhetoric. In February 1987 he declared that 'there should not be any blank pages in either our history or our literature', but, he added hastily, 'we must value each of the 70 years of our Soviet history. . . . There was both joy and bitterness. But whatever occurred we went forward and did not fall under the tanks of fascism. We overcame fascism not only with heroism and self-sacrifice, but also with better steel, better tanks, better soldiers.'[110] Everything else could be let go, indeed the more wicked were Stalin and the Stalinists the better, but Lenin, the Revolution, and the Great Patriotic War must remain sacred.

Though some observers detected hesitations and a turning back, a process had begun which seemed difficult now to stop. In October 1987 it was announced that *Ten Days that Shook the World* would finally be reprinted.[111] In 1988 *Pravda*, amid sustained controversy, took to publishing historical features every Friday. In February 1988, the sentences which had condemned Bukharin,[112] Rykov, Rakovsky and six others were overturned; in June, Zinoviev, Kamenev, Pyatakov and Radek were rehabilitated.[113] Of the Old Bolsheviks, only Trotsky[114] was still beyond the pale (and his foreign defenders, E.H. Carr and Deutscher, were still criticised).[115] *Repentance* earned Abuladze the Lenin Prize.

Among the historians, the leading radical pushing for further change was Yuri Afanasyev. (In 1990 he would join De Felice and others on the international editorial board of the *Journal of Contemporary History*.) Perhaps appropriately Afanasyev was an expert on the *Annales,* by the late 1980s ready to defend them in any circumstances but once their critic.[116] As if emboldened by his possession of a useful paradigm, Afanasyev now took to commenting on contemporary events. His views were clear: 'There is not and has never been in the world a people and a country with such a falsified history as ours.' Under Stalin and Brezhnev, he complained, 'history as a science was not needed; it was required only to justify the injustices which had been committed.' Now the USSR needed 'an objective view' of Stalin. Afanasyev did seem to realise that 'science' and 'objectivity' are somewhat embattled terms but he must have been pleased when, in 1987, Gorbachev admitted that the 'guilt' of Stalin and his entourage was 'huge and unforgivable'.

Afanasyev, along with Roy Medvedev, rapidly campaigned to make that admission concrete. Memorials to the victims of Stalinism should, he urged, be constructed throughout the Soviet Empire: 'The Memorial must be a permanent reminder to humanity that history does not leave any lawlessness unpunished, does not forget any evil, that no tyranny remains without exposure and condemnation.'[117]

In May 1988 came the final demonstration that Party history no longer had the answers. The State Committee for Education cancelled the final exams in history and social science. Afanasyev had declared 'the whole textbook is a lie' and now, it was announced, a new one would be composed.[118] By the end of 1991 the book had still not been published.

A critical commentator had remarked in 1988: 'the political legitimacy of the Soviet group derives largely from its historical role, and particularly from its ties to the Russian Revolution'[119] (or, he should have added, to the Great Patriotic War). What in essence these ties depended on was a single reading of the past. Now that past seemed irredeemably fragmented and the decline and fall of the Soviet Empire or its mutation into a naked form of military dictatorship seemed only a matter of time.

Meanwhile varieties of history grew apace, mocking the extreme totalitarianist theory that citizens of a totalitarian society were 'atomised' and had had their minds and their memories wiped clean by an all-intrusive regime. One growth area was 'nationalist' history. Everywhere non-Russian peoples remembered either how their 'freedom' (often it had been of a decidedly limited kind) had been snuffed out by the reconstitution of the Russian Empire in the early 1920s, or after the Ribbentrop–Molotov Pact. They also recalled other moments of 'national glory', which might stretch back to the Middle Ages. They imagined communities in the past which might lead to new political formations in the future. Even the Stalin regime at its height had given some protection to most local languages and cultures.[120] Now those languages and cultures coalesced into a history and each seemed likely to demand its own state in a way curiously or menacingly reminiscent of the successor states of the Habsburg Empire.

Among the new nationalists were also the Russians, who expressed their 'own' history most ominously in the xenophobic and anti-Semitic *Pamyat'*. This organisation had started as a sort of grouping of historic environmentalists, committed to restoring degraded national monuments, but turned into a fully-fledged nationalist movement. The attitude of politicians in the Russian segment of the USSR to its ideas and ambitions remained unclear. And in addition to *Pamyat'*, other national conservatives began to write romantic re-evocations of Tsarist life[121] (one argued that Russia had gone wrong because it had shown little sympathy to the ideals of the RSPCA). A right-wing paper greatly increased its circulation by publishing long extracts from the histories of the nineteenth-century Slavophile, Nikolai Karamzin.[122] In the press and even in learned circles, Stalin was not without his defenders, especially when controversy began to spread to Russia's military effort and achievement in the Great Patriotic War. As Dimitri Volkogonov, General and Professor of Philosophy, reminded his readers in an article in *Literaturnaya Gazeta* in December 1987, Stalin had committed indefensible crimes and yet

> in those years the foundations of all that we build on today were created. Those were the times of the supreme flight of the human spirit of the Soviet people, who stood firm and conquered fascism in the Great Patriotic War. It is wrong, when assessing Stalin or the people in his immediate entourage, mechanically to transfer these assessments to the party and to the millions of ordinary people whose faith in the rightness of revolutionary ideals was not shaken.[123]

Maybe both Stalin and Lenin could be buried but, for the moment, the Red Army was not willing to give up its war. In 1991, however, any popular base for this history collapsed. When, in August, they briefly seized power, Defence Minister Dimitri Yazov and his nostalgic comrades made no mention whatever of their birthright in Marxism and the Revolution, and were only half-hearted in their reference to the Great Patriotic War. They knew that the populace of Leningrad, a city which ostentatiously opposed the coup, had already voted to change its name back to St Petersburg and thus had denied any continuing significance to the epic wartime siege. In this new world, Yazov, Vladimir Kryuchkov and the rest had no past (and no future).

They may have been more helpless in their unmooring from history, but they were not alone in their failure to locate a usable past. The professional historians of the USSR were also bewildered. This bewilderment had been well displayed in a meeting organised in 1989 between experts associated with the *Journal of Modern History* and their Soviet colleagues. As A.A. Iskenderov stated in opening the proceedings: 'No one present here today will be surprised to hear me say that in recent years, or even in the last several decades, world historical scholarship has not been the unified process we thought it was.'[124] In the debate which followed, the old Soviet buddies, now themselves openly factionalised, besought a spare paradigm from the Americans. For, P.V. Volubuev remarked sadly, 'whenever a historian appears before any audience, he is beset by such a hail of questions that by the end of the evening he feels squeezed like a lemon.' Such exhaustion could not be alleviated because 'at the moment, we still do not have the answer'.[125] Yuri Afanasyev, too, maintained his belief that historians could find 'regular laws in the development of historical knowledge'.[126] And few of the Russians present seem much to have listened to the urgings of Fitzpatrick and Steve Kaplan about the multiplicity of truth, or to have accepted that the Americans did not have the final answer concealed somewhere in their conceptual kit.[127]

In one of the first English-language summaries of this continuing cultural crisis, R.W. Davies had contended that 'nothing like this has ever happened before in the history of the world. In the course of 1987 and 1988, tens of millions of Soviet citizens became passionately involved in studying their country's past, and in rethinking the principles and practice of Soviet socialism.'[128] At least in the first part of his statement, Davies exaggerated. As this book has shown, almost every society which endured the 'long Second World War' eventually had a reckoning with what had become its first prevailing myth or historical interpretation of that conflict. In this sense, historiographical *glasnost* and *perestroika* merely saw the USSR catching up with its Western European neighbours. And yet both the delay in this catching up and the horror, the horror of the Soviet people's actual experience of the 'long Second World War', carry a bitter legacy. Converting the revisionist ideas into an acceptance that history is a plural subject, a democratic argument without end, will not be an easy task.

None the less it must be admitted that, in 1991, history is alive and well in the USSR, often frighteningly so. As a recent commentator has concluded: 'The future of the Soviet Union is being determined by the fierce debate over its past.'[129] He might have added the hope that the debate will proceed and will become ever more committed to complexity, variety and pluralism. Then perhaps, the Great Patriotic War will not have been fought in vain and the decline and fall of the Soviet or Russian Empires will not become a story merely of the crimes, follies and misfortunes of humankind.

8

Hiroshima, *mon amour*: under eastern eyes

6 August 1945: The hour was early; the morning still, warm and beautiful.
... Clad in drawers and undershirt, I was sprawled on the living room floor
because I had just spent a sleepless night on duty as an air warden in my
hospital. Suddenly, a strong flash of light startled me —and then another.
... A stone lantern in the garden became brilliantly lit and I debated whether
this light was caused by a magnesium flare or sparks from a passing trolley.
... A profound weakness overcame me ... to my surprise I discovered that
I was completely naked. How odd! Where were my drawers and undershirt?[1]

So runs the diary entry for 6 August 1945 of Hachiya Michihiko, director of
Hiroshima Communications Hospital. By the next day, having reached his hospital
and sought some succour for himself, Hachiya was hearing still more hellish tales.
A friend had walked over the Misasa bridge near Hiroshima Castle. There many
thousands had died. The friend explained:

The sight of the soldiers, though, was more dreadful than the dead people
floating down the river. I came onto I don't know how many, burned from
the hips up; and where the skin had peeled, their flesh was wet and mushy.
... And they had no faces! Their eyes, noses and mouths had been burned
away, and it looked like their ears had melted off. It was hard to tell front
from back. One soldier, whose features had been destroyed and was left with
his white teeth sticking out, asked me for some water, but I didn't have any![2]

But even in this Dantesque world, momentary comfort could be found:

11 August: ... Following the news that Nagasaki had been bombed, a man
came in ... with the incredible story that Japan had the same mysterious
weapon, but until now, had kept it a strict secret and had not used it because
it was judged too horrible even to mention. This man went on to say that a
special attack squad had now used the bomb on the mainland of America.
... If San Francisco, San Diego and Los Angeles had been hit like Hiroshima,
what chaos there must be in those cities! At last Japan was retaliating! The
whole atmosphere in the ward changed, and for the first time since Hiroshima
was bombed, everyone became cheerful and bright. Those who had been hurt

167

the most were the happiest. Jokes were made, and some began singing the victory song.[3]

Alas, the news was false. On 15 August, Emperor Hirohito, in however arcane language and however ambiguous words, broadcast to his people the Imperial Japanese surrender. Dr Hachiya, ill but still trying to keep his hospital functioning, was appalled:

> I had been prepared for the broadcast to tell us to dig in and fight to the end, but this unexpected message left me stunned. . . . My psychic apparatus stopped working and my tear glands stopped too. . . . The one word – surrender – had produced a greater shock than the bombing of our city. . . . But the order to surrender was the Emperor's order and to this we could not object. His injunction to bear the unbearable could mean but one thing. As a nation we must be patient.[4]

As these passages from Dr Hachiya's diary imply, Japan is one of the enigmas of the contemporary world. For the Marxist Eric Hobsbawm, whose recent book, *Nations and Nationalism since 1780: Programme, Myth, Reality,* has been cited on a number of occasions in this study, the idea of the single and united nation no longer makes political or economic sense. 'Ethnic communities and groups in modern societies', he says, accompanied by their multiple histories, 'are fated to coexist, whatever the rhetoric which dreams of a return to an unmixed nation' and a single, unified, 'truthful' history. But Hobsbawm's Law has one exception: 'Probably the only functioning "national economy" of the late twentieth century', he notes, 'is the Japanese.'[5]

In making this assessment, Hobsbawm has an ally in the great liberal internationalist and generalist historian, William H. McNeill. In his Creighton Lectures of 1985, McNeill aimed to 'show polyethnicity as normal in civilized societies, whereas the ideal of an ethnically unitary state was exceptional in theory and rarely approached in practice. . . . Marginality and pluralism were and are the norm of civilised existence. . . . Only in remote and barbarous lands did ethnic homogeneity prevail.' But again there was one variant to his rule – Japan.[6]

That country by the 1990s is either the second or first greatest economic power in the world. Its parliament and press are free; its people consume and seem happy. It is true that there is something a little disturbing about endless administration by a single party, the Liberal Democrats, but perhaps the division and disputation natural in a democracy occur within and among the factions of the LDP rather than between the governing party and the feeble or fractious opposition. It is also true that there is something distinctive about contemporary Japan's relationship with its own past. Perhaps there is no relationship. After 1945 the US occupiers received, as it were, a Japan with its historical ears, mouth, nose and eyes melted into nothingness; post-war Japan did not know front from back. Then the plastic surgeons of American truth, American justice and American democracy fashioned a new Japan, which could face the world in a new way. Arguably, Japan, in a much more profound sense than Germany, Italy, France or the other combatants of the 'long Second World War', was born again in *Anno Zero*, or, at least, sloughed off, at that time, its historical skin. Perhaps its 'Fifteen Years' War' (1931–45)[7] has become merely of antiquarian interest. Perhaps Japan is not so much a post-modern as a post-historical society (and thus the better equipped for its many economic triumphs). Perhaps Japan's experience of the 'end of history' dates from 1945. Perhaps Japan's friends and competitors and the Japanese Establishment prefer it that way. Perhaps.

A historian trained as a modern Europeanist enters with trepidation into a discussion of an 'Asian' society. Paul Kennedy has provided one model in his survey of *The Rise and Fall of the Great Powers*, wherein he treats the 'coming power' of Japan no differently from that of past players in the international polity.[8] I am also aware, however, that, in the last generation, experts in 'Asian studies' have demanded that societies in this region be studied on their own terms. Their case was put most succinctly by Edward Said in his *Orientalism* (1978). For Said, the very use of the term 'Asia' bespoke an imperialist relationship in which Western scholars strove to understand the 'alien' and in that striving committed an original sin. Those who were outsiders would never understand what they were outside.[9] Maybe, subsequent commentators have noted, the very concept of 'rationality', on which most historical and other 'scientific' research is at least partially posited, is an imposed 'Western' construct.[10] Western history is by definition inapposite in a non-Western society and, as Said warned, Western historians will be automatic carriers of the values of European imperialism. Interpreting 'Asia' is not their business.

In the case of Japan, the claim for specificity can be strengthened further. It is commonplace that Japan has been, and is, 'the only non-Western society to industrialise fully'[11] and, at the same time, that the Japanese 'opening to the West has never been total and unambiguous'. The Japanese experience of 'modernity' includes a profound sense of isolation – on its own estimate, Japan stands alone.[12]

Moreover, any analyst of the Second World War rapidly realises that the Pacific conflict was not necessarily the same as the European one and perhaps was entirely separate from it.[13] For example, it is clear in retrospect that there were no inevitable or permanent reasons why Nazi Germany and Imperial Japan should have been allies, given their many contradictory interests and widely divergent world views.[14] Indeed, those who like to muse on what did not happen in history might fruitfully contemplate the fate of the world and the results of the various Second World Wars had Germany, under a Machiavellian leader more like Frederick II than Adolf Hitler, capitalised on the bombing of Pearl Harbor by declaring war not on the United States but on Japan.

Doubtless such speculations should be confined to the pages of *fantastoria*, but investigators still have some surprises in store when they consult the comparative literature of the Second World War in the Asia–Pacific region. They discover some explication of the differences between the US and British Imperial forces – those 'allies of a kind', as Christopher Thorne has deftly defined them.[15] But they also come up against a sort of 'convergence theory', emphasising across the battlefront the allegedly shared experiences of the United States and Japan. The latter, it is implied, entered the Pacific War in a fit of absent-mindedness while the former's reasons for joining the conflict had little that were praiseworthy about them. The Vietnam War, especially, encouraged its critics to seek 'origins' for the errors and ruthlessness of US policy at that time, and one obvious place to look was the 1930s. Crusading anarchist intellectual Noam Chomsky, in his sweeping denunciation of the covert aggressiveness of US liberalism, has pronounced that it was the USA which led those who 'encircled' Japan and drove it to found an empire. US opposition to Japan was, he says, 'in substantial measure, quite hypocritical'.[16]

Somewhat ironically, it has been American liberal historians who have taken up Chomsky's ideas most enthusiastically. Richard Minear has praised both Chomsky and Said,[17] and openly stated that the book which he wrote attacking the 1946–8 trial of Japanese 'war criminals' – he defined it as a case of 'victors' justice' – was composed in recoil from his country's bloody practices in Vietnam.[18] A decade later, John Dower denominated the Pacific conflict 'a war without mercy', a Manichean dispute of rival racisms, in which, paradoxically, the Japanese and American leadership constructed their enemy in a similar fashion. 'The Japanese', Dower notes, 'read Western history in much the same way that Westerners were reading the history of Japan: as a chronicle of destructive values, exploitative practices, and brutal war.'[19] The Americans detested the Japanese far more whole-heartedly than they did the Germans[20] – their servicemen cheerfully collected as trophies the ears or gold teeth of dead Japanese soldiers.[21] The Japanese fought on without serious thought of surrender – on Okinawa, as late as April–June 1945, 50,000 Japanese soldiers were killed; 227 were taken prisoner.[22] Battles like this, Dower alleges, were bitter and even 'total', because the Japanese and the Americans had so much in common, because, without knowing it, they were 'enemies of a kind'.

Iriye Akira, the Japanese-born US diplomatic historian, who would later become President of the American Historical Association, had earlier reached parallel conclusions if by a different route. His study not so much of public opinion as of the formal practice of diplomacy convinced him that Japanese and American policy-makers possessed 'a number of similar, and at times, parallel assumptions', 'an undercurrent of shared interests and outlooks'. When the bombs fell on Hiroshima and Nagasaki, Iriye has claimed, 'in a way it was symbolic that the Japanese–American differences came down to a matter of a few words on the institution of the emperor and that on almost all other issues Tokyo and Washington were in essential agreement.' 'The war's end', Iriye concluded cosily, 'showed that Japanese–American cooperation and interdependence were a more desirable framework than rivalry and conflict.'[23]

Even if curmudgeonly outsiders shrug their shoulders in some disbelief at the warm outer glow engendered by this sort of liberal theorising, and wonder why comparison is thought most apposite between Japan and the USA rather than Japan and Imperial and Nazi Germany or Japan and Liberal and Fascist Italy, they confront problems on other fronts. When they go back to consult the first Western analysts of wartime or post-Hiroshima Japan, they come up against an intrusion from present politics at least as pervasive as that already described in the work of a Namier on Germany or Friedrich and Brzezinski on the USSR. As both Dower and Minear have noted, the most typical academic experts on Shōwa Japan were anthropologists like Ruth Benedict, Geoffrey Gorer or Westen La Barre.[24] Though Benedict, for one, had campaigned actively against racial theoretics and thus earned the hostility of the US Right, she found the compulsions of her discipline hard to avoid and she herself soon crafted a model of 'Japanese culture'. Her pre-war expertise had been concentrated on native Americans but, in 1944, as 'Social Science Analyst, Foreign Morale Division' of the US Office of War Information, she drafted her classic text, *The Chrysanthemum and the Sword*. With some up-dating, it would be published in 1946 as a guide for US occupying forces. From its pages, a reader learned that Japan was a naturally bifurcated society. On the one side stood the *samurai*, the warrior, the fight-to-the-end; on the other, the chrysanthemum, beauty, and its gentle and elegant contemplation. 'The Japanese are, to the highest degree', Benedict explained, 'both aggressive and unaggressive, both militaristic and aesthetic, both insolent and polite, rigid and adaptable, submissive and resentful of being pushed around, loyal and treacherous, brave and timid, conservative and hospitable to new ways.' Their social system was based on a hierarchy of 'extreme explicitness' and yet it was also adaptable to talent or to force, and was productive of unity rather than European-style class conflict. As long as US occupiers did not insist on ridiculing them, the Japanese would be ready 'to sail a new course' and 'to wipe the slate clean'. 'What the United States cannot do – what no outside nation could do – is to create by fiat a free, democratic Japan.' And yet Japan would accept a new world order more reliably than would Germany. 'Japan's motivations are situational. She will seek her place within a world at peace if circumstances permit.'[25]

Such theorising was very useful for contemporary American 'planners' of a Japanese future, all the more because it built on a common pre-war belief that two souls contended for supremacy within the Japanese body politic.[26] If the sword could be blunted into some form of modern technology and defeat could be assumed to have purged 'militarism' from the Japanese mind, post-war Japan could be swiftly granted full membership of the democratic or capitalist 'West'. A sociologist of modernisation like Talcott Parsons and General Douglas MacArthur himself might concur in their conviction that the Japanese had once displayed 'adolescent' 'cultural patterns',[27] but fatherly US administrators and their 'value free' social scientist aides would educate Japanese society and lead it out on the paths of 'modernity'.

In the 1950s and 1960s, the most typical spokesperson of this line was Edwin O. Reischauer, an expert in Japanese studies who doubled as US Ambassador to Tokyo (1961–6), and a fertile historian of Japan. He had made his name with his 1950 study, *The United States and Japan*. This book carried many echoes from

Benedict's earlier work. Japan, unlike Germany, was not a natural leader in her part of the world and it was 'inconceivable that Japan could again threaten her neighbours'. The Japanese were a 'highly homogeneous race', with 'a very homogeneous culture'. Both before and after the war, they had behaved with 'unparalleled docility', but their behaviour had been conditioned by their history. They had 'a keen awareness of playing a role on the stage of history. As true Far Easterners, the Japanese have a much stronger sense of history than we do in the West.'[28]

Thus, although the Japanese were not native democrats, they were more Westernised than any other people in Asia. As US Under Secretary of State, Sumner Welles, put it in a preface which rather ruthlessly trampled over some of Reischauer's academic hesitations, 'that Japan can later become a mighty bulwark against Moscow's domination of Asia can no longer be questioned'.[29] Too much emphasis on violence and crime in the Japanese past, Welles, Reischauer and other US commentators agreed, would only play into the hands of those Marxists ambitious to kindle conflict in the Japanese present.[30] And, sure enough, this present, with its astonishingly rapid and sustained levels of growth, did seem to prove that there was something special about Japan and that its key was unity. If the present was 'unique', the view that Japan's history must have been unique was reinforced. Indeed, with the passage of the years, this claim to a unique unity became the most basic method by which the Japanese Establishment explained and understood Japan's contemporary triumphs. The giant Nippon Steel Company financed an introductory booklet entitled *Nippon: Its Land and its People* (1982), and distributed it to its managers and foreign clients to explain that Japan had followed, did follow and would follow its own 'special way'. Those morning ceremonies (*chōreikai*), in which Japanese workers sing the company song and cleanse themselves morally for the day ahead, still emphasise 'the unique features of Japanese society'.[31] Prime Minister Nakasone Yasuhiro, who had frequently spoken up for nationalist causes, got himself into hot water in 1986 when he said out loud what most of the Japanese elite presumably believe, that Japan's 'success' was explained by its 'homogeneity' and the USA's 'failure' by the presence in American society of 'blacks, Puerto Ricans and Hispanics'.[32]

It is, of course, obvious that this assertion of uniqueness has manipulative and self-interested aspects. A past, present and future unity in a Japanese *Sonderweg* seconds the cause of those who are doing well – and they may presently constitute the majority of the population. They want to deny any present or future inequalities or divisions,[33] and readily comprehend that the best justification of such a denial involves reading out of Japanese history any past disunity or conflict. But these theories of an eternal unity have one other plain purpose. 'Eternity' serves post-war Japan in much the same way that the concept of the *longue durée* helped post-war France. If Japan has a '2,600-year-old' history of unity, then the terror and the horror of the Japanese experience of the war and the war's experience of the Japanese can be muted and relativised. That conflict, it can be assumed, marked no real break in the rise and rise of Japan. Moreover, what may well have been unique about it – the atomic bombings of Hiroshima and Nagasaki – could, for a time at least, be forgotten, all the more because the too blatant recording of such fearful events might embarrass the American ally and competitor. Members of the present-day Japanese Establishment have many reasons not to think too hard about their nation's 'long Second World War'.

And yet, by most reckonings, a terrible war it was, so terrible that it urgently requires the asking of the same questions posed earlier in this book about the historicisation of other societies' wars. How did the war fit into the course of Japanese history and Japanese historiography? And what efforts have been made after the event to 'explain' and to 'understand' it?

Though the motives of the inter-war Japanese leadership in pursuit of their policy may have been mixed, the first point to make about Japan is that it was directly involved in military conflict longer than any of the other combatants. It does seem reasonable to date Japan's war from its seizure of Manchuria (Manchukuo) in 1931. Thereafter, Japanese forces would be engaged in an increasingly complex series of wars. There was the 'pacification' of Manchuria. There was Japan's involvement in 'restoring order' in a China itself beset by multiple civil wars. After 1937, this became something like a full-scale Japanese invasion of China. There was the Japanese conflict with the USSR, most ideologically satisfying to many Japanese politicians and intellectuals, but a war which the Japanese lost in what is perhaps the most forgotten conflict of the period, the Nomonhan campaign of August 1939.[34] And, finally, after 7 December 1941, there was the war with the United States and Britain which, in a curious sense, Japan entered because it had already lost or could not win those wars which affected it more nearly.[35]

It is not the purpose of this book to discuss the causes or character of this complex 'Fifteen Years' War'. And yet it is necessary to note events which have attracted, or look as though they ought to have attracted, historiographical debate.

First there is the question of atrocities. In this regard, the most flagrant or debated examples occurred not in the Pacific but in Asia. In December 1937, Japanese forces stormed the Chinese city of Nanjing and proceeded to sack it. In the next month, at least according to local accounts, some 200,000 died. So vicious was the rape, murder and pillage that a strict censorship in reporting the 'incident' was rapidly put in place.[36] In post-war Japan, the brutality continued to be denied and only belatedly became public knowledge although, even in the 1980s, nationalist writers disputed the death toll and rejected the view that the sacking was an exceptional event.[37]

A very similar story can be told about 'Unit 731' and its medical experts under Ishii Shirō who, by 1945, from a base in Manchuria, had developed bacteriological warfare to a level unequalled elsewhere in the world. Under the innocuous-sounding title of the Epidemic Prevention and Water Supply Unit of the Kwantung Army, Ishii's force,[38] from the mid-1930s, specialised in human experimentation. Prisoners called '*maruta*', or logs of wood, were deliberately given plague and other diseases, frozen to death or had vivisection practised on them.[39] As the Unit's historians have noted: 'so large was the production plant that in [its] heyday . . . it had the potential for creating sufficient bacteria to kill the world's population several times over.'[40] Inventing an appropriate 'delivery system' proved a challenge, though fleas offered an attractive line of investigation. After 1941, the Unit's products killed tens of thousands of Chinese even if, to Ishii's regret, it proved impossible to save Japanese soldiers from also falling victim to the artificial epidemics.[41]

The activities of Unit 731 appear to have been known and approved in the highest circles. From 1935 'motion pictures of human experiments were customarily being shown to senior staff officers of the Kwantung Army', though Tōjō Hidecki, the later wartime leader, seems to have been sickened by his sight of them.[42] Ishii himself came from a distinguished family and, by his marriage to a daughter of the President of Kyoto University, had a special entrée to university medical faculties. Many a promising young doctor helped in the work of Unit 731. Much of the ordinary policing at the secret base, by contrast, was done by loyal family retainers from the village of Kamo where Ishii had historical roots. Even members of the royal household were implicated in Unit 731's activities – the Emperor's brother came on a wartime visit and another prince, Takeda Tsuneyoshi, held executive responsibilities at Pingfan.[43]

To this story of atrocities and their condoning or encouragement was added concealment. In August 1945, Ishii made determined efforts to wipe out any trace of his experiments. The surviving prisoners were murdered as were some 600 local labourers.[44] Ishii ordered perpetual secrecy from his own men. Allied and Soviet intelligence had known what was going on but, although the Soviets staged a small show trial of some captured officers in December 1949, most news about Unit 731 was suppressed, apparently because US officials had learned things 'of great value' from Ishii and did not want to share them.[45] The horrifying tale was rarely mentioned in Japan, though in 1976 a TV documentary made for the Tokyo Broadcasting Commission revealed more than ever before. However, in the 1980s, a subsequent investigative programme was not screened in Japan[46] and, in 1984, officials at the Ministry of Education declared that it was impossible to talk seriously about Ishii, because historians were still 'in the process of collecting the historical data'.[47] By that time, many of Unit 731's members had gone on to distinguished post-war academic, business or political careers – Prince Takeda, for example, had become, in 1962, the President of the Japanese Olympic Committee. A more redolent future awaited Dr Yoshimura Hisato. That sometime experimenter in freezing processes was awarded the Order of the Rising Sun Third Class, became President of Kobe Women's University, and acted as a consultant to the Japanese frozen fish industry.[48] Unit 731, like some sections of the SS or other 'elite forces', had been composed of the Japanese 'best and the brightest' and they remained as natural a part of the Establishment after 1945 as they had been before.

Nor does the horror and obloquy of the Asian face of the Second World War end here. Japan which, already in 1940, had 1.1 million soldiers serving abroad and was spending 40 per cent of its budget on the China conflict,[49] would eventually suffer some 2.5 million casualties. Ten to fifteen million Chinese died as victims of the Japanese, as did hundreds of thousands of other Asian and Pacific peoples. Some 40 million Chinese were rendered homeless during the war's course, while the casual detritus of combat included Japanese, Korean and 'native' women forcibly prostituted as 'comfort girls' for the Japanese soldiery,[50] and Korean immigrant labourers. Some 670,000 of these last were transferred to the Japanese islands between 1939 and 1945, where they were a prey to extreme racial prejudice, hunger, disease, their terrible working conditions, and US bombers.[51] An estimated 67,000 died.[52]

Violence and brutality in the conduct of the war were accompanied by a rigorous control over domestic opinion. More than for any other combatant society, the generalisation holds that in Japan there was no such thing as a formal Resistance to the wartime regime. In waging its wars, Imperial Japan had earned a level of 'consensus' to which the allegedly 'totalitarian' regimes of Italy, the USSR or even Nazi Germany could only aspire. Ronald Dore, a British sociologist, has written a brilliant description of Shinohata, a village inland from Tokyo, in wartime. There, he avers, social control reached an intensity equalled only in post-1949 China.[53] Shinohata saw the consummation of 'the act of the"voluntary" organization that everyone automatically belongs to':

> There was, in this hamlet of sixty households, the Shinohata Youth Organization for those between seventeen and twenty-five, the Voluntary Fire Brigade for the next age group, the Army Reserve Association,[54] the Housewives' Association, the Hygiene Association (created in the nineteenth century to organize preventive measures against epidemic diseases), the School Parents' Association, the Shrine Worshippers' Association, the Cocoon Rearers' Association, the General Agriculture Practice Association – not to mention the general-purpose Shinohata Hamlet Association, together with its sub-organs, the five ten-to-twelve household neighbourhood groups into which the hamlet was divided. All were mobilized to play their full part in a Japan united for Victory – mobilized under the active leadership of the owner farmers and under the patronage of the landlords. The Housewives' Association learned patriotic songs and dances, and new ways of pickling otherwise inedible foods, knitted for the troops, sent them body-belts into which every woman in the village had put at least one prayerful 'come-home-safe-and-victorious' stitch. The Hygiene Association collected money to buy bandages. The Hamlet Association and the Youth Association organized the send-off parties for conscripts; the fire brigade did voluntary labour digging up pine roots in the forest and taking them to the railway for a factory on the coast which extracted from them pitifully small quantities of supposedly useful resin. The school-children were sent into the mountains to collect plants that only the very oldest people knew of as famine foods to be dried and sent to the towns.[55]

This institutional base to the Imperial regime doubtless explains much about what one radical critic has called the 'remarkable docility'[56] of the Japanese people in wartime. But, as Maruyama Masao, [57] an independent left liberal who, in 1946–7, provided the first and in some ways still the best Japanese analysis of the 'Fifteen Years' War', asked: 'What were the *internal* factors which drove Japan into her disastrous war?'[58] and how did Tōjō and the other leaders thereafter achieve the 'total mobilization of the people's spirit'?[59]

Maruyama, who had himself served as an infantryman in Korea but who was also the son of a distinguished liberal journalist and commentator, thought the answer lay in a Japanese version of fascism – 'cool fascism' as he called it, picking up terminology already used in the 1930s.[60] In so arguing, Maruyama was anxious to distinguish himself from those vulgar Marxists who, reviving in Japan after 1945, made the thesis that Imperial Japan was fascist commonplace. Japanese history, they said, moved like a locomotive down the tracks of history from the feudalism of the Tokugawa era through the Meiji 'bourgeois revolution' to a fascism which was the natural and inevitable accompaniment of industrialisation.[61] Maruyama, by contrast, sketched a more subtle picture, applying to Japan concepts comparable with those which would become famous through their later usage by scholars of European fascism.

Like De Felice, Maruyama urged the necessity of distinguishing between fascism as 'state structure' and fascism as 'movement'.[62] It was the latter, he said, which interested him most but, at the same time, he noticed that Nazi Germany was more popular or 'democratic' in its character[63] than was Imperial Japan. In Japan, radical fascists, for example those military plotters who unsuccessfully attempted a coup in the 'February 26 Incident' of 1936, were 'visionary, fanatic and lacking in plan'. Japan was a place of 'fascism from above' rather than 'fascism from below'.[64]

But Maruyama did not leave it at that. Though he made some attempt to excuse the Japanese intelligentsia who, 'essentially European in culture', tended, he claimed, to dislike the 'low tone' of fascism,[65] he was troubled by the lack of open opposition to the regime. The answer, he surmised, lay in the government's successful deployment of psychological coercion, in its achievement of what, in the 1960s and 1970s under the influence of Gramsci, would be called hegemony: 'ultra-nationalism succeeded in spreading a multi-layered, though invisible net over the Japanese people, and', Maruyama concluded somewhat pessimistically, 'even today they have not freed themselves from its hold.'[66]

Although he would have his devotees,[67] Maruyama has remained a somewhat isolated figure. Especially outside Japan, the idea of a 'Japanese fascism' has not made much headway. The most developed case for it was that advanced by the radical sociologist Barrington Moore in his *Social Origins of Dictatorship and Democracy* (1966) but, although Moore bracketed Germany and Japan as 'industrial-feudal' societies of 'repression at home and aggression abroad', he elided the difference between the active consensus granted to Nazism and the more passive support required by its predecessors. His Imperial Japan sounded more like Imperial Germany than like the Nazi regime.[68]

Other commentators have been more emphatic in rejecting any fascist model. There was, they say, no rupture in Japanese political history between the wars, no 1933, no 1922.[69] There were no deaths (or very few), no murderous street-fighters, no charismatic *Führer*, no concentration camps and no mobilising mass party. An organisation like the Imperial Rule Assistance Association was established in October 1940 from above; its mass base remained weak and fragmented. Even in wartime, the ordinary patterns of Japanese politics continued. Parliament met; an election was held; even the press was not censored directly. The Japanese 'thought police' could be brutal but they remained interested in 'rehabilitating' those they arrested and certainly were not employed to kill off a section of society.[70] Rather they were proud of the sort of figures provided by the Ministry of Justice in March 1943: then 2,440 'communists' had been prosecuted, 1,246 were said to be 'converted', 1,157 'semi-converted' and only 37 unreformed.[71] And presumably, at least sometimes, the Japanese police followed the charming advice of a 1920s prosecutor on how to deal with a student dissident:

> The police stationmaster should have a prisoner brought from the cell to the stationmaster's room, should sit him down in the stationmaster's chair and from his own pocket buy him a bowl of *oyako donburi* (chicken and eggs on rice). The name of this dish means, literally, 'parent–child bowl' and was intended to remind the prisoner of the parent–child relationship. The policeman should say nothing about ideology, but only 'Your mother is worried about you'. He should not mention the father as this might encourage the student's defiance of authority.[72]

In the face of such blandishments, the prosecutor stated, *tenkō,* or conversion back to the government way, would at once occur.

This sort of evidence has led many Western commentators to conclude that any comparison between Germany and Japan is a false one and that 'Japanese fascism' is a 'meaningless' term.[73] Japan should rather be defined as 'highly authoritarian',[74] a 'police state',[75] 'militarist'[76] or even a place pursuing in its own way 'modernisation' and technological progress.[77] As Gavin McCormack has noted, paradoxically, 'to most Japanese scholars Japan was fascist; to almost all Western scholars it was not'.[78] At least within the ivory tower, Japanese scholars seem more anxious than are many Western experts on Japan to confess a troubled past, especially in the inter-war period.

But in pondering the history and historiography of modern Japan, a student comes upon another familiar issue lurking not far below the surface – continuity. Was the Japanese Fifteen Years' War and the regime which fought it a 'parenthesis' in Japanese history? If there was no 'rupture' before 1931, did defeat and US occupation after 1945 make a real change? Or was the imposition of democracy on Japan a political and not a social revolution, an event which entailed no radical alteration in *mentalité*? Were the critical historians confined to the universities and was their expertise irrelevant to the assumptions held about the past by the Japanese ruling elite and the Japanese people?

Here scholarship seems remarkably united in its answer – if there was change after 1945, it was certainly incomplete. As early as 1951, Maruyama, fearing a revival of nationalism, warned that the occupation 'went no further than institutional and legal reforms in the State machinery. It did not reach the social structure or the people's way of life, much less the mental constitution of the people.'[79] Though less alarmist in their reading of present politics, later commentators concur. In the village of Shinohata, Dore says, the patterns of institutionalised village rule 'established in the 1930s – only modifications, in any case, of ancient customary patterns – have persisted'.[80] In the bureaucracy, too, especially that dealing with labour or education,[81] there was a major carry-over of personnel and ideas from the wartime years. Indeed, according to one critical analyst of the continuity from pre-war to post-war Japan, 'if one were to search for a Japanese equivalent to fascism or national socialism, its leaders would likely include those social bureaucrats who attempted to restructure industrial relations along corporatist lines.'[82] After 1945 these 'social bureaucrats' were briefly threatened by Japanese socialism but the Japanese Socialist Party, like so many of its European equivalents, split under the impact of the Cold War. In March 1948 the government of Katayama Tetsu fell and, since that time, the JSP has not regained office. The ex-corporatists had never been purged from the bureaucracy and, under successive conservative administrations, they were able to cement an alliance with post-war Japanese business. The alliance flourished most mightily in the 1980s. Four of the 'social bureaucrats' held Cabinet office after November 1982 and their past experience in combining 'labor and welfare administration with extensive police work' then set the tone of the Nakasone Government.[83]

No doubt many factors explain this continuity, just as there was multi-faceted support for the Imperial regime and its policies abroad and at home from 1931 to 1945. But the subject which lies nearest to the heart of the system certainly was, and perhaps still is, history. How did the Japanese read their history both before and after 1945? How were the Japanese masses nationalised? How did a Japanese tradition get invented? How were the Japanese persuaded to imagine themselves belonging to a certain sort of community?

Here the first focus must be on the 'Meiji restoration' of 1868, which some see as the Japanese 'Risorgimento',[84] that one apparent moment of at least formal political 'rupture'. Before 1868, there seems no particular reason to regard the Japanese as especially united or nationalised. Well into this century, Dore says, 'the people of Shinohata had never been much aware of being Japanese because no other kind of people had much impinged on their consciousness.'[85] In the 1870s, Mori Arinori, later to be the first national Minister for Education, actually mooted the abolition of the Japanese language in favour of English: 'our meagre language', he wrote, 'which can never be of any use outside our islands, is doomed to yield to the domination of the English tongue, especially when the power of steam and electricity shall have pervaded the land.'[86]

Those in favour of the changes of the Meiji period had not been a particularly compact group and had proffered a variety of recipes for Japan's future. None the less, even before 1868, they showed an interest in history. At present, some of their intellectuals said, 'the truly natural Way had been obscured and distorted by foreign doctrines'. Only a re-reading of history could re-compose the Japanese people and thus properly equip them for a dangerous future.[87] After the Meiji restoration, the impulsion to re-work the past grew. Despite his enthusiasm for technology and modernity, Mori, once he became Minister of Education, declared that schools must simply 'serve, after all, the purposes of the state'. 'Higher scholarship', with its fondness for debate, should be reserved for the elite few. The many, by contrast, needed careful policing. The Ministry should watch over the contents of textbooks, and pupils should be trained to obey their masters and revere the Emperor and national traditions. Compulsory military training completed an educational system which should eventually carry Japan 'to the foremost position in the entire world'.[88]

The teaching of universal rather than national Japanese history had been banned in 1880,[89] and ten years later, shortly after Mori's assassination, an Imperial Rescript on Education was promulgated. It defined a population 'united in loyalty and filial piety … from generation to generation'. The national way *(kokutai)* was 'infallible for all ages and true in all places'.[90] As a contemporary critic has put it, 'in the government's view, the sole purpose of teaching history [and, indeed, other things] was to foster reverence for the emperor'[91] and state system.

The American historian, Carol Gluck, has written a detailed study of this imposition of hegemony in Meiji Japan and has concluded: 'by 1915 Japan possessed a public language of ideology that retained currency through the end of the Second World War'.[92] And yet hegemony was not complete. Rather, she avers, in the 1930s 'ideological orthodoxy' was further 'rigidified' and was well expressed in the manual of patriotic education issued in 1937. There was reiterated the essence of the Japanese past, present and future, the official national Japanese version of history: 'The unbroken line of Emperors, receiving the Oracle of the Founder of the Nation, reign eternally over the Japanese Empire. This is our eternal and immutable *kokutai*.'[93]

In this concept of the *kokutai*, history, religion,[94] a philosophy of state and police practice merged. When, in May 1925, a government granted universal manhood suffrage, this apparent move towards democracy was bracketed with the Peace Preservation Law, legislation to be applied against any who denied either the *kokutai* or 'the private property system'.[95] Thereafter, it was urged, the police should systematically control 'all thought that might disturb the national polity'.[96] Japan had had '2,600 years' of history – on 10–11 November 1940, there would be grandiose celebrations of the anniversary.[97] As the Imperial line stretched back to the gods, so did Japanese national history. In a very real sense Japan's history was eternal. In turn, it was longevity which meant that, as one university professor had proclaimed in 1933, 'the Japanese could only serve humanity by making Japan the strongest country in the world' and, as had already been explained back in 1910, 'the world can enjoy peace only when all countries reach the same level of civilization. It cannot permit such a thing as low civilization countries.'[98] Japanese history was also unchanging – one Imperial era succeeded another (and the

Emperors, as the vessels of history, were known not by their own names or personalities but by their eras, the Meiji, Taishō or Shōwa rulers); one form of technology replaced another, but Japan went on forever.

At the heart of the Japanese system by the outbreak of war thus lay a single reading of history and the resultant absence of thorough-going historiographical debate. Of course, there were still divisions in Japanese society. In the 1930s junior army officers were frequently more 'radical' (that is, more chauvinist) than their seniors. The army and the navy pursued different, even contradictory, policies. The police were never a uniform body. For all their formal appearance of hierarchy, Japanese families, too, did not always function as official rhetoric claimed that they should.[99] In many ways, Japan remained a place with a complex and functioning civil society which was often a world away from high politics.[100] Neither popular nor high culture was ever reliably autarchic. As Reischauer noted, 'every artistic or philosophic current in the Western world produced its own little eddy in Japan'.[101]

After 1917, Marxism had appealed to quite a number of the young and intellectual. As late as 1932–3, a multi-authored, seven-volume Marxist history of the development of Japanese capitalism could be published and read.[102] Though Japanese socialism seems well enough defined as 'a movement of intellectuals for intellectuals',[103] it did obtain an influence in the higher schools and universities. Especially the latter remained places of very considerable autonomy even though, after 1941, students were generally as positive about the Pacific War as was the rest of Japanese society.[104]

For, despite these inconsistencies, the idea of the *kokutai* had penetrated deeply into Japanese minds. Recruits to the army and primary-school children would be flogged if they made mistakes in reciting the archaic wording of those 'Imperial Rescripts' or public statements which were held best to express it, and, as a not surprising result, the key words surfaced in everyday speech.[105] Japan's own professional historians, whether the classicists at Tokyo University who, in 1889, alleged that they had proof that Japanese gods ruled Korea in antiquity,[106] or experts in more recent fields, though they argued about whether the Imperial system could legitimately embrace parliamentarism, did little to rebut the *kokutai*. They, too, accepted and promulgated the myths of '2,600 years' of national history. In great majority,[107] Japan's historians were as committed agents of their regime as were the *Ostforschers* in Germany or Volpe and his school in Italy.

The most powerful bulwark of this single version of history was, however, bureaucratic. One of the basic aims of most Meiji reformers had been educational attainment. From 1899, the Emperor himself annually attended graduation ceremonies at Tokyo University[108] and, by the 1920s, 100 per cent literacy had been achieved among the populace. But the educational process was also the subject of strict controls. Most formidable was that exercised by the Ministry of Education in its centralised policing of textbooks. Except for that minority which reached university, Japanese students were frequently expected to concentrate on the factual and to learn by rote rather than through some freer system. In these circumstances, history was the most perilous subject of all. As a Minister of Education put it bluntly in 1928, instruction in history should have strict borders: 'we must teach . . . about our nation's creation and explain in clear terms the meaning of the *kokutai*.' [109]

The Ministry's desire to supervise text-books had steadily increased since Mori Arinori's time, and the educational bureaucrats readily accepted Japanese 'militarism' or 'fascism from above'. They happily sponsored the educational equivalent of 'mass politics from above' (as, after 1940, marshalled in the Imperial Rule Assistance Association) or 'organised labour from above' (after 1938, in the Industrial Patriotic Movement).[110] And, for a critic of Japanese policy in the 1930s like US Ambassador Grew, 'to await the hoped-for discrediting in Japan of the Japanese Army and the Japanese military system [was] to await the millennium', unless there were radical changes in the Japanese education system.[111]

In these circumstances, when General Douglas MacArthur reached Japan in September 1945, he said that his aim was to uplift 'a race long stunted by ancient concepts of mythological teaching'.[112] The occupation thus became, among other things, a conflict over education, a battle to write a new history for Japan.

Those moderate elements, who formed the first post-war governments and who treated with the Americans, were as anxious to cling to the *kokutai* as they were to prevent the deposition of the Emperor or his trial as a war criminal – they understood, however dimly, that, if he were tried, all of Japan's national history might also be judged and convicted.[113] Those 'few words over the institution of the emperor' which Iriye noted keeping the USA and Japan apart in August 1945 were words read from the book of the past, words expressing the established Japanese version of history. Thus, in September–October 1945, those officials of the Ministry of Education, who had remained at their desks or found their way back to them, insisted that reference to the *kokutai* should not be deleted from school texts and the Minister for Education, Maeda Tamon, even urged the preservation of the 1890 Imperial Rescript. The retention of a certain way of teaching history underpinned the defence of Imperial sovereignty and the survival of a Japanese political and social system which, despite its loss of the war, should not change too much.

At first, the US authorities were chary of these conservative ambitions. On 13 October 1945, the occupying authorities officially informed the Ministry of Education that they must accept sweeping changes, including 'a new Bureau of text-books to rewrite text-books'. In November, the Americans ordered the translation of all text-books in the most dangerous subjects – 'morals', geography and history – so that they could be systematically checked and, by the end of the year, MacArthur had suspended all courses on those subjects and was demanding 'the collection of all existing text-books'. History books, the Americans said, should be converted into 'an honest story of the Japanese people' (and a number of 'progressive' historians rapidly declared themselves available to write this new history).[114]

Matters, however, never quite went as officially planned. A paper shortage made new publication difficult. Many text-books survived with passages inked out or pages stapled together.[115] A number of teachers then and later decided that discretion was the best policy – even in the 1980s, high-school children were complaining that their courses, though theoretically coming through to the present, actually petered out with national victory in the Russo-Japanese War of 1904–5.[116] None the less, in November 1946, a few weeks after MacArthur had permitted history courses to resume, the Ministry did publish its *Guiding Principles for Instruction in Japanese History*, wherein, it declared, 'materials which propagate militarism, ultranationalism and State Shinto, shall be excluded, as well as antiforeign ideas'.[117] That sounded as clear as the Emperor's own renunciation of his divinity in his speech of 1 January 1946, but, in fact, ambiguities remained, both in the teaching of national history and in its surviving imperial embodiment.

Indeed, the Ministry's advice to teachers had carried its own equivocations. In teaching history, its guide had run on, 'stress should be put on concrete aspects of the development of national life from social, economic and cultural viewpoints rather than on the history of peace and war and the vicissitudes of powers and struggles for political power.'[118] History, especially contemporary history, was too hot and dangerous an issue to be handled – it would be best for all if history, for the foreseeable future, was relegated to being a study of facts. Presumably those officials would have been relieved to hear an account by an American observer a generation later of history classes in Japanese high schools:

> No hard choices are presented, and failings are ignored. No villains or heroes and no momentous moral or national imperatives emerge. History does not contain good and evil forces. . . . Every textbook I examined offer[ed] essentially the same account. It all began with the Great Depression, which destabilised many societies, including Japan. This led to militarism, which led, in turn, to the invasion of China. Japan's 'advance' (not 'imperialism') in China was not going well.

But whereas Europe was rent by Nazi aggression and expansion, Japan was only acting 'out of weakness'. Society, the implication seemed to be, is 'best run by technocrats who know how to adjust the gauges and valves to maintain the optimal mix. . . . The management of society is an economic, not a political science.'[119]

If the bureaucrats could look forward to eventual victory, the US occupiers had not long retained their commitment to radical change. The real enemy, it was soon manifest, was not fascism or 'militarism', which in any case had been defeated and destroyed in 1945; rather it was communism. While Mao and his forces moved to their triumph in China (1949), the Korean War commenced (1950), the USA and Japan signed their peace and mutual security treaties (1951) and the occupation ended (1952), Americans and Japanese found that they had much in common. Maybe the Pacific War had been a mistake on both sides and now would be best forgotten. As H.B. Schonberger has put it wrily:

Even though he recognized that the Japanese elites opposed the far-reaching reform program, MacArthur saw no acceptable alternative but to rely on them for the day-to-day administration of the country. To do otherwise, he feared, was to invite chaos, mass misery, communism, and the demise of his presidential aspirations.[120]

To the official mind, there were enemies within, after all. Someone like the Asian studies expert, Thomas A. Bisson, once a member of MacArthur's team but who had returned to the USA in 1947 complaining that the changes in Japan had been superficial, was duly persecuted by the McCarthyite congressional hearings and driven from his job at the University of California.[121] Worse, in Japan, the national Teachers Union had fallen to leftist elements. They expounded a vulgar Marxist interpretation of Japanese history and were delighted by evidence of riot and disunity in the national past. Some of their ideas had even penetrated the first text-books despatched to schools in the immediate post-war period.[122] In 1947, some 22 per cent of teachers had left the profession after a review of their wartime activities; two years later, however, it was left-wing teachers who faced a purge as the American occupiers and the Japanese authorities joined in a hunt for communist subversives.

Such events ensured that, in the 1950s, history was a subject of major contestation. The Japanese Teachers Union enthusiastically endorsed the slogan: 'never send our students to the battlefield again'.[123] And, throughout the decade, they could be relied on to lead those groups in Japan demanding that Hiroshima be recorded and publicised,[124] that wartime Japanese politicians returning to office give an account of their past misdeeds,[125] and that Japan not be the automatic and deferential ally of the USA.

Endorsing the teachers in their campaigns was a group of 'progressive intellectuals' including Tsurumi Shunsuke, Maruyama Masao and historian Hani Gorō.[126] For them, the key question was ethical and historical. Only the Japanese could build Japanese democracy; the buyers should beware before they cheerfully purchased the US import. The past should not be forgotten and the Japanese Establishment especially needed to be constantly reminded of its recent sins. Japan should be neutralist and independent in its foreign policy; its culture must be independent and new.

In Establishment circles, by contrast, discussion of pre-war policies had, for a time, been muted. As in so many other combatant societies, such groups 'preferred the refuge of amnesia'.[127] Predictably, however, the pressure to write the history of such momentous events was irresistible. In 1951, for example, Hayashi Saburō, once an army intelligence expert on the USSR, published a narrative history of the Japanese campaign in the Pacific in which the main hints of analysis lay in Hayashi's implicit regrets that Japan had not followed up its 1930s war plans against the USSR and his explicit statements that the real world was a tough place: 'After the Meiji Restoration in 1868, Japan set about satisfying her irrepressible longing, to achieve truly advanced statehood, second to none in the world. . . .

Wealth and armed might were the twin foundations. It followed that national defense was bound to exert dominance over domestic politics.'[128] Japan, it seemed, exhibited another case of the *Primat der Aussenpolitik* and Imperial Japanese foreign policy was as 'destined' as Gerhard Ritter deemed Imperial Germany's to have been.

In succeeding years, conservative and patriotic forces in Japan duly became more self-confident in expressing themselves. Popular magazines began to feature accounts of battle. Films also displayed Japan's military glory, if, at first, they concentrated on the victorious wars against Korea, China and Russia in the safer period of the 1890s and 1900s. By 1958, Kaya Okinori, a wartime minister who had resumed his seat in parliament, could state publicly: 'I believe that the Greater East Asia war was not premeditated by Japan. I believe that the war broke out by force of circumstances during the China Incident. It was not like the war which the Nazis started after painstaking planning.'[129]

As the decade came to a close the ruling elite proclaimed that the 'post-war era' was over. Already in 1956–7, the economic boom had led people to say 'not since the Emperor Jimmu … had things been so good'.[130] In 1957, Kishi Nobusuke, once a Class A war criminal and now a power among the conservative Liberal Democrats, became Prime Minister. He and his confrères talked of the need to curb the Teachers Union, to amend 'deplorable textbooks' and 'to strengthen morals education'.[131] At the same time, the Japanese Socialist Party flirted with revolutionary ideas, especially as expressed by the Marxist ideologue, Sakisaka Itsurō.[132] The battle-lines seemed to be being drawn for a major conflict over the Japanese present and the Japanese past.

In 1960 came 'Japan's worst post-war political crisis'.[133] The official issue was the renewal, favoured by Kishi, of the Security Treaty with the USA. Strikes in schools, walkouts from the Diet, massive public demonstrations and campus unrest[134] followed. In May 1960, after sensational scenes inside and outside the Diet, Maruyama formally demanded Kishi's resignation, arguing then and later that only popular protest against potential infractions of Japanese pacifism could construct a real democracy.[135] Kishi did, indeed, eventually resign after being forced to cancel an invitation to the US President, Dwight Eisenhower, to visit Japan. In the course of the political conflict, Kishi was stabbed and the chairman of the Socialist Party, Asanuma Inejirō, was assassinated. In 1960, the great moral issues raised by Japan's 'long Second World War' seemed as alive or more alive than in other combatant societies.

The next step, however, was not taken. No great historiographical controversy comparable with those over *Griff nach der Weltmacht* or *The Origins of the Second World War* emerged in Japan. The JSP did not follow the SPD's path to legitimation and government but instead remained 'encapsulated' in permanent opposition rather as the Social Democrats had been in Imperial Germany. Leftist or critical interpretations of Japan's 'long Second World War' failed to achieve the sort of public acceptance won by the 'myth of the Resistance' in 1960s and 1970s Italy.

Instead, the lineaments of a compromise which would increasingly work to the benefit of conservative Japan were already salient. The JTU and the Marxists could voice their ideas, they could have their own publications, their own journals and their own debating societies. They remain probably the dominant force in Japanese academic history writing but, increasingly, there were material rewards for them, too, in modern Japan. The fate of Marxist historians was to be confined in a gilded and permanent opposition. In that way hostile academic readings of Japanese history could be relied on not to upset the good order of Japanese society.

Some historians tried to find another path to the past. Especially in the 1970s a new school of 'people's history' (*minshushi*) developed. Leading figures such as Irokawa Daikichi rejected Marxism, the cosy modernisation theories of Reischauer and his Japanese adepts, and even the activist moralism of Maruyama. Japanese historiography, Irokawa said, should not degenerate into 'a branch store of European theory'.[136] For all this assertion of intellectual independence, the *minshushi* movement seemed, even at some remove, to reflect the influences of E.P. Thompson, Gramsci and the *Annales*. A proper scrutiny of the Meiji restoration, they advised, would make plain how it need not have been a *rivoluzione mancata*. Peasant *mentalité* was best studied in the long term and such study would both highlight the stubborn quest for freedom of the free-born Japanese and proffer 'a potential source of energy to revitalise a debilitated modern Japanese history'.[137]

But, rather as with some European social history, Japanese people's history did not greatly illuminate the politics of the recent past. Instead, conservative Japan gradually began to re-state its own interpretations. The success of the LDP in riding out the Security Treaty crisis gave nationalists a new confidence. During the events themselves, Nakasone had condemned a public anxious to be pro-American or pro-Russian when it should only be pro-Japanese.[138] In 1963 the Tokyo District Court ruled that the bombing of Hiroshima and Nagasaki had indeed violated international law and, a few months later, the government awarded posthumous decorations to those who had died fighting for Japan in the Second World War.[139] The national Yasukini shrine increased in prestige (though 20,000 Koreans are buried there, still to this day only Japanese may enter it).[140] The historian, Hayashi Fusao, argued that the Pacific conflict was only one incident in a 100 year US–Japan war.[141] And in 1966, formal recognition of National Foundation Day was renewed.

Conservative Japan was thus increasingly making it plain that, as far as it was concerned, the Pacific War had been, at most, a regrettable accident and that there was little to apologise for in any aspect of the national past. Doubtless it was proper for the *kokutai* to have been somewhat amended in the new technological society, but it still expressed the Japanese way and the innate distinctiveness of the 'Japanese race'. The young needed to hear more not less about this distinctiveness. As the LDP leader, Tanaka Kakuei, whose later career would be dogged by corruption charges, urged, not altogether obliquely, in 1974: 'Education today over-emphasises intellectual development. While we fatten our children's intellects, their morals starve.'[142]

Tanaka, and his Japan, did not want to hear what the Marxists or any other revisionists were saying. And there historiography has remained – as a sort of dialogue of the deaf. Japanese contemporary history does, as a consequence, have one special characteristic: the paradigm shift, described in this book as occurring in all the other combatant societies, has never happened in Japan. Emblematic is the story of Ienaga Saburō, a revisionist *mancato* and at least as idiosyncratic a figure as Maruyama.

Ienaga had been born in Nagoya in 1913. Between 1931 and 1935, while at higher school and then at university, he experienced a spiritual crisis, writing that 'the whole Japanese thought world generally has gone mad since the Manchurian incident' and despairing at 'the dry and lifeless university lectures without any real thought in them'.[143] His reaction was to withdraw as far as was possible from the contemporary world in order to study neo-Kantian philosophy and, especially, traditional Buddhism. He drew comfort from a seventh-century saying: 'the world is empty and false, only the Buddha is true', and from the writings of a thirteenth-century Buddhist, who emphasised the transcendental nature of faith in a world in which men cannot save themselves.[144]

Whether impelled by this religious other-worldliness, or by the stirrings of a more orthodox patriotism, Ienaga did not publicly dissent from the national cause in wartime. As he would later say in self-reproach: 'until the end of the Pacific War I was concerned only to preserve my own conscience.'[145] After 1945, he evinced suspicion at the swiftness of his fellow citizens' conversion to democracy and for a time was regarded as a reactionary. None the less, from a position at the Tokyo University of Education, which he would not relinquish until his retirement in 1977, Ienaga began to campaign for contemporary causes. As a historian of ideas he had switched his attention from the ancient and medieval to the post-Meiji period, and he also spoke up about university autonomy and legal reform, while staunchly opposing the 1960 renewal of the Security Treaty. Individualism he defined as 'an essential element of the modern spirit' and it and the other achievements of democracy, he believed, must be thoroughly institutionalised in contemporary Japan.[146] At the same time he was anxious that Japan regain its 'spiritual values', which, he feared, had been lost sight of both in the war and in the onrush of capitalist prosperity since 1945. It was almost as though he, too, in his way wanted to re-forge a tradition which might express the rights and duties of the 'free-born Japanese'.

His more straightforward ideas are summed up in the translated work, *Japan's Last War: World War II and the Japanese, 1931–1945*. Published in 1968, the book had begun life as a series of public lectures three years earlier. Ienaga argued that history had an essentially critical purpose: 'a generation raised on sugar-coated history', he warned, 'would be likely to repeat the errors of the past.'[147] Not for him would there be a recourse to the 'primacy of external policy', nor to the idea that Japan had stumbled over the brink into war. The events of the 'Fifteen Years' War' were, he stated, 'inseparable', while the conflict in the Pacific nakedly disclosed the Japanese military *mentalité*: 'recklessness, absurd persistence beyond the point of no return, and innumerable acts of savagery. That kind of war did not just happen.

It was not the result of accident or loss of control.' Indeed, expansion abroad and repression at home constituted a single mixture: 'It was a projection into international politics of the domestic suppression of communism by force. The fifteen years war may be seen as an attempt to impose the Peace Preservation Law on other nations.'[148]

At the centre of the system lay education. 'Every facet of the curriculum was permeated with emperor worship and militarism', while information about the Nanjing incident (an atrocity Ienaga thought comparable with Auschwitz), the defeat at Nomonhan and Ishii's bacteriological warfare was kept secret before and after 1945.[149] Post-war Japan had similarly failed to acknowledge its disgraceful policies towards Koreans and 'comfort girls', or the appalling nature of its imperialism in China, where, for example, 'rape was an accepted prerogative of the Imperial Army'.[150] Japan had both entered its wars and made peace without any popular consultation, but its 'fascism from above' had been as effective, as bloody and as tyrannous as that of Germany. Wartime Japan had offered 'barren ground for political dissidents' and the absence of concentration camps may only have meant that 'oppression was actually greater in Japan'.[151]

Many of Ienaga's theses were comparable with those raised in the other great controversies about the meaning of the 'long Second World War'. In particular, Ienaga implied that even in 'democratic' Japan, there was a potential for militarist continuity, a negative nationalist *Sonderweg*, unless committed intellectuals like himself went on demanding a more open and honest investigation of the past. Like Fischer in West Germany, Ienaga would find that the official mind viewed his strident moralising frostily. Given his views, it was almost inevitable that Ienaga should come into conflict with that great repository of the conservative 'truth' about the national past – the Ministry of Education.

The Ministry had gradually resumed control over publication for schools and culled those first textbooks of the post-war period which, officials presumed, carried too heavy an imprint of Marxism. They had systematised their processes. In the 1990s, this system still operates. It works as follows:

> First the publisher sends sample copies of its proposed textbook to the Ministry of Education. Then the Ministry's textbook inspection officials check the contents and indicate places that require rewriting. After revisions have been made, the publisher submits samples of the revised text to the Ministry, where an advisory council then decides whether to pass or reject the textbook. If a book does not pass inspection, all the money spent in preparation will have been wasted. And there is no way a book can pass inspection unless a publisher follows the suggestions of the textbook inspection officials.

Of all areas of study, history was the subject on which the officials took the most scrupulous or rigorous line.[152]

In the early 1960s, Ienaga had produced a textbook of his own, but in 1963 he was informed that the Ministry of Education had rejected his work as 'too gloomy'.

His reaction was to sue them for unwarranted interference in free debate.[153] For almost three decades the case has remained in the courts, which have moved with a languor that Oblomov might have envied.

None the less, for a time, radical critics like Ienaga could feel that they were still getting somewhere. Progress might not have been as swift as in the great German historiographical revolution of the 1960s, but some progress there had seemed to be. In 1972, for example, the Chinese Communist leader, Zhou Enlai, publicly lectured visiting Japanese Prime Minister Tanaka about the failure of school text-books to admit the dreadful nature of Japanese military policy in China. This threat of unpleasantness abroad engendered some soul-searching in officialdom, the more so because, it was feared, such talk might damage Japanese trade.[154] And, as has already been noted, it was in the 1970s that a number of previously hidden 'incidents' came to be discussed more openly in both scholarly and popular circles. But Ienaga won no outright victories comparable with those of Fischer. And Japanese historiography was in a weaker position as the next decade brought, in Japan, too, another conservative counter-attack. In June 1980, the LDP had achieved a surprisingly sweeping electoral victory, and in its aftermath, Okuno Seisuke, the Minister of Education, demanded that 'patriotism' be restored to Japanese text-books. Soon journalists were forecasting textual changes of which the key one was to be the replacement of the word 'aggression' by the word 'advance' in descriptions of Japanese policy in China before 1937.[155]

The result was a brief but bitter display of international discord about how to read the past. Both the Chinese and the Korean press again took up the issue of the interpretation of Japan's history in Asia. So serious did the exchanges become that the Chinese cancelled an invitation to the Japanese Education Minister to visit the People's Republic, the South Koreans issued an *aide-memoire* 'strongly demanding changes', and on 6 August 1982, the Chinese Ambassador in Tokyo returned to Peking for 'discussions'. There were rumours that the South Korean Ambassador would do likewise and that anxiety about Japanese history was spreading in North Korea, Taiwan and other Asian countries.[156]

The storm blew over. On 23 August, Prime Minister Suzuki Zenko used a press conference to accept responsibility for Japan's wartime deeds in Asia, and implied somewhat vaguely that any text-book revisions would not offend Japan's neighbours. Thereupon the Chinese leadership reluctantly allowed a state visit to go ahead, but they received Suzuki coolly, and on 12 October the Prime Minister resigned.[157]

Although the international disputation over the textbooks for a time subsided, the impetus within Japan for a more conservative reading of history had not been blunted. Ienaga might urge that:

textbooks should not be censored by the government. . . . The decision as to whether or not the content of a textbook is accurate from a scholarly point of view should be left to the free discussion and research of scientists, and not to the judgement of state power. . . . Patriotism also means to regret and feel sorrow for the wrongs that have been committed by your own country. Patriotism does not involve boasting or covering up your past mistakes. We should feel proud of our traditions and our accomplishments. But we should also admit what we have done to other peoples in the past and vow never to repeat it.[158]

But few in authority in Japan were impressed by his sort of humility. Rather, the tone for the 1980s was set by the new Prime Minister, Nakasone, whose background was that of a committed nationalist and who was personally anxious that history textbooks become more overtly patriotic. As long as international alarums could be averted, it was time, he said, for 'a complete reassessment of the post-war years' and a return to an educational system 'founded on Japanese tradition'.[159]

In the end, the Nakasone Government made fewer radical conservative changes than its rhetoric had promised.[160] Indeed, in September 1986, Nakasone was forced to drop an Education Minister who publicly defended Japanese imperialism in Korea.[161] However, though politicians might come and go, the bureaucrats went on for ever, stiffened in their views by the staunch patriotism and sense of particularity which seem to have remained strong in many sections of the Japanese populace. The Ministry of Education continued to assert its censorship rights[162] and in 1989 announced a seven-year plan for the preparation of new text-books. These works would emphasise 'respect for Japanese culture and tradition, ... [and] identity as Japanese'.[163]

The Japanese leadership's newly determined search for a usable past replicates those developments in Germany, Italy and elsewhere which have already been outlined in this book. But there is a major difference between the Japanese historicisation of the 'long Second World War' and that of other combatant societies. In Japan, revisionist historians like Maruyama and Ienaga have, in the final analysis, remained peripheral figures. The more ordinary academic world's Marxism has echoed, too, with the sounds of silence. As far as official Japan is concerned, only external events, American occupation, or later moments of exci-tation among the Chinese and South Koreans, have briefly prompted superficial criticism of the past. It may well be that the great majority of present-day Japanese youth think that *kokutai* is a mispronunciation of the term for the National Athletic Competition[164] and, like so many *praktiki,* happily get on with the business of production and consumption. A prospering Japan has many reasons to find tiresome any insistence on the lessons of the past. But, a historian may suspect, this past will not fade away and, especially if prosperity ends, may still impinge on the Japanese present or future.

Already the faltering prosperity of the USA has convinced many Japanese that they should say no[165] hereafter to their great and powerful friend of the post-war era (and that saying no in the past was not by itself a crime). No doubt each society must define its own politics and its own morality. And yet this book has repeatedly shown that the spread of liberty, equality and fraternity is well fostered by a continued reflection on the horrors of the various Second World Wars. There may still be a time to reflect that Japan's commitment to democracy at home and abroad remains enigmatic while so many who make up its political class and so many of its ordinary citizens signally fail to admit that their Fifteen Years War offers compelling evidence that history is or ought to be about 'criticism, criticism, again criticism and criticism once more'. It will be best if Eastern eyes are not completely averted from the terrible reality either of Hiroshima or of Nanjing and the experiments of Unit 731.

Conclusion

This analysis of the part played by the 'long Second World War' in the writing of history could be continued almost *ad infinitum*. In the historiography of Australia, my own country of birth and residence, for example, the most celebrated historian of the last generation was C.M.H. (Manning) Clark (1915–91). A curiously prophetic figure with a social role and prose style resembling that of some nineteenth-century 'forgers of the nation', it was Clark who 'made' Australian history or at least who gave it a new sense of self-respect and purpose. Clark preached that Australia was the 'new tree green' which should have its present, its future and its past separated from the 'old dead tree' of Britain and its Empire,[1] from what Australian historians are inclined loosely to denominate 'Europe'.

Clark's own life had taken him to Britain and to Europe. The child, on his mother's side, of an Australasian family born to rule and, on his father's, of an English one born to serve, Clark recoiled from his experience of the English class system at Oxford (1938–40) and returned to Australia without taking a degree.[2] This 'failure' seems to have made him all the more determined to shake the dust of the British Empire from his shoes and proclaim Australia's historiographical independence. But he had also seen the crisis of the 1930s, the torment of the 'Old World' and 'Auschwitz' more directly. As he recounted in a radio interview, he had happened to arrive in Germany on the morning after *Kristallnacht*:

> I came up out of Bonn railway station with my head stuffed with these myths about progress and so on, and the British and so on, and there I was confronted by the Stormtroopers – of course they didn't menace me or threaten me but I saw the fruits of evil, of human evil, before me on the streets of Bonn. From that time, over the next three or four years, I had to abandon all the myths I had grown up with. My world, my intellectual equipment, my spiritual equipment, could not cope with what I had seen in Germany.[3]

If the moral crisis of the 'long Second World War' intruded even into the historiography of distant Australia, it had a more direct effect in Spain. That nation had not, of course, entered the war, though Falangist 'volunteers' assisted German forces on the Eastern Front. But anyone who accepts A.J.P. Taylor's view that Guadalajara was part of the great crisis has to acknowledge that Spain, too, participated in 'Auschwitz'. For the thirty years after 1945, while its certainly authoritarian and perhaps Fascist[4] dictator Generalissimo Francisco Franco lived, Spain was the European society which endured most visibly a 'Second World War that never ended', even while it was protected against contemporary historiographical debate. Franco arrogantly incarnated past, present and future in his own person as he pronounced: 'We *are* . . . [Spanish] history.'[5] Until his death, any discussion of the meaning of the Spanish Civil War (1936–9) and its aftermath, any pluralist relativism, and any genuine democracy within Spain, were impossible. Meanwhile his regime manipulated documentation with an extreme ruthlessness and crudity.[6] Only after 1975 could Spaniards recommence a debate about their contemporary history.

Of course, the Spanish Civil War was also an international event and its 'myth' did not cease to divide historians outside Spain. The classic illustration of the ability of this facet of the 'long Second World War' to excite controversy came over Gabriel Jackson's *The Spanish Republic and the Civil War 1931–1939* (1965).[7] Jackson was a Left Democrat of an almost painful honesty – he would characteristically entitle his memoirs *Historian's Quest*.[8] He declared that a historian's task was to relate the 'truth' and that, in his major book, he had written 'an objective, nonpolemical account of the living experience of the Spanish people in the 1930s'.[9] But while specifically denying that history was an arena in which 'good guys' fought to the last paragraph against 'bad guys',[10] Jackson did direct his most obvious sympathies towards the moderate Republican cause. In so doing, he distanced himself from such conservative Anglo-American historians of Spain as Raymond Carr,[11] Stanley Payne[12] and Hugh Thomas[13] who, without endorsing Franco, saw much to deplore in the Republic.

But, in some imitation of what had happened to the Republicans between 1931 and 1939, the most dramatic dispute occurred within the Left. Noam Chomsky, as ready to argue matters to their logical or illogical conclusions over Spain as he was over Japan,[14] attacked Jackson as living proof that, from their elevated perspective, the 'best and the brightest' would never understand real people. For all his plangent favouring of the anti-Fascist cause, Jackson was, said Chomsky, churlish and prejudiced in his dealings with Spanish anarchism. From the very core of his liberal being, Jackson could not comprehend the positive nature of permanent social revolution. Chomsky took this denunciation one step further by linking the last civil war-with-international-ramifications to the contemporary one. Though Jackson opposed American policy in Vietnam and campaigned actively against it,[15] 'objectively speaking', Chomsky declared, it had been the Jacksonian variety of liberalism, with its basilear commitment to truth, justice (and the American way), which had spurred on American intervention in Asia.[16] 'Eurocentrist' and liberal principle, or vainglory, with its desire to re-make the world in its own image, ensured that the tragedy of Spain would be repeated in Vietnam.

Re-reading this dispute, it is hard not to conclude that any arrogance on the part of Jackson pales into insignificance compared with that of Chomsky. But the Chomsky–Jackson controversy is another reminder of how the 'long Second World

War' lived on in the United States. 'Spain' could still matter in US academic and political worlds just as could the Holocaust,[17] or particular interpretations of Russian history. The issues of 'Auschwitz' and 'Hiroshima' retained their relevance for contemporary political debate.

In this book, I have not devoted a specific chapter to American historiography. I have made this omission for two reasons – first, the United States has, in the post-war period, generally been the powerhouse of world historiography[18] in much the same way as it has driven the world economy. Look in any chapter of this book and reference to an American historian – a Genovese, a Maier, a Mayer, a Paxton, a Ledeen, a Pipes, a Reischauer – is invariably there. British history, German history, French history, Italian history, Russian and Japanese history are a natural part of American history, both because of American power and because of the immigrant base of American society, because little Britains, Germanies, Frances, Italies, Russias and Japans (and many more) survive and flourish in the USA.

At the same time, it is also true that the United States, for all the contribution of its technology, production lines and armed forces, for all its victories both in Europe and Asia, was not a participant in the Second World War to the degree that the other societies analysed in this book were. Studs Terkel[19] and Paul Fussell[20] may debate whether the second conflict was a 'good war' or not, but, for a visceral experience of war, the United States would have to await Vietnam. Only then would some Americans have a faint inkling of what it might mean for a nation to live in *Anno Zero*. Thus, though it is possible to find traces of the 'long Second World War' in the post-war writings of such varied students of America's own history as William Appleman Williams,[21] Daniel Boorstin[22] and Crane Brinton[23], the history of American history is not of central relevance to this book.

The segments of the world in which the 'long Second World War' has remained most palpably alive, by contrast, are the Middle East, and Central and Eastern Europe. In these latter regions, the sort of nuanced debates, the give and take which has been established in most ex-combatant societies, have scarcely begun. Rather, one single, 'truthful' interpretation of the war is proclaimed in academic or political discourse, though another sometimes remains in the hearts of the people. As the Kurt Waldheim affair indicated,[24] neither Austrian historiography nor the Austrian political Establishment are yet willing to admit Austria's special path to 'Auschwitz'. The enthusiasm with which the Nazis were welcomed in March 1938 and the active commitment to Nazism by large sections of both the Austrian ruling elite and the Austrian populace are obscured or ignored. Neither Austrian anti-Semitism, nor the still widespread Austrian belief that 'to be a Slav is [to be] some form of second-class citizen'[25] have been subjected to open debate and, as Richard Bassett has written, unlike the FRG, Austria has avoided 'any rational confrontation with the past'.[26] The Austrian historiography of 'Auschwitz' and 'Hiroshima' remains like that of Germany before the publication of Fischer's *Griff nach der Weltmacht*. But now that Austria, as a result of the events of 1989, has lost the justification for its neutralist present, it will be interesting to see if it will need to re-fashion its future and its past.

Nor in its region is Austria unique. At the time of writing, Serbs and Croats are killing each other with an ardour which seems to indicate that the post-war Yugoslav state, creation of the internationalist partisans, was no more than the keeper of a truce. Bosnians, Slovenians, Macedonians, Albanians and the other peoples who made wartime Yugoslavia the site of a complex of vicious small wars, all threaten to seek to impose a single past, present and future on their neighbours and themselves. Nor are Czechoslovakia, Hungary, Poland, Romania, Bulgaria, the Baltic states, let alone the potential successor states of a decolonised Russian Empire, exempt from the same problem. As Misha Glenny has remarked about a specific case, 'Hungary may have a proud history, but its democratic traditions would barely fill a school exercise book.'[27] I would contend that the best way to expand such an exercise book in Hungary and the other states will be by permitting historiographical debate and specifically by accepting a frank discourse about each of these societies' own participation in 'Auschwitz'. Arno Mayer's *Why did the Heavens not Darken?*, with its emphasis on the multiplicity of killings in the war and the willing aid often given to the Nazis by the peoples of Central and Eastern Europe,[28] might be a useful first text for the region. But a pessimist would predict that many of these states will prefer to promulgate a nationalist and even fascist version of their own past. As Glenny has suggested, 'history' has been re-born in that part of the world,[29] but it is not yet clear that it is the sort of history which fosters pluralist democracy.

In general, then, the historicisation of the Second World War has followed a twisted path. The war had been such an elemental force, the ethical crisis of the 'long Second World War' so profound, that, in its aftermath, 'Auschwitz' and 'Hiroshima' insistently demanded historical explanation. History was the most obvious and the best discipline to employ to work through the terror and the horror of those years. Only historical explanation, it seemed, could heal the trauma caused by the many Second World Wars, or revive some sort of optimism about progress and the continued spread of liberty, equality and fraternity.

Many of the first historians to ponder the war – A.J.P. Taylor in *The Course of German History*, Sir Lewis Namier, Jacob Talmon or Maruyama Masao – stressed that the causes of the disaster were not short-term but lay deep in the past. Other analysts, and perhaps Benedetto Croce was the classic example, tried instead to detach the evil of the 'long Second World War' from the ordinary process of history. If the cataclysm could be written off as a 'parenthesis', if Hitler or Mussolini were merely accidents in the works, then the fascist era need not trouble the future.

But the most characteristic approach to historicising 'Auschwitz' and 'Hiroshima' involved the familiar historical technique of comparison. Hitler and the Nazis, the most loathsome, murderous, irrational and pessimistic protagonists of the war, were almost universally agreed to be the common enemies of mankind. But, if they really were unique, then their uniqueness would act as a sort of intellectual parenthesis. Without some context, and therefore without some comparison, the Nazi assault on any belief in the perfectability of humankind could not be comprehended and overcome. Thus Nazism was increasingly 'explained' and understood by comparison with other regimes, if often at first with a blatantly instrumental purpose. Theoreticians of totalitarianism sought to merge the past evil of Nazism with what they perceived to be the continuing sins of the Cold War USSR. Stalinist Marxists instead matched Nazism with US 'imperialism', or with the liberal capitalist 'West'. At the same time, they reiterated Soviet society's special suffering in the Great Patriotic War and denied the concept of the 'Holocaust' in which, they feared, the conflict would be reduced to being merely a 'war against the Jews'. Anti-Fascist Italians utilised the model of fascism in order to bracket Mussolini's regime with that of Hitler. Japanese democrats and Marxists deployed the concepts of 'cool fascism' or 'fascism from above' to associate their pre-war regime with its German ally. A.J.P. Taylor urged, if only as an academic exercise, that Hitler should not be demonised but should have his actions as an executive analysed like those of any other opportunist politician. E.P. Thompson thought that the spirit which had moved the free-born people of Europe to resist Nazism expressed a goodness which had both deep roots and a long history, and which still must be nurtured against those with oppressive ambitions in the present world.

Of course the act of comparison exposed both similarity and dissimilarity. A German liberal like Ralf Dahrendorf could hymn the high way to 'modernity' pursued by liberal Britain and the liberal USA and explain the German deviation from it through the unique survival in Germany of feudal elements until their failed conspiracy in July 1944. Italian anti-Communists could underline the relatively mild nature of Fascist tyranny compared with that of Nazism or of Stalin's USSR. A.J.P. Taylor could warn that, if appeasement was once a mistake, it would not always be. French historians and their confrères, most intellectually subtle of all, decided that one sort of chronology did not bear comparison with another. In the fullness of time or in *longue durée*, what did a fleeting event like the fall of France matter?

In half a century of investigation, historians of the 'long Second World War' have thus produced a myriad of interpretations of that momentous event. Even though its ideal title might be *The Long Second World War: For and Against,* this book has not aimed, however, to be just a catalogue of the writing of one damn historian after another. Instead, I have often demonstrated how turning points in historical explanations are inextricably linked to changes in broader politics and society, just as I have shown, in despite of some post-modernist assumptions, that the authors of major history books have usually 'authorised' them. History books, it seems, will excite the most controversy and ensure paradigm shifts in understanding when the books are themselves 'time bombs'. Historians will play their most useful social role when they seek to understand both the present and the past. Thus, A.J.P. Taylor's *The Origins of the Second World War* was as much a signal of the end of the first Cold War as were the accession of Pope John XXIII or the election of President Kennedy, the pressing of the first Beatles record or the spread into Europe of blue jeans. Thus, Fritz Fischer's two great books on the First World War acted as a crucial backdrop to the legitimation of the SPD and the acceptance of *Ostpolitik* in West Germany. Thus, Renzo De Felice's massive biography of Mussolini, so similar in its methodology to Fischer's work, had the reverse effect as it provided historical justification first for the non-legitimation of the PCI and later for its destruction. Thus, Ienaga Saburō's interminable court cases about textbooks gave incessant testimony to the Japanese Establishment's failure to integrate the history of the Greater East Asian War into Japan's present. Thus, as the decline and fall of the Soviet and Russian Empires proceeded apace, citizens of the many Russias sought explanation and advice from the many histories which still exist in the USSR. Their seeking was all the more urgent because these histories had been too long kept from them by the Stalinist old soldiers of the Great Patriotic War and too long denied by Western Cold Warriors. In case anyone should ever doubt it, the peoples of the composite parts of the Soviet Empire are showing how extraordinarily difficult it is to wipe the history of the 'long Second World War' from human minds.

Some history, thus, is always contemporary history. And Spike Milligan, too, is right – when you ask that great question 'what's the time?' there never is a simple, single answer, unless it be given by those who have stopped the clock for their own immediate and self-interested reasons. In a free society, rather, men and women make and re-make their own historiography, both of their own free-will and under the given and inherited circumstances with which they are directly confronted. In the writing of history and the comprehension and experience of life, the traditions of the dead generations weigh, sometimes like a nightmare, sometimes like a glorious dream, on the minds of the living.

Spike Milligan, that soldier of the People's war, that Irish Englishman, that holy fool, that Dostoevskyian idiot bound for the lunatic asylum, that neo-surrealist, that *goaker* in the pack, acted as one of the inspirations of this book and the university course on which it is based. Another, less inspirational, starting-point was provided by Francis Fukuyama, with his heralding in 1989 of German re-unification and the completion of the 'post-war epoch'. With this victory of the West, he proclaimed the 'end of history' and the universal adoption of a single reading of past, present and the foreseeable future. In his renewed search for the absolute, Fukuyama was a man of his time, merely expressing more strikingly the contemporary philosophy of many conservative commentators. In the 1980s, Gertrud Himmelfarb, for one, had attacked a whole range of 'new historians' from Braudel[30] to E.P. Thompson and Eric Hobsbawn, and demanded that history and the nation be re-united. Only thus, she averred, could the USA, itself rent by what she saw as yawning divisions of class, ethnicity, gender and age, re-compose itself.[31] If one purpose could be restored to the past, she urged, one purpose would be located in the present and the future. In so arguing, her motto was, somewhat ironically, drawn from that very clever but not altogether morally trustworthy novelist, Milan Kundera:

> The past is full of life, eager to irritate us, provoke and insult us, tempt us to destroy or repaint it. The only reason people want to be masters of the future

is to change the past. They are fighting for access to laboratories where photographs are retouched and biographies and histories rewritten.[32]

In Reagan's America, it seemed, Himmelfarb's mastery of the present would give her an opportunity to amend historiography, to cut through its complexities and attach a simpler and allegedly better past to the monetarist future. Nor was Himmelfarb alone in these hopes. Rather, in the late 1980s, a chorus of voices paradoxically and even perversely intoned the thesis that it was relativism which had absolute ambitions and which was closing the American or 'Western' mind.[33] Such American commentators were impelled by similar beliefs and had similar plans to those of Hillgruber and Stürmer in the FRG, the De Feliceans in Italy, or their conservative equivalents in Britain, France, Japan and, ironically, shared much with the few surviving nostalgics for Stalinism in the USSR. All believed that a factual, objective and patriotic history would restore their Second World War to its proper place in cultural discourse. The ultimate ambition of the free market, whose protagonists are so commonly derisory of the humanities, was to win a historiographical monopoly.

These new conservatives sometimes had unlikely allies, for example among those 'post-modernists' who, when pressed, want to 'return to the Middle Ages', grow dewy-eyed at the sublime virtue of peasant society, presumably wish to preserve Common Market agricultural subsidies, and innocently affirm the special history of their own nations. Pierre Nora, that concocter of *ego-histoire* mentioned in chapter 5, has, for example, recently contrasted 'memory' and 'history', and awarded laurels to the former and condemnation to the latter. Peasant culture, 'that quintessential repository of collective memory', he opines, is regrettably falling victim to 'democratisation and mass culture on a global scale'. 'Memory is life' but history, an arid and academic activity, is 'the reconstruction, always problematic and incomplete, of what is no longer'. History's target is 'not to exalt but to annihilate what has in reality taken place'. 'In a country such as France', Nora states, 'the history of history cannot be an innocent operation; it amounts to the internal subversion of memory-history by critical history' (though such a process, he adds, is less worrying in the United States which, his French perspective reveals, may not possess a 'real' tradition anyway). 'Memory', Nora concludes, in words which Himmelfarb might approve, 'is absolute, while history can only conceive the relative.'[34]

But, ideally, the Second World War achieved more than the making of the world safe for French intellectuals and their adepts. Indeed, my argument throughout this book has been that the war's first lesson is that the yearning for the absolute by successive generations of 'terrible simplifiers' must be resisted. In the preface, I asked whether 1989 and all that, the re-unification of Germany and the final end (in most places) of the 'long Second World War' were a cause for sadness or rejoicing, optimism or pessimism. In the pages which followed, I have asserted that the war either was itself enough of a People's war, or was explained and understood sufficiently as such, for it frequently to have advanced the cause of liberty, equality and fraternity and for the post-war era to have been, on balance, one in which the greatest happiness of the greatest number markedly increased. It is too soon to judge whether the completion of the post-war epoch in 1989 will mean the abandonment of these gains, and the forgetting of the lessons of 'Auschwitz' and 'Hiroshima'.

Historians are highly unreliable predictors of the future – as A.J.P. Taylor advised, 'men see the past when they peer into the future'.[35] None the less, it is unnerving to think that the world which, in Central and Eastern Europe, coped so badly with the collapse of the Austro-Hungarian Empire after 1918, and which, thereafter set the task of making new nation states coincide with reality, took up the many varieties of fascism, will now have to deal with the demise of the Soviet and Russian Empires. Since it is my belief that, of all the approaches to understanding how civilisation reached its nadir at 'Auschwitz' and 'Hiroshima', some version of the model of fascism is the most suggestive and elucidatory, and since mass society has produced only three ideologies of government – socialism, which is now 'dead'; liberalism, which often seems but a fair-weather friend; and fascism – I find it impossible to be unrestrainedly optimistic about the latest 'new world order'. If the European Second World Wars were partly fought for the Austro-Hungarian succession, and if the Pacific War contested the British succession,[36] it is devoutly to be hoped that history will not repeat itself, now that the Russian succession will need to be organised both in Europe and Asia.

These hints of menacing historical parallels are, of course, merely speculative. One thing, however, is certain. In *The Name of the Rose*, Umberto Eco promulgated a semiotician's or a post-modernist's credo: 'In the beginning was the Word, and the Word was with God, and the Word was God.'[37] Historians need to be careful before accepting completely the implications that 'it is all in the mind, you know', or that there is always a con in the context. Instead, they should respond with a refrain of their own: 'Historical debate without end. Amen.' If the messages of the People's war are to survive 'the end of history', historians, proudly accepting the burden of their own 'authority', must go on explaining to our societies that our task in exploring the history of the Second World War, and any other issue, is to assess the evidence, find an answer, write it down on a piece of paper, and humbly acknowledge that it is wrong.

Notes

Preface

1 For a more detailed summary of the course, see R. Bosworth, 'The *Decennale* of Late Modern European History I (LME I) or teaching war and revolution in East and West 1978–88', *Australian Historical Association Bulletin*, 59–60, 1989, pp. 5–26.

2 He used the term in his British Open University film series. Cf. also his comments in A. Marwick, *The Nature of History*, London, 1970, p. 321 on 'squeezing the last drop' out of the evidence.

3 In the second week of each fortnight, the course offered students the chance to choose from an array of primary sources. See R. Bosworth, op. cit., p. 8 for some examples.

4 The author was Angelo Rognoni. See M. Kirby, *Futurist Performance*, New York, 1971, p. 301.

5 U. Eco, *The Name of the Rose*, London, 1983, p. 316.

6 P. Geyl, *Encounters in History*, London, 1963, p. 401.

7 It is a rather pleasant irony that the polymathic Fernand Braudel (see chapter 5 below) thought white settlement commenced in Australia in 1789 not 1788 – bicentennial alliances that might have been. See F. Braudel, *Civilization and Capitalism 15th–18th Century*, vol. III, *The Perspective of the World*, London, 1985, p. 382. Braudel also got wrong the name and rank of Captain Arthur Phillip, the first governor. The French edition, vol. III, p. 327 speaks of 'commodore Philipps' reaching Australia 'à la fin de 1789'.

Introduction

1 Bluebottle and Eccles from 'The Mysterious Punch-up-the-conker', TLO 23090, first broadcast 7 February 1957; Greenslade from 'The Thing on the Mountain', TLO 45929, first broadcast 6 January 1958 (and from other *Goon Shows*).

2 Like a good Rankean, Milligan, in his prefaces, repeatedly noted his ambition to record 'what actually happened', to get his 'facts' and his dates 'right'. Ironically, it seems to me that, in his later and less surreal volumes, Milligan's war becomes far less interesting and far less 'real'. S. Milligan, *Adolf Hitler: My Part in His Downfall*, London, 1971; *Rommel? Gunner Who?*, London, 1974; *Monty, His Part in My Victory*, London, 1976; *Mussolini, His Part in My Downfall*, London, 1978; *Where Have All the Bullets Gone?*, London, 1985; *Goodbye Soldier*, London, 1986.

3 For a still most evocative account of this in Britain, see A. Calder, *The People's War: Britain 1939–45*, London, 1969.

4 There is a semi-official biography, P. Scudamore, *Spike Milligan: A Biography*, London, 1985. It contains a somewhat garbled reference to LME I (pp. 248–9) and is

generally literal in its reading of evidence. For a more nuanced account, see also D. Behan, *Milligan: The Life and Times of Spike Milligan*, London, 1988.

5 He made an exception if the officer, Major Chater Jack for example, was 'modern', that is, technologically competent and reasonably democratic in his attitude to the men. Somewhat appropriately for the themes of this book, Milligan, after the war, would, in 1947, join the Italian Communist Party (PCI) 'because this was the only way [he] could get a meal' when on tour near the Yugoslav border, and, in the late 1950s, the Campaign for Nuclear Disarmament (CND). See D. Behan, op. cit., pp. 131, 147.

6 See, for example P. Scudamore, op. cit., pp. 146–7. It must be concluded, however, that BBC officialdom did not really understand how bitter was Milligan's attack on Britain's *ancien régime* as exemplified in the gigantic and explosive musical fart which heralded the character Major Bloodnok. That cowardly reprobate reflected all of Milligan's detestation of the officer caste. D. Behan, op. cit., p. 139 notes acutely: 'much as Milligan hated the Conservative Party he was shrewd enough to realise that *The Goon Show* would have . . . no real focus without them in power.'

7 See P. Scudamore, op. cit., pp. 102–6; D. Behan, op. cit., p. 115.

8 G. Mosse, 'Two World Wars and the myth of the war experience', *Journal of Contemporary History*, 21, 1986, pp. 491–513; cf. his further development of these ideas in his *Fallen Soldiers. Shaping the Memory of the World Wars*, New York, 1990.

9 F. Fukuyama, 'The End of History?', *National Interest*, 16, 1989, pp. 3–4, 9, 18; for Fukuyama as historian, see also F. Fukuyama, *The Soviet Union and the Third World: The Last Three Decades*, Ithaca, NJ, 1987; cf. his 'A reply to my critics', *National Interest*, 18, 1989–90, pp. 21–8.

10 P. Geyl, *Napoleon: For and Against*, rev. edn, Harmondsworth, 1965, p. 18.

11 G. Mosse, 'Two World Wars and the myth of the war experience', pp. 496, 498.

12 For some autobiographical comments, see G. Mosse, *Nazism: a Historical and Comparative Analysis of National Socialism*, New Brunswick, NJ, 1978, pp. 21–31. The interviewer was Michael Ledeen, for whom see chapter 6.

13 It is a commonplace, as A.J.P. Taylor noted long ago, that 'The second World war [sic] was, in large part, a repeat performance of the first', A.J.P. Taylor, *The Origins of the Second World War*, rev. edn, Harmondsworth, 1964, p. 41.

14 See A. J. Mayer, *Why did the Heavens not Darken? The 'Final Solution' in History*, New York, 1988 and chapter 4 below.

15 A.J. Mayer, *Wilson versus Lenin: Political Origins of the New Diplomacy, 1917–8*, New Haven, Conn., 1959.

16 D. Behan, op. cit., p. 16.

17 E. Gibbon, *The Decline and Fall of the Roman Empire*, London, 1910, vol.I, p. 78. In the original quote Domitian replaces Hitler while happiness elapses with the accession of Commodus.

18 B. Bettelheim, *Surviving the Holocaust*, London, 1986, p. 21.

19 See Taylor's wonderfully nuanced use of this phrase, A.J.P. Taylor, op. cit., p. 235 and his explanation of the nuances in his 'Second Thoughts', pp. 7–8 and cf. chapter 2 below.

The Second World War and the historians

1 S. Milligan, *Rommel? Gunner Who?*, London, 1974, p. 13.

2 See A.J.P. Taylor, *The Origins of the Second World War*, rev. edn, Harmondsworth, 1964, p. 7 and chapter 2 below.

3 G.J. Whitrow, *Time in History: Views of Time from Prehistory to the Present Day*, Oxford, 1989, pp. 43–5.

4 For some introductory statistics, see G. Wright, *The Ordeal of Total War 1939–1945*, New York, 1968, pp. 263–5.

5 K. A. Schleunes, *The Twisted Road to Auschwitz: Nazi Policy Toward German Jews, 1933–1939*, Urbana, 1970, p. i.

6 This is one of the American satirist-mathematician Tom Lehrer's 'songs for World War III'. See T. Lehrer, 'That was the year that was: TW3 songs and other songs of the year', sung at the *Hungry I*, San Francisco, 1965 and T. Lehrer, *Too Many Songs*, London, 1981, pp. 116–19.

7 R.A.C. Parker, *Struggle for Survival: The History of the Second World War*, Oxford, 1990, p. 281.

8 P. Fussell, *The Great War and Modern Memory*, London, 1975; for Fussell's doubts about the 'goodness' of the USA's Second World War, see his *Wartime: Understanding and Behavior in the Second World War*, New York, 1989.

9 For a further development of this matter, at least in regard to Germany, see chapter 3 below.

10 H.S. Hughes, *The Sea Change: The Migration of Social Thought, 1930–1965*, New York, 1975; cf. also H. Lehmann and J.J. Sheehan (eds), *An Interrupted Past: German-speaking Refugee Historians in the United States after 1933*, Cambridge, 1991.

11 Gilbert has written an evocative memoir of his life journey from posy-giver to Franz Josef, through Nazi Germany and the OSS, to being a leading early and late modern Europeanist. See F. Gilbert, *A European Past: Memoirs 1900–1945*, New York, 1988.

12 For a preliminary account, see B.M. Katz, 'The criticism of arms: the Frankfurt school goes to war', *Journal of Modern History*, 59, 1987, pp. 439–78.

13 When I was an undergraduate my most inspiring teacher was Ernest Bramsted, one of the few distinguished European refugee historians who found their way to Australia. Harry Hinsley supervised my PhD. For Bramsted, see J. Hooper, 'Ernest K. Bramsted (1901–1978): a European historian in Germany, England and Australia', *Australian Journal of Politics and History*, 31, 1985, pp. 397–407; for Hinsley of Bletchley Park, see the essays by Richard Langhorne, Jonathan Steinberg and Christopher Andrew, three of his students who have had successful careers at Cambridge, in R. Langhorne (ed.), *Diplomacy and Intelligence During the Second World War: Essays in Honour of F.H. Hinsley*, Cambridge, 1985, pp. 3–40. For some autobiographical writing by Davidson, by contrast, see B. Davidson, *Scenes from the Anti-Nazi War*, New York, 1980.

14 R. Cobb, *French and Germans, Germans and French: A Personal Interpretation of France under Two Occupations 1914–1918/1940–1944*, Hanover, 1983, pp. xv, xviii–xx.

15 For an introduction, see his own autobiographical comments, P. Geyl, *Encounters in History*, London, 1963, pp. 399–424 and H.W. Von Der Dunk, 'Pieter Geyl: history as a form of self-expression', in A.C. Duke and C.A. Tamse (eds), *Clio's Mirror. Historiography in Britain and the Netherlands*, Zutphen, 1985.

16 A.J.P. Taylor, *Europe: Grandeur and Decline*, rev. edn, Harmondsworth, 1967, p. 16.

17 P. Geyl, *Napoleon: For and Against*, rev. edn, Harmondsworth, 1965, pp. 15, 18.

18 P. Geyl, *Encounters in History*, p. 340.

19 He concealed his work in toothpaste tubes; see A.E.C. Simoni, 'Dutch clandestine printing, 1940–1945', *Library*, 5th series, xxvii, 1972, pp. 17–19.

20 V. Mehta, *Fly and the Fly-bottle: Encounters with British Intellectuals*, rev. edn, New York, 1983, pp. 156–7.

21 P. Geyl, *The Revolt of the Netherlands 1555–1609*, London, 1932, rev. edn, 1958; cf. also his *Netherlands in the Seventeenth Century*, 2 vols, London, 1936, rev. edn, 1961–4.

22 See, for example, P. Geyl, *Debates with Historians*, London, 1955, pp. 222–6.

23 ibid., pp. 9–29 and cf. chapter 3 below.
24 H.W. Von Der Dunk, op. cit., pp. 187, 205. Probably on the advice of Ritter, the FRG gave him the *Pour le Mérite*, an award which he much treasured.
25 A. Toynbee, *A Study of History*, 12 vols, London, 1934–61; cf., for example W.H. McNeill, *Arnold J. Toynbee: A Life*, Oxford, 1989.
26 V. Mehta, op. cit., p. 156.
27 P. Geyl, *Debates with Historians*, p. 201; for a typical example of his unyielding nature in polemic, see his chapter in reply to Toynbee in P. Geyl, *Encounters in History*, pp. 276–305.
28 Cf. also P. Geyl, *Use and Abuse of History*, New Haven, Conn., 1955, which is a brief charter for the cause of scepticism.
29 P. Geyl, *Napoleon: For and Against*, p. 7.
30 ibid. He does emphasise that 'History does not repeat itself. Between noticing a parallel and establishing an identity there is a wide gap' (p. 8).
31 Cf. his musing on what might be called his 'Napoleon 2', a study of the historiography of the French Revolution proper. P. Geyl, *Encounters in History*, pp. 115–87. It was originally published, perhaps appropriately, in 1956.
32 For his recollection of the key significance of this phrase, and his accompanying rejection of Toynbee and determinism, see V. Mehta, op. cit., pp. 158–9.
33 See, for example, Geyl's deft depiction of Napoleon, the historian/propagandist of himself, anxious to argue that 'he had been obliged to conquer Europe in self-defence' (P. Geyl, *Napoleon: For and Against*, p. 25) or Geyl's repetition of the young soldier's racist statement in 1797 that France was 'peopled by men, Italy by children, Holland by pot-bellied merchants, Germany by herds enclosed within fences which their masters shift at will' (p. 239).
34 R. Cobb, *The Police and the People: French Popular Protest 1789–1820*, London, 1972, p. 197. But cf. L. Bergeron, *France under Napoleon*, Princeton, NJ, 1981 (first published in Paris, 1972). This latter work, written self-consciously from the *Annales* school, none the less contains a Napoleon who keeps breaking through the structures. For more on French historiography, see chapter 5 below.
35 E. Hobsbawm, *Nations and Nationalism since 1780: Programme, Myth, Reality*, Cambridge, 1990, p. 133.
36 H.W. Von Der Dunk, op. cit., pp. 193, 198, 204.
37 P. Geyl, *Encounters in History*, p. 408.
38 When the USSR invaded Hungary in 1956, Geyl would have welcomed war to expel the Soviets but for the existence of nuclear weapons. He thought Indonesia's Sukarno both a demagogue and a traitor. H.W. Von Der Dunk, op. cit., p. 204.
39 V. Mehta, op. cit., p. 163.
40 For Geyl's critique of Namier, ironically for Freudian irrationalism, see ibid., pp. 162–3.
41 L. Namier, *The Structure of Politics at the Accession of George III*, London, 1929 (rev. edn, London, 1957); *England in the Age of the American Revolution*, London, 1930.
42 See chapter 2 below.
43 In its 1976 edition, the *Oxford English Dictionary* accepted the verb 'to namierise'. L. Colley, *Lewis Namier*, London, 1989, p. 1.
44 He co-ordinated the massive project of writing a namierised history of parliament and, on his death, had almost finished his own three volumes covering the period 1754–90. For some account of this Namier, see the eulogistic essay by his pupil and colleague J. Brooke, 'Namier and Namierism', *History and Theory*, III, 1964, pp. 331–46; cf. also the debate in H.C. Mansfield, 'Sir Lewis Namier considered', *Journal of British Studies*, II, 1963, pp. 28–55; 'Sir Lewis Namier again considered', *Journal of British Studies*, III, 1964, pp. 109–19; R. Walcott, 'Sir Lewis Namier considered considered', *Journal of British Studies*, III, 1964, pp. 85–108; or, of special interest because of its author's own background, H.R. Winkler, 'Sir Lewis Namier', *Journal of Modern History*,

XXXV, 1963, pp. 1–19. Ancient historians also took to prosopography with a will as, more predictably, did students of US colonial history.

45 For his biography, see L. Colley, op. cit.; N. Rose, *Lewis Namier and Zionism*, Oxford, 1980; J. Namier, *Lewis Namier: A Biography*, London, 1971. This last work, written by Julia, Namier's second wife, needs to be treated with some caution; cf. A.J.P. Taylor, *Letters to Eva 1969–1983* (ed. E. Haraszti Taylor), London, 1991, pp. 251–2.

46 J. Namier, op. cit., p. 54.

47 Quoted by N. Davies, *God's Playground: A History of Poland*, Oxford, 1981, p. 393.

48 N. Rose, op. cit., p. 10.

49 For a further, muted but resonant example, see the obituary by H. Butterfield, 'Sir Lewis Namier as historian', *Listener*, 18 May 1961, pp. 873–6 which reiterates the advantages Namier gained from his 'cosmopolitan background'.

50 V. Mehta, op. cit., p. 267.

51 A.J.P. Taylor, *A Personal History*, London, 1983, p. 112.

52 V. Mehta, op. cit., p. 264 quoting J. Namier.

53 R. Bruce Lockhart, *Diaries* (ed. K. Young), London, 1973, vol. I, p. 252.

54 ibid., vol. I, p. 311.

55 L. Namier, *Skyscrapers and Other Essays*, New York, 1931, p. 92.

56 See below pp. 155–8.

57 J.L. Talmon, 'The ordeal of Sir Lewis Namier: the man, the historian and the Jew', *Commentary*, 33, 1962, p. 238.

58 L. Namier, *Skyscrapers, and other essays*, p. 47.

59 N. Rose, op. cit., p. 155.

60 L. Namier, *1848: The Revolution of the Intellectuals*, London, 1946.

61 N. Rose, op. cit., p. 60.

62 For a curious misreading of Namier to endorse the idea that 1989 was, at last, the real springtime of the peoples, see T.G. Ash, *We, the People*, Cambridge, 1990, p. 134.

63 L. Namier, *1848: The Revolution of the Intellectuals*, pp. 24, 33.

64 ibid., p. 31.

65 ibid., p. 124.

66 L. Namier, *Facing East: Essays on Germany, the Balkans, and Russia in the Twentieth Century*, London, 1947, p. 9.

67 According to John Kenyon, Namier was nicknamed by his enemies 'Constipation', 'the big shit we can't get rid of'. J.P. Kenyon, *The History Men*, Pittsburgh, Penn., 1984, p. 255.

68 A.J.P. Taylor, *A Personal History*, p. 126.

69 L. Namier, *1848: The Revolution of the Intellectuals*, p. 7.

70 I. Berlin, 'L.B. Namier: a personal impression', *Encounter*, XXVII, 1966, p. 33.

71 L. Namier, *Facing East*, pp. 111–12.

72 E.g. L. Namier, *Conflicts: Studies in Contemporary History*, London, 1942, pp. 40–1 (article of May 1940).

73 L. Schapiro, *Totalitarianism*, London, 1972 provides a brief and not very satisfactory introduction.

74 His wife was expected thus to address him until after the birth of their fourth child. R. Mussolini, *The Real Mussolini*, Farnborough, 1973, p. 66.

75 For the best introduction, see A. Aquarone, *L'organizzazione dello stato totalitario*, Turin, 1965.

76 In English, see C.F. Delzell (ed.), *Mediterranean Fascism, 1919–1945*, New York, 1970, pp. 93–4.

77 For further evidence on this matter, see chapter 6 below.

78 L. Schapiro, op. cit., pp. 13–14. In the late 1930s, some Italian commentators hopeful, perhaps as a way of countering the German ally, that Stalin was a 'Russian fascist' again applied the term in what they deemed a positive manner.

79 In a huge literature, an introduction to the theoretics may be found in W. Laqueur (ed.),

Fascism: A Reader's Guide, London, 1976; M. Kitchen, *Fascism*, London, 1976; R. De Felice, *Interpretations of Fascism*, Cambridge, Mass., 1977; P. Ayçoberry, *The Nazi Question: An Essay on the Interpretation of National Socialism (1922–1975)*, London, 1981.

80 See, for example, P. Togliatti, *Lectures on Fascism*, London, 1976, p. 1. Many of Togliatti's lectures were devoted, characteristically, to demonstrating that this definition was not a very adequate one.

81 H. Rauschning, *The Beast from the Abyss*, London, 1941, p. 13.

82 ibid., p. 122.

83 ibid., pp. 139–40.

84 H. Arendt, *The Origins of Totalitarianism*, London, 1951; J.L. Talmon, *The Origins of Totalitarian Democracy*, London, 1952; C.J. Friedrich and Z.K. Brzezinski, *Totalitarian Dictatorship and Autocracy*, Cambridge, Mass., 1956. Carl Friedrich also edited the proceedings of an important conference on totalitarianism held at the American Academy of Arts and Sciences in March 1953. Among a long list of speakers were Hannah Arendt, Erik Erikson, Merle Fainsod, Alexander Gerschenkron, Michael Karpovich, George Kennan, Harold Lasswell, J.P. Nettl, Sigmund Neumann, Adam Ulam, Bertram Wolfe and Friedrich himself. See C.J. Friedrich (ed.), *Totalitarianism*, London, 1954.

85 R. De Felice, *Interpretations of Fascism*, pp. 21–3, somewhat oddly, gives pride of place as a totalitarianist to another emigré, Hans Kohn, a fine liberal historian of nationalism. Kohn had been born in Prague in 1891 and fled the Old World in 1933, finding a position at Smith College from 1934. For his own autobiography (and some philosophising), see H. Kohn, *Living in a World Revolution: My Encounter with History*, New York, 1964. 'The very air of Prague', he remarks, 'made me a student of history and of nationalism' and his bourgeois Jewish origins similarly assisted him to see that the course of history did not move with 'Hegelian-Marxian' rationality (p.19). Kohn, a POW in Russia 1915–20 and one who rejected Zionist rigidity after the experience of living in Jerusalem, was a sort of 'inverted Namier'.

86 C.J. Friedrich and Z. Brzezinski, op. cit., pp. vii–ix.

87 The clause about weapons has had a major impact in US politics given the long-standing debates in that country about gun control. See, for example, ibid., pp. 11–2.

88 ibid., pp. 9–10.

89 ibid., p. 63.

90 J.L. Talmon, *The Myth of the Nation and the Vision of Revolution: The Origins of Ideological Polarization in the Twentieth Century*, London, 1981, p. 535.

91 J.L. Talmon, *The Origins of Totalitarian Democracy*, p. 1.

92 ibid., p. 249.

93 Cf. the second volume of the trilogy with its concentration on Marx and on Mazzinian nationalism, J.L. Talmon, *Political Messianism: The Romantic Phase*, London, 1960.

94 H. Arendt, *The Origins of Totalitarianism*, rev. edn, London, 1967, pp. xxxi, 3. For an introduction to Arendt's thought, see, for example, M. Canovan, *The Political Thought of Hannah Arendt*, London, 1974; G.T. Kaplan and C.S. Kessler (eds), *Hannah Arendt: Thinking, Judging, Freedom*, Sydney, 1989.

95 H. Arendt, *The Origins of Totalitarianism*, pp. 54, 290–1.

96 ibid., pp. 107–8, 125, 222, 307, 317. Arendt's views were not so different from Namier's distinction between (good) territorial and (bad) linguistic nationalism.

97 ibid., p. 415.

98 See L.K. Adler and T.G. Paterson, 'Red Fascism: the merger of Nazi Germany and Soviet Russia in the American image of totalitarianism 1930s–1950s', *American Historical Review*, LXXV, 1970, pp. 1046, 1051, 1058, 1060.

99 K.F. Shteppa, *Russian Historians and the Soviet State*, New Brunswick, NJ, 1962, pp. 347–8. In 1952 *Voprosy Istorii* excoriated the (conservative) *Catholic Historical*

Review for opening its pages to the 'vile fabrications of Ukrainian national degenerates' (p. 349).

100 For a useful introduction, see N. Thompson, *The Anti-Appeasers: Conservative Opposition to Appeasement in the 1930s*, Oxford, 1971.

101 A. Bullock, *Hitler: A Study in Tyranny*, London, 1952.

102 K.G. Feiling, *The Life of Neville Chamberlain*, London, 1946. Feiling had access to the Chamberlain papers and diaries and published many extracts from them.

103 H.R. Trevor-Roper, 'The Mind of Adolf Hitler', foreword to his edition of *Hitler's Table Talk 1941–4*, London, 1953, p. xxviii. For an autobiographical defence, cf. also his 'Hitler revisited: a retrospective', *Encounter*, LXXI, December 1988, pp. 17–19.

104 H. Arendt, *Eichmann in Jerusalem: A Report on the Banality of Evil*, rev. edn, New York, 1965; for a recent comment on the book's influence, see D. Diner, 'Historical experience and cognition: perspectives on National Socialism', *History and Memory*, II, 1990, pp. 92–3.

105 E.H. Carr, *What is History?*, rev. edn, Harmondsworth, 1987, p. 3.

106 E.H. Carr, *The Twenty Years' Crisis 1919–1939*, London, 1939; *International Relations between the Two World Wars (1919–1939)*, rev. edn of original 1937 work, London, 1947; *The Bolshevik Revolution, 1917–23*, 3 vols, London, 1950–3; *The Interregnum 1923–4*, London, 1954; *Socialism in One Country 1924–6*, 3 vols, London, 1958–64; (with R.W. Davies), *Foundations of a Planned Economy 1926–9*, 3 vols, London, 1969–78.

107 N. Stone, 'Grim eminence', *London Review of Books*, 20 January 1983, p. 982. Some replies to Stone defending Carr were published in subsequent issues.

108 E.H. Carr, *What is History?* Harmondsworth, 1964, p. 55.

109 ibid., pp. 10–11, 30.

110 ibid., pp. 23–4.

111 W.H. McNeill, 'Mythistory or truth, myths, history and historians', *American Historical Review*, 91, 1986, p. 7.

112 ibid., p. 8.

113 The classic English language statement against historiographical relativism in this period is that of G.R. Elton, *The Practice of History*, Sydney, 1967. Elton, born in Prague in 1921 but become a major conservative historian of Tudor England, was another who carried the strains of Central Europe in his cultural baggage. For a portrait of Elton, see J.P. Kenyon, op. cit., pp. 209–12. For a more direct, if unconvincing, attack on Carr, see J.H. Hexter, *Doing History*, London, 1971, pp. 77–106, and for further comments on modern Rankeanism, see chapters 3 and 6 below.

114 R. Barthes, *Mythologies*, London, 1973 (first published in French, 1957).

115 T. Eagleton, *Literary Theory: An Introduction*, Oxford, 1983, p. 142.

116 See, for example, ibid., p. 145 or, in recent controversy, David Lehman, *Signs of the Times: Deconstruction and the Fall of Paul de Man*, New York, 1991.

117 In the narrow field of historiography, this matter is examined in chapter 5 below.

118 For an extraordinarily vivid recent example of this sort of nostalgia, see P. Nora, 'Between memory and history: *les lieux de mémoire*', *Representations*, 26, 1989, pp. 7–25, and p. 197 below.

The origins of the Third World War and the making of English social history

1 S. Milligan, *Adolf Hitler: My Part in His Downfall*, London, 1971, p. 13.

2 R.R. James (ed.), *Chips: The Diaries of Sir Henry Channon*, Harmondsworth, 1970, p. 265.

3 D.C. Watt, *How War Came: The Immediate Origins of the Second World War, 1938–1939*, London, 1989 repeatedly alleges that the war was 'willed to happen' (p. 2).

It was Hitler who 'willed, desired, lusted after war' (p.610). Donald Cameron Watt has been Stevenson Professor of International History at the University of London since 1981 and is very much an 'old-fashioned diplomatic historian'.

4 ibid., pp. 385, 616.

5 A.J.P. Taylor, *The Trouble Makers: Dissent over Foreign Policy 1792–1939*, London, 1957, p. 176.

6 C.B. Otley, 'The social origins of British army officers', *Sociological Review*, 18, 1970, pp. 233–4.

7 For a fascinating introduction to the political side of cinema, see A. Aldgate, *Cinema and History: British Newsreels and the Spanish Civil War*, London, 1979.

8 Cricket was, of course, a marvellous symbol of the survival of 'two nations'. *Wisden's Cricketers Almanack*, the annual 'bible' of the sport, in 1940 still distinguished 'amateurs' or 'gentlemen' from 'professionals' or 'players' by placing an amateur's initials and title before the name on a score-card; a professional's initials were only recorded, and then in brackets, after the name.

9 A.J.P. Taylor, *English History 1914–1945*, Oxford, 1965, p. 597.

10 T. Lloyd, *Empire to Welfare State: English History 1906–76*, rev. edn, Oxford, 1979, pp. 267–8.

11 A. Calder, *The People's War: Britain 1939–45*, London, 1971, pp. 47, 49.

12 Calder says that in the week after Dunkirk production rose 25 per cent, though it was almost back to normal a month later: ibid., p. 136.

13 See, for example, A. Marwick, *War and Social Change in the Twentieth Century: A Comparative Study of Britain, France, Germany, Russia and the United States*, London, 1974, pp. 153–6.

14 See, for example, N. Frankland, *The Bombing Offensive against Germany: Outlines and Perspectives*, London, 1965; cf. his *The Strategic Air Offensive against Germany 1939–1945*, London, 1961.

15 For some figures, see A. Milward, *War, Economy and Society 1939–1945*, Harmondsworth, 1987, pp. 89–92.

16 A. Calder, op. cit., p. 354. Incidence of absenteeism, suicide and drunkenness also fell (pp. 251, 257).

17 ibid., pp. 323–4. During the war, women left domestic service in droves for the factory floor while female union membership doubled (pp. 454–5).

18 A.J.P. Taylor, *English History 1914–1945*, pp. 596, 600.

19 For an introduction, see K.O. Morgan, *Labour in Power 1945–1951*, Oxford, 1984.

20 A.J.P. Taylor, *The Origins of the Second World War*, London, 1961. Mostly my citations will be from the revised edition which includes the Foreword 'Second Thoughts', London, 1963, issued as a Penguin paperback, Harmondsworth, 1964.

21 His Hungarian third wife, misleadingly, calls it instead his 'joke book'. E. Haraszti Taylor, *A Life with Alan; The Diary of A.J.P. Taylor's Wife Eva from 1978 to 1985*, London, 1987, p. 41; but cf. Taylor's own, not altogether adequate explanation of his usage, A.J.P. Taylor, *Letters to Eva 1969–1983* (ed. E. Haraszti Taylor), London, 1991, p. 333.

22 A.J.P. Taylor, *A Personal History*, London, 1983, p. 234. A great deal of this autobiography is replicated in the recently published collection of Taylor's love letters, A.J.P. Taylor, *Letters to Eva 1969–1983*.

23 A.J.P. Taylor, *Politicians, Socialism and Historians*, London, 1980, pp. 3–5. (The autobiographical chapter, 'Accident prone, or what happened next?' was originally published in the *Journal of Modern History*, 49, 1977, pp. 1–18. This same issue has a number of useful, critical essays on Taylor.) The working-class mistress of Taylor's father always called him 'Mr Taylor', even after a decade of relationship. A.J.P. Taylor, *Letters to Eva 1969–1983*, p. 267.

24 A.J.P. Taylor, *The Trouble Makers*, p. 14.

25 A.J.P. Taylor, *Politicians, Socialism and Historians*, p. 6.

26 A.J.P. Taylor, *A Personal History*, p. 84.

27 ibid.

28 ibid., pp. 41–2, 53–4, 60, 76–8; A.J.P. Taylor, *Politicians, Socialism and Historians*, p. 7.

29 A.J.P. Taylor, *A Personal History*, p. 56.

30 ibid., p. 78.

31 ibid., pp. 80–2.

32 ibid., p. 88. For examples of Pribram's work, see A.F. Pribram, *The Secret Treaties of Austria-Hungary, 1879–1914*, 2 vols, Cambridge, Mass., 1920–1; *Austria-Hungary and Great Britain, 1908–1914*, London, 1951.

33 A.J.P. Taylor, *The Italian Problem in European Diplomacy, 1847–1849*, Manchester, 1934.

34 See, for example, his remarkable footnote to his textual comment 'there were few real secrets in the [pre-1914] diplomatic world, and all diplomatists were honest, according to their moral code'. The footnote then runs: 'It becomes wearisome to add "except the Italians" to every generalisation. Henceforth it may be assumed.' A.J.P. Taylor, *The Struggle for Mastery in Europe 1848–1918*, Oxford, 1954, p. xxiii fn. 4. I have always considered my own 537-page *Italy, the Least of Great Powers: Italian Foreign Policy before the First World War*, Cambridge, 1979 as no more than an explication of this *goak*. On Trieste, see A.J.P. Taylor, *A Personal History*, p. 158.

35 A.J.P. Taylor, *A Personal History*, p. 123; *Germany's First Bid for Colonies, 1884–5*, London, 1938.

36 A.J.P. Taylor, *Politicians, Socialism and Historians*, p. 10.

37 ibid., p. 19; A.J.P. Taylor, *A Personal History*, pp. 214–17. It is perhaps appropriate that Trevor-Roper's 'best book' is a biography of a Lancastrian-Quaker-gone-wrong. H.R. Trevor-Roper, *Hermit of Peking: The Hidden Life of Sir Edmund Backhouse*, rev. edn, London, 1986.

38 See, for example, A.J.P. Taylor, *Essays in English History*, Harmondsworth, 1976, pp. 49–54; *The Trouble Makers*, pp. 35–6.

39 A.J.P. Taylor, *Politicians, Socialism and Historians*, pp. 62–3.

40 A.J.P. Taylor, *A Personal History*, p. 153.

41 ibid., p. 165.

42 ibid., p. 161; A.J.P. Taylor, *The Habsburg Monarchy, 1809–1918*, rev. edn, London, 1948; also Harmondsworth, 1964.

43 A.J.P. Taylor, *The Habsburg Monarchy, 1809–1918*, Harmondsworth, 1964, pp. 9–10.

44 A.J.P. Taylor, *The Course of German History: A Survey of the Development of German History since 1815*, London, 1945; rev. edn, London, 1961; *A Personal History*, p. 172.

45 A.J.P. Taylor, *The Course of German History*, rev. edn, pp. 110, 154–5; Taylor would also later write a psychologically acute biography of Bismarck, A.J.P. Taylor, *Bismarck: The Man and the Statesman*, London, 1955.

46 Taylor would hold to this interpretation and thus refuse to accept the more extreme claims of the 'Fischer revolution'. See, for example, A.J.P. Taylor, *Politicians, Socialism and Historians*, pp. 12–14 where he also notes 'at least I had read Eckhart Kehr, which most English historians at the time had not' and chapter 3 below.

47 A.J.P. Taylor, *The Course of German History*, rev. edn, p. 186.

48 ibid., pp. 238–9.

49 ibid., p. 240.

50 ibid., pp. 257, 260.

51 ibid., p. vii.

52 See chapter 3 below.

53 A.J.P. Taylor, *The Course of German History*, rev. edn, p. 259.

54 ibid., p. 2.

55 A.J.P. Taylor, *Europe: Grandeur and Decline*, rev. edn, Harmondsworth, 1967, p. 7.

56 Of his books, apart from those already listed in these footnotes, see, for example, *The*

First World War: An Illustrated History, London, 1963; *Beaverbrook*, London, 1972; *The Second World War: An Illustrated History*, London, 1975 and the wonderfully evocative photographic collection, *The Last of Old Europe: A Grand Tour*, London, 1976. Some of the reviews are collected in A.J.P. Taylor, *Europe: Grandeur and Decline*, and *Essays in English History*. For a preliminary listing, see also C. Wrigley, *A.J.P. Taylor: A Complete Annotated Bibliography and Guide to his Historical and Other Writings*, Brighton, 1980.

57 A.J.P. Taylor, *A Personal History*, p. 220.

58 ibid., pp. 211–14.

59 ibid., p. 225.

60 R. Taylor and C. Pritchard, *The Protest Makers. The British Nuclear Disarmament Movement of 1958–1965: Twenty Years On*, Oxford, 1980, pp. 7, 17.

61 A.J.P. Taylor, *Politicians, Socialism and Historians*, p. 16.

62 A.J.P. Taylor, *A Personal History*, p. 233. My thanks even more than usual hereabouts to Tony Cahill who, as an undergraduate, attended these lectures.

63 *Time*, 12 January 1962 as cited in W.R. Louis (ed.), *The Origins of the Second World War: A.J.P. Taylor and his Critics*, New York, 1972, pp. 104–5. The book was similarly welcomed by German neo-Nazis and by Oswald Mosley. Many Italian scholars continue naively to read it as a defence of Hitler.

64 According to Taylor, Namier had indeed recommended Trevor-Roper for the chair, after Taylor refused an ultimatum that he desist writing for the *Sunday Express*! A.J.P. Taylor, *A Personal History*, pp. 215–17.

65 H.R. Trevor-Roper, 'A.J.P. Taylor, Hitler and the war', *Encounter*, XVII, July 1961, pp. 88–96 as republished in W.R. Louis (ed.), op. cit., pp. 57–8.

66 A.J.P. Taylor, 'How to quote: exercises for beginners', *Encounter*, XVII, September 1961, pp. 72–3, again in W.R. Louis, op. cit., pp. 58–61. In the same issue, Trevor-Roper published another, characteristically portentous, 'reply' (pp. 61–3). The same extracts and that of fn.65 are also re-published in E.M. Robertson (ed.), *The Origins of the Second World War: Historical Interpretations*, London, 1971, pp. 83–104.

67 See W.R. Louis (ed.), op. cit., pp. 69–81 (Hinsley), 110–14 (Craig), 117–45 (Bullock).

68 T. Mason, 'Some origins of the Second World War', *Past and Present*, 29, 1964, pp. 67–87 as reproduced in E.M. Robertson (ed.), op. cit., pp. 106-123. For Taylor's own generous reply to Mason, see pp. 136–41 or *Past and Present*, 65, 1965, pp. 110–13.

69 For a much more detailed exposition of these terms and their place in the historiography, see chapter 4 below.

70 S.A. Schuker, 'The end of Versailles' in G. Martel (ed.), *'The Origins of the Second World War' Reconsidered: The A.J.P. Taylor Debate after Twenty-five Years*, Boston, Mass., 1986, pp. 50, 52, 54.

71 E. Ingram, 'Epilogue: a patriot for me' in ibid., p. 245.

72 Ingram, in my opinion, is completely mistaken in his assessment of *A Personal History*. He has much more of a case against the jejune A.J.P. Taylor, *An Old Man's Diary*, London, 1984.

73 E. Ingram, op. cit., p. 248.

74 Cowling, a Tory, 'namierised' politics at the accession of George VI. See, for example, M. Cowling, *The Impact of Hitler: British Politics and British Policy 1933–1940*, Cambridge, 1975.

75 P. Kennedy, 'Appeasement' in G. Martel, op. cit., p. 145; cf. also his sensible comments, seconding Tim Mason and Hinsley, about the weakness of Taylor's reconciliation of what should now be called 'structures' and 'events', and what he saw as determinism and the freedom of the individual. P. Kennedy, 'A.J.P. Taylor and "profound forces" in history' in C. Wrigley (ed.), *Warfare, Diplomacy and Politics: Essays in Honour of A.J.P. Taylor*, London, 1986, pp. 14–28. Taylor is perhaps the only historian to have been accorded a *Festschrift* on his 60th, 70th and 80th birthdays.

76 R. Young, 'A.J.P. Taylor and the problem with France', in ibid., p. 97.
77 V. Mehta, *Fly and the Fly-bottle: Encounters with British Intellectuals*, rev. edn, New York, 1983, pp. 168–9.
78 C. Wrigley, *A.J.P. Taylor: A Complete Annotated Bibliography . . .*, pp. 94–8 lists some reviews as well as the translation of his book into Finnish and Sinhalese among other languages.
79 A.J.P. Taylor, *Politicians, Socialism and Historians*, p. 10.
80 ibid., p. 23 where he defines him as 'perhaps the greatest of English historians', *Essays in English History*, p. 19 where he removes the perhaps.
81 ibid., p. 5.
82 A.J.P. Taylor, *Essays in English History*, p. 17.
83 A.J.P. Taylor, *A Personal History*, p. 235.
84 W.R. Louis (ed.), op. cit., pp. 47, 105.
85 A.J.P. Taylor, *The Origins of the Second World War*, rev. edn, p. 235 (cf. Taylor's own signalling of the *goak* in 'Second Thoughts', pp. 7–8).
86 A.J.P. Taylor, *A Personal History*, p. 234.
87 A.J.P. Taylor, *The Origins of the Second World War*, rev. edn, p. 27.
88 See A.J.P. Taylor, *Politicians, Socialism and Historians*, p. 211; for Havel and his colleagues' own evocation of history, see M. Glenny, *The Rebirth of History: Eastern Europe in an Age of Democracy*, Harmondsworth, 1990, pp. 25–6.
89 A.J.P. Taylor, *The Origins of the Second World War*, rev. edn, p. 27.
90 A.J.P. Taylor, *Politicians, Socialism and Historians*, pp. 210–11, quoting Keith Robbins.
91 ibid., p. 41.
92 E. Haraszti Taylor, op. cit., p. 84.
93 A.J.P. Taylor, *A Personal History*, pp. 234, 236; for a very similar sense of hurt, cf. A.J.P. Taylor, *Letters to Eva 1969–1983*, pp. 93, 236.
94 A.J.P. Taylor, *An Old Man's Diary*, p. 121.
95 A.J.P. Taylor, *Essays in English History*, p. 15.
96 A.J.P. Taylor, *Politicians, Socialism and Historians*, p. 20.
97 ibid., p. 18.
98 ibid., p. 3.
99 A.J.P. Taylor, *The Origins of the Second World War*, rev. edn, p. 42.
100 A.J.P. Taylor, *Politicians, Socialism and Historians*, p. 3.
101 E.H. Carr, *What is History?*, Harmondsworth, 1964, p. 95.
102 For a further development of this debate, see chapter 5 below and for a spectacular rebuttal of the more extreme versions of social history, cf. T. Judt, 'A clown in regal purple: social history and the historians', *History Workshop*, 7, 1979, pp. 66–94.
103 E.P. Thompson, *The Making of the English Working Class*, London, 1963; rev. edn, Harmondsworth, 1980.
104 For some introduction to Thompson see B.D. Palmer, *The Making of E.P. Thompson: Marxism, Humanism and History*, Toronto, 1981; H.J. Kaye, *The British Marxist Historians: An Introductory Analysis*, Cambridge, 1984, pp. 167–220; T.W. Heyck, 'E.P. Thompson: moralist as Marxist historian' in W.L. Arnstein (ed.), *Recent Historians of Great Britain: Essays on the Post-1945 Generation*, Ames, Iowa, 1990, pp. 121–45; and, in his own writing, E.P. Thompson, 'Interview' in H. Abelove *et al.* (eds), *Visions of History*, Manchester, 1983. Specifically on Frank, see E.P. and T.J. Thompson, *There is a Spirit in Europe: A Memoir of Frank Thompson*, London, 1948.
105 E.P. Thompson, *The Heavy Dancers*, New York, 1985, pp. 199–200.
106 E.P. Thompson, *The Sykaos Papers*, London, 1988.
107 See, for example, D. Thompson, *The Chartists: Popular Politics in the Industrial Revolution,* Aldershot, 1984.
108 E.P. Thompson, *William Morris: Romantic to Revolutionary*, rev. edn, New York, 1977.

109 E.P. Thompson, *The Heavy Dancers*, p. 194.
110 E.P. Thompson, *The Making of the English Working Class*, rev. edn, pp. 9, 12, 213.
111 See, for example, chapter 4 of ibid. but the phrase is reiterated throughout Thompson's work.
112 ibid., p. 10; E.P. Thompson, *The Poverty of Theory and Other Essays*, London, 1978, p. 85 enlarges on this point.
113 Thompson dismissed Namier as 'that inverted – [vulgar] Marxist'. ibid., p. 48.
114 For example, E.P. Thompson, *The Making of the English Working Class*, rev. edn, p. 110.
115 See ibid., pp. 916–39 for the Postscript; pp. 221, 231 for reading statistics.
116 See K. Marx, *Political Writings,* vol. II: *Surveys from Exile* (ed. D. Fernbach), Harmondsworth, 1973, p. 146.
117 E.P. Thompson, *The Poverty of Theory*, pp. 230–2, 262, 384.
118 E.P. Thompson, *The Making of the English Working Class*, p. 19.
119 See chapter 7 below.
120 For an introduction, see H.J. Kaye, op. cit..
121 See chapter 6 below. In *The Making of the English Working Class,* Thompson analyses 'hegemony' before that Gramscian concept became a familiar one in historiography. See, for example, G. Eley, 'Reading Gramsci in English: observations on the reception of Antonio Gramsci in the English-speaking world 1957–82', *European History Quarterly*, 14, 1984, pp. 441–78; E.J. Hobsbawm, 'Labour history and ideology', *Journal of Social History*, 7, 1974, pp. 371–81; in the preface to E.P. Thompson, *The Poverty of Theory*, p. iv, Thompson can be found ascribing Gramscian 'national populism' to himself.
122 E. Genovese, *Roll, Jordan, Roll*, New York, 1974.
123 See, for example, H.J. Kaye and K. McClelland (eds), *E.P. Thompson: Critical Perspectives*, Cambridge, 1990 for accounts from many different viewpoints of Thompson's influence and impact. In the United States, the chief missionary of the Thompsonian gospel was the labour historian, Herbert Gutman.
124 E.P. Thompson, *The Poverty of Theory*, p. 30.
125 ibid., p. 195.
126 ibid., p. 13.
127 E.P. Thompson, 'Notes on exterminism: the last stage of civilization', *New Left Review*, 121, 1980, p. 15; with D. Smith (eds), *Protest and Survive*, Harmondsworth, 1980, p. 52. The grouchy elderly Taylor wrote off Thompson's exterminism as 'sheer gibberish'; A.J.P. Taylor, *Letters to Eva 1969–1983*, p. 439.
128 E.P. Thompson, *Writing by Candlelight*, London, 1980, pp. 13–37; cf. E.P. Thompson (ed.), *Warwick University Ltd.: Industry, Management and the Universities*, Harmondsworth, 1970.
129 See, for example, E.P. Thompson, *Whigs and Hunters: the Origin of the Black Act*, Harmondsworth, 1975. Thompson (p. 258) briefly defines the Hanoverian Whigs as 'a hard lot of men'; cf. also Thompson's chapter, 'The crime of anonymity' in D. Hay *et al.*, *Albion's Fatal Tree: Crime and Society in Eighteenth Century England*, Harmondsworth, 1975. In his evocation of the law's potential and 'mythical' virtue, Thompson was attacking the post-structuralism of Foucault and his supporters and that of much French historiography. He wrote derisively (*Whigs and Hunters,* p. 268) of 'those universal thinkers, impatient of all except the *longue durée*, who cannot be bothered with cartloads of victims at Tyburn'. Cf. M. Foucault, *Discipline and Punish: The Birth of the Prison*, Harmondsworth, 1977 (first published in French, 1975); and chapter 5 below.
130 See, for example, E.P. Thompson, *Writing by Candlelight*; with D. Smith (eds), *Protest and Survive: Beyond the Cold War*, London, 1982; *Zero Option*, London, 1982; with B. Thompson, *Star Wars: Self-destruct Incorporated*, London, 1985; with M. Kaldor *et al.* (eds), *Mad Dogs: The U.S. Raids on Libya*, London, 1986 {as an interesting sign

of fame, the front cover of this book cites Thompson and Kaldor as editors, the frontispiece instead refers to Kaldor and Paul Anderson}; with D. Smith (eds), *Prospectus for a Habitable Planet*, Harmondsworth, 1987.

131 H. Abelove *et al.* (eds), op. cit., p. 6.

132 E.P. Thompson, 'The rituals of enmity' in D. Smith and E.P. Thompson (eds), *Prospectus for a Habitable Planet*, p. 17.

133 E.P. Thompson, *The Heavy Dancers*, London, 1985, pp. 338–9. For some reason the poem is excluded from the American edition of this book which is otherwise cited.

134 See, for example, J.C.D. Clark, *English Society, 1688–1832*, Cambridge, 1985; *Revolution and Rebellion: State and Society in England in the Seventeenth and Eighteenth Centuries*, Cambridge, 1986; '1688 and all that: *The English Revolution*', *Encounter*, LXXII, January 1989, pp. 14–17. Clark is especially severe on Thompson and what he calls the Marxist 'Old Guard' and also believes Namier to have been a 'fine though overrated historian'. See J.C.D. Clark, *Revolution and Rebellion*, pp. 13, 48–50.

135 See, for example, C. Barnett, *The Audit of War: The Illusion and Reality of Britain as a Great Nation*, London, 1986. The US edition, published by the Free Press in New York, is instead entitled *The Pride and the Fall*.

136 For a left-wing analysis of the historiographical resonance of this painting and the 'event' which lay behind it, see H. Southworth, *Guernica! Guernica! A Study of Journalism, Propaganda, and History*, Berkeley, Calif., 1977.

Germany and the Third, Second and First World Wars

1 G. Grass, *The Tin Drum*, Harmondsworth, 1965, p. 57.

2 G. Grass, *Two States — One Nation? The Case Against German Reunification*, London, 1990, pp. 5, 13, 94, 123; cf. also T.W. Adorno's famous question asked in 1959, 'What does coming to terms with the past mean?': see A. Rabinbach, 'The Jewish question in the German question' in P. Baldwin (ed.), *Reworking the Past: Hitler, the Holocaust, and the Historians' Debate*, Boston, Mass., 1990, p. 54.

3 E. Nolte, *Marxism, Fascism, Cold War*, Assen, 1982, p. 54; for some preliminary comments on East German historiography, see R.J. Evans, *Rethinking German History: Nineteenth Century Germany and the Origins of the Third Reich*, London, 1987, pp. 25, 35; cf. H. Schleier, 'German Democratic Republic' in G.G. Iggers and H.T. Parker (eds), *International Handbook of Historical Studies: Contemporary Research and Theory*, Westport, Conn., 1979, pp. 326–7.

4 As first sung by Toni Fisher in 1962.

5 For a useful study of the background, see H.W. Koch (ed.), *The Origins of the First World War: Great Power Rivalry and German War Aims*, London, 1972.

6 F. Fischer, *Germany's Aims in the First World War*, London, 1967; German edition, Düsseldorf 1961 (with three further editions 1962, 1964, 1967).

7 The basic English-language account is J.A. Moses, *The Politics of Illusion: The Fischer Controversy in German Historiography*, St Lucia, 1975; cf. R. Fletcher, 'Introduction' to F. Fischer, *From Kaiserreich to Third Reich: Elements of Continuity in German History, 1871–1945*, London, 1986, pp. 1–32; see also Fischer's own account, F. Fischer, *World Power or Decline: The Controversy over 'Germany's Aims in the First World War'*, London, 1975 (first published in German, Frankfurt, 1965).

8 R.J. Evans, op. cit., p. 3.

9 F. Fischer, *World Power or Decline*, p. 95; cf. also K.H. Janssen, 'Gerhard Ritter: a patriotic historian's justification' in H.W. Koch (ed.), op. cit., pp. 257–60.

10 J. Joll, 'The 1914 debate continues: Fritz Fischer and his critics', in H.W. Koch, op. cit., pp. 15–16.

11 J.A. Moses, op. cit., p. xii.

12 F. Fischer, *Germany's Aims in the First World War*, p. ix.
13 E.g. R.J. Evans, op. cit., p. 8.
14 K. Epstein, 'Gerhard Ritter and the First World War' in H.W. Koch (ed.), op. cit., p. 288.
15 F. Fischer, *Germany's Aims in the First World War*, pp. 475–509, 515–23.
16 ibid., pp. 98–119. There is now a full-scale biography in English of Bethmann Hollweg, K.H. Jarausch, *The Enigmatic Chancellor: Bethmann Hollweg and the Hubris of Imperial Germany*, New Haven, Conn., 1973.
17 F. Fischer, *War of Illusions: German Policies from 1911 to 1914*, London, 1975. The fuller and more satisfactory German edition was published in Düsseldorf, 1969.
18 Perhaps the most drastic statement of all is Fischer's *From Kaiserreich to Third Reich*, first published in German, Düsseldorf, 1979.
19 L. Albertini, *The Origins of the War of 1914*, 3 vols, Oxford, 1952–7.
20 For this Albertini, see R. Bosworth, *Italy and the Approach of the First World War*, London, 1983, pp. 31–2.
21 R.J. Evans, op. cit., p. 32.
22 W.P. Maehl, 'Gerhard Ritter', in H.A. Schmitt (ed.), *Historians of Modern Europe*, Baton Rouge, La, 1971, pp. 151–62.
23 For Felix Gilbert's fascinating and redolent description of Kehr and his departure, see F. Gilbert, op. cit., pp. 70–1, 84; and for Kehr's posthumous influence in the United States, see A.L. Skop, 'The primacy of domestic politics: Eckart Kehr and the intellectual development of Charles A. Beard', *History and Theory*, XIII, 1974, pp. 119–31.
24 H.-U. Wehler, 'Historiography in Germany today', in J. Habermas (ed.), *Observations on the 'Spiritual Situation of the Age': Contemporary German Perspectives*, Cambridge, Mass., 1984, p. 225.
25 W.H. Maehl, op. cit., pp. 162–7.
26 The best analysis of this is I. Kershaw, *The 'Hitler Myth': Image and Reality in the Third Reich*, Oxford, 1987.
27 W.H. Maehl, op. cit., p. 166.
28 ibid., p. 172.
29 W.H. Maehl, op. cit., pp. 168–9.
30 There is an English-language edition, G. Ritter, *The Sword and the Sceptre: The Problem of Militarism in Germany*, 4 vols, Coral Gables, Fla, 1969–73.
31 In Anglo-Saxon historiography, the Fischer debate was followed up by a series of investigations into other states' policies to 1914 asking Fischerite questions about the relationship between internal and external policies. For these accounts, which generally reinforce Fischer's conclusion that there was indeed something special about Germany, see V.R. Berghahn, *Germany and the Approach of War in 1914*, London, 1973; Z.S. Steiner, *Britain and the Origins of the First World War*, London, 1977; D.C.B. Lieven, *Russia and the Origins of the First World War*, London, 1983; J.F.V. Keiger, *France and the Origins of the First World War*, London, 1983; and R. Bosworth, op. cit.
32 In English see, for example, I. Geiss, 'Origins of the First World War', in H.W. Koch (ed.), op. cit., pp. 36–78 or *German Foreign Policy 1871–1914*, London, 1976. This latter work, especially, is more extreme than Fischer in its 'social imperialist' thesis.
33 K. Riezler, *Tagebücher, Aufsätze, Dokumente* (ed. K.D. Erdmann), Gottingen, 1972 has the fullest account.
34 The best general review in English is G. Iggers, *The German Conception of History: The National Tradition of Historical Thought from Herder to the Present*, Middletown, Conn., 1968.
35 H.S. Hughes, *Consciousness and Society: The Reorientation of European Social Thought 1890–1930*, London, 1974, p. 185.
36 P. Novick, *That Noble Dream. The 'Objectivity Question' and the American Historical Profession*, Cambridge, 1988, pp. 26–30. Novick argues that Americans drastically over-estimated Ranke's commitment to empiricism (and nationalism) while under-estimating his religious and philosophical idealism and his universalism.

37 See, for example, G. Iggers, op. cit., pp. 122–3 on Mommsen's concerns in old age that the Bismarckian version of nationalism which he had at first favoured was not after all so beneficial to a liberal society.

38 H. Kohn, *Prophets and Peoples: Studies in Nineteenth-Century Nationalism*, New York, 1952, pp. 105–26; H.S. Hughes, op. cit., p. 232.

39 See, e.g. H. von Treitschke, *Politics* (ed. H. Kohn), New York, 1963, pp. xiv, xvi, 8, 13, 20, 25, 38–9, 101, 117, 126, 134, 152, 241.

40 For a review of his career and reputation, see G. Iggers, op. cit., pp. 195–228.

41 L. Namier, *Facing East: Essays on Germany, the Balkans, and Russia in the Twentieth Century*, New York, 1966, p. 9. (This work was first published London, 1947.)

42 W.A. Maehl, op. cit.., pp. 171–2, 178. H. Graml, 'Resistance thinking on foreign policy', in H. Graml *et al.*, *The German Resistance to Hitler*, Berkeley, Calif., 1970, p. 1 notes that Goerdeler thought Alsace-Lorraine, Austria, the Sudetenland and the South Tyrol ought to remain in German hands and Germany should also receive 'colonial justice'. Von Hassell, another leading conspirator, was von Tirpitz's son-in-law.

43 See, for example, H. Rothfels, *The German Opposition to Hitler*, Chicago, 1948; cf. G. Iggers, op. cit., pp. 257–9. Rothfels, a Jewish convert, lost his chair in 1934. See L. Dawidowicz, *The Holocaust and the Historians*, Cambridge, Mass., 1981, p. 61.

44 F. Meinecke, *The German Catastrophe: Reflections and Recollections*, Boston, 1950. S.B. Fay, the distinguished historian of the origins of the First World War, acted as translator (and eulogist of Meinecke's values).

45 See chapter 6 below.

46 See, for example, R. D'O. Butler, *The Roots of National Socialism*, London, 1941; A.J.P. Taylor, *The Course of German History*, London, 1945; E. Vermeil, *Germany's Three Reichs: Their History and Culture*, London, 1944; cf. also E. Vermeil et al., *Quelques aspects du problème allemand*, Paris, 1945.

47 See R. Bosworth, 'Mito e linguaggio nella politica estera italiana', in R. Bosworth and S. Romano (eds), *La politica estera italiana 1860–1985*, Bologna, 1991, p. 55.

48 F. Meinecke, op. cit., pp. 1, 32, 51–6; G. Iggers, op. cit., p. 224.

49 H. Rauschning, *The Beast from the Abyss*, London, 1941.

50 F. Meinecke, *The German Catastrophe*, pp. 9–10; 13–14; 25.

51 R.J. Evans, op. cit., p. 66.

52 ibid., pp. 25–8.

53 ibid., p. 45.

54 P. Ayçoberry, *The Nazi Question: An Essay on the Interpretations of National Socialism (1922–1975)*, London, 1981, pp. 136–7.

55 K. Sontheimer, 'Weimar culture' in M. Laffan (ed.), *The Burden of German History*, London, 1989, p. 4.

56 F. Gilbert, *A European Past: Memoirs 1905–45*, New York, 1988, p. 75; F. Meinecke, op. cit., p. 32.

57 See below p. 127.

58 G. Iggers, op. cit., pp. 223–4; F. Meinecke, op. cit., pp. 74–5.

59 H.-U. Wehler, 'Historiography in Germany today', p. 253, fn.12.

60 K.A. Schleunes, *The Twisted Road to Auschwitz: Nazi Policy toward German Jews, 1933–1939*, Urbana, 1970.

61 M. Burleigh, *Germany Turns Eastwards: A Study of 'Ostforschung' in the Third Reich*, Cambridge, 1988; cf. M. Burleigh, 'Albert Brackmann (1871–1952) "Ostforscher": the years of retirement', *Journal of Contemporary History*, 23, 1988, pp. 573–88.

62 M. Burleigh, *Germany Turns Eastwards*, pp. 21–2.

63 ibid., p. 7.

64 Oskar's still-to-be-born ghost would not have been pleased by a Leipzig historian's observation in 1920 that 'precisely the lack of history of the Sorbs is a guarantee for the acceleration of their desired disappearance into Germandom:' ibid., p. 119.

65 ibid., p. 9.
66 ibid., pp. 49, 62–4.
67 ibid., p. 137.
68 ibid., p. 145.
69 ibid., p. 248.
70 The moderate and courteous Gordon Craig has even remarked that there were no institutions in Germany 'more resistant to change' than the universities, G.A. Craig, *The Germans*, Harmondsworth, 1984, p. 170.
71 For the best example of his work in English, see H.-U. Wehler, *The German Empire, 1871–1918*, Leamington Spa, 1985.
72 In the 1980s Geiss would become a somewhat unlikely ally of the conservatives in the *Historikerstreit*. In English, see for an introduction to his more recent ideas, I. Geiss, 'The Weimar Republic between the Second and the Third Reich: continuity and discontinuity in the German question', in M. Laffan (ed.), op. cit., pp. 56–79.
73 See, most recently, J. Kocka, 'German history before Hitler: the debate about the German *Sonderweg*', *Journal of Contemporary History*, 23, 1988, pp. 3–16. Cf. also in English his *Facing Total War: German Society, 1914–18*, Leamington Spa, 1984 and especially his fascinating excursion into the *Sonderweg* of the USA, *White Collar Workers in America, 1890–1940: A Social Political History in International Perspective*, London, 1980.
74 T. Prittie, *Willy Brandt: Portrait of a Statesman*, London, 1974, p. 153. 'Willy Brandt' was actually only a 'combat name'. He had been christened Herbert Ernst Karl Frahm. For an English-language edition of his writings in these years, see W. Brandt, *In Exile: Essays, Reflections and Letters 1933–1947*, London, 1971 (first published in German, 1966).
75 J.D. Nagle, *The National Democratic Party: Right Radicalism in the Federal Republic of Germany*, Berkeley, Calif., 1970, p. 75. They were also delighted by an opinion poll in 1967 which showed 43 per cent of Germans agreeing 'it is high time to get rid of the claim that Germany was to blame for the outbreak of World War II'(!) (p. 76).
76 ibid., p. 121.
77 T. Prittie, op. cit.., p. 222.
78 E.J. Hobsbawm, *Nations and Nationalism since 1780: Programme, Myth, Reality*, Cambridge, 1990, p. 133.
79 For the great statement of this thesis, see A.J. Mayer, *Wilson vs. Lenin: Political Origins of the New Diplomacy, 1917–18*, New Haven, Conn., 1959.
80 So till the early 1970s did the *Statistisches Jahrbuch*, the FRG's 'standard source of official statistics', also define the borders. See D. Forsythe, 'German identity and the problem of history' in E. Tonkin *et al.* (eds), *History and Ethnicity*, London, 1989, pp. 139–40, 155. According to Forsythe, even in the 1980s, 'German' weather reports on TV gave no precise borders to 'Germany' but merely set it somewhere between France and Russia (p. 140).
81 V.R. Berghahn, *Modern Germany: Society, Economy and Politics in the Twentieth Century*, Cambridge, 1982, p. 229.
82 T. Prittie, op. cit.., p. 253. In 1971 *Time* made Brandt its 'Man of the Year' as a result of these foreign policy successes. He was legitimate outside Germany, too.
83 A.J.P. Taylor, *Politicians, Socialism and Historians*, London, 1980, p. 41 (citing 1959 review); in 1951, by contrast, a poll found university professors accorded the highest status out of thirty-eight categories in the FRG; see R. Dahrendorf, *Society and Democracy in Germany*, New York, 1967, p. 81.
84 R. Dahrendorf, *Society and Democracy in Germany*, p. 58. It was Malcolm Bradbury who satirised sociology in his novel *The History Man*, London, 1975.
85 R. Dahrendorf, *The New Liberty: Survival and Justice in a Changing World*, London, 1975, pp. 3–4; *Reflections on the Revolution in Europe: In a Letter intended to have been sent to a Gentleman in Warsaw, 1990*, London, 1990, pp. 48–9, 109–10.

86 R. Dahrendorf, *On Britain*, London, 1982, p. 10; cf. that most brilliant of urban histories, R.J. Evans, *Death in Hamburg: Society and Politics in the Cholera Years 1830–1910*, Oxford, 1987.

87 R. Dahrendorf, *Class and Class Conflict in Industrial Society*, rev. edn, Stanford, 1959.

88 R. Dahrendorf, *Society and Democracy in Germany*, p. 5.

89 From the period, see, for example K.D. Bracher, 'The technique of the National Socialist seizure of power' in L. Wilson (ed.), *The Road to Dictatorship: Germany 1918–1933*, London, 1964. Bracher's great work remains the still very valuable analysis of inter-war German politics, *The German Dictatorship: The Origins, Structure, and Effects of National Socialism*, Harmondsworth, 1973.

90 R. Dahrendorf, *Society and Democracy in Germany*, p. 18.

91 ibid., pp. 46, 262, 377–8.

92 Of this last he is particular critical, condemning its 'illiberalism' and 'fatal love for the state' and defining it as 'the protestantism of the Prussian state': ibid., pp. 180–1.

93 ibid., p. 382.

94 ibid., pp. 390–1.

95 ibid., pp. 400, 426.

96 *Observer*, 16 January 1983.

97 For example *L'Espresso*, XXXV, 29 January 1989 (on the meaning of the French Revolution 200 years after); 25 June 1989 (on the 'state of Europe').

98 See C. Hardyment, 'On Dahrendorf', *Oxford Today*, 1, 1989, pp. 39–40 on his view of that job.

99 For Deakin the historian, see F.W.D. Deakin, *The Brutal Friendship*, London, 1962; with G.R. Storry, *The Case of Richard Sorge*, London, 1966; *The Embattled Mountain*, London, 1971; with H. Shukman and H.T. Willetts, *A History of World Communism*, London, 1975.

100 R. Dahrendorf, *Professor Ralf Dahrendorf in Australia*, Sydney, 1978.

101 See R. Dahrendorf, *Reflections on the Revolution in Europe*, pp. 25, 37, 104–6. The parallel with Burke is of course intentional, as is his debt to Karl Popper. Sensitive antipodeans might be troubled by Dahrendorf's choice of metaphor when he praises Hayek for liberating Popper from his 'New Zealand exile' (p. 25).

102 Dahrendorf interview in *Corriere della Sera*, 14 May 1987.

103 L. Namier, *1848: The Revolution of the Intellectuals*, London, 1946, p. 57.

104 R.J. Evans, op. cit., pp. 1–54; cf. also I. Kershaw, *The Nazi Dictatorship: Problems and Perspectives of Interpretation*, rev. edn, London, 1989, pp. 7–8.

105 D. Blackbourn and G. Eley, *The Peculiarities of German History: Bourgeois Society and Politics in Nineteenth-Century Germany*, Oxford, 1984. Geoff Eley has been an especially fertile and effective writer about German (and other) historiography, see, for example, his 'Recent work in modern German history', *Historical Journal*, 23, 1980, pp. 463–79; 'Nationalism and social history', *Social History*, 6, 1981, pp. 83–107; 'James Sheehan and the German liberals: a critical appraisal', *Central European History*, XIV, 1981; *From Unification to Nazism: Reinterpreting the Nazi Past*, Boston, Mass., 1986; 'Labor History, Social History, "Alltagsgeschichte": experience, culture, and the politics of everyday — a new direction for German social history?' *Journal of Modern History*, 61, 1989, pp. 297–343.

106 S.M. Lipset, *Political Man: The Social Bases of Politics*, New York, 1963, pp. 127–79.

107 There is an unending literature on this problem. One commentator has reckoned that, between 1977 and 1981, at least twenty-four doctoral theses were written on Nazism before 1933 in Franconia, J.H. Grill, 'Local and regional studies on National Socialism: a review', *Journal of Contemporary History*, 21, 1986, p. 261; for a clever over-view of developments by the author of the first and still very useful analysis of Nazism in a small town, see W.S. Allen, 'Farewell to class analysis in the rise of Nazism: comment', *Central European History*, XVII, 1984, pp. 54–62.

108 R. Dahrendorf, *Reflections on the Revolution in Europe*, p. 94.

The *Historikerstreit* and the relativisation of Auschwitz

1 K.D. Erdmann, *Die Oekumene der Historiker: Geschichte der Internationalen Historikerkongresse und des Comité International des Sciences Historiques*, Göttingen, 1987. For an English-language introduction, see his 'A History of the International Historical Congress. Work in progress', *Storia della Storiografia*, 8, 1985, pp. 3–23.

2 Comité international des sciences historiques, XVIe congrès international des sciences historiques, *Rapports,* 2 vols, Stuttgart, 1985.

3 One of the short articles which launched the *Historikerstreit* was entitled '*Vergangenheit, die nicht vergehen will'* ('A past that will not pass away'). It was written by Ernst Nolte and published in *Frankfurter Allgemeine Zeitung*, 6 June 1986. See also p. 82.

4 B. Heuser, 'Museums, identity and warring historians — observations on History in Germany', *Historical Journal*, 33, 1990, p. 421.

5 For an introduction, see, for example, C.S. Maier, *The Unmasterable Past: History, Holocaust and German National Identity*, Cambridge, Mass., 1988, pp. 43–4.

6 R.J. Evans, 'The New Nationalism and the Old History: perspectives on the West German *Historikerstreit'*, *Journal of Modern History*, 59, 1987, p. 788; cf. also his further development of the matter under the same title, *German History*, 6, 1988, pp. 63–4.

7 See J. Habermas, 'Defusing the past: a politico-cultural tract' in G.H. Hartman (ed.), *Bitburg in Moral and Political Perspective*, Bloomington, Ind., 1986, p. 44.

8 See, for example, C.S. Maier, op. cit., pp. 121–3; for the tension between FRG and GDR usable history, see also M. Fulbrook, 'From "*Volksgemeinschaft*" to Divided Nation: German national identities and political cultures since the Third Reich', *Historical Research*, 62, 1989, pp. 193–213.

9 B. Heuser, op. cit.., p. 427.

10 Ironically, Martin Broszat (see p. 80) was one of those most publicly hostile to Kohl's committee. See R.J. Evans, *In Hitler's Shadow: West German Historians and the Attempt to Escape from the Nazi Past*, London, 1989, pp. 18–19. For an account of the relationship of the *Historikerstreit* to the silences of the film, *Heimat*, see E.L. Santner, 'On the difficulty of saying "We": the Historians' Debate and Edgar Reitz's *Heimat*', *History and Memory*, II, 1990, pp. 76–96.

11 C.S. Maier, op. cit.., pp. 124–8.

12 See the trilingual (French, English, German but not Russian) catalogue of the exhibition, issued by the GDR's Ministry of Culture. M. Krille (ed.), *Luther 1483–1983*, n.p., 1983. In 1988 the GDR would also bizarrely try to annex the Prussian tradition to itself by celebrating the 300th anniversary of the death of the 'Great Elector', Frederick William, founder of the Hohenzollern dynasty.

13 C.S. Maier, op. cit., p. 44.

14 ibid., p. 121.

15 For the most developed summary of this event and a collection of useful translations of articles on it, see G.H. Hartman (ed.), op. cit.

16 G.H. Hartman, 'Introduction – 1985', in ibid., p. 6; A.H. Rosenfeld, 'Another revisionism: popular culture and the changing image of the Holocaust', also in ibid., pp. 93–4.

17 For a splendid analysis of this Reagan, see M.P. Rogin, *Ronald Reagan, the Movie and Other Episodes in Political Demonology*, Berkeley, Calif., 1987, pp. 1–43.

18 A.H. Rosenfeld, op. cit., p. 92.

19 T.G. Ash, 'Germany after Bitburg', in G.H. Hartman (ed.), op. cit., p. 199.

20 See for example, C. Streit, *Keine Kameraden. Die Wehrmacht und die sowjetischen Kriegsgefangenen 1941–5*, Stuttgart, 1978 or, in English, O. Bartov, *The Eastern Front, 1941–5: German Troops and the Barbarisation of Warfare*, New York, 1986 and his,

'The Missing Years: German workers, German soldiers', *German History*, 8, 1990, pp. 46–65.

21 See, for example, R. Hilberg, 'Bitburg as symbol', in G.H Hartman (ed.), op. cit., pp. 15–26 and cf. his massive, pioneering work, R. Hilberg, *The Destruction of the European Jews*, New York, 1961.

22 See, for example, S. Friedländer, 'Some German struggles with memory' in G.H. Hartman (ed.), op. cit., pp. 27–42; 'Some reflections on the historicization of National Socialism' in P. Baldwin (ed.), *Reworking the Past: Hitler, the Holocaust, and the Historians' Debate*, Boston, Mass., 1990, pp. 88–101; with M. Broszat, 'A controversy about the historicization of National Socialism' in ibid., pp. 102–34.

23 H. Rousso, 'The reactions in France: the sounds of silence', in G.H. Hartman (ed.), op. cit., p. 62.

24 G.H. Hartman, 'Introduction – 1985', p. 5.

25 A.H. Rosenfeld, op. cit., p. 93.

26 C.S. Maier, op. cit., p. 11.

27 J. Habermas, op. cit., p. 47.

28 As translated in G.H. Hartman (ed.), op. cit., pp. 246–7.

29 See E. von Weizsäcker, *Memoirs*, London, 1951.

30 G.H. Hartman (ed.), op. cit., pp. 262–6; cf. also R. von Weizsäcker, *A Voice from Germany: Speeches*, London, 1986.

31 See I. Kershaw, *The Nazi Dictatorship: Problems and Perspectives of Interpretation*, London, 1985; rev. edn, London, 1989.

32 I. Kershaw, *The Nazi Dictatorship*, rev. edn, p. 184.

33 E.N. Peterson, *The Limits of Hitler's Power*, Princeton, NJ, 1969.

34 For a review of the debate, see I. Kershaw, op. cit., pp. 61–81.

35 But cf. the moving account of being a part-Jewish success story in the Hitler youth, I. Koehn, *Mischling, Second Degree: My Childhood in Nazi Germany*, Harmondsworth, 1981.

36 D. Schoenbaum, *Hitler's Social Revolution: Class and Status in Nazi Germany 1933–9*, New York, 1966, pp. 273–5.

37 *Observer*, 12 June 1977; cf. D. Irving, *Hitler's War*, London, 1977. Karl May's writings were, in the post-war period, still popular in the Germanies (and especially in the GDR). H.W. Koch, 'Introduction' to H.W. Koch (ed.), *Aspects of the Third Reich*, London, 1985, p. 12.

38 For an introduction, see I. Kershaw, op. cit., pp. 150–67.

39 D.J.K. Peukert, *Inside Nazi Germany: Conformity, Opposition and Racism in Everyday Life*, Harmondsworth, 1989, p. 22.

40 ibid., pp. 31, 33, 77.

41 See p. 140. But Peukert, op. cit., p. 251 fn. 6, praises De Felice's 'subtle and expert' understanding of Italian Fascism.

42 D. Peukert, op. cit., pp. 49, 154, 159, 167.

43 ibid., pp. 14–15, 44, 180, 182.

44 M. Broszat, op. cit., pp. 77, 84; cf. I. Kershaw, 'Martin Broszat: Obituary', *German History*, 8, 1990, pp. 310–6.

45 M. Broszat, op. cit., p. 83.

46 Ibid., p. 79.

47 S. Friedländer, 'Some reflections on the historicization of National Socialism', p. 98; M. Broszat and S. Friedländer, 'A controversy about the historicization of National Socialism', p. 116.

48 See C.S. Maier, op. cit., pp. 39–47.

49 In English, see, for example, J.C. Fest, *Hitler*, Harmondsworth, 1977; *The Face of the Third Reich*, Harmondsworth, 1972. Fest, it seems, had also helped to ghost the memoirs of Albert Speer which, at least according to their critics, were the cleverest

effort at exculpation by any survivor of the regime. See M. Schmidt, *Albert Speer: The End of a Myth*, London, 1984, pp. 3, 12.

50 Cited by C.S. Maier, op. cit., p. 30.

51 Cited by R.J. Evans, *In Hitler's Shadow*, p. 28.

52 See, for example, E. Nolte, *Three Faces of Fascism: Action Française, Italian Fascism, National Socialism*, New York, 1965.

53 See, for example, H. Rogger and E. Weber (eds), *The European Right*, London, 1965; *Journal of Contemporary History*. Its first issue in 1966 was a thematic one devoted to the problem of fascism. Among members of the early editorial board of the journal were K.D. Bracher, G. Craig, P. Geyl, F.H. Hinsley, J. Joll, P. Renouvin, J.L. Talmon, and L. Valiani.

54 E. Nolte, op. cit., p. 537.

55 See E. Fromm, *The Fear of Freedom*, London, 1942.

56 Among many others, probably his most famous work remains G. Mosse, *The Nationalisation of the Masses: Political Symbolism and Mass Movements from the Napoleonic Wars through the Third Reich*, New York, 1975.

57 See p. 134-40.

58 E. Nolte, op. cit., p. 46.

59 E. Nolte, *Marxism, Fascism, Cold War*, Assen, 1982, p. 175; cf. his highly arguable comment, 'there can be no doubt that of all the fascist movements of the period between the two World Wars, national socialism was one of the furthest from the university' (p.108); C.S. Maier, op. cit., p. 28. In English, cf. also E. Nolte, 'The problem of fascism in recent scholarship' in H.A. Turner (ed.), *Reappraisals of Fascism*, New York, 1975, pp. 26–42; and his 'Between myth and revisionism? The Third Reich in the perspective of the 1980s', in H.W. Koch (ed.), *Aspects of the Third Reich*, pp. 17–38.

60 R.J. Evans, 'The New Nationalism and the Old History', p. 767.

61 E. Nolte, *Marxism, Fascism and Cold War*, p. 81.

62 R.J. Evans, *In Hitler's Shadow*, p. 27.

63 E. Nolte, *Marxism, Fascism and Cold War*, pp. 170, 175. In his *Germany and the Cold War,* he had accepted the inevitability of *Ostpolitik* but also defined it as 'self-surrender'; R.J. Evans, *In Hitler's Shadow*, p. 28.

64 For a eulogistic introduction to Hillgruber's work, see H.H. Herwig, 'Andreas Hillgruber: Historian of "Grossmachtpolitik" 1871–1945', *Central European History*, XV, 1982, pp. 186–98. Herwig notes Hillgruber's commitment to the traditional idea of the 'primacy of external politics' (p. 196).

65 R.J. Evans, *In Hitler's Shadow*, pp. 47–54; A. Hillgruber, 'Le discussioni sul "primato della politica estera" e la storia delle relazioni internazionali nella storiografia tedesca dal 1945 a oggi' in S. Pizzetti (ed.), *La storia delle relazioni internazionali nella germania contemporanea*, Milan, 1987, pp. 77–97.

66 This was published in Berlin in 1986; see C.S. Maier, op. cit., pp. 19–23.

67 Cited by R.J. Evans, *In Hitler's Shadow*, p. 51.

68 ibid., p. 17.

69 J. Joffe, 'The battle of the historians: a report from Germany', *Encounter*, LXIX, June 1987, pp. 74, 76.

70 See P. Baldwin, '*The Historikerstreit* in context' in P. Baldwin (ed.), op. cit., p. 10. For some of Baldwin's own, controversial, intellectual and historiographical assumptions, see his 'Social interpretations of Nazism: renewing a tradition', *Journal of Contemporary History*, 25, 1990, pp. 5–37.

71 In English, see, for example, H. Schulze, 'Explaining the German catastrophe: the use and abuse of historical explanations' in P. Baldwin (ed.), *Reworking the Past*, pp. 185–95. In the same book cf. H. Mommsen, 'Reappraisal and Repression: the Third Reich in West German historical consciousness', pp. 173–84; H.-U. Wehler, 'Unburdening the German past? A preliminary assessment', pp. 214–23.

72 I. Kershaw, *The Nazi Dictatorship*, rev. edn, p. 170, fn.6.

73 R.J. Evans, *In Hitler's Shadow*, pp. 21–2.

74 I. Kershaw, *The Nazi Dictatorship*; R.J. Evans, *In Hitler's Shadow*; P. Baldwin (ed.), *Reworking the Past*; C.S. Maier, *The Unmasterable Past*; cf. also R.J. Evans, *Rethinking German History*, London, 1987 and M.R. Marrus, *The Holocaust in History*, London, 1988.

75 S. Pizzetti (ed.), *La storia delle relazioni internazionali nella germania contemporanea.*

76 I. Kershaw, 'Nuova inquietudine tedesca? Le reazioni internazionali', *Passato e presente*, 16, 1988, pp. 151–64; 'Le "mythe du Fuhrer" et la dynamique de l'État nazi', *Annales ESC*, 43, 1988, pp. 593–614. The obverse of this foreign interest in German history had long been the enthusiasm displayed by the FRG for divulging abroad the views of its historians, for example through the establishment of Historical Institutes in Paris, Washington, London and Rome. See K. Robbins, 'National identity and history: past, present and future', *History*, 75, 1990, p. 371.

77 I. Kershaw, *The Nazi Dictatorship*, rev. edn, p. 170.

78 ibid., p. 169.

79 He also cites Stürmer regretting that German historiography cannot produce a book like Braudel's *The Identity of France* (ibid., p. 182). For the *Annales*, see chapter 5 below.

80 C.S. Maier, *The Unmasterable Past*, p. ix. Maier had made his name with the insightful, if lengthy, comparative study *Recasting Bourgeois Europe: Stabilization in France, Germany, and Italy in the Decade after World War I*, Princeton, NJ, 1975. It was an account of what might be deemed 'three faces of capitalism'.

81 D. Abraham, *The Collapse of the Weimar Republic: Political Economy and Crisis*, rev. edn, New York, 1986, p. xiii, fn. 1 has a bibliographical introduction; cf. I. Kershaw, *The Nazi Dictatorship*, rev. edn, pp. 42–3, fn. 1.

82 H.A. Turner, *German Big Business and the Rise of Hitler*, New York, 1985, p. 100.

83 ibid., pp. 350–1.

84 ibid., p. 351.

85 ibid., p. 359.

86 C.S. Maier, *The Unmasterable Past*, pp. 5, 119.

87 ibid., p. 3.

88 ibid., p. 1.

89 ibid., p. 5.

90 ibid., p. 2. Of course the choice of the word 'resonates' resonates, too.

91 ibid., p. 123.

92 ibid., p. 149.

93 ibid., p. 136.

94 ibid., p. 151.

95 ibid., pp. 74–5, 77–8.

96 ibid., pp. 164–6.

97 See, for example, R. Payne, 'Israel: Jewish identity and competition over "tradition"' in E. Tonkin *et al.* (eds), *History and Ethnicity*, London, 1989, pp. 121–8 on the many Israels in both present and past.

98 The best introduction is still C.E. Schorske, *Fin de Siècle Vienna: Politics and Culture*, New York, 1980, chapter III; this was first published with a different metaphor as 'Politics in a new key: an Austrian Triptych', *Journal of Modern History*, 39, 1967, pp. 343–86.

99 E. Hobsbawm, *Nations and Nationalism since 1780: Programme, Myth, Reality*, Cambridge, 1990, p. 118. Cf. p. 76 for his views on Zionism's lack of historicity.

100 L.S. Dawidowicz, *From that Place and Time: A Memoir, 1938–1947*, New York, 1989, p. 7.

101 ibid., p. 3.

102 ibid., pp. 257, 277.

103 L.S. Dawidowicz, *The War against the Jews 1933–45*, rev. edn, Harmondsworth, 1987. (The first edition was published London, 1975.) In her introduction she strongly attacks Broszat, Hans Mommsen and other functionalist historians (pp. xxiii–xxxiii).
104 L.S. Dawidowicz, *The Holocaust and the Historians*, Cambridge, Mass., 1981, pp. 31, 33, 57, 61, 66–7, 71–2, 109, 137.
105 ibid., p. 125. cf. M.R. Marrus, op. cit., pp. 39, 202 who, in specific counter to Dawidowicz, urges that historians need to approach the Holocaust from a number of perspectives.
106 L.S. Dawidowicz, 'Perversions of the Holocaust', *Commentary*, 88, 1989, pp. 56–60. Dawidowicz was a frequent contributor to this journal of the intellectual right which she had helped to found in 1945.
107 A.J. Mayer, *Why did the Heavens not Darken? The 'Final Solution' in History*, New York, 1988. Mayer, famously or notoriously, did not use footnotes. He would defend himself against what he described as a 'fetish [that] very often interferes with careful intellection [sic] and rumination', *Newsweek*, 15 May 1989.
108 A.J. Mayer, *Why did the Heavens not Darken?* pp. viii–xiii; cf. his interview by S. Terkel, *'The Good War': An Oral History of World War II*, New York, 1984, pp. 465–71.
109 A.J. Mayer, *Why did the Heavens not Darken?* p. viii.
110 See, for example, A.J. Mayer, *Wilson versus Lenin: Political Origins of the New Diplomacy 1917–1918*, New Haven, Conn., 1959; *Politics and Diplomacy of Peacemaking: Containment and Counter-Revolution at Versailles, 1918–19*, London, 1968; *Dynamics of Counter-Revolution in Europe, 1870–1956: An Analytic Framework*, New York, 1971; *The Persistence of the Old Regime: Europe to the Great War*, London, 1981.
111 A.J. Mayer, *Why did the Heavens not Darken?* p. vii.
112 ibid., p. 3.
113 ibid., p. 107.
114 ibid., pp. xiii–xiv.
115 ibid., p. 234.
116 A.J. Mayer, *Why did the Heavens not Darken?*, rev. edn, New York, 1990, p. 463.
117 A.J. Mayer, *Why did the Heavens not Darken?*, p. 3.
118 E. Nolte, *Marxism, Fascism, Cold War*, p. 322.
119 A.J. Mayer, *Why did the Heavens not Darken?* rev. edn, p. 465.

The sorrow and the pity of the fall of France and the rise of French historiography

1 C.S. Maier, *The Unmasterable Past: History, Holocaust, and German National Identity*, Cambridge, Mass., 1988, pp. 168–9.
2 For example, M. Bloch, *The Royal Touch: Sacred Monarchy and Scrofula in England and France*, London, 1973 (first published in French, 1923).
3 F. Braudel, *The Mediterranean and the Mediterranean World in the Age of Philip II*, 2 vols, London, 1973 (first published in French, 1949, rev. edn, 1966); cf. also the mammoth *Civilization and Capitalism 15th–18th century*, 3 vols, Glasgow, 1985 (first published in French, 1979).
4 E. Le Roy Ladurie, *Montaillou: Cathars and Catholics in a French Village 1294–1324*, London, 1978 (first published in French, 1975); *Carnival in Romans: A People's Uprising at Romans 1579–1580*, Harmondsworth, 1981 (first published in French, 1979); and for his theoretical writings, see, for example, *The Territory of the Historian*, Hassocks, 1979 (first published in French, 1973).
5 See, as the ultimate in grandiosity, F. Braudel, *The Identity of France*, 2 vols, London, 1988–1990 (first published in French, 1986); for a sympathetic analysis, see

S.L. Kaplan, 'Long-run lamentations: Braudel on France', *Journal of Modern History*, 63, 1991, pp. 341–53.

6 F. Furet (ed.), *Unanswered Questions: Nazi Germany and the Genocide of the Jews*, New York, 1989.

7 M.R. Marrus and R.O. Paxton, 'The Nazis and the Jews in occupied Western Europe 1940–1944', in ibid.

8 P. Vidal-Naquet, 'Theses on revisionism', in ibid. (see especially p. 313).

9 In English, see M. Ophuls, *The Sorrow and the Pity: Chronicle of a French City under German Occupation*, St Albans, 1975. See also pp. 109-13.

10 For his comments on France, see A. Marwick, *War and Social Change in the Twentieth Century: A Comparative Study of Britain, France, Russia and the United States*, London, 1974, pp. 185–212.

11 See chapter 6 and cf. R. Cobb's recollection from the 1930s that his French friends then both had a special animus against Italians and regarded them as objects of 'high comedy' because they were believed to be enemies who could be beaten. R. Cobb, *Promenades: A Historian's Appreciation of Modern French Literature*, Oxford, 1986, pp. 137–8. Cobb himself is another historian massively conditioned by the Second World War, a sort of Tunbridge Wells equivalent of 'Chips' Channon — Kipps as Chips. See especially *Still Life: Sketches of a Tunbridge Wells Childhood*, London, 1984; *A Classical Education*, Harmondsworth, 1985; *People and Places*, Oxford, 1985 for his commitment to fine writing and his hostility to the Second World War and revolution.

12 For a moving evocation of this war using this metaphor, see N. Davies, *God's Playground: A History of Poland*, Oxford, 1981, vol. II, pp. 435–91. It is perhaps predictable, given the matters discussed in this chapter, that contemporary Polish historiography should be much influenced by the *Annales*. P. Burke, *The French Historical Revolution: the 'Annales' School, 1929–89*, Oxford, 1990, p. 95. See also below, p. 164 for the relationship of the *Annales* to the new Soviet historiography.

13 R.A.C. Parker, *Struggle for Survival: The History of the Second World War*, Oxford, 1990, p. 34.

14 D. Pryce-Jones, 'Paris during German occupation', in G. Hirschfeld and P. Marsh (eds), *Collaboration in France: Politics and Culture during the Nazi Occupation 1940–1944*, Oxford, 1989, p. 16.

15 ibid.

16 Naturally enough the local papers were flattered by this prospect. See J.F. Sweets, *Choices in Vichy France: The French under Nazi Occupation*, Oxford, 1986, p. 4.

17 For a recent review of this debate, see R.J. Soucy, 'French Fascism and the Croix de Feu: a dissenting interpretation', *Journal of Contemporary History*, 26, 1991, pp. 159–88.

18 See, for example, R. Rémond, *Les Droites en France*, Paris, 1982 and his self-analysis in P. Nora (ed.), *Essai d'ego histoire*, Paris, 1987, pp. 293–347. He concluded this by condemning the 'arrogant simplifications of the new majority [after the Socialist victory in 1981] and their absurd misunderstanding of the positive work accomplished in the two preceding decades'.

19 The major historian of the regime is R.O. Paxton. See his *Parades and Politics at Vichy: The French Officer Corps under Marshal Pétain*, Princeton, NJ, 1966; *Vichy France: Old Guard and New Order 1940–1944*, New York, 1972; with M.R. Marrus, *Vichy France and the Jews*, New York, 1981; cf. also A. Shennan, *Rethinking France: Plans for Revival 1940–6*, Oxford, 1986.

20 A.S. Milward, *War, Economy and Society 1939–1945*, Harmondsworth, 1987, pp. 137–46; *The New Order and the French Economy*, Oxford, 1970.

21 G. Hirschfeld, 'Collaboration in Nazi-occupied France: some introductory remarks' in G. Hirschfeld and P. Marsh (eds), op cit., p. 14.

22 Milward has estimated that, during the war, the Germans extracted from France 42 per cent of their total income from occupied territories. A.S. Milward, *War, Economy and Society 1939–1945*, p. 138.

23 P. Marsh, 'The Theatre: compromise or collaboration?' in G. Hirschfeld and P. Marsh (eds), op. cit., p. 142.

24 E. Haraszti Taylor, *A Life with Alan: The Diary of A.J.P. Taylor's Wife Eva from 1978 to 1985,* London, 1987, p. 16.

25 See, for example, R. Armes, 'Cinema of paradox: French film-making during the occupation' in G. Hirschfeld and P. Marsh (eds), op. cit., pp. 126–41.

26 P. McCarthy, *Céline*, London, 1975, p. 206.

27 In English, see, for example, W.R. Tucker, *The Fascist Ego: A Political Biography of Robert Brasillach*, Berkeley, Calif., 1975 on this self-styed 'anarchofascist' (p.5).

28 M.R. Marrus and R.O. Paxton, *Vichy France and the Jews*, p. 3.

29 R.I. Cohen, *The Burden of Conscience: French Jewish Leadership during the Holocaust*, Bloomington, Ind., 1987, pp. 31, 50, 75. This book also predictably tells the sad story of the attempts by 'French Jews' to dissociate themselves from 'foreign ones'.

30 M.R. Marrus and R.O. Paxton, *Vichy France and the Jews*, p. xi.

31 J. Steinberg, *All or Nothing: The Axis and the Holocaust, 1941–3*, London, 1990, pp. 105–16 on the Italian zone.

32 M.R. Marrus and R.O. Paxton, *Vichy France and the Jews*, p. xi.

33 ibid., p. 4.

34 For the relative tables see R. Hilberg, *The Destruction of the European Jews*, New York, 1961, p. 670.

35 M. Ophuls, op. cit., p. 139.

36 M.R. Marrus and R.O. Paxton, 'The Nazis and the Jews in occupied Western Europe 1940–1944', p. 180.

37 For some introduction, see H. Michel, 'The psychology of the French resister', *Journal of Contemporary History*, 5, 1970, pp. 159–75; S. Hawes and R. White (eds), *Resistance in Europe 1939–1945*, Harmondsworth, 1976, pp. 77–134; H.R. Kedward, *Resistance in Vichy France: A Study of Ideas and Motivation in the Southern Zone 1940–1942*, Oxford, 1978.

38 P. Calvocoressi and G. Wint, *Total War: Causes and Courses of the Second World War*, Harmondsworth, 1972, p. 267.

39 H. Footitt and J. Simmonds, *France 1943–1945*, Leicester, 1988, p. 70.

40 ibid., p. 63. He preferred the flag used in the invasion merely to have *La France* inscribed on it.

41 ibid., p. xii.

42 The official food ration by then was down to 1,200 calories per day. A. Marwick, op. cit., p. 193.

43 H.R. Lottman, *The People's Anger: Justice and Revenge in Post-Liberation France*, London, 1986, p. 15.

44 ibid., p. 33.

45 ibid., pp. 85, 163–4, 198–9, 259–60, 273. Piaf, on investigation, was not only exonerated but publicly congratulated for her work at the time.

46 ibid., pp. 177–9.

47 For an account, see M. Ferro, *Pétain*, Paris, 1987, pp. 615–62. Pétain's defence lawyer, Jacques Isorni, became one of the more extraordinary figures of post-war France. See J. Isorni, *Souffrance et mort du Maréchal*, Paris, 1951; *Mémoires, 1911–1945*, Paris, 1984.

48 J.F. Sweets, op. cit., p. 84.

49 H. Rousso, *Le Syndrome de Vichy (1944–198. . .)*, Paris, 1987, pp. 51–4. The racist leader of the later Front National, Jean-Marie Le Pen, would be a member of this last body. By contrast, since 1945, Febvre, Renouvin and Henri Michel had belonged to a

Comité d'histoire de la guerre. In 1951 this fused with the *Commission d'histoire de l'Occupation et de la Libération de France* under G. Lefebvre among others, to form the *Comité d'histoire de la Deuxième Guerre Mondiale* (p. 256). Rousso's book has now appeared in English translation under the title *The Vichy Syndrome: History and Memory in France since 1944*, Cambridge, Mass., 1991.

50 H. Rousso, *Le Syndrome de Vichy (1944–198. . .)*, p. 51; cf. M. Ferro, *Pétain*, pp. 278–9.

51 Cf. the fine E. Weber, *Peasants into Frenchmen*, Stanford, 1976.

52 P. Geyl, *Napoleon: For and Against*, rev. edn, Harmondsworth, 1965, pp. 319–23, 333–5, 376–400.

53 Cobb says, somewhat maliciously, 'Lefebvre looked forward with great eagerness to a time after his death, when every imaginable historical problem would be able to be solved scientifically'. R. Cobb, *People and Places*, p. 45.

54 P. Geyl, op. cit., p. 399.

55 ibid., pp. 336–59. Both Charles Maurras and Philippe Pétain were also members of the *Académie Française*. This fact would cause some embarrassment after 1945 although the pro-Vichy faction was basically able to sit out the *épuration*. See H. Rousso, op. cit., especially pp. 76–80 over the candidature of the 1930s anti-Semitic novelist, Paul Morand, a diplomat reintegrated into the service in 1953, but vetoed by De Gaulle as an academician.

56 In English see W.R. Keylor, *Jacques Bainville and the Renaissance of Royalist History in the Twentieth Century*, Baton Rouge, La, 1979.

57 For an English-language introduction, see J.S. McClelland (ed.), *The French Right (from De Maistre to Maurras)*, London, 1970, pp. 213–304.

58 H.R. Kedward, 'The Vichy of the other Philippe' in G. Hirschfeld and P. Marsh (eds), op. cit., p. 33. In 1941 Vichy would also launch the series *Collection des grands redressements de l'Histoire*, A. Shennan, op. cit., p. 103.

59 My copy of J. Carcopino, *Daily Life in Ancient Rome: The People and the City at the Height of the Empire*, Harmondsworth, 1956 (first published in French, 1941) intriguingly lists his other biographical achievements but omits his career as Minister of National Education. For Madelin and Fascist Italy, see E. Decleva, *L'incerto alleato: ricerche sugli orientamenti dell'Italia unità*, Milan, 1987, pp. 197–8, 216–18.

60 J.F. Sweets, op. cit., p. 46.

61 H.R. Lottman, op. cit., p. 80; for a recent review of the Drancy camp's earlier history, see M. Rajsfus, *Drancy: un camp de concentration très ordinaire 1941–1944*, Paris, 1991.

62 For biographical details, see, for example, C. Fink, 'Introduction' to M. Bloch, *Memoirs of War, 1914–15*, Ithaca, N.Y., 1980. (F. Braudel helped the English publication of this work); cf. in more detail, C. Fink, *M. Bloch: A Life in History*, Cambridge, 1989.

63 C. Fink, 'Introduction', p. 52.

64 For an introduction to this founding, see P. Burke, op. cit., pp. 12–13. The sort of collective openness to neighbouring disciplines (which none the less should accept the leadership of history), favoured by the early *Annales,* seems a little like an intellectual version of the French perception of the League of Nations or the Kellogg–Briand Pact of the late 1920s.

65 M. Bloch, *Strange Defeat*, London, 1949 (first published in French, 1946); cf. his *The Historian's Craft*, Manchester, 1954 (in French, 1949) and P. M. Rutcoff, 'Letters to America: the correspondence of Marc Bloch, 1940–41', *French Historical Studies*, 12, 1981, pp. 277–303 for the reasons why Bloch did not then make the 'sea change' to the USA.

66 C. Fink, 'Introduction', p. 62.

67 ibid., p. 64.

68 Andrew Shennan has remarked both that 'the most striking characteristic of all wartime planning … was the desire for a complete break with the pre-war status quo' and that,

with apparent paradox, 'reformers of all shades generally insisted on a continuity between France's past and their vision of her future' (A. Shennan, op. cit., pp. 10, 103). The problem for the French, before and after 1944, was to find a usable past and usable historians to relate it.

69 For detailed study of the story at least to 1958, see J.-P. Rioux, *The Fourth Republic 1944–1958*, Cambridge, 1987.

70 For a bitter account of this 'betrayal', see G. Bidault, *Resistance*, London, 1967 (p. 249 parallels De Gaulle in 1940 with those generals who, after 1958, wanted Algeria to stay French).

71 J. Glénisson, 'France' in G.G. Iggers and H.T. Parker (eds), *International Handbook of Historical Studies: Contemporary Research and Theory*, Westport, Conn., 1979, p. 176.

72 For an *Annaliste* introduction to the concept of *mentalité*, see M. Vovelle, *Ideologies and Mentalities*, Cambridge, 1990 (first published in French, 1982). Vovelle, like M. Agulhon (see p. 108) is an *Annaliste* with a background in Marxism.

73 J.H. Hexter, 'Fernand Braudel and the *Monde Braudellien* . . .', *Journal of Modern History*, 44, 1972, p. 493. This issue of the *JMH* was devoted to the *Annales*. Among others writing in Braudel's praise was H.R. Trevor-Roper, 'Fernand Braudel, the *Annales* and the Mediterranean', pp. 468–79. Febvre had been French delegate to UNESCO after 1945, see P. Burke, op. cit., p. 31.

74 J.H. Hexter, op. cit., p. 493. Richard Cobb's acid pen describes a different side to the *Annales*. One matter on which he agreed with the Communist, Albert Soboul, was rejecting the '*chapelle braudélienne*'. Soboul's criticisms, Cobb said, 'were entirely justified . . . I fully shared Soboul's personal dislike of the *mafiosi*; they were a uniformly unpleasant lot. There was something quite sickening about the sycophancy of Braudel's Renaissance Court.' R. Cobb, *People and Places*, p. 71. Braudel, who had taught in Algeria (and Brazil), was another *Annaliste* with imperial experience (as was Ferro). It is a mutuality of background which deserves further analysis.

75 Cf. B. Vian, *Froth on the Day Dream*, Harmondsworth, 1970. The manuscripts of Jean Pulse Heartre prove a terrible temptation for one of the protagonists of this novel.

76 E. Le Roy Ladurie, *The Territory of the Historian*, Hassocks, 1979, pp. 255–72, 293–319. Le Roy Ladurie had been a youthful member of the PCF but now is bitterly disillusioned. See his autobiographical account *Paris–Montpellier: PC–PSU 1945–63*, Paris, 1983.

77 F. Braudel, *Civilization and Capitalism 15th–18th Century*, vol. I, p. 23. There are odd and very pessimistic references in the text to the oil crisis of 1973–4 which he depicted as leading to 'the development of a modern version of the non-market economy'. See, for example, vol. I, p. 23; vol. III, p. 81 (there he suggested 1973–4 would be 'more sinister' than the 'hurricane' of 1929–30 — 'all the foundations of economic life and all the lessons of experience past and present seem to be being challenged'); p. 88; p. 614 (the crisis, now dated 1972–4, he thought would be the moment of decline, the entry point into a new secular trend); p. 631 (where he appears to endorse the small firm as the third way between capitalism and socialism).

78 F. Braudel, *The Identity of France*, vol. I, p. 15.

79 H. Rousso, op. cit., p. 95 adroitly relates Astérix to the 'Vichy syndrome'. The Gaul's axe, or *francisque,* was a symbol of Vichy and distinguished from the (Roman) *fasces* of Fascist Italy. F. Braudel, *The Identity of France*, vol. II, p. 71 remarks that French blood today is the same as in prehistory though 'historical haematology is still in its infancy'. He also argues that 'Nordic', 'Alpine', 'Mediterranean' and Lorrainer racial groups compose France's population. The millions of immigrants might be surprised and alarmed by these conclusions (see vol. II, pp. 32, 67).

80 F. Braudel, *The Identity of France*, vol. I, pp. 19–21.

81 See, for example, C. Ginzburg, 'Mythologie germanique et nazisme. Sur un livre ancien de Georges Dumézil', *Annales ESC*, 40, 1985, pp. 695–715 which attacks the geopolitical ideas of Dumézil but notes his influence on Bloch and, by implication, on the Braudellian *Annales*.

82 F. Braudel, *The Identity of France*, vol. I, pp. 24, 72–3, 316; cf. also vol. II, p. 21 on France and eternity; vol. II, p. 203 on immigration (and Braudel's own credentials as an unprejudiced observer); p. 210 for Braudel's personal encounters with skate-board riders and taxi drivers.

83 ibid., vol.I., pp. 24–5.

84 F. Braudel, *On History*, Chicago, 1980, p. 47.

85 P. Nora (ed.), op. cit., p. 5.

86 E.H. Carr, *What is History?*, Harmondsworth, 1964, p. 23.

87 P. Nora (ed.), op. cit., pp. 139–72, 293–347. Girardet's staunch nationalism displays something of the traditions of French diplomatic history. Of a military family, he very much defines himself as a child of the First World War. Like Philippe Ariès, Girardet was a youthful member of *Action Française*.

88 P. Chaunu (with H. Chaunu), *Séville et l'Atlantique*, 12 vols, Paris, 1955–60; P. Chaunu et al., *La mort à Paris,* Paris, 1978, cf. E. Le Roy Ladurie, *The Territory of the Historian*, pp. 273–84; perhaps appropriately, Chaunu is a staunch opponent of legalised abortion. F. Braudel, *The Identity of France*, vol. II, pp. 188–9.

89 P. Chaunu, 'Le fils de la morte' in P. Nora (ed.), op. cit., pp. 61, 63, 65.

90 ibid., p. 77.

91 M. Agulhon, 'Vu des coulisses' in ibid., pp. 10, 13.

92 ibid., p. 25.

93 ibid., pp. 25–6; cf. Rémond's comment that, in the 1950s, there was a 'mistrust or reserve by university people towards history judged as too recent' (p. 323). But Agulhon has recently at last written genuinely contemporary history. M. Agulhon, *La République: de Jules Ferry à François Mitterrand. 1880 à nos jours*, Paris, 1991.

94 The English version of the thesis is M. Agulhon, *The Republic in the Village*, Cambridge, 1982; cf. also his witty historical deconstruction of the symbol of France, *Marianne into Battle*, Cambridge, 1981 (first published in French, 1979).

95 J. Le Goff, 'L'appétit de l'histoire' in P. Nora (ed.), op. cit., p. 205. For Le Goff cf. also J. Le Goff and P. Nora (eds), *Constructing the Past*, Cambridge, 1985 (first published in French, 1974).

96 J. Le Goff, 'L'appétit de l'histoire', pp. 177–8, 208–9.

97 ibid., pp. 216, 224.

98 ibid., p. 234.

99 J. Le Goff, 'Is politics the backbone of history?', *Daedalus*, 100, 1971, pp. 2, 11–12. In the same issue another *Annaliste* proselytised for 'cliometrics', F. Furet, 'Quantitative history', pp. 151–67.

100 See, for example, R. Armes, *French Cinema*, New York, 1985, pp. 223–4.

101 Then on the nights of 28–9 October 1981, it showed to an estimated audience of 5 million. H. Rousso, op. cit., p. 125. Georges Pompidou, by contrast, had served out the war as a teacher in Paris.

102 ibid. In Woody Allen's *Annie Hall,* however, trendy New Yorkers queue to see it.

103 P. Geyl, *Encounters in History*, London,1963, p. 411.

104 R. Armes, *French Cinema*, pp. 77, 89, 146, 155; cf. also Marcel's revealing comments on his 'left-wing father' who was shaken by the quality of Moscow hotels in 1937. S. Terkel, *'The Good War': An Oral History of World War II*, New York, 1984, pp. 247–53.

105 J.F. Sweets, op. cit., pp. 3–5.

106 Stanley Hoffmann provides the English-language version of the text with a fine and by no means uncritical introduction. S. Hoffmann, 'In the looking glass', in M. Ophuls, op. cit., pp. vii–xxvi.

107 J.F. Sweets, op. cit., p. viii.
108 H. Rousso, op. cit., p. 26.
109 ibid., p. 27.
110 ibid., p. 34.
111 ibid., pp. 32–4 making the subtle point that the absence of commemoration is what really shows that the Second World War was remembered in France.
112 H. Rousso, op. cit., p. 27.
113 R. Aron, *The Vichy Regime 1940–1944*, London, 1958 (first published in French, 1954). Cf. also his memoirs *Fragments d'une vie*, Paris, 1981, noting (pp. 144–5) that, even as a Jew, he could still find reasons to defend Laval.
114 C. De Gaulle, *War Memoirs,* 3 vols, London, 1954–9.
115 M. Ophuls, op. cit., pp. 96–100.
116 ibid., p. 118. This comment makes Sweets especially cross, see J.F. Sweets, op. cit., p. 208 (cf. also p. 165 with an alternative view to that of Tausend). For D'Astier, cf. also J.H. King, 'Emmanuel d'Astier and the nature of the French Resistance', *Journal of Contemporary History*, 8, 1973, pp. 25–45.
117 The most redolent moment occurs when Eden portentously recalls how moved the House of Commons was when its members stood in silence at news of the fate of the Jews. It is not recorded in the English-language text of *The Sorrow and the Pity*.
118 Simone Weil, herself a Jewish ex-deportee, thought the documentary was 'masochism'. H. Rousso, op. cit., p. 125.
119 R.O. Paxton, *Vichy France: Old Guard and New Order 1940–1944*.
120 H. Rousso, op. cit., p. 269. The journalist was Dominique Jamet, writing in *Aurore*.
121 On Barbie, see, for example, M. Linklater et al., *The Fourth Reich: Klaus Barbie and the Neo-Fascist Connection,* London, 1984.
122 F. Furet and M. Ozouf (eds), *A Critical Dictionary of the French Revolution*, Cambridge, Mass., 1989; for a well crafted review, see I. Woloch, 'On the latest illiberalism of the French Revolution', *American Historical Review*, 95, 1990, pp. 1452–70.
123 For a somewhat equivocal review, see *Cahiers du cinéma*, 406, 1988, p. 18.
124 Cf. for example F. Furet, 'Beyond the *Annales*', *Journal of Modern History*, 55, 1983, pp. 389–410; M. Harsgor, 'Total history: the *Annales* school', *Journal of Contemporary History*, 13, 1978, pp. 1–13.
125 L. Hunt, 'French history in the last twenty years: the rise and fall of the *Annales* paradigm', *Journal of Contemporary History*, 21, 1986, pp. 209–24.
126 For some autobiographical introduction, see M. Ferro, *Histoires de Russie et d'ailleurs: entretiens avec Jules Chancel et Jean-François Sabouret*, Paris, 1990; it is odd that Peter Burke, an enthusiastic proponent of the *Annales*, virtually omits Ferro from his discussion. P. Burke, op. cit., pp. 43, 87, 108.
127 In English, see, for example, M. Ferro, *The Great War*, London, 1973 (first published in French, 1969); 'Film as an agent, product and science of history', *Journal of Contemporary History*, 18, 1983, pp. 357–64.
128 F. Braudel, *Civilization and Capitalism*, vol. III, p. 619.
129 M. Ferro, *The Use and Abuse of History: Or How the Past is Taught*, London, 1984, p. vii (first published in French, 1981). This curious book preaches an internationalisation of history teaching but ends (p. 240) with a re-assertion of the fundamental requirement to teach the 'national past'.
130 ibid., p. 238.
131 ibid., p. 19; M. Ferro, *Histoires de Russie et d'ailleurs*, pp. 9, 39.
132 D. Peschanski, 'Vichy au singulier, Vichy au pluriel. Une tentative avortée d'encadrement de la société (1941–1944)', *Annales ESC*, 43, 1988, pp. 639, 658.
133 M. Ferro, 'Ouverture', *Annales ESC*, 43, 1988, pp. 561–3. He also denies the usefulness of the totalitarian model (p. 564).

134 M. Ferro, *Suez, naissance d'un tiers monde: 1956*, Paris, 1983. Ferro has recently published a biographical study of the last Tsar, *Nicolas II*, Paris, 1990.

135 M. Ferro, *Pétain*, pp. i–iii.

136 ibid., p. iii.

137 ibid., p. ix; Ferro's mother was a victim of deportation and this personal suffering, he admits, also influenced his choice of subject, M. Ferro, *Histoires de Russie et d'ailleurs*, p. 10. He also acknowledges that the peasantry did not always view the Resistance with total enthusiasm (p. 32). For further information on the FFI's 'uneven' nature, see H. Footitt and J. Simmonds, op. cit., p. 155.

138 Or is it something about the survival of the 'Vichy syndrome'? In a book acclaimed by E. Le Roy Ladurie among others, Henry Rousso has done a sort of dramatic or melodramatic reconstruction of the 'last days of Vichy', H. Rousso, *Pétain et la fin de la collaboration: Sigmaringen 1944–1945*, Brussels, 1984. Ferro's *Pétain* has 403 'scenes'.

139 M. Ferro, *Pétain*, pp. 718–20. Paxton gave the book a fine review, *Times Literary Supplement*, 13–19 November 1987.

140 M. Ferro, *Pétain*, p. 721.

141 E. Le Roy Ladurie, *Montaillou*, p. 155.

142 C. Ginzburg, *The Cheese and the Worms*, London, 1980 (first published in Italian, 1976). Cf. Dominick La Capra's explanation of the book which appears to notice everything except the key context of the 'long Second World War'. D. La Capra, *History and Criticism*, Ithaca, N.Y., 1985, pp. 45–69.

143 A visiting Frenchman thus famously described the Australian labour movement c. 1900 (antipodean socialists' great aim being to install a piano in every front room). See A. Métin, *Socialism without Doctrine*, Sydney, 1977. For the 'piano irréductible', cf. E. Ginzburg, *Within the Whirlwind*, London, 1989, p. 322.

144 Mitterrand had escaped from his POW camp and joined the Resistance. But, after 1944, he was most active as an organiser of pressure groups for ex-POWs. In this regard, S. Fishman, 'Grand delusions: the unintended consequences of Vichy France's prisoner of war propaganda', *Journal of Contemporary History*, 26, 1991, pp. 229–54, makes interesting points about the way returning POWs were greeted by a hostile and suspicious French public opinion. France was not totally different from Stalin's USSR.

145 F. Braudel, *The Identity of France*, vol. II, p. 182.

146 ibid., vol. II, p. 679.

147 M. Ferro, *The Use and Abuse of History*, p. 238.

The eclipse of anti-Fascism in Italy

1 For the best introduction to the possibilities, see P. Ginsborg, *A History of Contemporary Italy: Society and Politics 1943–1988*, Harmondsworth, 1990.

2 For an English-language introduction to the Communism of the Emilia-Romagna, see M. Jaggi *et al.*, *Red Bologna*, London, 1976; D.I. Kertzer, *Comrades and Christians: Religion and Political Struggle in Communist Italy*, Cambridge, 1980; R.H. Evans, *Coexistence: Communism and its Practice in Bologna, 1945–1965*, Notre Dame, 1967.

3 Z. Brzezinski, *Power and Principle*, New York, 1985, pp. 311–13 expresses the adamantine opposition of the (liberal) Carter administration to any such process.

4 For Moro's thought at this time, characteristically expressed in his labyrinthine speeches, see A. Moro, *L'intelligenza e gli avvenimenti: testi 1959–78*, Milan, 1979. Mosse's role in introducing these works deserves to be remarked.

5 For some introduction, see, for example, D. Moss, *The Politics of Left-Wing Violence in Italy, 1969–85*, London, 1988; R. Lumley, *States of Emergency: Cultures of Revolt in Italy from 1968 to 1978*, London, 1990.

6 See, for example, K. Luria and R. Gandolfo, 'Carlo Ginzburg: an interview', *Radical History Review*, 35, 1986, pp. 91, 105–6, 109.

7 T.J. Jackson Lears, 'The concept of cultural hegemony: problems and possibilities', *American Historical Review*, 90, 1985, p. 567.

8 See, for example, D. Betti, 'Il partito editore: libri e lettori nella politica culturale del PCI 1945–53', *Italia contemporanea*, 175, 1989, pp. 53–74 and, for Gramsci's writings in English, note especially A. Gramsci, *Letters from Prison* (ed. L. Lawner), New York, 1975; the major English-language editions of his books are *Selections from the Prison Notebooks* (ed. Q. Hoare and G. Nowell Smith), London, 1971; *Selections from Political Writings*, 2 vols (ed. Q. Hoare), London, 1977–8; *Selections from Cultural Writings* (ed. D. Forgacs and G. Nowell Smith), London, 1985.

9 There is a vast literature on Gramsci. For English-language introduction, see J. Joll, *Gramsci*, London, 1977; J.V. Femia, *Gramsci's Political Thought: Hegemony, Consciousness, and the Revolutionary Process*, Oxford, 1981.

10 See P. Spriano, *Le passioni di un decennio 1946–56*, Milan, 1986, p. 66. The speech was delivered to the Chamber of Deputies on 26 September 1947. Spriano is a decidedly enlightened PCI party historian whose most renowned book is his *Storia del Partito Comunista Italiano*, 5 vols, Turin, 1970–5. For some autobiographical comments, see also P. Spriano, *Intervista sulla storia del PCI*, Bari, 1979.

11 For a typical example, see I. Montanelli, 'Ai comunisti fa comodo dare del fascista a tutta', *Oggi illustrato*, 27 October 1975, p. 7. Montanelli, an ex-Fascist journalist turned independent radical conservative, has also been the republic's best-selling popular historian. In that capacity, he has typically argued that Imperial Rome won not because of its strength but because of its belief in itself. It was another triumph of the will. I. Montanelli, *Rome: The First Thousand Years*, London, 1962 (first published in Italian, Milan, 1959). This sort of history, its populism and its popularity, deserve analysis.

12 For a musical introduction, see the emblematic protest song 'Per i morti di Reggio Emilia', G. Vettori (ed.), *Canzoni italiane di protesta 1794–1974*, Rome, 1974, pp. 185–6.

13 L. Valiani, *Tutte le strade conducono a Roma*, Bologna, 1983, p. 18.

14 See L. Valiani, *Dall'antifascismo alla resistenza*, Milan, 1959; *Sessant' anni di avventure e battaglie: riflessioni e ricordi*, Milan, 1983; cf. also L. Valiani and R. De Felice, 'Il dibattito sul fascismo', *Nuova antologia*, f. 2165, January–March 1988, pp. 167–71; and for another fine memoir by a leading Marxist historian see P. Alatri, 'Minima personalia', *Belfagor*, XLI, 1986, pp. 455–65.

15 The term was utilised by the journalist George Seldes in his account of the Ethiopian war. See G. Seldes, *Sawdust Caesar: The Untold History of Mussolini and Fascism*, London, 1936.

16 A.J.P. Taylor, *The Origins of the Second World War*, rev. edn, Harmondsworth, 1964, pp. 84–5.

17 For a critical review, see R. Bosworth, 'Denis Mack Smith and the Third Italy', *International History Review*, XII, 1990, pp. 782–92.

18 The Spanish allegedly told each other that 'CTV', the initials of the Italian force, stood for 'when will you go home?' For a full analysis, see J.F. Coverdale, *Italian Intervention in the Spanish Civil War*, Princeton, NJ, 1975.

19 Jonathan Steinberg's account *All or Nothing: The Axis and the Holocaust 1941–3*, London, 1990, unfortunately does not cover this period of 'the last days of Mussolini'.

20 For an introduction, see R. Bosworth, 'Mito e linguaggio nella politica estera italiana', in R.J.B. Bosworth and S. Romano (eds), *La politica estera italiana (1860–1985)*, Bologna, 1991, pp. 49–54, 67.

21 For a splendid evocation of the emotions of a then adolescent Fascist true believer who turned into a fine liberal democratic historian, see E. Di Nolfo, *Le paure e le speranze degli Italiani* (1943–1953), Milan, 1986.

22 See E. Hobsbawm and T. Ranger (eds), *The Invention of Tradition*, Cambridge, 1983; and cf. the thesis of B. Anderson, *Imagined Communities*, London, 1983, which, although developed in regard to new Asian states, could easily be applied to Italy.

23 Cited by R. Romano, *La storiografia italiana oggi*, Rome, 1978, p. 9 and noting that Foscolo was not suggesting the ideal of objectivity.

24 J. Mazzini, *The Duties of Man and Other Essays,* London, 1907, pp. 222, 245.

25 In the present historiography, this interpretation is mostly abandoned in favour of some version of the Gramscian '*rivoluzione mancata*' thesis in which the Risorgimento was a time when things changed in order to remain the same, a political and not a social revolution. In English-language historiography, see S. Woolf, *A History of Italy 1700–1860*, London, 1979 and, especially, J.A. Davis, *Conflict and Control: Law and Order in Nineteenth-century Italy,* London, 1988, both of which are more interested in the *longue durée* of society than in political 'events'. But evidence that there is still life in the *rivoluzione nazionale* thesis came in 1982, with the commemoration of the centenary of the death of Giuseppe Garibaldi. Chief enthusiast of that hero of heroes was the rotund Giovanni Spadolini, then Republican Party Prime Minister. Spadolini, an ex-editor of *Corriere della sera*, is another enormously fertile popularist or belle-lettrist historian. See the very lavish collection of papers, A.A. Mola (ed.), *Garibaldi: generale della libertà*, Rome, 1984, e.g. p. 14 where Spadolini avers that the 'Italian passion' of the heroes of the Risorgimento is a precious patrimony to be transmitted to the new generation. It is the essence of Italian history.

26 For an English-language description of this world, see R. Drake, *Byzantium for Rome: The Politics of Nostalgia in Umbertian Italy*, Chapel Hill, 1980.

27 G. Fortunato, *Carteggio 1865–1911* (ed. E. Gentile), Bari, 1978, p. 235.

28 B. Croce, *History of the Kingdom of Naples* (ed. H.S. Hughes), Chicago, 1970, pp. 41, 195–6. This book was originally published by Laterza in 1925.

29 A. Lyttelton (ed.), *Italian Fascisms from Pareto to Gentile,* London, 1973, p. 213. For recent analyses, each of which, however, is a little too anxious to treat the Futurists on their own terms, see G.L. Mosse, 'The political culture of Italian Futurism: a general perspective', *Journal of Contemporary History*, 25, 1990, p. 257; cf. W.L. Adamson, 'Modernism and Fascism: the politics of culture in Italy 1903–1922', *American Historical Review,* 95, 1990, pp. 359–90.

30 As quoted by E. Gentile, *Le origini dell' ideologia fascista, 1918–25*, Bari, 1975, p. 346.

31 The most recent example is M. Eksteins, *Rites of Spring: The Great War and the Birth of the Modern Age,* New York, 1989.

32 As early as 1921, Italian politicians were already trying to police foreign accounts of Caporetto in school texts. L. Couder, 'Manuels scolaires et, diplomatie: une controverse franco-italienne dans les années 1920', *Risorgimento,* III, 1982, p. 41.

33 G. Corni, 'L'occupazione austro-germanica del Veneto nel 1917–18: sindaci, preti, austriacanti e patrioti', *Rivista di storia contemporanea*, XVIII, 1989, pp. 380–408.

34 M. Clark, *Modern Italy 1871–1982,* London, 1984, p. 200.

35 A. Asor Rosa, *Scrittori e popolo*, Rome, 1972, pp. 83–4.

36 For some comments, see R. Bosworth, 'Italian foreign policy and its historiography' in R. Bosworth and G. Rizzo (eds), *Altro Polo: Intellectuals and their Ideas in Contemporary Italy,* Sydney, 1983, pp. 72–3; it was also predictable that the translation of the revisionist R.J.B. Bosworth, *Italy, the Least of the Great Powers*, should be published by Riuniti, high culture publishing house of the PCI (*La politica estera dell'Italia giolittiana*, Rome, 1985.)

37 R. Romeo, *L'Italia unita e la prima Guerra mondiale*, Bari, 1978, p. 157.

38 For an introduction, see P. V. Cannistraro (ed.), *Historical Dictionary of Fascist Italy,* Westport, Conn., 1982, pp. 167–8.

39 A. Casali, *Storici italiani fra le due guerre: la 'Nuova Rivista Storica' 1917–43,* Naples, 1980, pp. 153–4.

40 C.M. De Vecchi di Val Cismon, *Il quadrumviro scomodo* (ed. L. Romersa), Milan, 1983, pp. 230–1.

41 M. Isnenghi, *Intellettuali militanti e intellettuali funzionari: appunti sulla cultura fascista,* Turin, 1979, p. 54.

42 See G. Turi, 'Ruolo e destino degli intellettuali nella politica razziale del fascismo', *Passato e presente,* 19, 1989, pp. 35–6, 41.

43 R. De Felice, 'Fascism and culture in Italy: outlines for further study', *Stanford Italian Review,* VIII, 1990, p. 9.

44 M. Isnenghi, *L'educazione dell'italiano: il fascismo e l'organizzazione della cultura,* Bologna, 1979, p. 94.

45 B. Croce, *History as the Story of Liberty,* London, 1941, p. 17.

46 Cf. De Felice's similar defence of the record of his father-in-law, Guido De Ruggiero, R. De Felice, 'Il Magistero di Guido De Ruggiero', *Nuova antologia,* f. 2161, 1987, pp. 79–97.

47 D. Mack Smith, 'Benedetto Croce: History and Politics', *Journal of Contemporary History,* 8, 1973 pp. 41–61.

48 See D.D. Roberts, 'Croce and beyond: Italian intellectuals and the First World War', *International History Review,* III, 1981, p. 212.

49 Cited by D. Mack Smith, 'Benedetto Croce: History and Politics', p. 46.

50 E. Santarelli, *Fascismo e Neofascismo,* Rome, 1974, p. xiv. Volpe, by contrast, had argued that it was the Liberal era which was the real 'parenthesis'. G. Volpe, *L'Italia in cammino,* Milan, 1928, p. 267.

51 For a review, see R. Bosworth, 'Italy's historians and the myth of fascism', in R. Langhorne (ed.), *Diplomacy and Intelligence during the Second World War,* Cambridge, 1985, pp. 88–93. By contrast, cf. the comments in B. Vigezzi (ed.), *Federico Chabod e la 'Nuova Storiografia' italiana dal primo al secondo dopoguerra,* Milan, 1984, pp. 432, 490, 690. In this last instance, De Felice admitted Volpe was a Fascist but argued also that he was 'the greatest historian of the first half of this century'.

52 M. Isnenghi, *Intellettuali militanti e intellettuali funzionari,* p. 24; cf. also Togliatti's famous and wise comment that Fascism conquered nationalism in the way Rome did Greece and that, whenever there was a clash between the two, 'the substance of the solution . . . has always come from the Nationalist Party'. P. Togliatti, *Lectures on Fascism,* London, 1976, p. 36.

53 The most detailed study of Italian war entry is M. Knox, *Mussolini Unleashed 1939–41,* Cambridge, 1982 (though it is perhaps a little literal in its reading of the evidence).

54 See M. Ferrarotto, *L'accademia d'Italia: intellettuali e potere durante il Fascismo,* Naples, 1977.

55 G. Volpe, *Storia della Corsica italiana,* Milan, 1939, p. 10. (He emphasised typically that Mazzini had regarded Corsica as Italian 'per spirti generosi di patria', p. 77. At the same time he did specifically reject the idea that, in the present circumstances, Italy should pursue its 'irredentisms', p. 215.) Cf. also his article on Corsica in the PNF's *Dizionario di politica,* Rome, 1940, vol. 1, pp. 646–56.

56 R. Truffi (ed.), *Precursori dell'impero africano,* Rome, 1936, Volpe introduction.

57 Cf. also the menacing establishment of a *Centro studi per la svizzera italiana* in 1941 under the nationalist A. Solmi. G. Turi, 'Le istituzioni culturali del regime fascista durante la seconda guerra mondiale', *Italia contemporanea,* XXXII, 1980, p. 10.

58 G. Volpe, *Guerra, dopoguerra, Fascismo,* Venice, 1928, p. 414.

59 G. Volpe, *Nel regno di Clio,* Rome, 1977, pp. 19–20, 80.

60 See comments of P. Treves in B. Vigezzi (ed.), op. cit., p. 629 noting that, after 1943, Volpe did not resile from these views.

61 E. Gentile, 'La natura e la storia del partito nazionale fascista nelle interpretazioni dei contemporanei e degli storici', *Storia contemporanea,* XVI, 1985, p. 534.

62 See, for example, his speech to the Academy in 1931 in which he talked about the need

for both Science and Art to work for the 'grandeur of the Nation'. *dizionario della dottrina fascista,* Turin, 1934, p. 3.

63 On 9 May 1936, Volpe, Chabod, Morandi, Ghisalberti, Sestan and Maturi attended the great victory demonstration in which the creation of a Fascist Empire was celebrated. They hugged each other with joy at the national triumph. B. Vigezzi (ed.), op. cit., p. 583.

64 M. Isnenghi, 'La guerra civile nella pubblicista di destra', *Rivista di storia contemporanea,* XVII, 1989, p. 111; for a recent, much fuller development of this theme, see C. Pavone, *Una guerra civile: saggio storico sulla moralità nella resistenza,* Turin, 1991; cf. by contrast, the moving account of creative and humane disloyalty in R. Absalom, *A Strange Alliance: Aspects of Escape and Survival in Italy 1943–45,* Florence, 1991.

65 G. Volpe, *Nel regno di Clio,* p. 100; for the admiration, see, for example, N. Rodolico review in *Nuova antologia,* f. 1822, October 1952, p. 194.

66 P. Silva, *Io difendo la monarchia,* Rome, 1946, pp. 14, 89. Silva had associated himself with the anti-Fascist Manifesto of the Intellectuals in 1925. For this, and the Fascist Manifesto, see E.R. Papa, *Fascismo e cultura,* Venice, 1974.

67 G. Pintor, *Doppio diario 1936–1943,* Turin, 1978, p. 201.

68 E. Serra, *I tempi duri della speranza,* Rome, 1982, pp. 10, 27, 43–4, 81, 87.

69 See R. Bosworth, 'Italy's historians and the myth of Fascism', pp. 99–100; N. Ajello, *Intellettuali e PCI 1944–58,* Bari, 1979, pp. 439, 545–6.

70 D. Cantimori, *Studi di storia* (rev. edn), Turin, 1976, vol. I, p. xix.

71 R. Zangheri, historian of peasant Italy, sometime Mayor of Bologna and member of the PCI's Central Committee, argued that the peasantry was a key force behind the Resistance. See R. Zangheri, 'Movimento contadino e storia d'Italia. Riflessioni sulla storiografia del dopoguerra', *Studi storici,* 17, 1976, pp. 5–33.

72 See, for example, P. Brunette, *Roberto Rossellini,* New York, 1987, pp. 41–60. Rossellini would, in 1947, make *Germania: anno zero,* a film version of the end of (German) history.

73 See F. Chabod, *Storia dell'idea d'Europa,* Bari, 1961; S. Soave, *Federico Chabod politico,* Bologna, 1989.

74 See R. Bosworth, 'Italy's historians and the myth of Fascism', pp. 85–6.

75 F. Chabod, *Lezioni di metodo storico,* Bari, 1976, pp. 51, 241, 257.

76 F. Chabod, *Storia della politica estera italiana,* 2 vols, Bari, 1951. An English translation is about to be published by Princeton University Press as part of a scheme for cultural exchange favoured by the Italian government.

77 Spadolini, for one, believes the book is 'the summit of Italian lay historiography'. B. Vigezzi (ed.), op. cit., p. 555.

78 F. Chabod, *Machiavelli and the Renaissance,* London, 1958, p. 1.

79 D. Mack Smith, *Italy: A Modern History,* Ann Arbor, Mich., 1959.

80 G. Volpe, *Nel regno di Clio,* p. 220.

81 N. Ajello, 'Cavour contro Cavour', *L'Espresso,* XXX, 4 November 1984.

82 R. Romeo, *Dal Piemonte sabaudo all'Italia liberale,* Bari, 1974, p. 319.

83 For a super-radical, '68-ist effort at history, see R. Del Carria, *Proletari senza rivoluzione: storia delle classi subalterne italiane dal 1860 al 1950,* 2 vols, Milan, 1970.

84 Umberto Eco, for example, published in 1967 *Towards a Semiotic Guerrilla Warfare,* translated into English as U. Eco, *Faith in Fakes,* London, 1986, pp. 135–44.

85 It was ironical that, in his search for a euphemism, Battaglia should come up with the same word which Croce had used to express his detachment from Fascism. R. Battaglia, *Un uomo, un partigiano,* Turin, 1965, p. 9. For Battaglia as historian, see R. Battaglia and G. Garritano, *La resistenza italiana: lineamenti di storia,* Rome, 1973. This is an enlarged version of Battaglia's *Breve storia della resistenza italiana,* Rome, 1955

(available in English as *The Story of the Italian Resistance*, London, 1957). The 1973 publication was distributed free to subscribers of the PCI daily *L'Unità*. It was prefaced by Gian Carlo Pajetta, a member of the PCI Central Committee and ex-Garibaldi Brigade fighter for the anti-Fascist cause in the Spanish Civil War.

86 R. Battaglia, *Un uomo, un partigiano*, p. 154.

87 The most famous admission in this regard during the De Felice affair came from Giorgio Amendola, another member of the PCI directorate. G. Amendola, *Intervista sull'antifascismo*, Bari, 1976, pp. 13, 155–6.

88 R. Battaglia, *Un uomo, un partigiano*, pp. 13–14.

89 *L'Espresso*, XXVIII, 26 December 1982, p. 20.

90 R. Lumley, op. cit., p. 103.

91 G. Quazza, *Resistenza e storia d'Italia*, Milan, 1976, p. 7 (he added, with a characteristic combination of professorial sense of responsibility and good form, that a proper history of the Resistance had not been written and that it would need a generation to research; its namierisation, he thought, might be a good starting-point, pp. 19–21, 442); G. Quazza, 'Il Fascismo: esame di coscienza degli italiani' in G. Quazza *et al.*, *Storiografia e Fascismo*, Milan, 1985, p. 7. The recent revelations about the Masonic Lodge, P2, and '*Operazione Gladio*' do seem to indicate that there was indeed a Fascist threat to egalitarian democracy in 1970s Italy.

92 R. Del Carria, op. cit., vol. II, p. 362. For a vituperative attack on this book, see R. De Felice, 'Italian historiography since the Second World War' in R. Bosworth and G. Cresciani (eds), *Altro Polo: A Volume of Italian Studies*, Sydney, 1979, pp. 175–7.

93 The last phrase is repeated five times in the sung version, just to make it heard. 'Il bastone e la carota: canti di rebellione dei giorni nostri', *Canzoniere internazionale*, Milan, 1971.

94 R. De Felice, *Mussolini il rivoluzionario 1883–1920*, Turin, 1965; *Mussolini il Fascista: la conquista del potere 1921–5*, Turin, 1966; *Mussolini il Fascista: l'organizzazione dello stato fascista 1925–9*, Turin, 1968; *Mussolini il Duce: gli anni del consenso 1929–36*, Turin, 1974; *Mussolini il Duce: lo stato totalitario 1936–40*, Turin, 1981; *Mussolini l'alleato 1940–5: L'Italia in guerra 1940–3*, 2 vols, Turin, 1990. By these last volumes, the work had almost reached its 6,000th page, a total which means that De Felice has devoted a page to every three days of Mussolini's life. For some examples of De Felice's work in English, see R. De Felice, *Interpretations of Fascism*, Cambridge, Mass., 1977; *Fascism, an Informal Introduction to its Theory and Practice*, New Brunswick, NJ, 1977; 'Italian fascism and the middle classes' in S.U. Larsen *et al.* (eds), *Who were the Fascists?* Bergen, 1980 and 'Varieties of Fascism' in G.R. Urban (ed.), *Eurocommunism: Its Roots and Future in Italy and Elsewhere*, London, 1978. For further comments, see R. Bosworth, 'Italian foreign policy and its historiography', pp. 67–71 or, in very bland tones, B.W. Painter, 'Renzo De Felice and the historiography of Italian Fascism', *American Historical Review*, 95, 1990, pp. 391–405. See, by contrast, contemporary, if rival, English-language assessments, R. Bosworth, 'In the green corner, Denis Mack Smith, in the red? black? corner Renzo De Felice: an account of the 1976 contest in the historiography of Italian fascism', *Teaching History*, 11, 1977, pp. 29–43; A.J. Gregor, 'Professor Renzo De Felice and the Fascist phenomenon', *World Politics*, 30, 1978, pp. 433–49; M.A. Ledeen, 'Renzo De Felice and the controversy over Italian Fascism', *Journal of Contemporary History*, 11, 1976, pp. 269–83; for an Italian-language summary, see P. Meldini (ed.), *Un monumento al Duce?* Florence, 1976.

95 See G. Volpe, *Ritorno al paese (Paganica): memorie minime*, Rome, 1963 for a romantic re-evoction.

96 His major work is a lengthy biography of Cavour, R. Romeo, *Cavour e il suo tempo*, 3 vols, Bari, 1977–84.

97 Gentile is of the new generation. He has begun what looks like being an exhaustive

history of the Fascist Party in neo-Rankean mode. E. Gentile, *Storia del Partito fascista: 1919–22 movimento e milizia,* Bari, 1989; cf. also his appearance in the *Annales,* E. Gentile, 'Le rôle du parti dans le laboratoire totalitaire italien', *Annales ESC,* 43, 1988, pp. 567–92.

98 See, for example, D. Cantimori and R. De Felice (eds), *Giacobini italiani,* 2 vols, Bari, 1964.

99 R. De Felice, *Storia degli ebrei italiani sotto il Fascismo,* Turin, 1961. There has been recent controversy over De Felice's omission in a new edition of the somewhat critical introduction by Cantimori. See R. Cotroneo, 'Renzo e Benito', *L'Espresso,* XXXVI, 11 November 1990, pp. 112–21.

100 See for example, R. Vivarelli, *Il dopoguerra in Italia e l'avvento del Fascismo (1918–22),* vol. 1, *Dalla fine della guerra all'impresa di fiume,* Naples, 1967. For a recent re-statement of the fundamentally anti-liberal character of Fascism (and an attack on what is perceived as Anglo-Saxon downplaying of Italian history), see R. Vivarelli, 'Interpretations of the origins of Fascism', *Journal of Modern History,* 63, 1991, pp. 29–43 and cf. his *Storia delle origini del Fascismo: L'Italia dalla grande guerra alla marcia su Roma,* vol. II, Bologna, 1991, which is characteristically dedicated to Salvemini and Chabod.

101 But see M. Knox, 'I testi "aggiustati" dei discorsi segreti di Grandi', *Passato e presente,* 13, 1987.

102 For an English-language example, see S.J. Woolf, 'Mussolini as revolutionary', *Journal of Contemporary History,* I, 1966, pp. 187–96.

103 E.g. R. De Felice, *Mussolini il rivoluzionario,* pp. 659–60.

104 R. De Felice, *Intervista sul Fascismo,* Bari, 1975. The English-language version is *Fascism, an Informal Introduction,* cited above.

105 Ledeen had recently published M.A. Ledeen, *Universal Fascism: The Theory and Practice of the Fascist International 1928–1936,* New York, 1972; see further R. Bosworth, 'In the green corner Denis Mack Smith, in the red? black? corner Renzo De Felice', pp. 33–4.

106 With hindsight, however, it is hard to accept that Ledeen is a praeternaturally objective person. His career has led through Billygate to murky dealings with Israel, Iran and factions of the Italian secret service. The Italian press described him as the middle man connecting Craxian socialism to the Reagan regime. For hostile English-language accounts, see L. Gurwin, *The Calvi Affair,* London, 1983; T. Draper, 'The rise of the American junta', *New York Review of Books,* 8 October 1987, pp. 47–58; R.J. Lambrose, 'The Abusable Past', *Radical History Review,* 39, 1987, pp. 171–2. For Ledeen's own voluminous expressions of his world view see, for example, M.A. Ledeen, *Grave New World,* Oxford, 1985, or his many articles in *Commentary, New Republic* and elsewhere. Redolent early examples are M. Ledeen and C. Sterling, 'Italy's Russian Sugar Daddies', *New Republic,* 174, 3 April 1976, pp. 16–21; M. Ledeen, 'Roman roulette', *New Republic,* 175, 3 July 1976, pp. 14–17; 'Inertia in Italy', *New Republic,* 175, 31 July 1976, pp. 14–16; 'Europe's sickest man', *New Republic,* 176, 12 February 1977, pp. 8–9: cf. his 'Italy in crisis', *The Washington Papers,* V, 1977 published in Italian as *Il complesso di Nerone.* 'The West' and its Italian friends were fiddling while Rome burned.

107 M. Clark, D. Hine and R.E.M. Irving, 'Divorce — Italian Style', *Parliamentary Affairs,* XXVII, 1974, p. 349.

108 For some over-statement in this regard, see the work of one of De Felice's pupils, R. Quartararo, *Roma tra Londra e Berlino,* Rome, 1980. Quartararo's book was published by Bonacci in a series edited by De Felice and subsidised by the Italian Ministry of Foreign Affairs.

109 R. De Felice, *Fascism, an Informal Introduction,* p. 26; cf. p. 37 where De Felice says the study of Fascism in 1970s Italy has reached the same position as Mme de Staël's interpretation of the French Revolution.

110 See M. Ambri, *I falsi fascismi: Ungheria, Jugoslavia, Romania 1919–1945,* Rome, 1980 and De Felice preface, pp. 6–20.

111 *Corriere della sera,* 27 December 1987.

112 I. Montanelli, 'Ai comunisti fa comodo dare del fascista a tutta', p. 7.

113 R. De Felice, 'Varieties of Fascism', p. 115.

114 N. Tranfaglia, 'Fascismo e mass media: dall'intervista De Felice agli sceneggiati televisivi', *Passato e presente,* 3, 1983, p. 136; cf. N. Tranfaglia (ed.), *L'Italia unita nella storiografia del secondo dopoguerra,* Milan, 1980; J. Jacobelli (ed.), *Il Fascismo e gli storici oggi,* Bari, 1988, pp. 114–20.

115 A malicious commentator might add that De Felice's participation in the 'baronial', patron-client relationships of Italian academic life was less crass than that of some of his left-wing critics. For an introduction to these patterns in the cultural life of the Italian Republic, see B.R. Clark, *Academic Power in Italy: Bureaucracy and Oligarchy in a National University System,* Chicago, 1977.

116 T. Mason, 'Il fascismo "Made in Italy": mostra sull' economia italiana tra le due guerre', *Italia contemporanea,* 158, 1985, pp. 14, 23–4; or, in English-language version, 'The Great Economic History Show', *History Workshop,* 21, 1986, pp. 3–35.

117 For his eulogy on Romeo's death, see R. De Felice, 'Rosario Romeo: il grande storico, il grande amico', *Nuova antologia,* f. 2162, April–June 1987, pp. 9–11.

118 *L'Espresso,* XXVII, 2 May 1982; XXIX, 30 June 1985; XXXIII, 18 October 1987. For imperialism, see the De Felice preface to L. Calabrò, *Intermezzo africano,* Rome, 1988, a memoir which itself proffers dubious clichés about the 'non-racist' behaviour of almost all Italians and is nostalgic for the 'good', nationalist side of AOI.

119 *Corriere della Sera,* 27 December 1987.

120 See, for example, *Corriere della sera,* 28 December 1987 (Spriano); 29 December (Valiani and Galli della Loggia); 30 December (Mack Smith and M. Salvadori); 31 December (Andreotti); 7 January and 18 March 1988 (De Felice); *Resto del carlino,* 29 December (Colletti); 8 January (Settembrini); *La Repubblica,* 29 December (Asor Rosa); 2 January (Tranfaglia); *Il Giornale Nuovo,* 29 December (Montanelli); *Il Giorno,* 29 December (Mack Smith). A book-length summary of the controversy also soon appeared. J. Jacobelli, op. cit.; cf. also M. Legnani, 'Al mercato del revisionismo: un inopinato dibattito su fascismo e antifascismo', *Italia contemporanea,* 170, 1988, pp. 97–101.

121 R. De Felice, *Mussolini l'alleato,* pp. ix–xi.

122 ibid., pp. 770–1.

123 Cf. L. Passerini, *Fascism in Popular Memory: The Cultural Experience of the Turin Working Class,* Cambridge, 1987. One, somewhat ironical, way to read De Felice's position in Italian historiography is regional — he stands for Rome against the more radical traditions of the Turin of Quazza and Passerini. Similarly, he represents political history (and has doubted the probity of both oral and contemporary history) against social history and its accompaniments. For an important summary of Passerini's methodological views which are radically different from De Felice's, see L. Passerini, *Storia e soggettività: le fonti orali, la memoria,* Florence, 1988 and also cf. her moving and highly individualist memoirs, *Autoritratto di gruppo,* Florence, 1988.

124 P. Di Cori, 'Soggettività e pratica storica', *Movimento operaio e socialista,* 10, 1987, p. 89.

125 S. Pertini, *Sei condanne, due evasioni,* Milan, 1978; cf. the natural anti-Fascism frequently expressed in R. Uboldi, *Il cittadino Sandro Pertini,* Milan, 1982.

126 F. Cossiga, 'Sono pronto a liberare Curcio', *L'Espresso,* XXXVII, 11 August 1991, pp. 28–9.

127 A. Gramsci, *Letters from Prison* (ed. L. Lawner), New York, 1975, p. 273.

128 B. Croce, *History as the Story of Liberty,* p. 45.

Glasnost Reaches Soviet historiography

1 *Izvestia*, 7 May 1985 in G. H. Hartman (ed.), *Bitburg in Moral and Political Perspective*, Bloomington, Ind., 1986, p. 210.

2 O. Bartov, *The Eastern Front, 1941–5: German Troops and the Barbarisation of Warfare*, New York, 1986, p. 173.

3 R.A.C. Parker, *Struggle for Survival: The History of the Second World War*, Oxford, 1990, p. 1.

4 M. Lewin, *The Gorbachev Phenomenon: A Historical Interpretation*, London, 1989, argues this point strongly.

5 M. Ferro, *October 1917: A Social History of the Russian Revolution*, London, 1980, pp. viii, 1.

6 T.H. von Laue, 'Stalin in focus', *Slavic Review*, 42, 1983, p. 383.

7 E. Wilson, *To the Finland Station: A Study in the Writing and Acting of History*, London, 1960, p. 375.

8 R.A. Rosenstone, *Romantic Revolutionary: A Biography of John Reed*, Harmondsworth, 1982, p. 298; cf. J. Reed, *Ten Days that Shook the World*, Harmondsworth, 1966.

9 J. Bergman, 'The perils of historical analogy: Leon Trotsky and the French Revolution', *Journal of the History of Ideas*, XLVIII, 1987, p. 81; cf. D. Schlapentokh, 'The images of the French Revolution in the February and Bolshevik Revolutions', *Russian Review*, 16, 1989, pp. 31–54.

10 S. Fitzpatrick, *Education and Social Mobility in the Soviet Union 1921–34*, Cambridge, 1979, pp. 24–5; J. Barber, *Soviet Historians in Crisis, 1928–1932*, London, 1981, p. vii. For Pokrovsky's biography, see pp. 20–3.

11 N. Tumarkin, *Lenin Lives! The Lenin Cult in Soviet Russia*, Cambridge, Mass., 1983, p. 76.

12 ibid., pp. 241–2.

13 ibid., p. 179.

14 ibid., p. 255.

15 S. Alliluyeva, *Twenty Letters to a Friend*, Harmondsworth, 1968, p. 161; for another way in which peasants felt historically at a loss in these years, therefore seeking comfort and meaning from the Apocalypse, see L. Viola, 'The Peasant Nightmare: visions of Apocalypse in the Soviet countryside', *Journal of Modern History*, 62, 1990, pp. 747–70.

16 J. Barber, 'The establishment of intellectual orthodoxy in the USSR 1928–1934', *Past and Present*, 83, 1979 says (p. 148) that the proletarian element among students rose from 25 per cent (1928) to 58 per cent (1932); cf. also S. Fitzpatrick, 'Stalin and the making of a new elite 1928–1939', *Slavic Review*, 38, 1979.

17 J. Barber, *Soviet Historians in Crisis, 1928–1932*, p. 12.

18 ibid., p. 41.

19 See, for example, R. Medvedev, *All Stalin's Men*, Oxford, 1983, pp. 114–15.

20 Cited by J. Barber, *Soviet Historians in Crisis, 1928–32*, p. 124.

21 G.M. Enteen, 'Marxist historians during the Cultural Revolution: a case study of professional infighting' in S. Fitzpatrick (ed.), *Cultural Revolution in Russia*, Bloomington, Ind., 1978, pp. 155, 165; cf. also his 'Writing party history in the USSR: the case of E.M. Iaroslavskii', *Journal of Contemporary History*, 21, 1986, pp. 321–39; J. Barber, *Soviet Historians in Crisis 1928–1932*, pp. 126–9.

22 S. Fitzpatrick, *Education and Social Mobility in the Soviet Union*, pp. 230–1.

23 G.S. Counts, *The Challenge of Soviet Education*, New York, 1957, pp. 65–6.

24 My copy of this tome was printed and published in distant Sydney in 1942 by 'Current Book Distributors'.

25 S. Fitzpatrick, *Education and Social Mobility in the Soviet Union*, p. 323; for some detailed examples of Stalin's editing, see N.N. Maslov, 'Short course of the history

of the All-Russian Communist Party (Bolshevik) – an encyclopaedia of Stalin's person-ality cult', *Soviet Studies in History*, 28, 1989–90, pp. 41–68.

26 M. Ferro, *October 1917*, p.vii.

27 E. Ginzburg, *Within the Whirlwind*, London, 1989, p. 68; the earlier volume of this historian-purgee's memoirs, *Into the Whirlwind*, Harmondsworth, 1968 is perhaps the most remarkable and moving of the genre.

28 S. Fitzpatrick, *Education and Social Mobility in the Soviet Union*, p. 118.

29 See generally M. Lewin, *The Making of the Soviet System: Essays in the Social History of Inter-war Russia*, London, 1985.

30 ibid., pp. 63–5.

31 ibid., p. 38 and for a fine developed account, see L.H. Siegelbaum, *Stakhanovism and the Politics of Productivity in the USSR 1935–41*, Cambridge, 1988.

32 N. Mandelstam, *Hope Abandoned: A Memoir*, London, 1974, pp. 59, 161.

33 *History of the Communist Party of the Soviet Union – Bolsheviks: Short Course*, Sydney, 1942, p. 347.

34 O. Bartov, op. cit., p. 153; for a fine recent summary by a new social historian of the impact of the war, see S. Fitzpatrick, '*War and Society* in Soviet context: Soviet labor before, during and after World War II', *International Labor and Working-Class History*, 35, 1989, pp. 37–52; in more detail, cf. S.J. Linz (ed.), *The Impact of World War II on the Soviet Union*, Totowa, 1985 which also has a chapter by Fitzpatrick (pp. 129–56); and for the army in the Civil War, cf. O. Figes, 'The Red Army and mass mobilization during the Russian Civil War', *Past and Present*, 129, 1990, pp. 168–211.

35 A. Nove, 'Soviet peasantry in World War II', in S.J. Linz (ed.), op. cit., p. 81; for an attempt at comparison, see A. Marwick, *War and Social Change in the Twentieth Century*, London, 1974.

36 C. Malaparte, *Kaputt*, London, 1948, pp. 206–11.

37 J. Barber, *Soviet Historians in Crisis, 1928–32*, p. 140; cf. K. Shteppa, *Russian Historians and the Soviet State*, New Brunswick, N.J.,1962 which lists at great length the able work done in some non-controversial fields during the Stalin period.

38 See, for example, I. Deutscher, *Stalin: A Political Biography*, Harmondsworth, 1966, pp. 349, 357–8; or for Ivan, I. Grey, *Ivan the Terrible*, London, 1964.

39 M. Seton, *Sergei M. Eisenstein*, London, 1978, pp. 17–23.

40 ibid., p. 36.

41 ibid., p. 75.

42 ibid., pp. 96–7.

43 S.M. Eisenstein, *Complete Films (Together with an Unpublished Essay)*, London, 1974, p. 51. John Reed's book, on which the film was loosely based, also fell out of favour under Stalin. For a characteristically pungent assessment of it and the event it described, see A.J.P. Taylor, 'Introduction' to J. Reed, *Ten Days that Shook the World*, rev. edn, Harmondsworth, 1977. The publication of this introduction was delayed by more than a decade because of the hostility of the British communist publishing house, Lawrence & Wishart (p. vii).

44 M. Seton, op. cit., p. 254.

45 S.M. Eisenstein, op. cit., pp. 89–97. It was later claimed that the film was 'lost' to German bombing in 1942 but it was probably destroyed by Soviet officials in 1937. It has only been very partially reconstituted.

46 M. Seton, op. cit., p. 379.

47 ibid., p. 386.

48 M. Le Fanu, 'Writing in images: the Eisenstein enigma', *Encounter*, LXXII, February 1989, p. 48.

49 M. Perrie, *The Image of Ivan the Terrible in Russian Folklore*, Cambridge, 1987, pp. 21–2; cf. also her 'Folklore as evidence of peasant *mentalité*: social attitudes and values in Russian popular culture', *Russian Review*, 45, 1989, pp. 119–43. Ironically,

the revolutionaries of November 1917 were, at least according to John Reed, attacked by their enemies as *oprichniki*. J. Reed, 1966, op. cit., p. 148.

50 M. Perrie, *The Image of Ivan the Terrible*, p. 114.

51 ibid., p. 22.

52 So was its sexual morality. The portrayal of Ivan's relationship with his wife Anastasia ought to have pleased *True Romance* readers and is splendid evidence on the abandonment of the Revolution's early enthusiasm for sexual equality. Actually Ivan had seven wives, cf. I. Grey, *Ivan the Terrible*.

53 S. Eisenstein and N. Cherkasov, 'A conversation in the Kremlin. Stalin on *Ivan the Terrible*', *Encounter*, LXXII, February 1989, p. 3.

54 See S. M. Eisenstein, *Ivan the Terrible: A Screenplay*, New York, 1962.

55 M. Seton, op. cit., pp. 462–3.

56 For this snide comment, see W. Laqueur, *Soviet Realities: Culture and Politics from Stalin to Gorbachev*, New Brunswick, NJ, 1990, p. xiii; Laqueur had earlier published a useful if predictably hostile narration about the impact of *glasnost, The Long Road to Freedom: Russia and 'Glasnost'*, London, 1989.

57 S. Fitzpatrick, 'A Student in Moscow, 1966', *Wilson Quarterly*, VI, 1982, p. 134.

58 I. Deutscher, *Stalin* was first published by OUP in 1949. It went into a Penguin edition in 1966 and was reprinted ten times in the next twenty years; cf. *The Prophet Armed. Trotsky: 1879–1921*, Oxford, 1954; *The Prophet Unarmed. Trotsky: 1921–9*, Oxford, 1959; *The Prophet Outcast. Trotsky: 1929–40*, Oxford, 1963. Perhaps fittingly, Deutscher never did complete his other projects, a life of Lenin and a history of the Russian Revolution.

59 See I. Deutscher, *The Non-Jewish Jew and Other Essays*, Oxford, 1968.

60 ibid., p. 18.

61 D. Horowitz, 'Introduction' to *Isaac Deutscher: The Man and His Work*, London, 1971, p. 11; I. Deutscher, *Marxism, Wars and Revolutions: Essays from Four Decades* (ed. T. Deutscher), London, 1984, pp. 1–16.

62 I. Deutscher, *Stalin*, Harmondsworth, 1966, p. 11.

63 I. Deutscher, *The Non-Jewish Jew and Other Essays*, p. 27.

64 ibid., pp. 33–5.

65 ibid., p. 120; I. Deutscher, *Marxism, Wars and Revolutions*, pp. 243–4. In this as in almost every other matter, Deutscher was the obverse of Sir Lewis Namier. Cf. chapter 1 above.

66 L. Labedz, 'Deutscher as historian and prophet II', *Survey*, 23, 1977–8, pp. 148, 153. This article has recently been re-published in a collection of Labedz's essays. L. Labedz, *The Use and Abuse of Sovietology*, New Brunswick, NJ, 1989. Brzezinski provides a foreword.

67 I. Deutscher, *Stalin*, p.44.

68 ibid., p. 11.

69 ibid., p. 379. Deutscher did not become involved in what have become the steadily more arcane debates about how many actually died in the purges (though there is a rather jejune posthumous pictorial history, I. and T. Deutscher, *The Great Purges*, Oxford, 1984).

70 ibid., pp. 296–7, 553.

71 ibid., p. 328.

72 ibid., pp. 335–6. Such a prefiguring was not seen by all as an advantage, cf. D. Orlovsky, 'Social history and its categories', *Slavic Review*, 47, 1988, p. 621.

73 T. Deutscher, 'Work in Progress' in D. Horowitz (ed.), op. cit., p. 74.

74 I. Deutscher, *The Great Contest: Russia and the West*, London, 1960, pp. 65, 79–80.

75 L. Labedz, op. cit., p. 164.

76 M. Ferro, *The Russian Revolution of February 1917*, London, 1972; *October 1917: A Social History of the Russian Revolution*, London, 1980 (and translated by Norman Stone). A paperback edition of *October* has now appeared. It is somewhat confusedly

entitled, *The Bolshevik Revolution: A Social History of the Russian Revolution*, London, 1985; cf. also his 'third volume', not translated into English, *Des Soviets au communisme bureaucratique*, Paris, 1980; cf. also his personal recollections of penetrating Soviet history in his *Histoires de Russie et d'ailleurs: entretiens avec Jules Chancel et Jean-François Sabouret*, Paris, 1990, pp. 39–43.

77 M. Ferro, *October 1917*, p. 231.

78 ibid., p. 265.

79 See B.N. Ponomarov *et al.*, *History of the Communist Party of the Soviet Union*, Moscow, 1960.

80 B. Pasternak, *Doctor Zhivago*, London, 1958. The book was first published by the left-wing Italian publishing house Feltrinelli in 1957. This connection between anti-Stalinism in the USSR and the 'myth of the Resistance and anti-Fascism' in Italy deserves further analysis. For a brief introduction, see P. Levi, *Boris Pasternak*, London, 1990, pp. 241–2.

81 A. Solzhenitsyn, *One Day in the Life of Ivan Denisovich*, London, 1963 (first published in *Novy Mir*, November 1962). Solzhenitsyn, assisted by figures like Labedz, would of course earn enormous fame in the West and write a succession of historical novels, some with a decidedly nineteenth-century, Russian nationalist, Slavophile air. See L. Labedz (ed.), *Solzhenitsyn: A Documentary Record*, Harmondsworth, 1972, but cf. a recent critique of Solzhenitsyn's enthusiasm for authority, M. Confino, 'Solzhenitsyn, the West, and the new Russian nationalism', *Journal of Contemporary History*, 26, 1991, pp. 611–36.

82 E. Ginzburg, *Into the Whirlwind*; cf. fn.19 above.

83 R.W. Davies, *Soviet History in the Gorbachev Revolution*, London, 1989, pp. 3–4; G. Lyons (ed.), *The Russian Version of the Second World War: The History of the War as Taught to Soviet School Children*, London, 1976, p. 87; Susan Linz has estimated that, by 1985, 15,000 books had been written about the Great Patriotic War. See S.J. Linz, op. cit., p. 1.

84 See B. Kagarlitsky, *The Thinking Reed: Intellectuals and the Soviet State 1917 to the Present*, London, 1988, pp. 291–2, 297. T. Deutscher was again one of the foreign patrons of this dissident.

85 D. Joravsky, 'Introduction' to R. Medvedev, *Let History Judge*, London, 1975, p. ix.

86 R. Medvedev and G. Chiesa, *Time of Change: An Insider's View of Russia's Transformation*, New York, 1989. It was appropriate that Medvedev's collaborator in this book was Chiesa, long-time correspondent of the PCI's paper, *L'Unità*, in Moscow. A revised and expanded edition of *Let History Judge*, Oxford, 1989 has now appeared. A Russian-language edition had come out in the USA in 1974 and Peking also published a Chinese version.

87 See, for example, Z.A. Medvedev, *Rise and Fall of T.D. Lysenko*, New York, 1969; *Andropov*, Oxford, 1983; *Gorbachev*, Oxford, 1987, and especially, his account, in collaboration with his brother, of his persecution by Brezhnevite psychiatrists, Z.A. and R.A. Medvedev, *A Question of Madness*, London, 1971. Among those who campaigned for the release of Zhores were Sakharov and Solzhenitsyn.

88 D. Joravsky, op. cit., p. x.

89 See, for example, R. Medvedev, *Political Essays*, Nottingham, 1976; *Khrushchev, a Biography*, New York, 1983; *All Stalin's Men*. This last is a 'real intellectual's' denunciation of such unlettered or under-trained Stalinist left-overs as Voroshilov, Mikoyan, Suslov, Molotov, Kaganovitch and Malenkov.

90 R. Medvedev, *Let History Judge*, p. 566; cf. R. Medvedev (ed.), *The Samizdat Register*, New York, 1977 both for Medvedev's continued defence of Lenin and the October Revolution (pp. 1–71) and for the distancing from Solzhenitsyn.

91 For a typical example, see K.D. Bracher, *The Age of Ideologies: A History of Political Thought in the Twentieth Century*, London, 1984.

92 The basic text is R. Conquest, *The Great Terror: Stalin's Purge of the Thirties*, London, 1968.

93 See, for example, S. Rosefielde. 'An assessment of the sources and use of Gulag forced labour 1929–56', *Soviet Studies,* XXXIII, 1981, pp. 51–87; 'Excess mortality in the Soviet Union: a reconsideration of the demographic consequences of forced industrialization 1929–49', *Soviet Studies,* XXXV, 1983, pp. 385–409. 'Excess deaths and industrialization: a realist theory of Stalinist economic development in the 1930s', *Journal of Contemporary History*, 23, 1988, pp. 277–89.

94 J.A. Getty, *Origins of the Great Purges: The Soviet Communist Party Reconsidered, 1933–8,* Cambridge, 1985, p. 7; for a more technical reply to Rosefielde, see S. Wheatcroft, 'New demographic evidence on excess collectivization deaths: yet another *Kliukva* from Steven Rosefielde', *Slavic Review*, 44, 1985, pp. 505–8 and letter, *Slavic Review*, 45, 1986, pp. 298–9; B.A. Anderson and B.D. Silver, 'Demographic analysis and population catastrophes in the USSR', *Slavic Review*, 44, 1985, pp. 517–36 and Rosefielde's re-statement 'New demographic evidence on collectivization deaths: a rejoinder to Stephen Wheatcroft', pp. 509–16.

95 R. Pipes, *Russia under the Old Regime*, Harmondsworth, 1977, p. xvii.

96 See, for example, R. Pipes, 'Why the Soviet Union thinks it could fight and win a nuclear war', *Commentary,* 64, July 1977, pp. 21–34 (the answer was the survival of such enormous losses in the Great Patriotic War); 'Soviet global strategy', *Commentary*, 69, April 1980, pp. 31–9 (the regime could only survive while it kept up a 'history' of advances. It thus played to win and, anyway, Russia had always been the most tenacious imperial power); cf. R. Pipes, *Survival is Not Enough: Soviet Realities and America's Future*, New York, 1984; 'Solzhenitsyn and the Russian intellectual tradition', *Encounter*, LII, June 1979; 'How vulnerable is the West: survival is not enough', *Survey*, 28, 1984 (and subsequent debate). Pipes has reiterated his historical theses in a massive new book, R. Pipes, *The Russian Revolution*, London, 1991. Cf. also G. Hosking, *The Awakening of the Soviet Union,* Cambridge, Mass., 1990, p. 6. A historian (the biographer of both Lenin and Stalin) with a somewhat comparable world view is Adam Ulam. See A.B. Ulam, *Lenin and the Bolsheviks*, Glasgow, 1966; *Stalin, the Man and His Era*, London, 1974; 'What is "Soviet" – What is "Russian" ', *Encounter*, LXXIV, May 1990, pp. 47–59 (a discussion with George Urban) or his bitter attack on the post-1968 university, *The Fall of the American University*, London, 1972.

97 Z. Brzezinski, *Power and Principle,* London, 1983, p. 382; he was also pleased that Carter accepted the idea of there being totalitarian states (p. 527).

98 For his defence of political science in spite of it all, see J.F. Hough, 'The "Dark Forces", the Totalitarian Model and Soviet history', *Russian Review,* 46, 1987, pp. 397–403 and more generally with M. Fainsod, *How the Soviet Union is Governed*, Cambridge, Mass., 1979, his 'notorious' re-working of the original totalitarianist M. Fainsod, *How Russia is Ruled*, Cambridge, Mass., 1953.

99 For a review of the famous Smolensk archive and the historiography, see J.A. Getty, op. cit., pp. 7–8, 211–20; and for an account of the continuing difficulties confronting a historian in pursuit of the 'facts', see S. Fitzpatrick, 'A closed city and its secret archives: notes on a journey to the Urals', *Journal of Modern History*, 62, 1990, pp. 771–81.

100 S. Fitzpatrick, 'Afterword: revisionism revisited', *Russian Review,* 45, 1986, pp. 411–12. In his recent survey of the historiography of the 1917 Revolution, Edward Acton has also plumped for the 'revisionists', while often implying what he calls 'liberal' (i.e. conservative and totalitarianist) accounts are less helpful than the Soviet regime's own orthodox historiography. See E. Acton, *Rethinking the Russian Revolution*, London, 1990.

101 See *Russian Review*, 45–6, 1986–7; *Slavic Review*, 47, 1988; cf. also S. Fitzpatrick, 'L'identité de classe dans la société de la NEP', *Annales ESC*, 44, 1989, pp. 251–72. This issue of *Annales* included a number of articles on the problem of Stalinism.

102 P. Kenez, 'Stalinism as humdrum politics', *Russian Review*, 45, 1986, p. 396.

103 G.T. Rittersporn, 'History, commemoration and hectoring rhetoric', *Russian Review,* 46, 1987, p. 422.

104 M.S. Gorbachov [sic], *Speeches and Writings,* Oxford, 1986, p. 160. Speech of 8 May 1985 (in answer to Reagan at Bitburg) celebrating 'The Immortal Exploit of the Soviet People', i.e. victory in the Second World War. Gorbachev also preached that it had been the USSR which had first opposed Fascism, and condemned nameless re-writers of history who denied that (p.176). Many of these themes are reiterated in M. Gorbachev, *Perestroika: New Thinking for Our Country and the World,* New York, 1987.

105 See M. Heller, 'Current politics and current historiography', *Survey,* 30, 1989, p. 1.

106 L.H. Siegelbaum, 'Historical revisionism in the USSR', *Radical History Review,* 44, 1989, p. 45. Cf. J. Barber, *Soviet Historians in Crisis, 1928–32,* pp. 15, 134.

107 B. Kagarlitsky, op. cit., p. x.

108 Denise Youngblood has recently remarked of the film: 'One learns *nothing* factual from it — and *everything* that matters about the Stalin period.' See D.J. Youngblood, 'Review of *Repentance*', *American Historical Review,* 95, 1990, pp. 1133–6. I suspect none the less that it will tell historians more about the 1980s than the 1930s. Cf. P. O'Meara, '*Glasnost,* Soviet culture and the debate on history', in R. J. Hill and J.A. Dellebrant (eds), *Gorbachev and 'Perestroika': Towards a New Socialism,* Aldershot, 1989, pp. 112–15.

109 R.W. Davies, *Soviet History in the Gorbachev Revolution,* p. 8; for a droll account of how previously banned foreign novels penetrated Gorbachev's USSR, see E. Tall, 'Behind the scenes: how *Ulysses* was finally published in the Soviet Union', *Slavic Review,* 49, 1990, pp. 183–99.

110 R.W. Davies, *Soviet history in the Gorbachev Revolution,* p. 130.

111 S. Wheatcroft, 'Steadying the energy of history and probing the limits of *glasnost*: Moscow, July to December 1987', *Australian Slavonic and East European Studies,* 1, 1987, p. 74.

112 On a visit to the USA, Gorbachev told the moderate totalitarianist, Stephen Cohen, that he had read his biography of Bukharin but did not agree with all of it! L.H. Siegelbaum, 'Historical revisionism in the USSR', p. 39; cf. S.F. Cohen, *Bukharin and the Bolshevik Revolution,* New York, 1973.

113 R.W. Davies, op. cit., pp. 146, 151.

114 But see the recent and very naive comments of V. Danilov (and what appears their excessive appreciation) in *History Workshop,* V. Danilov, 'We are starting to learn about Trotsky', *History Workshop,* 29, 1990, pp. 136–46; T. Shanin, 'Introduction: Victor Danilov, a profile of a Historian-Discoverer', *History Workshop,* 29, 1990, pp. 134–5.

115 R.W. Davies, op. cit., p. 147.

116 J.W. Boyer and J. Kirshner (eds), 'Roundtable, Moscow, January 1989: Perestroika, history and historians', *Journal of Modern History,* 62, 1990, pp. 799, 805, 807, 829; cf. also D.J. Raleigh (ed.), *Soviet Historians and Perestroika: The First Phase,* Armonk, N.Y., 1989 and M. Rediker, 'The Old Guard, the New Guard, and the people at the gates: new approaches to the study of American history in the USSR', *William and Mary Quarterly,* XLVIII, 1991, pp. 580–97.

117 R.W. Davies, op. cit., pp. 56, 150, 157; P. O'Meara, op. cit., p. 122; cf. also the very bland description of the movement by D.B. Yaroshevski, 'Political participation and public memory: the memorial movement in the USSR, 1987–1989', *History and Memory,* 2, 1990, pp. 5–31.

118 R.W. Davies, op. cit., pp. 182–4; L.H. Siegelbaum, 'Historical revisionism in the USSR', p. 33. The whole board of the leading academic journal, *Voprosy Istorii,* was replaced at the beginning of 1988, V. Danilov becoming one of its editors.

119 J. Hochman, 'The Soviet historical debate', *Orbis,* 32, 1988, p. 369.

120 G. Hosking, op. cit., pp. 79–81, 95–6; for an attack on the alleged absence of non-Russians in Western historiography see A.J. Motyl, ' "Sovietology in one country" or comparative nationality studies?', *Slavic Review*, 48, 1989, pp. 83–8.
121 G. Hosking, op. cit., p. 105.
122 W. Laqueur, op. cit., p. 42.
123 I.J. Tarasulo (ed.), *Gorbachev and Glasnost: Viewpoints from the Soviet Press*, Wilmington, 1989, p. 30; cf. also D. Volkogonov, *Stalin: Triumph and Tragedy*, London, 1991.
124 J.W. Boyer and J. Kirshner (eds), op. cit., p. 786.
125 ibid., pp. 787, 790.
126 ibid., p. 799.
127 ibid., pp. 797–8, 827–8.
128 R.W. Davies, op. cit., p. vii.
129 I.J. Tarasulo (ed.), op. cit., p. 1.

Hiroshima, *mon amour*: under eastern eyes

1 Hachiya Michihiko, *Hiroshima Diary: The Journal of a Japanese Physician August 6–September 30, 1945*, (ed. W. Wells), Chapel Hill, NC, 1955, p. 1. (Note: Japanese ordinarily reverse the Western system of first name, then family name. I have followed their practice in this chapter.)
2 ibid., p. 15.
3 ibid., p. 48.
4 ibid., pp. 81–2. The classic and deeply moving account of the event remains J. Hersey, *Hiroshima*, New York, 1946. For a recent English-language evocation of Hiroshima, of a more literary nature, see R.H. Minear (ed.), *Hiroshima: Three Witnesses*, Princeton, NJ, 1990 (pp. 389–91 lists other English language accounts of the event); cf. M. Selden, 'The United States, Japan, and the Atomic Bomb', *Bulletin of Concerned Asian Scholars*, 23, 1991, pp. 3–12; for a graphic account of the Nagasaki bombing, see *Japan Interpreter*, XII, 1978, pp. 54–93 (account by Hayashi Kyoko).
5 E. Hobsbawm, *Nations and Nationalism since 1780: Programme, Myth, Reality*, Cambridge, 1990, pp. 157, 174; cf. also the not dissimilar views of the conservative journalist, Karel Van Wolferen (his book is dedicated to Leo Labedz). K. Van Wolferen, *The Enigma of Japanese Power: People and Politics in a Stateless Nation*, London, 1989.
6 W.H. McNeill, *Polyethnicity and National Unity in World History*, Toronto, 1986, pp. 4, 6, 15, 17.
7 Tsurumi Shunsuke, *An Intellectual History of Wartime Japan 1931–1945*, London, 1986, p. vii gives the war this title. Actually, the naming of Japan's war is itself a matter of controversy. It varies between 'the Great East Asian War' (the government's official title after December 1941), the blander 'Pacific War' (emphasising the US–Japan conflict) and Tsurumi's radical 'Fifteen Years' War'.
8 P. Kennedy, *The Rise and Fall of the Great Powers: Economic Change and Military Conflict from 1500 to 2000*, London, 1988, especially pp. 591–608.
9 E.W. Said, *Orientalism*, London, 1978. Said's concentration is very much on the Arab 'Near East' but he implies that what is true there is true elsewhere in 'Asia'.
10 See, for example, D.D. Buck, 'Editor's introduction: forum on universalism and relativism in Asian Studies', *Journal of Asian Studies*, 50, 1991, pp. 29–34.
11 R. Mouer and Sugimoto Yoshio, *Images of Japanese Society: A Study in the Structure of Social Reality*, London, 1986, p. 17. The Singapore, South Korea and Taiwan of the 1990s may want to dispute this claim.
12 J. Hunter, *The Emergence of Modern Japan: An Introductory History since 1853*, London, 1989, pp. 36–7.

13 The comments of R.A.C. Parker, *Struggle for Survival: The History of the Second World War*, Oxford, 1990, p. 1 in this regard have already been noted. See p. 142 above.

14 For basic narratives, see J.M. Meskill, *Hitler and Japan: The Hollow Alliance*, New York, 1966; J.P. Fox, *Germany and the Far Eastern Crisis 1931–1938: A Study in Diplomacy and Ideology*, Oxford, 1982.

15 C. Thorne, *Allies of a Kind: The United States, Britain and the War against Japan, 1941–1945*, London, 1978; cf. his *The Far Eastern War: States and Societies 1941–5*, London, 1986.

16 N. Chomsky, 'The revolutionary pacifism of A.J. Muste: on the backgrounds of the Pacific War' in his *American Power and the New Mandarins*, Harmondsworth, 1969, p. 130.

17 R.H. Minear, 'The wartime studies of Japanese national character', *Japan Interpreter*, XIII, 1980, p. 54; *Victors' Justice: The Tokyo War Crimes Trial*, Princeton, NJ, 1971, p. 150.

18 R.H. Minear, *Victors' Justice*, p. x where he noted 'many Japanese acts on the continent of Asia before and during the war are as repugnant to me as current American acts in Indochina.' Minear pursued his relativisation further by paralleling the US bombing of Nagasaki with the belated Soviet declaration of war against Japan (p. 99).

19 J. Dower, *War without Mercy: Race and Power in the Pacific War*, New York, 1986, pp. ix, 24.

20 In this regard, Dower notes the example of the pamphlet 'How we felt about the war', published in 1946 by Allan Nevins, a very distinguished historian of the USA. J. Dower, op. cit., pp. 33–4.

21 ibid., p. 65. Dower argues (p. 68) that the Japanese fought to the death because they were convinced that the Americans (and, even more, the Australians) would kill them anyway.

22 R.A.C. Parker, op. cit., p. 232.

23 Iriye Akira, *Power and Culture: The Japanese–American War 1941–5*, Cambridge, Mass., 1981, pp. vii, 264–5; cf. also the comment by G.M. Berger, 'The three-dimensional empire: Japanese attitudes and the new order in Asia, 1937–45', *Japan Interpreter*, XII, 1979, pp. 357–8 that the Japanese were searching for a 'third way'; 'the concepts of a new order in Asia and the Co-Prosperity Sphere were the final products of an ongoing effort in Imperial Japan to resolve the dilemma of standing between Asia and the West'. For Iriye's presidential address as 1988 President of the AHA, see Iriye Akira, 'The internationalisation of history', *American Historical Review*, 94, 1989, pp. 1–10.

24 J. Dower, op. cit., pp. 119–22; R.H. Minear, 'The wartime studies of Japanese national character', pp. 39–44.

25 R. Benedict, *The Chrysanthemum and the Sword: Patterns of Japanese Culture*, Rutland, 1954 (first published Boston, 1946), pp. 2, 70, 73, 300, 306–7, 309, 316; cf. her *Race and Racism*, London, 1942.

26 For typical comments, see J.C. Grew, *Ten Years in Japan: A Contemporary Record Drawn from the Diaries and Private and Official Papers*, New York, 1944, pp. xi, 84, 149; and, for an intelligent survey of Grew's career and post-war role, see H.B. Schonberger, *Aftermath of War: Americans and the Remaking of Japan*, Kent, Ohio, 1989, pp. 11–39.

27 J. Dower, op. cit., p. 132; Nishi Toshio, *Unconditional Democracy: Education and Politics in Occupied Japan 1945–1952*, Stanford, 1982, p. 41.

28 R.H. Minear, 'The wartime studies of Japanese national character', p. 52; E.O. Reischauer, *The United States and Japan*, Cambridge, Mass., 1950, pp. 35, 49, 51, 101, 143 (p. 129 also says the Nazis were ridiculous when they tried to revive 'long dead cults' but, in Japan, this ancient and medieval history was still 'alive'.) In 1948–9, Reischauer, then an Associate Professor of Far Eastern languages at Harvard, had been a member of the

US Cultural Science mission in Japan. See Nishi Toshio, op. cit., pp. 230–2. He would also strongly defend US policy in Vietnam; and cf. also his *Japan Past and Present*, London, 1964 (first published 1946).

29 E.O. Reischauer, *The United States and Japan*, pp. xiii, 51, 183. In the 1970s, Zbigniew Brzezinski strayed from his normal fields of operation to write a surprisingly pessimistic report on Japan. See Z. Brzezinski, *The Fragile Blossom: Crisis and Change in Japan*, New York, 1972.

30 For some comment, see Kawamura Nozumu, 'The historical background of arguments emphasizing the uniqueness of Japanese society', *Social Analysis*, 5–6, 1980, pp. 52–3; or, for a detailed recent study of the 1919 rice riots and their historiography, see M. Lewis, *Rioters and Citizens: Mass Protest in Imperial Japan*, Berkeley, Calif., 1990.

31 R. Mouer and Sugimoto Yoshio, op. cit., p. 170.

32 See, for example, S. K. Johnson, *The Japanese through American Eyes*, Stanford, 1988, p. 169. Nakasone subsequently apologised and asserted that he had been misquoted.

33 Though the sociologists Mouer and Sugimoto, writing in the early 1980s, claimed that inequality of income distribution in Japan then actually paralleled that of the USA. R. Mouer and Sugimoto Yoshio, op. cit., pp. 127–8.

34 For a very detailed account see A.D. Coox, *Nomonhan: Japan against Russia 1939*, 2 vols, Stanford, 1985. The 18,000 Japanese casualties at Nomonhan were kept hidden until 1966. Ienaga Saburo, *Japan's Last War: World War II and the Japanese, 1931–1945*, Oxford, 1979, p. 82 (first published in Japanese, 1968).

35 Tsurumi Shunsuke, op. cit., p. 30; cf. G.M. Berger, op. cit., p. 355 who notes the ironical relief, after Pearl Harbor, that the time of confusion was over.

36 Ienega Saburo, op. cit., p. 101. The use of the weak term 'incident' in this and other cases also had a deliberately obfuscating purpose.

37 Daqing Yang, 'A Sino-Japanese controversy: the Nanjing atrocity as history', *Sino-Japanese Studies*, III, 1990, pp. 17–18, 20–1. China's new memorial claims the death toll was 300,000 (p. 25). *Pace* the Grandi diaries (see p. 233, n101 above), a number of 'amendments' were now revealed in a Japanese general's account of Nanjing (p. 23).

38 P. Williams and D. Wallace, *Unit 731: Japan's Secret Biological Warfare in World War II*, New York, 1989, p. 16; cf. Ienaga Saburo, op. cit., pp. 188–9.

39 P. Williams and D. Wallace, op. cit., pp. 48–9.

40 ibid., p. 23.

41 ibid., pp. 68–9.

42 ibid., p. 32.

43 ibid., pp. 31, 77–9.

44 ibid., pp. 84–6; Ienaga Saburo, op. cit., p. 189.

45 P. Williams and D. Wallace, op. cit., pp. 181–2, 196, 209.

46 J.W. Powell, 'Japan's germ warfare: the US cover-up of a war crime', *Bulletin of Concerned Asian Scholars*, 12, 1980, p. 4. Japanese did assist in the research of this latter documentary. See the acknowledgements at the start of P. Williams and D. Wallace, op. cit.

47 S. Leavenworth, 'Revising the truth', *Japanalysis*, November–December 1984, p. 8.

48 P. Williams and D. Wallace, op. cit., pp. 238, 240.

49 C. Thorne, *The Far Eastern War*, pp. 15, 82.

50 The story of the 1989 documentary *Senso's Daughters* about these women is similar to the tale of the investigation of Unit 731. Its producer, Sekiguchi Noriko, made it in Australia since it was impossible to imagine disclosing such a taboo subject in Japan. Cf., however, Ienaga Saburo, op. cit., pp. 159, 166.

51 Probably the most death-dealing air-raid of the war was the US firebombing of Tokyo on 9–10 March 1945: 100,000 died in the resultant firestorm; one million were rendered homeless. J. Dower, op. cit., pp. 40–1.

52 ibid., p. 47; from 1939, all Koreans were expected to adopt Japanese names and their culture was derided or suppressed. See, for example, Tsurumi Shunsuke, op. cit., p. 56 (after the 1923 Tokyo earthquake, some 6,000 Koreans were hunted down and massacred by local Japanese, p. 54); cf. also M. Weiner, *The Origins of the Korean Community in Japan 1910–1923,* Manchester, 1989.

53 R. Dore, *Shinohata: A Portrait of a Japanese Village*, London, 1978, p. 49.

54 Such a body, set up in 1910 and thereafter 'a leading force in village life', seems to parallel those Imperial German patriotic leagues studied by Geoff Eley whose work is mentioned in chapter 3 above. See J. Hunter, op. cit., p. 272 (cf. p. 145 for the Patriotic Women's Association).

55 R. Dore, op. cit., pp. 49–50.

56 Ienaga Saburō, *op. cit.*, p. 223; cf. fn.28 for Reischauer's use of the same word.

57 For a recent example of his writing, see Maruyama Masao, 'The structure of the *Matsurigoto:* the *basso ostinato* of Japanese political life', in S. Henny and J.-P. Lehmann (eds), *Themes and Theories in Modern Japanese History: Essays in Memory of Richard Storry*, London, 1988, pp. 27–43. For a useful analysis of Maruyama as a 'modernist', see A.E. Barshay, *State and Intellectual in Imperial Japan: The Public Man in Crisis*, Berkeley, Calif., 1988, especially pp. 224–52.

58 Maruyama Masao, *Thought and Behaviour in Modern Japanese Politics*, London, 1963, p. xii.

59 Maruyama Masao, 'Theory and psychology of ultra-nationalism' (first published May 1946), in ibid., p. 9.

60 G. McCormack, '1930s Japan. Fascist?', *Social Analysis*, 5–6, 1980, p. 134; cf. also the subtle comparative analysis in G.J. Kasza, *The State and the Mass Media in Japan, 1918–1945,* Berkeley, Calif., 1988.

61 For a droll example of a Japanese Marxist's reverence for the dead Marx, see G.C. Allen, *Appointment in Japan: Memories of Sixty Years*, London, 1983, p. 67.

62 Maruyama Masao, 'The ideology and dynamics of Japanese fascism' (first given as a lecture to Tokyo University in 1947), published in his *Thought and Behaviour in Modern Japanese Politics*, p. 25.

63 ibid., p. 56. Maruyama also made some fascinating comments about the diffuse nature of power in the Imperial elite. He talked about 'a war without planning' and declared Japanese imperialism to have sprung from 'a vast accumulation of illogical decisions'. In other words, he implied that the first problem about Japanese policy at Pearl Harbor lay in the question 'who ruled in Tokyo?' and in the difficulty of answering it. He was saying something very like what A.J.P. Taylor and other historians would say about Imperial Germany when they asked 'who ruled in Berlin?' in 1914.

64 ibid., p. 56.

65 ibid., pp. 59–60.

66 Maruyama Masao, 'Theory and psychology of ultra-nationalism', in ibid., pp. 1–2.

67 See, for example, H. Conroy, 'Concerning Japanese fascism', *Journal of Asian Studies*, XL, 1980, p. 327; A.E. Barshay, op. cit., p. xv.

68 Barrington Moore, *Social Origins of Dictatorship and Democracy: Lord and Peasant in the Making of the Modern World,* Harmondsworth, 1967, pp. 228–313 on 'Asian Fascism: Japan'.

69 See, for example, P. Duus and D.I. Okimoto, 'Fascism and the history of pre-war Japan: the failure of a concept', *Journal of Asian Studies*, XXXIX, 1979, p. 70.

70 In her analysis, Elise Tipton emphasises the bureaucratic complexity of policing in Japan. 'Thought control' was never only in the hands of the *Tokkō,* the thought police, and especially from the mid-1930s, they suffered the rivalry of the Army's *Kempeitai.* This sort of institutional confusion might not astonish a 'functionalist' analyst of Nazi Germany but, for Tipton, the parallel is more with Bismarckian Germany. See E.K. Tipton, *The Japanese Police State: The 'Tokkō' in Interwar Japan*, Sydney, 1990,

pp. 33, 107, 120, 137. She does note the 1933 death of the dissident novelist, Kobayashi Takiji, probably at police hands. 'Besides wounds from beating and kicking, there were traces of hot tongs on his forehead, over a dozen holes in his thigh as if made by a nail or drill, broken fingers and numerous other gruesome injuries' (p. 26).

71 R.H. Mitchell, *Thought Control in Prewar Japan*, Ithaca, N.Y., 1976, p. 147.

72 Tsurumi Shunsuke, op. cit., p. 12.

73 P. Duus and D.I. Okimoto, op. cit., p. 66; cf. also J.K. Fairbank, E.O. Reischauer and A.M. Craig, *East Asia: The Modern Transformation*, New York, 1962, as cited by H. Lubasz (ed.), *Fascism: Three Major Regimes*, New York, 1973, p. 183; cf. the recent P. Brooker, *The Faces of Fraternalism: Nazi Germany, Fascist Italy, and Imperial Japan*, Oxford, 1991, which deploys the concept of 'fraternalism' to re-state the similarities of these regimes.

74 R.H. Mitchell, op. cit., p. 189; cf. G.M. Wilson, *Radical Nationalist in Japan: Kita Ikki 1883–1937*, Cambridge, Mass., 1969, as a study of the potential for Peronism in Japan (or 'left fascism' on the model of S.M. Lipset) and G. Kasza, 'Fascism from below? A comparative perspective on the Japanese Right, 1931–1936', *Journal of Contemporary History*, 19, 1984, pp. 607–29. Kasza uses models from the historiography of Europe, and notably those of conservative, Stanley Payne, to argue that mainstream Japanese politics were merely of the 'authoritarian Right'.

75 E.K. Tipton, op. cit., p. 13.

76 This was the term especially favoured by 'value-free' 1950s US scholarship anxious that Japan be re-admitted to full membership of the capitalist 'West'. See G. McCormack, op. cit., p. 136.

77 See, for example, M. Fletcher, 'Intellectuals and fascism in early Shōwa Japan', *Journal of Asian Studies*, XXXIX, 1979, pp. 62–3; cf. B.-A. Shillony, *Revolt in Japan: The Young Officers and the February 26, 1936 Incident*, Princeton, NJ, 1973; 'Universities and students in wartime Japan', *Journal of Asian Studies*, XLV, 1986, pp. 769–87 and, more generally, his *Politics and Culture in Wartime Japan*, Oxford, 1981.

78 G. McCormack, op. cit., p. 142.

79 Maruyama Masao, 'Nationalism in Japan: its theoretical background and prospects' in his *Thought and Behaviour in Modern Japanese Politics*, p. 152. Again note Maruyama's perceptive use of something like the notion of *mentalité*, without actually employing the term.

80 R. Dore, op. cit., p. 207.

81 For a detailed if disjointed study, see Nishi Toshio, op. cit.

82 S.M. Garon, 'The imperial bureaucracy and labor policy in postwar Japan', *Journal of Asian Studies*, XLIII, 1984, p. 442, cf. also his *The State and Labor in Modern Japan*, Berkeley, Calif., 1987.

83 S.M. Garon, 'The imperial and labor policy in postwar Japan', pp. 453–5.

84 The Japanese term for this event, *ishin*, apparently means 'renovation' rather than 'restoration', despite that common English-language usage. J. Hunter, op. cit., p. 9. For a recent attempt to search out parallels between the Meiji restoration and the Italian Risorgimento, see E. Morelli (ed.), *Lo Stato liberale italiano e l'Età Meiji*, Rome, 1987.

85 R. Dore, op. cit., p. 41.

86 I.P. Hall, *Mori Arinori*, Cambridge, Mass., 1973, p. 189; cf. J. Hunter, 'Language reform in Meiji Japan: the views of Maejima Hisoka' in S. Henny and J.-P. Lehmann, op. cit., p. 104.

87 J.V. Koschmann, *The Mito Ideology: Discourse, Reform, and Insurrection in Late Tokugawa Japan 1790–1864*, Berkeley, Calif., 1987, p. 114. The aims of such ideologists to unite thought and action echo matters familiar in the Italian Risorgimento. Similarly, if momentary troubles were hard to keep out of Japanese history, unity could always be explained as the product of the *longue durée*.

88 I.P. Hall, op. cit., pp. 352, 397–9, 411, 424; cf. H. Wray, 'The lesson of the textbooks',

in H. Wray and H. Conroy (eds), *Japan Examined: Perspectives on Modern Japanese History,* Honolulu, Hawaii, 1983, pp. 282–90.

89 Yamazumi Masami, 'Educational democracy versus state control' in G. McCormack and Sugimoto Yoshio (eds), *Democracy in Contemporary Japan,* Sydney, 1986, p. 90.

90 B.C. Duke, *Japan's Militant Teachers: A History of the Left-wing Teachers' Movement,* Honolulu, Hawaii, 1973, p. 11.

91 Yamazumi Masami, op. cit., p. 90.

92 C. Gluck, *Japan's Modern Myths: Ideology in the Late Meiji Period,* Princeton, NJ, 1985, pp. 3, 247.

93 ibid., pp. 281–2; cf. C. Blacker, 'Two Shinto myths: the Golden Age and the chosen people' in S. Henny and J.-P. Lehmann, op. cit., pp. 64–77 in which she argues that the Japanese sense of being a 'chosen people' was greater even than that of the Jews.

94 Cf. R. Benedict, *The Chrysanthemum and the Sword,* pp. 87–8.

95 E.K. Tipton, op. cit., pp. 23, 62.

96 ibid., p. 17.

97 For a description of the ceremonies, see J.C. Grew, op. cit., pp. 352–3. In the wartime Japanese empire, 1942 was proclaimed the year 2602.

98 Tsurumi Shunsuki, op. cit., pp. 28–9. He was Minodo Kyōki, Professor of Logic and Psychology at Keiō University; M. Weiner, op. cit., p. 21, quoting the Tokyo paper, *Mainichi Shimbun.*

99 The classic study is the beautifully nuanced novel Tanizaki Junichirō, *The Makioka Sisters,* London, 1983, first published in Japanese, 1943–8. (The book was the object of wartime censorship.) German phrases like *Auf Wiedersehen,* German beer and Schubert songs in the 1930s gradually penetrate the world of this declining upper-class family. They are told you can make money in Tientsin but are too well bred to do that, 'with the China incident in progress, people no longer wore jewels', and by 1941 their German ex-neighbour is worrying in her letters about the servant problem and the need to economise on stockings (pp.215, 249, 303, 352, 377, 452, 521–3).

100 For a fine account of one area of developing thought control, see S. Garon, 'State and religion in Imperial Japan', *Journal of Japanese Studies,* 12, 1986, pp. 273–302. After 1935, the 'popular' religions (some 1,029 of them!) were doubtless all the more unpopular with officialdom, because the dissident, if generally patriotic, creeds were also vessels of popular history.

101 E.O. Reischauer, *The United States and Japan,* p. 192; cf. G.C. Allen, op. cit., pp. 70, 86 for the huge influence of US film in inter-war Japan.

102 It was entitled *Nihon Shihonshugi Hattasushi Kōza (Lectures on the History of the Development of Japanese Capitalism).* See Hattori Shiso, 'Absolutism and historiographical interpretation', *Japan Interpreter,* XIII, 1980, pp. 15–35; Tsuzuki Chushichi, 'Tenkō or Teikō : the dilemma of a Japanese Marxist between the wars' in S. Henny and J.-P. Lehmann (eds), op. cit., p. 221.

103 J. Hunter, op. cit., p. 244.

104 D. Roden, *Schooldays in Imperial Japan: A Study in the Culture of a Student Elite,* Berkeley, Calif., 1980, pp. 222, 226–7, 235–6, 241–2.

105 Tsurumi Shunsuke, op. cit., pp. 24–7. Ruth Benedict alleged that there were instances of suicide by those who made a slip of the tongue in their recitation. R. Benedict, *The Chrysanthemum and the Sword,* p. 151.

106 Chong-Sik Lee, *Japan and Korea: The Political Dimension,* Stanford, 1985, p. 155. The basis of the claim was a stele discovered by the Japanese military in 1884. The tale of mistranslation and outright forgery typically was not publicised in Japan until the 1970s (see pp. 155–9). Lee adds that the history of Manchuria was similarly distorted.

107 For a recent and rather unconvincing attempt to locate a genuine liberal continuity from pre-war to post-war, see S.H. Nolte, *Liberalism in Modern Japan: Ishibashi Tanzan and his Teachers, 1905–1960,* Berkeley, Calif., 1987.

108 C. Gluck, op. cit., pp. 84–5.

109 Quoted by R.H. Mitchell, op. cit., p. 92.

110 For a remarkably 'value-free' or naive defence of this organisation, see E.J. Notar, 'Japan's wartime labor policy: a search for method', *Journal of Asian Studies*, XLIV, 1985, pp. 311–28.

111 J.C. Grew, op. cit., pp. 177, 303.

112 Nishi Toshio, op. cit., p. 42. MacArthur added his opinion that a 'practical demonstration of Christian ideals' would do the trick.

113 For a fine analysis, see J.W. Dower, *Empire and Aftermath: Yoshida Shigeru and the Japanese Experience, 1878–1954,* Cambridge, Mass., 1979.

114 ibid., pp. 148, 154–6, 164, 176–7, 180–2; cf. W. Edwards, 'Buried discourse: the Toro archaeological site and Japanese national identity in the early postwar period', *Journal of Japanese Studies,* 17, 1991, pp. 1–23 for a fascinating account of the impulse given to 'scientific' archaeology in the post-war years.

115 R. Dore, op. cit., p. 56.

116 *Asia Week*, 20 August 1982, p. 30.

117 Nishi Toshio, op. cit., pp. 183–4.

118 ibid., p. 184.

119 T.P. Rohlen, *Japan's High Schools*, Berkeley, Calif., 1983, pp. 250–6.

120 H.B. Schonberger, op. cit., p. 6.

121 ibid., pp. 90–110.

122 R. Dore, op. cit., p. 56.

123 B.C. Duke, op. cit., p. 102.

124 Cf., for example the case of the poet Tōge Sankichi (R.N. Minear [ed.], *Hiroshima: Three Witnesses*, pp. 277–91). For an account of some later difficulties confronting those anxious to preserve a pictorial representation of the bombings, see H.B. Schonberger, 'People's art as history: Hiroshima survivors and the atomic bomb', *Japan Interpreter*, XII, 1978, pp. 43–53. The first international anti-nuclear conference was convened at Hiroshima in 1955. It was also typical that the US authorities should, after 1945, suppress a Japanese effort to film the effects of the bombing of Hiroshima and Nagasaki. The film was not returned to Japan until 1967 and then the Japanese Ministry of Education decided that it would be best for all concerned if it were not freely released to the public. Nishi Toshio, op. cit., p. 102.

125 A characteristic example was Shigemitsu Mamoru, condemned to seven years gaol in the Tokyo war crimes trial, released after four and a half years and, by December 1954, back at the Ministry of Foreign Affairs. For his extraordinarily disjointed memoirs which, none the less, adroitly place all blame for the 'mistakes' of the 1930s on the militarists, bad luck and the encirclement of Japan, see Shigemitsu Mamoru, *Japan and her Destiny: My Struggle for Peace*, London, 1958. Shigemitsu also praises the heroism and dedication of Japanese servicemen and believes that the spirit of their dead will watch over the next generation.

126 G.R. Packard, *Protest in Tokyo: The Security Treaty Crisis of 1960,* Princeton, NJ, 1966, pp. 26–8.

127 A.D. Coox, 'Foreword' to Hayashi Saburō, *Kogun: The Japanese Army in the Pacific War*, Westport, Conn., 1959, p. v (Hayashi's book was first published in Tokyo, 1951).

128 Hayashi Saburō, op. cit., pp. 1, 4; cf. also Hanayama Shincho's *The Way of Deliverance* (1950) which defended those arraigned before the war crimes tribunal. Hanayama was a Buddhist chaplain (A.D. Coox, 'Foreword', p. viii).

129 A.D. Coox, 'Foreword', pp. v–ix.

130 G.R. Packard, op. cit., p. 34.

131 B.C. Duke, op. cit., pp. 131–44.

132 G.R. Packard, op. cit., pp. 126–7 and cf. J.A.A. Stockwin, *The Japanese Socialist Party and Neutralism: A Study of a Political Party and its Foreign Policy,* Melbourne, 1968.

133 G.R. Packard, op. cit., p. vi.

134 For a semi-autobiographical account of being a first-year university student at this time, see Nishi Toshio, op. cit., pp. xxxi–xxxiii.

135 G.R. Packard, op. cit., pp.272–3, 328–9. At this time, Tsurumi Shunsuke publicly resigned his position at the Tokyo Institute of Technology as his protest against the government's policies (p. 275).

136 C. Gluck, 'The people in history: recent trends in Japanese historiography', *Journal of Asian Studies,* XXXVIII, 1978, p. 30.

137 ibid., pp. 28, 38–9, 44–5.

138 G.R. Packard, op. cit., p. 335.

139 ibid., p. 337.

140 G. McCormack and Sugimoto Yoshio, 'Introduction: democracry and Japan', in G. McCormack and Sugimoto Yoshio (eds), *Democracy in Contemporary Japan,* p. 15.

141 G.R. Packard, op. cit., p. 337.

142 Yamazumi Masami, op. cit., p. 98.

143 R.N. Bellah, 'Ienaga Saburō and the search for meaning in modern Japan' in M.B. Jansen (ed.), *Changing Japanese Attitudes towards Modernization*, Princeton, NJ, 1965, pp. 371–3, 376.

144 M. Fletcher, 'Intellectuals and fascism in early Shōwa Japan', p. 43; R.N. Bellah, *Beyond Belief: Essays on Religion in a Post-Traditional World,* New York, 1970, pp. 112–13, 119, 128.

145 R.N. Bellah, 'Ienaga Saburō and the search for meaning in modern Japan', p. 400.

146 ibid., pp. 402–6, 411, 417–20.

147 Ienaga Saburō, op. cit., p. viii.

148 ibid., pp. xiii–xiv, 46–7, 84, 97.

149 ibid., pp. 82, 101, 107, 181, 188–9.

150 ibid., pp. 156–9, 166.

151 ibid., pp. 112–14, 217, 229.

152 Yamazaki Masato, 'History textbooks that provoke an Asian outcry', *Japan Quarterly*, XXXIV, 1987, p. 53. The major text-book publishers allegedly were munificent donors to the coffers of the LDP. *Japan Times,* 5 August 1981.

153 Ienaga Saburō, op. cit., pp. 255–6. He was duly backed by the JTU. See B.C. Duke, op. cit., p. 178.

154 See Chong-Sik Lee, op. cit., p. 151; J. Holliday and G. McCormack, *Japanese Imperialism Today*, Harmondsworth, 1973, pp. 187–90. They say that the official in the Ministry responsible for text-books stated: 'I prefer to be called a rightist. I am an ultranationalist.'

155 Chong-Sik Lee, op. cit., pp. 141–3.

156 ibid., pp. 144–5; cf. for example, *The People's Korea*, 31 July, 14, 21, 28 August, 11 September 1982.

157 Chung-Sik Lee, op. cit., pp. 147–9.

158 Quoted by S. Leavenworth, op. cit., p. 9.

159 Nishimura Hidetoshi, 'Educational reform: commissioning a master plan', *Japan Quarterly*, XXXII, 1985, p. 21. For Nakasone's earlier career, see, for example, *Asia Week*, 10 December 1982, which noted that he had volunteered for war service and, in 1945, been a leading member of the 'Blue Cloud School', sporting a black tie in mourning for Japan's 'lost sovereignty'.

160 For a description, see Murumatsu Michio, 'In search of national identity: the politics and policies of the Nakasone administration', *Journal of Japanese Studies*, 13, 1987, pp. 307–42, or, in the same issue but more inclined to defend Nakasone, K.B. Pyle, 'In pursuit of a grand design: Nakasone betwixt the past and the future', pp. 243–70. For Pyle, Nakasone's nationalism was 'based on the realization that it is now in Japan's national interest, as a new leading nation, to be internationalist' (p. 265); cf. also his

earlier article, 'The future of Japanese nationality: an essay in contemporary history', *Journal of Japanese Studies,* 8, 1982, pp. 233–63 which accepts the legitimacy of Japanese nationalism and claims that it has a changed social base which in turn implies that its proponents will be more forward-looking than in the past.

161 Yamazaki Masuto, op. cit., pp. 50–2. The Minister, Fujio Masayuki, the next year asked a reporter in disgust: 'Aggression, aggression, is Japan the only country to commit these evil acts called aggression?' In August 1985, Nakasone had undertaken a Japanese version of Bitburg by becoming the first post-war Prime Minister officially to visit the Yasukuni shrine for the war dead (which included the burial places of some convicted war criminals) (p. 54); cf. Kim Hong-Nack, 'Perspectives on recent Sino-Japanese relations', *Journal of East Asian Affairs,* IV, 1990, pp. 410–14.

162 See, for example, Ikuhito Hata, 'When ideologues rewrite history', *Japan Echo,* XIII, 1986, pp. 73–8 giving examples of the Ministry's insistence on changes to a right-wing *New History of Japan.* In 1985 the Ministry made 241 mandatory revisions to this text and 478 recommended ones.

163 *Far Eastern Economic Review,* 23 March 1989. I am particularly grateful to Gavin McCormack for his generosity in letting me consult his file, built up over several years, on the text-book question.

164 C. Gluck, *Japan's Modern Myths,* p. 284.

165 See, for example, Ishihara Shintarō, *The Japan Which Can Say NO,* New York, 1991.

Conclusion

1 This was the title of the last volume of his massive, six-volume history of Australia. See C.M.H. Clark, *A History of Australia,* Melbourne, 1962–87.

2 For an introductory biography, see S. Holt, *Manning Clark and Australian History 1915–1963,* St Lucia, 1982.

3 As quoted in R. Bosworth, (Australian) ABC radio programme on '*Kristallnacht*', first broadcast 8 November 1988.

4 There is a vast literature on whether Spanish Fascism was 'Spanish' or 'Fascist'. For some introduction, see P. Preston, 'War of words: the Spanish Civil War and the historians' in P. Preston (ed.), *Revolution and War in Spain 1931–1939,* London, 1984, pp. 1–13.

5 J.P. Fusi, *Franco: A Biography,* London, 1987, p. 171. In so saying (in November 1964), Franco was denying that his regime marked any sort of parenthesis in Spanish history.

6 The classic exposé is H. Southworth, *Guernica! Guernica! A Study of Journalism, Propaganda and History,* Berkeley, Calif., 1977.

7 G. Jackson, *The Spanish Republic and the Civil War, 1931–1939,* Princeton, NJ, 1965. The book won the 1966 American Historical Association prize for European history.

8 G. Jackson, *Historian's Quest,* New York, 1969.

9 G. Jackson, *The Spanish Republic and the Civil War, 1931–1939,* pp. v–vi; *Historian's Quest,* p. 234; *A Concise History of the Spanish Civil War,* London, 1974, p. 7.

10 G. Jackson, *A Concise History of the Spanish Civil War,* p. 7.

11 See, for example, R. Carr, *Spain 1808–1939,* Oxford, 1966; R.Carr (ed.), *The Republic and the Civil War in Spain,* London, 1971 and cf. R.Carr, *English Fox Hunting: A History,* London, 1976.

12 See, for example, S.G. Payne, *Falange: A History of Spanish Fascism,* Stanford, 1961; *Franco's Spain,* London, 1968; *The Spanish Revolution,* London, 1970 and, among his many articles, 'Fascism and Right Authoritarianism — the Iberian world — the last twenty years', *Journal of Contemporary History,* 21, 1986, pp. 163–77.

13 See, for example, H. Thomas, *The Spanish Civil War,* rev. edn, Hardmondsworth, 1965. As Lord Thomas of Swynneston, he, with Stanley Payne, is a member of the editorial board of the *Journal of Contemporary History.*

14 See above p. 170.

15 See, for example, G. Jackson, *Historian's Quest*, pp. 231–3.

16 N. Chomsky, 'Objectivity and liberal scholarship' in his *American Power and the New Mandarins*, Harmondsworth, 1969, pp. 63–105.

17 As with some of the other matters traced in this book, the historicising of the Holocaust has a history of its own and especially flourished after the Arab–Israeli War of 1967. Peter Novick is preparing what should be a fascinating study of this subject and I am grateful to him for a discussion of it.

18 Another reason is that Novick's own analysis of the history of history of the USA is so superior to that available on any other national historiography and it seemed pointless to write some pale imitation of it. See P. Novick, *That Noble Dream: The 'Objectivity Question' and the American Historical Profession*, Cambridge, 1988 and the subsequent debate in the *American Historical Review*, 96, 1991, pp. 675–708.

19 S. Terkel, *'The Good War': An Oral History of World War II*, New York, 1984.

20 P. Fussell, *Wartime: Understanding and Behavior in the Second World War*, New York, 1989. See p. 15 for his bitter comments on the antecedents of the bombing of Hiroshima and Nagasaki.

21 See, for example, the interview with Williams in H. Abelove *et al.* (eds), *Visions of History*, Manchester, 1983, pp. 125–31.

22 Cf. D. Boorstin, *The Americans*, 3 vols, New York, 1958–73, with that Boorstin who had been a Communist and was forced to name names at the McCarthyite Congressional hearings. For the latter, see, for example, E.W. Schrecker, *No Ivory Tower: McCarthyism and the Universities*, New York, 1986, p. 339. Natalie Zeman Davis, that magnificent historian of popular culture, was far less transformed by her persecution in this period (H. Abelove et al., op. cit., pp. 100–8).

23 Brinton, the anatomiser of revolution, was another who served in the OSS. See B.M. Katz, 'The criticism of arms: The Frankfurt school goes to war', *Journal of Modern History*, 59, 1987, p. 446. Cf. also C. Brinton, *The Anatomy of Revolution*, London, 1953.

24 See, for example, M. Palumbo, *The Waldheim Files: Myth and Reality*, London, 1988.

25 R. Bassett, *Waldheim and Austria*, London, 1988, p. 2

26 ibid., p. 144.

27 M. Glenny, *The Rebirth of History: Eastern Europe in the Age of Democracy*, Harmondsworth, 1990, p. 72.

28 See above pp. 90–3.

29 M. Glenny, op. cit.

30 Her brief analysis of Braudel's *Mediterranean* is not very different from that given in chapter 5 above. See G. Himmelfarb, *The New History and the Old*, Cambridge, Mass., 1987, p. 11.

31 ibid., pp. 82–5, 91, 121; cf. also G. Himmelfarb, 'Some reflections on the new history', *American Historical Review*, 94, 1989, especially p. 664 and the accompanying debate in the rest of this issue of the *AHR*.

32 G. Himmelfarb, *The New History and the Old*.

33 For the most contradictory example, see A. Bloom, *The Closing of the American Mind*, New York, 1987.

34 P. Nora, 'Between memory and history: *Les lieux de mémoire*', *Representations*, 26, 1989, pp. 7–10.

35 A.J.P. Taylor, *The Origins of the Second World War*, rev. edn, Harmondsworth, 1964, p. 64.

36 A.J.P. Taylor, *Politicians, Socialism and Historians*, London, 1980, p. 216.

37 U. Eco, *The Name of the Rose*, London, 1983, p. 11.

Index